lonely planet

Rhodes &
the Dodecanese

Paul Hellander

LONELY PLANET PUBLICATIONS
Melbourne • Oakland • London • Paris

RHODES & THE DODECANESE

Ikaria

IKARIAN SEA

Agathonisi

To İzmir
& İstanbul

Marathi
Arki
Arki

Agios
Georgios

Skala

Lipsi Town

Farmako

*Mandalya
Gulf*

PATMOS
The stunning island of St John,
where God delivered the Book
of Revelations; an island with an
inimitable spirit of place

Patmos

Lipsi

Leros

Platanos
Lakki

Agia Marina

THE ASKLIPION
Kos' religious sanctuary, a
healing centre and a school of
medicine, where the teachings of
Hippocrates were followed

Bodrum

Kinaros

Kalymnos

37° N

Pothia
Pserimos

Kos
Town

Amorgos

Mastihari

Zia

A E G E A N

S E A

Kefalos

Kos

Mesa Vathy

Astypalea

Mandraki

Astypalea
Town

Nisyros

ASTYPALEA
A butterfly-shaped island with
a sparkling Cycladic Hora and
imposing Venetian castle

Tilos

Livadia

Halki

NISYROS
One of the strangest and most
beautiful of all Greek islands,
an unusual mixture of lush
vegetation and barren volcanic
moonscapes

Emborios

*KARPATHIAN
SEA*

36° N

Saria

OLYMBOS
A remote Karpathian mountain
village, where women still
wear traditional dress and
speak in a language akin
to that spoken by Homer

Diafani

Olymbos

Karpathos

SEA OF CRETE

26° E

27° E

Pigadia

AMMOÖPI BEACH
A Karpathian highlight, with
some of the best swimming
and skin diving in the whole
of the Dodecanese

Ammoöpi

Fry

Kasos

Dionisades

ELEVATION

1000m
700m
500m
300m
0

TURKEY

Kerme Gulf

Marmaris

Dalaman

SYMI
A picturesque island with a horseshoe-shaped harbour and colourful, neoclassical mansions; home to the annual Symi Cultural Festival

Fethiye

KASTELLORIZO
The beginning, or end of Europe, a tiny rock in the sun, Greece's farthest outpost and location for the cult film Mediterraneo

Gialos

Symi

Rhodes

RHODES' OLD TOWN
A splendid fortress city built by the Knights of St John, the largest inhabited medieval town in Europe

Alimia
Skala Kamirou

Petaloudes

Kaş

Rhodes

Kastellorizo

Monolithos

Laerma

Kastellorizo Town

Lindos

LINDOS
The Acropolis of Lindos, spectacularly perched atop a 116m-high rock, overlooking its picture postcard village

MEDITERRANEAN

SEA

Kattavia

Cape Prasonisi

GREECE

AEGEAN SEA

Chios

TURKEY

ATHENS
Piraeus

Andros

Samos

Kea

Tinos

Ikaria

Patmos

Kythnos

Syros

Mykonos

Leros

SARONIC GULF ISLANDS

Paros

Naxos

Kalymnos

Kos

MIRTOÖN SEA

Ios

Amorgos

Astypalea

Milos

Nisyros

Symi

Rhodes

28° E

CYCLADES

Santorini (Thira)

Anafi

Tilos

Halki

Rhodes

Kythira

DODECANESE

Kastellorizo

Antikythira

SEA OF CRETE

Kasos

Karpathos

CRETE

Rhodes & the Dodecanese
1st edition – June 2001

Published by
Lonely Planet Publications Pty Ltd ABN 36 005 607 983
90 Maribyrnong St, Footscray, Victoria 3011, Australia

Lonely Planet Offices
Australia Locked Bag 1, Footscray, Victoria 3011
USA 150 Linden St, Oakland, CA 94607
UK 10a Spring Place, London NW5 3BH
France 1 rue du Dahomey, 75011 Paris

Photographs
All of the images in this guide are available for licensing from
Lonely Planet Images.
email: lpi@lonelyplanet.com.au

Front cover photograph
Decorative bell, Kyra Panagia beach, Karpathos (Stella Hellander)

ISBN 1 86450 117 0

Contents – Text

Contents – Maps

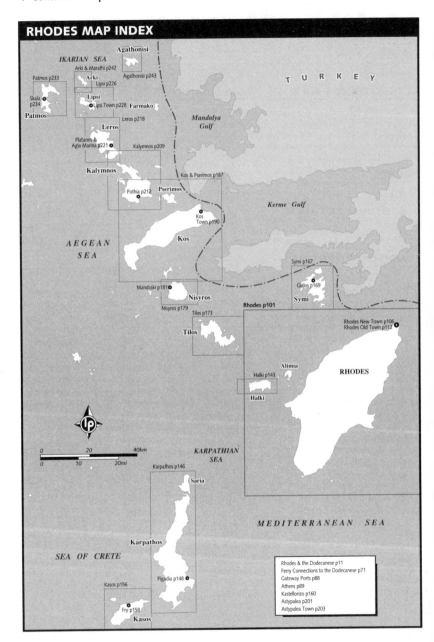

RHODES MAP INDEX

IKARIAN SEA

Agathonisi

Arki & Marathi p242

Arki

Lipsi p226

Patmos p233

Skala
p234

Patmos

Lipsi

Lipsi Town p228 Farmako

Leros p218

Leros

Platanos &
Agia Marina p221

Kalymnos p209

Kalymnos

Pothia p212

Pserimos

Kos & Pserimos p187

TURKEY

Mandalya
Gulf

Kerme Gulf

Kos
Town p190

Kos

AEGEAN
SEA

Symi p167

Gialos p169

Symi

Mandraki p181

Nisyros

Nisyros p179

Tilos p173

Tilos

Rhodes p101

Rhodes New Town p106
Rhodes Old Town p112

Alimia

Halki p143

Halki

RHODES

KARPATHIAN
SEA

0   20   40km
0   10   20mi

Karpathos p146

Saria

Karpathos

SEA OF CRETE

Pigadia p148

MEDITERRANEAN   SEA

Kasos p156

Fry p158

Kasos

The Author

Paul Hellander

Paul has never really stopped travelling since he first looked at a map in his native England. He graduated from Birmingham University with a degree in Greek before heading for Australia. He taught Modern Greek and trained interpreters and translators for many years before donning the hat of a travel writer. Paul has contributed to over 20 LP titles including guides to Greece, Greek Islands, Cyprus, France, Israel & the Palestinian Territories, Europe, Eastern Europe, Western Europe, Mediterranean Europe, SE Asia, Singapore and Central America. For this first edition of Rhodes & the Dodecanese Paul once more found himself back in his spiritual home – Greece. When not travelling with his Mac and Nikons, he lives in Adelaide, South Australia, where he studies the history of political intelligence, listens to Neil Young, cooks Thai food and grows hot chillies. He was last seen heading for the Inca ruins of Macchu Pichu in Peru.

FROM THE AUTHOR

Writing a travel guide invariably involves the input of many people. I would like to mention some who helped in ways big and small to make this book possible. Thanks again to my wife Stella for her unstinting assistance on the trip around the Dodecanese and for her excellent photography, to Louiza Maragozidis and Sofia Arhontoulis (Adelaide) for proofreading and Anatoli Kourtidis (Adelaide) for assistance with the research in Greece.

Thanks also to Geoff Harvey of Driveaway (Sydney) and Peugeot (Paris) for organising yet another flawless Peugeot 306; Minoan Lines (Patra & Venice) for swift and efficient transport to and from Greece; and Dodecanese Express (Rhodes) for first class transport on the best catamaran in the Dodecanese.

Ευχαριστώ to Nikos & Anna Hristodoulou (Lipsi); Faith Warn (Kalymnos); Emmanouil Manousos (Kasos); Dr Jürgen Franke (Nisyros); Detlef Wydra (Astypalea); Lakis, Mihail & Stefania Angelou (Rhodes); Paul & Helen Nuttall (Tilos); Dimitris Antonoglou (Symi); Alex & Christine Sakellaridis (Halki); Effie Antonaras (Rhodes); DANE (Rhodes); the GNTO (Rhodes); Road Editions (Athens); Demetres Dounas (Athens); Byron & Marcus Hellander (Athens & Ioannina) – this one is especially for you.

This Book

FROM THE PUBLISHER

The 1st edition of Rhodes & the Dodecanese was produced in the Melbourne office, and was coordinated by Susie Ashworth (editorial) and Yvonne Bischofberger (mapping and design). Editing and proofing assistance was provided by Susannah Farfor, and mapping assistance by Agustín Poó y Balbontin, Csanád Csutoros, Cris Gibcus, Sally Morgan, Adrian Persoglia, Jacqui Saunders, Ray Thompson and Celia Wood. Tony Davidson, Kieran Grogan and Elizabeth Swan also provided invaluable help during production.

Quentin Frayne prepared the Language chapter, Yvonne Bischofberger produced the climate chart, Maria Vallianos designed the cover and Mark Germanchis provided expert Quark support. Matt King organised the illustrations and they were drawn by Clint Curé (Q-ray), Martin Harris (MH), Margaret Jung (MJ) and Kelli Hamblet (KH). Photographs were supplied by Lonely Planet Images.

ACKNOWLEDGMENTS

Lonely Planet gratefully acknowledges the supply of the reference map for Astypalea Town: Detlef Wydra, Germany ©2000

Foreword

ABOUT LONELY PLANET GUIDEBOOKS

The story begins with a classic travel adventure: Tony and Maureen Wheeler's 1972 journey across Europe and Asia to Australia. Useful information about the overland trail did not exist at that time, so Tony and Maureen published the first Lonely Planet guidebook to meet a growing need.

From a kitchen table, then from a tiny office in Melbourne (Australia), Lonely Planet has become the largest independent travel publisher in the world, an international company with offices in Melbourne, Oakland (USA), London (UK) and Paris (France).

Today Lonely Planet guidebooks cover the globe. There is an ever-growing list of books and there's information in a variety of forms and media. Some things haven't changed. The main aim is still to help make it possible for adventurous travellers to get out there – to explore and better understand the world.

At Lonely Planet we believe travellers can make a positive contribution to the countries they visit – if they respect their host communities and spend their money wisely. Since 1986 a percentage of the income from each book has been donated to aid projects and human rights campaigns.

Updates Lonely Planet thoroughly updates each guidebook as often as possible. This usually means there are around two years between editions, although for more unusual or more stable destinations the gap can be longer. Check the imprint page (following the colour map at the beginning of the book) for publication dates.

Between editions up-to-date information is available in two free newsletters – the paper *Planet Talk* and email *Comet* (to subscribe, contact any Lonely Planet office) – and on our Web site at www.lonelyplanet.com. The *Upgrades* section of the Web site covers a number of important and volatile destinations and is regularly updated by Lonely Planet authors. *Scoop* covers news and current affairs relevant to travellers. And, lastly, the *Thorn Tree* bulletin board and *Postcards* section of the site carry unverified, but fascinating, reports from travellers.

Correspondence The process of creating new editions begins with the letters, postcards and emails received from travellers. This correspondence often includes suggestions, criticisms and comments about the current editions. Interesting excerpts are immediately passed on via newsletters and the Web site, and everything goes to our authors to be verified when they're researching on the road. We're keen to get more feedback from organisations or individuals who represent communities visited by travellers.

Lonely Planet gathers information for everyone who's curious about the planet – and especially for those who explore it first-hand. Through guidebooks, phrasebooks, activity guides, maps, literature, newsletters, image library, TV series and Web site we act as an information exchange for a worldwide community of travellers.

Research Authors aim to gather sufficient practical information to enable travellers to make informed choices and to make the mechanics of a journey run smoothly. They also research historical and cultural background to help enrich the travel experience and allow travellers to understand and respond appropriately to cultural and environmental issues.

Authors don't stay in every hotel because that would mean spending a couple of months in each medium-sized city and, no, they don't eat at every restaurant because that would mean stretching belts beyond capacity. They do visit hotels and restaurants to check standards and prices, but feedback based on readers' direct experiences can be very helpful.

Many of our authors work undercover, others aren't so secretive. None of them accept freebies in exchange for positive write-ups. And none of our guidebooks contain any advertising.

Production Authors submit their raw manuscripts and maps to offices in Australia, USA, UK or France. Editors and cartographers – all experienced travellers themselves – then begin the process of assembling the pieces. When the book finally hits the shops, some things are already out of date, we start getting feedback from readers and the process begins again …

WARNING & REQUEST

Things change – prices go up, schedules change, good places go bad and bad places go bankrupt – nothing stays the same. So, if you find things better or worse, recently opened or long since closed, please tell us and help make the next edition even more accurate and useful. We genuinely value all the feedback we receive. A well travelled team reads and acknowledges every letter, postcard and email and ensures that every morsel of information finds its way to the appropriate authors, editors and cartographers for verification.

Everyone who writes to us will find their name in the next edition of the appropriate guidebook. They will also receive the latest issue of *Planet Talk*, our quarterly printed newsletter, or *Comet*, our monthly email newsletter. Subscriptions to both newsletters are free. The very best contributions will be rewarded with a free guidebook.

Excerpts from your correspondence may appear in new editions of Lonely Planet guidebooks, the Lonely Planet Web site, *Planet Talk* or *Comet*, so please let us know if you *don't* want your letter published or your name acknowledged.

Send all correspondence to the Lonely Planet office closest to you:

Australia: Locked Bag 1, Footscray, Victoria 3011
USA: 150 Linden St, Oakland, CA 94607
UK: 10A Spring Place, London NW5 3BH
France: 1 rue du Dahomey, 75011 Paris

Or email us at: talk2us@lonelyplanet.com.au

For news, views and updates see our Web site: www.lonelyplanet.com

HOW TO USE A LONELY PLANET GUIDEBOOK

The best way to use a Lonely Planet guidebook is any way you choose. At Lonely Planet we believe the most memorable travel experiences are often those that are unexpected, and the finest discoveries are those you make yourself. Guidebooks are not intended to be used as if they provide a detailed set of infallible instructions!

Contents All Lonely Planet guidebooks follow roughly the same format. The Facts about the Destination chapters or sections give background information ranging from history to weather. Facts for the Visitor gives practical information on issues like visas and health. Getting There & Away gives a brief starting point for researching travel to and from the destination. Getting Around gives an overview of the transport options when you arrive.

The peculiar demands of each destination determine how subsequent chapters are broken up, but some things remain constant. We always start with background, then proceed to sights, places to stay, places to eat, entertainment, getting there and away, and getting around information – in that order.

Heading Hierarchy Lonely Planet headings are used in a strict hierarchical structure that can be visualised as a set of Russian dolls. Each heading (and its following text) is encompassed by any preceding heading that is higher on the hierarchical ladder.

Entry Points We do not assume guidebooks will be read from beginning to end, but that people will dip into them. The traditional entry points are the list of contents and the index. In addition, however, some books have a complete list of maps and an index map illustrating map coverage.

There may also be a colour map that shows highlights. These highlights are dealt with in greater detail in the Facts for the Visitor chapter, along with planning questions and suggested itineraries. Each chapter covering a geographical region usually begins with a locator map and another list of highlights. Once you find something of interest in a list of highlights, turn to the index.

Maps Maps play a crucial role in Lonely Planet guidebooks and include a huge amount of information. A legend is printed on the back page. We seek to have complete consistency between maps and text, and to have every important place in the text captured on a map. Map key numbers usually start in the top left corner.

Although inclusion in a guidebook usually implies a recommendation we cannot list every good place. Exclusion does not necessarily imply criticism. In fact there are a number of reasons why we might exclude a place – sometimes it is simply inappropriate to encourage an influx of travellers.

Introduction

If ever there was a chain of islands with an instant, magnetic pull, it is a group known as the Dodecanese. Strung like jewels upon the sea, this scattered domain of rocks, mountains, beaches, castles, cobalt blue seas and azure coves is closer to mainland Asia than Europe and has, over the centuries, attracted settlers, conquerors, adventurers and travellers alike. A part of Greece only as recently as 1948, the 18 inhabited islands that make up the Dodecanese constitute a vibrant and colourful legacy of the many peoples that have passed by and lived here.

Through these scattered, but well-connected islands have passed Karians, Minoans, Mycenaeans, Dorians, Romans, Genoese, Venetians, Ottomans, Italians, Germans and the British, each leaving in some distinct way their own brand of imbued cultural traits.

As a geographical and political entity the Dodecanese are known to relatively few travellers, yet tourists in their thousands descend on at least two of the major islands for up to eight months of the year. Smaller discerning groups seek out quieter islands and come back year after year. Travellers in search of those 'undiscovered' Greek islands may still find them in the Dodecanese, and lovers of history and archaeology will enjoy some of the most impressive historical sites in Greece today. Beachcombers won't be disappointed: the southern Aegean boasts some of the cleanest beaches and bluest seas in the whole Mediterranean basin. Windsurfers, hikers, scuba divers, yachties and extreme sport enthusiasts will all find their

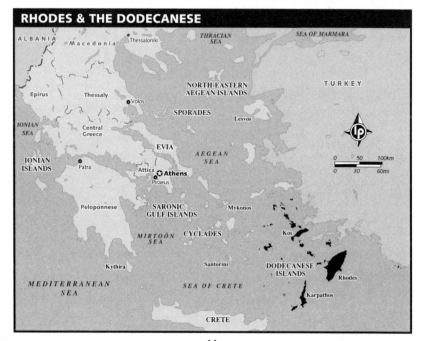

RHODES & THE DODECANESE

niche in the Dodecanese, with activities to suit all tastes and ages. If you are simply looking for some quality chill-out time with a pile of novels under seemingly endless sunny skies, look no further.

Rhodes, with its Unesco-listed medieval Old Town, is the crown jewel. There are few places in Europe where you can wander back in time as easily as this ever-fascinating labyrinth of alleyways and walls. Kos, with more beaches than days in a month, appeals to both hedonists and hermits. Patmos, a Cycladic-like rock in the north, has a spirit of place unparalleled by any island in the Aegean, and remote and rocky Agathonisi and Arki will appeal to latter-day Robinson Crusoes. Lipsi, almost forgotten, is a pearl appreciated by those curious enough to call in and who then forget to move on. Languid Leros sees relatively few visitors yet draws an increasingly curious stream of voyagers seeking something different. Kalymnos, the home of sponge divers, beckons travellers with an enticing mix of nightlife, solitude, hiking and sailing. Butterfly-shaped Astypalea is a Cycladic sapphire grafted onto a Dodecanese crown, proud, almost aloof in its isolation and attracting the seriously travel-struck.

If it's a volcano you want to see, make a beeline for solemn Nisyros. If it's solitude, space, sun and sand don't miss demure Tilos. Rocky and barren Halki and Symi are photographers' favourites, commanding a growing fan club that returns time and time again. Many stay on for good. True travellers will seek out quiet retreats like Kasos or Kastellorizo, two of the remotest islands in the Aegean, yet each with its own tragic history and quietly active present. Karpathos is a must for travellers who want it all without the excess: beaches, sports, mountains, good food, culture and music.

The varied richness of Rhodes and the Dodecanese Islands is an enticing mix for travellers looking for an experience that combines elements rarely found in such a geographically compact region. These jewels of the south-eastern Aegean will not disappoint and, like the lure of lost treasure, will tempt you back time and time again. You never know, you too may end up staying for good.

Facts about Rhodes & the Dodecanese

HISTORY

The name 'Dodecanese' derives from the Greek *Dodekanisa* meaning 'Twelve Islands'. A glance at the map will demonstrate how initially confusing this appears to be since there are in fact some 18 inhabited islands in the Dodecanese archipelago. They are, in rough north to south order: Agathonisi, Arki, Marathi, Patmos, Lipsi, Leros, Kalymnos, Astypalea, Kos, Nisyros, Tilos, Symi, Halki, Rhodes, Karpathos, Kasos and Kastellorizo. In addition, there are the two dependencies of Telendos (the 18th inhabited isle) and Pserimos, both close to Kalymnos.

The name Dodecanese derives from the time of the Ottoman Empire when 12 of the 18 islands were granted special privileges for willingly submitting to the new Ottoman overlords, a rule which began in earnest in 1478. Intriguingly, the original Dodecanese did not include the largest and richest islands of Rhodes and Kos as they had unwillingly been subjugated to the Ottomans. Instead, they consisted only of Patmos, Lipsi, Leros, Kalymnos, Astypalea, Nisyros, Tilos, Symi, Halki, Karpathos, Kasos and Kastellorizo.

While the history of the Dodecanese shares much in common with wider Greek history, it has its own twists and turns, with occupation by a richer than usual list of invaders, including Karians, Dorians, Romans, Genoese, Venetians, Knights Hospitallers, Italians Germans and British, as well as the aforementioned Ottomans. This rich tapestry of cultural infusion has given the Dodecanese Islands a unique flavour and feel. The scattered island archipelago only became part of the Greek State in 1948 and, in some respects, is still coming to terms with it.

Neolithic, Minoan & Mycenaean Era

People first came to the Dodecanese archipelago from the nearby Asian mainland, rather than the Greek mainland. Archaeological finds dating back to the 6th century BC on Halki, Tilos, Rhodes and Kalymnos testify to human activity on the islands from this time. Little is known otherwise about these settlers commonly know as Karians, but they gave way in time to successive waves of settlement from farther afield. The Dodecanese was settled or briefly visited by Phoenicians, Minoans from Crete and Mycenaeans from the Peloponnese mainland, the natural successors to the Minoans who were thought to have perished in the Santorini volcano eruption some time around 1400 BC. The Mycenaean presence is particularly well-documented in Rhodes where much pottery has been found dating to the time of their own collapse around 1200 BC.

Dorian & Archaic Eras

The disappearance of the Mycenaeans is widely attributed to the so-called 'Dorian invasion'. The Dorians were a lighter-skinned northern people who swept down into the Aegean heartland and islands some time in the 12th century BC. While the Dorians primarily established themselves in the Peloponnese, they also headed to the southeastern Aegean and colonised an area loosely centred on Rhodes, Kos, and the Anatolian mainland in present-day Turkey. It is here that they formed the Dorian Hexapolis, a commercial alliance made up of the cities of Kamiros, Lindos, Ialysos (all on Rhodes), Astypalea (on Kos) and the cities of Halicarnassus and Knidos on the Anatolian mainland. The Dorian Hexapolis had the good fortune to prosper and developed wide trade connections across the Mediterranean basin. This prototype European Union is also credited with bringing the Greek alphabet into common usage and it is in the 7th century BC that Lindos, under the benevolent tyrant Kleoboulos, reached its peak of supremacy.

The Dorian era, also known as the Greek Dark Ages, gradually gave way to more enlightened political and cultural development, as the rise of the *polis* or city-state replaced impoverished agrarian settlements, and the citizens began to take part in government. It is during this time that the two most prominent city-states, Athens and Sparta, emerged and were to dominate Greek history for the next 500 years. In the Dodecanese, city-states were founded at Lindos in Rhodes and Astypalea on Kos. While the former still figures prominently in archaeological tourism, the latter has all but faded to total insignificance.

Classical & Hellenistic Eras

Prefacing the classical period of Greek history was a concerted campaign by the Persians to subjugate the rising power of Athens and its influence over the Hellenic mainland. The Persian Wars, waged by Darius and Xerxes, sorely tested Greek will. While Rhodes managed to resist the first Persian invasion in 491 BC, the island-state was later obliged to contribute to the war against the mainland being waged by the Persians. It was the Persian land campaign that witnessed the famous battles of Marathon and Thermopylae against the Greek forces. The subsequent decisive naval battles and Greek victories at Salamis and Mykale, near Samos, finally saw off the Persian threat once and for all. Rhodes accordingly realigned itself with the interests of Athens by joining the newly-founded Delian league. While this new naval alliance, based on the island of Delos in the Cyclades, clipped Rhodes' commercial wings to some degree, it also assured its ongoing security in a rapidly expanding Hellenic world.

During the ensuing Golden Age (461–429 BC), the Parthenon was commissioned by Pericles, Sophocles wrote *Oedipus the King*, and Socrates taught young Athenians to think. At the same time, the Spartans were creating a military state. The Golden Age ended with the Peloponnesian War (431–404 BC), in which the militaristic Spartans defeated the Athenians. So embroiled were they in this war that they failed to notice the expansion of Macedonia to the north under King Philip II, who easily conquered the war-weary city-states. Meanwhile, on the island of Rhodes in 408 BC, the three original island city-states of Kamiros, Lindos and Ialysos joined forces and populations and moved lock, stock and barrel to a new site on the northernmost tip of the island, and thus was born the new City of Rhodes.

Philip II's ambitions were surpassed by those of his son, Alexander the Great, who marched triumphantly into Asia Minor, Egypt, Persia and what are now parts of Afghanistan and India. After Alexander's untimely death in 323 BC at the age of 33, his generals divided his empire between themselves. The Dodecanese became part of the kingdom of Ptolemy I of Egypt. In the ensuing chaos following Alexander's death, Antigonus of Macedonia, a former general of Alexander, sought to bring Rhodes into an alliance against the Rhodians' own protectors, the Ptolemies. When they refused, he tried to bring them into line by instigating a year-long siege. He dispatched his son, Demetrios I Poliorkites, on a mission that became one of the greatest and longest drawn-out sieges in history in 306–305 BC. The end result was a stalemate and Demetrios withdrew leaving all his war machinery behind. This was melted down and in triumph the Colossus of Rhodes was erected near the port of Rhodes. (See the boxed text in the Rhodes chapter.)

Rhodes enjoyed a subsequent century and a half of prosperity and developed a powerful and rich trading fleet whose maritime code is still being used as a standard today.

Roman Rule & the Byzantine Empire

Roman incursions into Greece began in 205 BC. By 146 BC the mainland had become the Roman provinces of Greece and Macedonia. Crete fell in 67 BC, and the southern city of Gortyn became the capital of the Roman province of Cyrenaica, which included a large chunk of North Africa. Rhodes held out until AD 70.

In the 1st century AD, St Paul made numerous trips to mainland Greece and the islands, including the Dodecanese, with plans to convert the masses to Christianity. The Greeks embraced the new religion with great enthusiasm, turning temples into churches, and the number of followers increased rapidly over the next 300 years.

In AD 330 Emperor Constantine, a Christian advocate, chose Byzantium as the new capital of the Roman Empire and renamed the city Constantinople. After the subdivision of the Roman Empire into Eastern and Western Empires in AD 395, Greece became part of the Eastern Roman Empire, leading to the illustrious Byzantine age.

In the centuries that followed, Venetians, Franks, Normans, Slavs, Persians, Arabs and, finally, Turks all took their turns to chip away at the Byzantine Empire. The Persians captured Rhodes in 620, but were replaced by the Saracens (Arabs) in 653. The Arabs also captured Crete in 824.

Other islands in the Aegean remained under Byzantine control until the sack of Constantinople in 1204 by renegade Frankish crusaders in cahoots with Venice. The Venetians were rewarded with the Cyclades, and they added Crete and Rhodes to their possessions in 1210.

Genoese & the Knights of St John

In 1248 Rhodes was seized by the Genoese from Latin rivals, the Venetians, and so began two centuries of further ownership transfer of Rhodes and the southern Dodecanese. The Genoese held sway in Rhodes for 58 years until the Knights Hospitaller of St John, recently expelled from Jerusalem, arrived from Cyprus to add their own brand of commercial colonialism to the Dodecanese. It took the Knights three years to wrest Rhodes from the Genoese and five years later they added Kos to their list of Dodecanese possessions. Meanwhile, Astypalea, Karpathos and Kasos remained firmly in the Venetian camp. The Knights, though ostensibly a chivalric Christian order, soon established themselves as purveyors of legitimate and illegitimate practices. While building a formidable set of fortifications for the cities of Rhodes and Kos they set about engaging themselves in

piracy, primarily against Ottoman shipping and pilgrims.

This naturally irked the sultan of the Ottoman Empire, Süleyman the Magnificent, who in 1512 acquired the island of Kastellorizo and then in 1522 set about besieging and dislodging the miscreant Knights from Rhodes. This second siege of Rhodes was more successful, but only just. The siege lasted six months, despite the fact that the Rhodians were outnumbered 30 to one – they were only defeated when a traitor Knight let it be known to the Sultan's forces how under-protected Rhodes really was. A final series of assaults was launched and Rhodes capitulated in 1523. The Knights were dispersed, only to re-emerge seven years later in Malta, where they continued to harass the Ottomans.

The Ottoman Empire & Independence

The Byzantine Empire finally came to an end in 1453 when Constantinople fell to the Turks. Once more Greece became a battleground, this time fought over by the Turks and Venetians. Eventually, with the exception of Corfu, Greece became part of the Ottoman Empire.

Much has been made of the horrors of the Turkish occupation in Greece. However, in the early years, people probably marginally preferred Ottoman to Venetian or Frankish rule. The Venetians, in particular, treated their subjects little better than slaves. But life was not easy under the Turks, not least because of the high taxation they imposed. One of their most hated practices was the taking of one out of every five male children to become janissaries, the personal bodyguards of the sultan. Many janissaries became infantrymen in the Ottoman army, but the cleverest could rise to high office – including grand vizier (chief minister).

Ottoman power reached its zenith under Sultan Süleyman the Magnificent (ruled 1520–66), who expanded the empire to the gates of Vienna. His successor added Cyprus to their dominions in 1570, but his death in 1574 marked the end of serious territorial expansion.

Ottoman rule in the Dodecanese was marked by a general malaise and creeping decay. The Ottomans rarely bothered to interfere with everyday life as long as their omnipresent taxes were paid. Only the larger islands of Rhodes and Kos attracted any permanent settlement by mainland Ottomans, while islands like Symi and Kastellorizo made fortunes by constructing merchant shipping fleets – many for the Ottomans themselves. Other islands like Kalymnos and Halki made their own fortunes from sponges. The by now firmly Orthodox Patmos had long enjoyed a high degree of autonomy and even ran its own merchant fleet.

The long-heralded War of Independence finally began on 25 March 1821, when Bishop Germanos of Patras hoisted the Greek flag at the monastery of Agias Lavras in the Peloponnese. Fighting broke out almost simultaneously across most of Greece and the occupied islands, with the Greeks making big early gains. The fighting was savage, with atrocities committed on both sides. The islands weren't spared the horrors of war. In 1822, Turkish forces massacred 25,000 people on the island of Chios, while another 7000 were butchered on Kasos in 1824 by Ottomans from Egypt.

Eventually, the Great Powers – Britain, France and Russia – intervened on the side of the Greeks, defeating the Turkish-Egyptian fleet at the Battle of Navarino in 1827. The island of Aegina was proclaimed the temporary capital of an independent Greek state, and Ioannis Kapodistrias was elected the first president. The capital was soon moved to Nafplio in the Peloponnese, where Kapodistrias was assassinated in 1831.

Amid anarchy, the European powers stepped in again and declared that Greece should become a monarchy. In January 1833, 17-year-old Prince Otto of Bavaria was installed as king of a nation (established by the London Convention of 1832) that consisted of the Peloponnese, Sterea Ellada (Central Greece), the Cyclades and the Sporades.

King Othon (as his name became) displeased the Greek people from the start, arriving with a bunch of upper class Bavarian cronies to whom he gave the most presti-

gious official posts. He moved the capital to Athens in 1834.

Patience with his rule ran out in 1843 when demonstrations in the capital, led by the War of Independence leaders, called for a constitution. Othon mustered a National Assembly which drafted a constitution calling for parliamentary government consisting of a Lower House and a senate. Othon's cronies were whisked out of power and replaced by War of Independence freedom fighters, who bullied and bribed the populace into voting for them.

By the end of the 1850s, most of the stalwarts from the War of Independence had been replaced by a new breed of university graduates (Athens University had been founded in 1837). In 1862 they staged a bloodless revolution and deposed the king. But they weren't quite able to set their own agenda, because in 1863 Britain returned the Ionian Islands (a British protectorate since 1815) to Greece. Amid the general euphoria that followed, the British were able to push forward young Prince William of Denmark, who became King George I.

His 50-year reign brought stability to the troubled country, beginning with a new constitution in 1864, which established the power of democratically elected representatives and pushed the king further towards a ceremonial role. An uprising in Crete against Turkish rule was suppressed by the sultan in 1866–68, but in 1881 Greece acquired Thessaly and part of Epiros as the result of another Russo-Turkish war.

Although the Ottoman Empire was in its death throes at the beginning of the 20th century, it was still clinging onto Macedonia. It was a prize sought by the newly formed Balkan countries of Serbia and Bulgaria, as well as by Greece, and this led to the Balkan wars. The first, in 1912, pitted all three against the Turks; the second, in 1913, pitted Serbia and Greece against Bulgaria. The outcome was the Treaty of Bucharest (August 1913), which greatly expanded Greek territory by adding the southern part of Macedonia, part of Thrace, another chunk of Epiros, and the North-Eastern Aegean Islands, as well as recognising the union with Crete.

In March 1913, King George was assassinated by a lunatic, and his son Constantine became king.

WWI & Smyrna

King Constantine, who was married to the sister of the German emperor, insisted that Greece remain neutral when WWI broke out in August 1914. As the war dragged on, the Allies (Britain, France and Russia) put increasing pressure on Greece to join forces with them against Germany and Turkey. They made promises that they couldn't hope to fulfil, including land in Asia Minor. Venizelos, the Prime Minister of Greece, favoured the Allied cause, placing him at loggerheads with the king. Tension between the two came to a head in 1916, and Venizelos set up a rebel government, first in Crete and then in Thessaloniki. Meanwhile the pressure from the Allies eventually persuaded Constantine to leave Greece in June 1917. He was replaced by his more amenable second son, Alexander.

Greek troops served with distinction on the Allied side, but when the war ended in 1918 the promised land in Asia Minor was not forthcoming. Venizelos took matters into his own hands and, with Allied acquiescence, landed troops in Smyrna (present-day Izmir) in May 1919 under the guise of protecting the half a million Greeks living in that city (just under half its population). With a firm foothold in Asia Minor, Venizelos now planned to push home his advantage against a war-depleted Ottoman Empire. He ordered his troops to attack in October 1920 (just weeks before he was voted out of office). By September 1921, the Greeks had advanced as far as Ankara.

The Turkish forces were commanded by Mustafa Kemal (later to become Atatürk), a young general who also belonged to the Young Turks, a group of army officers pressing for western-style political reforms. Kemal first halted the Greek advance outside Ankara in September 1921 and then routed them with a massive offensive the following spring. The Greeks were driven out of Smyrna and many of the Greek inhabitants were massacred. Mustafa Kemal was now a national hero, the sultanate was abolished and Turkey became a republic.

The outcome of the failed Greek invasion and the revolution in Turkey was the second Treaty of Lausanne of July 1923. This gave eastern Thrace and the islands of Imvros and Tenedos to Turkey, while the Italians kept the Dodecanese which they had temporarily acquired in 1912.

The treaty also called for a population exchange between Greece and Turkey to prevent any future disputes. Almost 1.5 million Greeks left Turkey and almost 400,000 Turks left Greece. The exchange put a tremendous strain on the Greek economy and caused great hardship for the individuals concerned. Many Greeks abandoned a privileged life in Asia Minor for one of extreme poverty in shantytowns in Greece.

King Constantine, restored to the throne in 1920, identified himself too closely with the war against Turkey, and abdicated after the fall of Smyrna. He was replaced by his first son, George II.

Italians, Germans & the British

The Dodecanese became an Italian possession in 1912 almost by accident. The Italians moved in on the Dodecanese as a pretext to getting the Ottomans out of what is today Libya. They claimed to be willing to leave the Dodecanese once Libya was vacated by the Ottomans. This was stipulated in the first Treaty of Lausanne signed in the same year, but the promises were never realised. In 1915 the Italians nullified the treaty, preferring instead the territorially more advantageous Treaty of London, which gave them full sovereignty over their new possessions. Thus, the Dodecanese slipped from Ottoman hands almost by default – a fact that recent Turkish governments have not easily forgotten.

The Greek disgrace after the failed invasion of Asia Minor, coupled with the rise of Italian Fascism saw the Dodecanese firmly in Italy's grip for much longer than initially planned. Italian rule was firm and often oppressive, where Ottoman rule had been liberal. The Orthodox Church and the Greek language were suppressed and Mussolini embarked on a campaign to create an Italian Aegean Empire, with grandiose public works and buildings, many of which remain to this day. The Italians capitulated to the Allies in 1943 following their failed war effort and were hastily replaced by the British. They only managed to hold on to Kos, Leros and Kastellorizo for a short time before being beaten in turn by the invading Germans. German rule was brutal, but short-lived. After their surrender, the British briefly moved back in to try to bring order to what was now chaos, but finally set in motion the mechanism that saw the Dodecanese Islands' formal union with the Greek State in March 1948.

The Civil War

A bloody civil war followed on from WWII, lasting until 1949 and leaving the country in chaos. More people were killed in the civil war than in WWII and 250,000 people were left homeless. The sense of despair that followed became the trigger for a mass exodus. Almost a million Greeks headed off in search of a better life elsewhere, primarily to Australia, Canada and the USA. Villages – whole islands even – were abandoned as people gambled on a new start in cities like Melbourne, Chicago and New York. While some have drifted back, the majority have stayed away.

The Colonels

Continuing political instability resulted in the colonels' coup d'état in 1967, led by Georgos Papadopoulos and Stylianos Pattakos. King Constantine (son of King Paul, who succeeded George II) staged an unsuccessful counter coup, then fled the country. The colonels' junta distinguished itself by inflicting appalling brutality, repression and political incompetence upon the people.

In 1974 the colonels' junta attempted to assassinate Cyprus' leader, Archbishop Makarios. When Makarios escaped, the junta replaced him with the extremist Nikos Sampson, a convicted murderer. The Turks, who comprised 20% of the population, were alarmed at having Sampson as leader. Consequently, mainland Turkey sent in troops and occupied North Cyprus; its continued occupation is one of the most contentious issues in Greek politics today. The junta, by now in a shambles, had little choice but to hand power back to the civilians.

In November 1974 a plebiscite voted 69% against restoration of the monarchy, and Greece became a republic. An election brought the right-wing New Democracy (ND) party into power.

The Socialist 1980s

In 1981 Greece entered the European Community (EC; now the EU). Andreas Papandreou's Panhellenic Socialist Movement (PASOK) won the next election, giving Greece its first socialist government. PASOK promised removal of US air bases and withdrawal from NATO, which Greece had joined in 1951.

Six years into government these promises remained unfulfilled, unemployment was high and reforms in education and welfare had been limited. Women's issues had fared better, however – the dowry system was abolished, abortion legalised, and civil marriage and divorce were implemented. The crunch for the government came in 1988 when Papandreou's affair with air stewardess Dimitra Liani (whom he subsequently married) was widely publicised and PASOK became embroiled in a financial scandal involving the Bank of Crete.

In July 1989 an unprecedented conservative and communist coalition took over to implement a *katharsis* (campaign of purification) to investigate the scandals. It ruled that Papandreou and four ministers should stand trial for embezzlement, telephone tapping and illegal grain sales. It then stepped down in October 1990, stating that the katharsis was complete.

Recent History

An election in 1990 brought the ND party back to power with a majority of only two seats. The tough economic reforms that Prime Minister Konstandinos Mitsotakis was forced to introduce to counter a spiralling foreign debt soon made his government deeply unpopular. By late 1992, allegations began to emerge about the same sort of government corruption and dirty tricks that had brought Papandreou unstuck. Mitsotakis himself was accused of having a secret hoard of Minoan art. He was forced to call an election in October 1993.

Greeks again turned to PASOK and the ageing, ailing Papandreou, who had been cleared of all the charges levelled in 1990. He marked his last brief period in power with a conspicuous display of the cronyism that had become his trademark. He appointed his wife as chief of staff, his son Giorgos as deputy foreign minister and his personal physician as minister of health.

Papandreou had little option but to continue with the same austerity program begun by Mitsotakis, quickly making his government equally unpopular. He was finally forced to hand over the reins in January 1996 after a lengthy spell in hospital. He was replaced by Kostas Simitis, an experienced economist and lawyer and outspoken critic of Papandreou, who surprised many by calling a snap poll in September 1996, and campaigned hard in support of his Mr Clean image. He was rewarded with a comfortable parliamentary majority.

Simitis belongs to much the same school of politics as Britain's Tony Blair. Since he took power, PASOK policy has shifted right, to the extent that it now agrees with the opposition ND party on all major policy issues. His government has focused almost exclusively on further integration with Europe, which has meant more tax reform and further austerity measures. It's rare for a day to pass without a protest of some sort from the electorate. Simitis has stuck to his guns, though, and on 1 January 2001, Greece became the 12th member of the eurozone. Euro membership enjoys strong popular support and Simitis was particularly pleased, announcing that inclusion in the European Monetary Union will ensure greater stability and open up new opportunities for the country.

Foreign Policy

Greece's foreign policy is dominated by its extremely sensitive relationship with Turkey, its giant Muslim neighbour to the east. These two uneasy NATO allies seem to delight in niggling each other in an ongoing war of one-upmanship. Incidents that might appear trivial to the outsider frequently bring the two to the brink of war – such as when Turkish journalists symbolically replaced the Greek flag on the tiny rocky outcrop of Imia (Kardak to the Turks) in February 1996 (see the boxed text 'The Imia Incident').

The massive earthquake that devastated the Izmit area of western Turkey in August 1999 sparked a remarkable turnaround in relations between the warring neighbours. According to geologists, the quake moved Turkey 1.5m closer to Greece. Greek rescue teams were among the first on the scene, a favour the Turks were quick to return after the Athens quake which followed on 7 September 1999.

The Imia Incident

Greek-Turkish relations have had their ups and downs. Most of the time they are up, but when they are down, things can get sticky. Take the case of the rocky islet of Imia, 12 nautical miles east of Kalymnos and four nautical miles from the Turkish coast. Known by the Turks as Kardak, this 10-acre rock, inhabited only by goats and topped by a Greek flag, became the focus of a nasty incident in 1996 that almost led to war between the two former enemies. After the 1947 convention that saw the Italians cede the Dodecanese to Greece, Imia became part of Greece. The trouble was that the Italians had taken the Dodecanese from the Turks in 1912, so as far as the Turks were concerned Imia/Kardak was still theirs. A test of wills took place when a Turkish freighter ran aground on Imia in January 1996 and refused Greek coastguard help. The island was 'Turkish' after all. A group of Turkish journalists took down the Greek flag on Imia and replaced it with the Turkish flag. Greek and Turkish warships converged on the scene, only to back down after a US-sponsored deal that saw the retention of the status quo. And so the goats of Imia still graze under a Greek flag.

While Turkey remains the top priority for Greece, it has also recently had to cope with events to the north, precipitated by the break-up of the former Yugoslavia and the collapse of the communist regimes in Albania and Romania, and succeeded by wars in Bosnia-Hercegovina and NATO attacks on Yugoslavia. However, the Dodecanese's proximity to the Turkish coastline will continue to keep strategic policy watchers on their toes. Perhaps with Turkey's pressing insistence on accession to the EU, threats – imagined or otherwise – by Turkey to the Dodecanese's territorial sovereignty will evaporate once and for all.

GEOGRAPHY

Between the Cyclades and the Turkish coast, the Dodecanese group, with Rhodes the largest of a dozen major islands, has a varied geologic structure ranging from the grey limestones of Kalymnos, Symi and Halki to the complete ancient volcanic cone that forms Nisyros. A further half dozen islands complete the picture and each shares the general geologic structure of the main islands. Kos is the flattest, though the Mt Dikeos (843m) range at the eastern end allows some relief from an otherwise low and mainly scrub-covered island.

The main islands lie on average about 20 nautical miles off the Turkish coastline and share more geographical features with the Anatolian hinterland than with mainland Greece. The Dodecanese Islands encompass an area of some 8500 sq km. From the farthest point north (Agathonisi) to the farthest point south (Kasos) the distance is 112km. The easternmost point is marked by the diminutive island of Kastellorizo, while at the westernmost point lies the island of Astypalea, around 142km away.

Mountainous terrain is found mainly on the islands of Rhodes, Kalymnos and the easternmost quadrant of Kos. The highest mountain in the Dodecanese is Mt Atavyros (1216m) on Rhodes. No lakes or major river systems distinguish the greater majority of these islands and with the notable exception of Rhodes, all islands suffer from water shortages ranging from chronic to extreme.

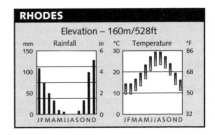

CLIMATE

The Dodecanese Islands enjoy some of the best climatic conditions in the whole of Greece, with a typically Mediterranean climate of hot, dry summers and milder winters. While it can be cold and rainy in Thessaloniki as early as October, it is usually still warm and balmy in Rhodes. Winter is short and it is during this time that the Dodecanese gets its only predictable annual rain. Spring comes quickly, with wildflowers blooming as early as February on some islands. The southern Dodecanese Islands tend to have warmer weather sooner and later than their counterparts in the north of the archipelago.

July and August are also the months of the *meltemi*, a strong northerly wind that sweeps the eastern coast of mainland Greece (including Athens) and the Aegean Islands, especially the Cyclades. The wind is caused by air pressure differences between North Africa and the Balkans. The wind is a mixed blessing: it reduces humidity, but plays havoc with ferry schedules and sends everything flying, from beach umbrellas to washing hanging out to dry. Beaches on the northern side of Dodecanese islands tend to be affected more by the meltemi.

ECOLOGY & ENVIRONMENT

The Dodecanese is belatedly becoming environmentally conscious; regrettably, it is often a case of closing the gate after the horse has bolted. Deforestation and soil erosion are problems that go back thousands of years. Olive cultivation and goats have been the main culprits, but firewood gathering, shipbuilding, housing and industry have all taken their toll.

Forest fires are also a major problem, with an estimated 25,000 hectares destroyed throughout Greece every year. The result is that the forests of ancient Greece have all but disappeared. Rhodes and Karpathos are now the only places where extensive forests remain. This loss of forest cover has been accompanied by serious soil erosion. The problem is finally being addressed with the start of a long overdue reafforestation program.

General environmental awareness remains at a very low level, especially where litter is concerned. The problem is particularly bad in rural areas, where roadsides are strewn with soft-drink cans and plastic packaging hurled from passing cars. Environmental education has begun in schools, but it will be some time before community attitudes change. See boxed text, 'Bin there, done that!'

Water shortages are a major problem on many islands, particularly smaller islands without a permanent water supply. These islands import their water by tanker, and visitors are urged to economise on water use wherever possible: small things, like turning the tap off while you brush your teeth, can make a big difference. The water supplies in Leros and Kalymnos have been tainted by seawater, resulting in very saline tap water that is impossible to drink or use for cooking.

FLORA

Greece and the Dodecanese are endowed with a variety of flora unrivalled in Europe. The wildflowers are spectacular. There are over 6000 species, some of which occur nowhere else, and more than 100 varieties of orchid, with around 50 blooming on Rhodes alone. They continue to thrive because most of the land is too poor for intensive agriculture and has escaped the ravages of chemical fertilisers.

The mountains of the Dodecanese, particularly the slopes of Mt Dikeos in Kos and Mt Atavyros in Rhodes, boast some of the finest displays in the country. During spring the hillsides are carpeted with flowers, which seem to sprout everywhere, even from the rocks. Spring flowers include anemones, white cyclamens, irises, lilies, poppies, gladioli, tulips, countless varieties of daisy and many more. Autumn brings flowers too, especially crocuses.

However, tourism is having its predictable effect on flora as native land is cleared to make way for yet more apartment blocks and bars.

FAUNA

You're unlikely to encounter much in the way of wildlife on most of the islands of the Dodecanese. Reptiles are well represented however, with multitudes of small lizards seen basking on rocks. The Rhodes dragon is a fairly long (up to 30cm) iguana-like reptile with rough, greyish-brown skin. It can be spotted in central Rhodes, more often than not eyeing you up before quietly disappearing into a crevice.

Snakes present include several viper species, which are poisonous, however the island of Astypalea is snake-free. Tortoises

Bin there, done that!

While Greeks in general keep spotless homes, the state of affairs in the streets and back-blocks can be an entirely different affair. Plastic bags and bottles, glass, paper, drink and food cartons are often tossed away with abandon in the curious belief that public property is also dumping property. Rubbish can be a nuisance in Greece, and the Dodecanese are no exception. It is both an eyesore and a health hazard. There is always some forgotten corner of an island that is home to the most unwanted property – the *homateri*, or rubbish tip. This is quite often an abandoned cliff face where waste is dumped without a care for aesthetics or proper disposal. As a visitor you have no excuse to follow suit. Set a good example and take with you all that you take in to a secluded beach, if only to keep the place clean for the next visitors. When in the town or village square, make a point of using waste paper bins and of being seen to do so. Things *will* get better, but it will take time and patience. Do your bit to help things along and bin it!

and terrapins may also be found – the former more or less anywhere in mountain undergrowth and the latter at river mouths on Kos and Rhodes in winter.

The Dodecanese has all the usual Mediterranean small birds – wagtails, tits, warblers, bee-eaters, larks, swallows, flycatchers, thrushes and chats – as well as some more distinctive species such as the hoopoe.

A large number of migratory birds pass by on their way from winter feeding sites in North Africa to summer nesting grounds in Eastern Europe. One very visible visitor is the stork.

A strikingly colourful species of butterfly (actually moths) flocks to a small valley in Rhodes where it feeds on the resin of styrax trees and rests up prior to mating. Unfortunately, its numbers are dropping due to increasing numbers of tourists who come to watch – and disturb it. See Petaloudes in the Rhodes chapter for details.

One of the pleasures of island-hopping in Greece is watching the dolphins as they follow the boats. Although there are many dolphins in the Aegean, the striped dolphin has recently been the victim of murbilivirus, a sickness that affects the immune system.

GOVERNMENT & POLITICS

Since 1975, democratic Greece has been a parliamentary republic with a president as head of state. The president and parliament, which has 300 deputies, have joint legislative power. The PASOK party of Prime Minister Simitis holds 163 seats in the current parliament.

Greece is divided into regions and island groups. The regions of the mainland are Attica (which includes Athens), the Peloponnese, Central Greece (officially called Sterea Ellada), Epiros, Thessaly, Macedonia and Thrace. The island groups are the Cyclades, the Dodecanese, North-Eastern Aegean, Sporades and Saronic Gulf, all in the Aegean Sea, and the Ionian, which is in the Ionian Sea. The large islands of Evia and Crete do not belong to any group.

For administrative purposes these regions and groups are divided into 51 prefectures (*nomi* in Greek) and one autonomous region.

The Dodecanese constitutes one *nomos* – that of the Dodekanisos.

ECONOMY

Although Greece has the second-lowest income per capita of all the EU countries (after Portugal), its long-term economic future looks brighter now than for some time. Tough austerity measures imposed by successive governments had cut inflation to 2.6% by 1999. The Greek stock market has been booming since 1997 and investor confidence appears high.

Initially, problems emanated from the NATO war against Serbia. The fighting,

---

The Price of Fish

When you next sit down at a waterside fish taverna on your favourite island and decide to have a romantic dinner, be prepared. Fish is expensive in Greece. The price you see on the menu – anywhere from 5000 dr to 10,000 dr – is *per kilo* of fish. What you will eventually pay for your fish depends on its weight, but will commonly be around 3000 dr to 4000 dr per serve for a decent fish like red mullet *(barbouni)*.

Fish is expensive for a few reasons. What you will normally get – and what Greeks demand – is fresh fish, taken from the sea near your island in the last 24 hours. What appears on a fish taverna's menu reflects what has been caught. Demand usually exceeds supply and according to the laws of economics, the price remains high.

There is, however, a more sinister aspect to all of this. The Aegean is being overfished and there is an ever-diminishing supply of fresh Aegean fish to meet growing diner demand. Large fishing boats have replaced small fishing smacks and fish caught by the larger concerns is not necessarily heading towards your waterside taverna table. A lot of it heads north to hungry diners in Europe. Fish farms, such as those spotted in Kalymnos and Agathonisi, also feed this consumer demand. Fish may be a renewable resource, but when it is consumed faster than it is renewed, one day it may all be gone: a heavier price to pay indeed.

combined with reports of anti-NATO sentiments in Greece, hit tourism particularly hard in 1999. However, with democracy of sorts restored to Yugoslavia and with the Balkans relatively quiet for once, the economy of the region looks set for a slow revival. Greece has been accepted into the European Monetary Union and will adopt the euro as its currency in line with the policies of the other EU euro states in January 2002.

Tourism is Greece's biggest earner, contributing an estimated $US9 billion a year in foreign exchange. It accounts for a large part of the 50% of the workforce employed in service industries (contributing 59% of GDP). The importance of agriculture has declined rapidly since WWII, with 22% of the workforce now engaged in the agricultural sector (contributing 15%). Tourism is also a major money-spinner in the Dodecanese, having more or less completely supplanted agriculture as the mainstay of the local economy.

POPULATION & PEOPLE

Of an estimated population of 10,601,527 living in Greece today, some 186,800 people reside in the Dodecanese Islands. Rhodes, the largest island, has a population of around 100,000; Kos has around 27,000 inhabitants; and Kalymnos has 18,200 locals. Smaller islands, such as Kastellorizo in the south, have around 275 permanent residents, while in the north, the tiny island of Arki and its satellite island of Marathi have a mere 50 and four locals respectively.

There are small numbers of Turks on Kos and Rhodes, as well as a small Jewish community on Rhodes which dates back to the Roman era. In 1943, the Germans overtook the Dodecanese and virtually destroyed Rhodes' Jewish community. Today there are only about 5000 Jews living in Greece.

The collapse of the communist regimes in Albania and Romania produced a wave of economic refugees across Greece's poorly guarded northern borders, with an estimated 300,000 arriving from Albania alone. They can be found on virtually every Dodecanese island. These refugees have been a vital source of cheap labour for the agricultural sector; fruit and vegetable prices have actually gone down as a result of their contribution. Albanians also have a reputation as fine stonemasons, and their influence can be seen everywhere. Georgians, Armenians and Ukrainians have also been finding their way to the Dodecanese and can often be found working in the service industries.

EDUCATION

Education in Greece is free at all levels of the state system, from kindergarten to tertiary. Primary schooling begins at the age of six, but most children attend a state-run kindergarten from the age of five. Private kindergartens are popular with those who can afford them. Primary school classes tend to be larger than those in most European countries – usually 30 to 35 children. Primary school hours are short (8 am to 1 pm), but children get a lot of homework.

At 12, children enter the *gymnasio*, and at 15 they may leave school or enter the *lykio*, from where they take university-entrance examinations. Although there is a high level of literacy, many parents and pupils are dissatisfied with the education system, especially beyond primary level. The private sector therefore flourishes, and even relatively poor parents struggle to send their children to one of the country's 5000 *frontistiria* (intensive coaching colleges) to prepare them for the very competitive university-entrance exams.

ARTS
Architecture

Of all the ancient Greek arts, architecture has perhaps had the greatest influence. The Dodecanese Islands, like the rest of the country, has many fine architectural examples worth exploring, particularly in Rhodes' impressive Old Town, with its Greek, Roman, Venetian, Turkish and Italian influences. The region also boasts a number of archaeological remains, including the Acropolis of Lindos in Rhodes and the Hellenistic and Roman ruins on Kos.

One of the earliest known architectural sites of ancient Greece is the huge palace and residential complex at Knossos on Crete, built in the Minoan period. Its excavation and reconstruction was begun by Sir Arthur Evans in 1900. Visitors today can see the ruins of the second residential palace built on this site (the first was destroyed by an earthquake in 1700 BC), with its spacious courtyards and grandiose stairways. They can also marvel at the many living rooms, storerooms and bathrooms that give us an idea of day-to-day Minoan life.

The Minoan period was followed by the Mycenaean. Instead of the open, labyrinthine palaces of the Minoans, the Mycenaeans used their advanced skills in engineering to build citadels on a compact, orderly plan, fortified by strong walls.

The next great advance in ancient Greek architecture came with the building of the first monumental stone temples in the Archaic and classical periods. From this time, temples were characterised by the famous orders of columns, particularly the Doric, Ionic and Corinthian. These orders were applied to the exteriors of temples, which retained their traditional simple plan of porch and hall but were now regularly surrounded by a colonnade or at least a columnar facade.

During the Hellenistic period, private houses and palaces, rather than temples and public buildings, were the main focus of building. Some well-preserved examples of Hellenistic houses can be seen at the vast Doric city ruins of ancient Kamiros on the island of Rhodes.

Sculpture

Some of the best examples of sculpture from the Dodecanese Islands can be viewed in the Archaeological Museum in Rhodes; marble exhibits include the beautiful *Aphrodite of Rhodes* and the *Aphrodite of Thalassia*. The renowned statue of Hippocrates, found at the Roman ruins on Kos, is kept in the Archaeological Museum in Kos Town.

The prehistoric art of Greece has been discovered only recently, notably in the Cyclades and on Crete. The pared-down sculptures of this period, with their smooth and flattish appearance, were carved from the high-quality marble of Paros and Naxos in the middle of the 3rd millennium BC. Their primitive and powerful forms have inspired many artists since, particularly those of the 20th century.

Displaying an obvious debt to Egyptian sculpture, the marble sculptures of the Archaic period are the true precursors of the famed Greek sculpture of the classical period. The artists of this period moved away from the examples of their Oriental predecessors and began to represent figures that were true to nature, rather than flat and stylised. Seeking to master the depiction of both the naked body and of drapery, sculptors of the period focused on figures of naked youths *(kouroi)*, with their set symmetrical stance and enigmatic smiles. At first the classical style was rather severe; later, as sculptors sought ideal proportions for the human figure, it became more animated.

Unfortunately, little original work of the classical period survives. Most freestanding classical sculpture described by ancient writers was made of bronze and survives only as marble copies made by the Romans. Fortunately, a few classical bronzes, lost when they were being shipped abroad in antiquity, were recovered from the sea in the 20th century, including a 2m statue found near Kalymnos by a local fisherman. These bronze sculptures are now in the collection of the National Archaeological Museum in Athens.

The sculpture of the Hellenistic period continued the Greeks' quest to attain total naturalism in their work. Works of this period were animated, almost theatrical, in contrast to their serene Archaic and classical predecessors. The focus was on realism. Just how successful the artists of this period were is shown in the way later artists, such as Michelangelo, revered them. Michelangelo, in fact, was at the forefront of the rediscovery and appreciation of Greek works in the Renaissance. He is said to have been at the site in Rome in 1506 when the famous Roman copy of the *Laocoön* group, one of the iconic sculptural works of the Hellenistic period, was unearthed.

Pottery

Say the words 'Greek art' and many people immediately visualise a painted terracotta pot. Represented in museums and art galleries throughout the world, the pots of ancient Greece have such a high profile for a number of reasons, chief among these being that there are lots of them around!

Practised from the Stone Age, pottery is one of the most ancient arts. At first, vases were built with coils and wads of clay but the art of throwing on the wheel was introduced in about 2000 BC and was then practised with great skill by Minoan and Mycenaean artists.

The 10th century BC saw the introduction of the Protogeometric style, with its substantial pots decorated with blackish-brown horizontal lines around the circumference, hatched triangles, and compass-drawn concentric circles. This was followed by the new vase shape and more crowded decoration of the pots of the Geometric period. By the early 8th century, figures were introduced, marking the introduction of the most fundamental element in the later tradition of classical art – the representation of gods, men and animals.

Music

Singing and the playing of musical instruments have also been an integral part of life in Greece since ancient times. Cycladic figurines holding instruments resembling harps and flutes date back to 2000 BC. Musical instruments of ancient Greece included the lyre, lute, *piktis* (pipes), *kroupeza* (a percussion instrument), *kithara* (a stringed instrument), *aulos* (a wind instrument), *barbitos* (similar to a violin cello) and the *magadio* (similar to a harp).

If ancient Greeks did not have a musical instrument to accompany their songs, they imitated the sound of one. It is believed that unaccompanied Byzantine choral singing derived from this custom.

The *bouzouki*, which you will hear everywhere in Greece, is a mandolin-like instrument similar to the Turkish *saz* and *baglama*. It is one of the main instruments of *rembetika* music – the Greek equivalent of the American Blues. The name rembetika may come from the Turkish word *rembet* which means outlaw. Opinions differ as to the origins of rembetika, but it is probably a hybrid of several different types of music. One source was the music that emerged in the 1870s in the 'low life' cafes, called *tekedes* (hashish dens), in urban areas and especially around ports. Another source was the Arabo-Persian music played in sophisticated Middle Eastern music cafes *(amanedes)* in the 19th century. Rembetika was popularised in Greece by the refugees from Asia Minor.

The regional music of the Dodecanese was never dependent on the sound of the bouzouki for its own expression, relying instead on the more muted sounds of the *lyra*, a three-stringed fiddle, the more wooden sounds of the *laouto*, like an oversized bouzouki and the somewhat primitive *tasmbouna*, a kind of droneless bagpipe. The lyra is just as likely to be replaced these days by what is essentially a western violin, the *violi,* and you will occasionally come across the difficult-to-learn hammered dulcimer or *sandouri*.

Dodecanese music developed more or less in isolation from the mainland influences, but has assumed musical similarities from neighbouring Crete and the Anatolian mainland. On Kasos and Karpathos in particular you will come across the lyra and laouto and a musical style more reminiscent of Crete than the lilting, spirited melodies of the

Everywhere you go you'll see and hear the bouzouki.

violin found in the central Aegean. The bagpipes are more likely to be heard on Patmos, Kalymnos and Karpathos, though bagpipes in general have appeared in musical cultures from as wide apart as Scotland and Central Asia.

Mandinadhes are songs made up of short rhyming couplets, heard often on Karpathos, while *helidonismata* are so-called 'swallow songs' – demotic songs peculiar to Halki and Nisyros.

Although you can buy Dodecanese music on CD or tape in specialised record stores you will have to look hard to find it. If you are looking for live music, it is best to look out for weddings or *paniyria* (festivals) which spring up all over the Dodecanese in summer.

Dance

The folk dances of today derive from the ritual dances performed in ancient Greek temples. One of these dances, the *syrtos*, is depicted on ancient Greek vases. There are references to dances in Homer's works. Many Greek folk dances, including the syrtos, are performed in a circular formation; in ancient times, dancers formed a circle in order to seal themselves off from evil influences.

Each region of Greece has its own dances, but one dance you'll see performed everywhere is the *kalamatianos*, originally from Kalamata in the Peloponnese. It's the dance in which dancers stand in a row with their hands on one another's shoulders. The more common island version is the *syrtos* – mentioned above – a circle dance where participants dance in a circle clasping each other's shoulders, while the lead dancer performs improvised kicks and twirls. The *ballos* is an island dance that originates from the Cyclades where two dancers execute their steps facing each other.

The Dodecanese has a series of dances, each differing in pace and steps from island to island, but generally characterised by a lightness in melody and rhythm. One poignant dance is particular to Kalymnos and is known as the *mihanikos*, the sponge diver's dance. The following description of

this dance is from a recent book on sponge diving in Greece.

The *mihanikos* is performed by proud, handsome young men full of athletic energy and fire. In the traditional style and dress of the islands, they circle, swirl and kick with prowess and comradely skill – until their dark-eyed leader suddenly falls to the ground. Watched with pity and fear by his friends, he can only drag himself up painfully slowly with the aid of a stick and a terrible force of will over the barely controllable shaking of his pathetic useless legs. His fine strong body has been crippled in its prime. He tries to continue dancing but all the fire has gone and in its place is angry despair and frustration at his helpless limbs.

As you listen to the sorrowful cry of the violin and watch the dance progress, the hairs on your neck start to rise and shivers tremble down your spine. Your stomach tightens to a knot and you dare not speak for fear of betraying such overwhelming emotion.

Eventually the dance ends in a climax of triumphant bravado. Today's performer is free to throw away his stick and kick and swirl once more with his friends. But that's not the part that stays with you. For moments the sponge diver who danced so proudly became like a broken shell. You watched him with pain and dread and now his image will not leave your mind.

Faith Warn, *Bitter Sea – The Real Story of Sponge Diving* (Guardian Angel Press, 2000)

Literature

The first, and greatest, ancient Greek writer was Homer, author of the *Iliad* and *Odyssey*. Nothing is known of Homer's life; where or when he lived, or whether, as it is alleged, he was blind. The historian Herodotus thought Homer lived in the 9th century BC, and no scholar since has proved nor disproved this.

Herodotus (5th century BC) was the author of the first historical work about western civilisation. His highly subjective account of the Persian Wars has, however, led him to be regarded as the 'father of lies' as well as the 'father of history'. The historian Thucydides (5th century BC) was more objective in his approach, but took a high moral stance. He wrote an account of the Peloponnesian Wars, and also the famous

Melian Dialogue, which chronicles the talks between the Athenians and Melians prior to the Athenian siege of Melos.

Pindar (c.518–438 BC) is regarded as the pre-eminent lyric poet of ancient Greece. He was commissioned to recite his odes at the Olympic Games. The greatest writers of love poetry were Sappho (6th century BC) and Alcaeus (5th century BC), both of whom lived on Lesvos. Sappho's poetic descriptions of her affections for other women gave rise to the term 'lesbian'.

In Byzantine times, poetry, like all of the arts, was of a religious nature. During Ottoman rule, poetry was inextricably linked with folk songs, which were not written down but passed on by word of mouth. Many of these songs were composed by the klefts, and told of the harshness of life in the mountains and of their uprisings against the Turks.

Dionysios Solomos (1798–1857) and Andreas Kalvos (1796–1869), who were both born on Zakynthos, are regarded as the first modern Greek poets. Solomos' work was heavily nationalistic and his *Hymn to Freedom* became the Greek national anthem. The highly acclaimed poet Constantine Cavafy (1863–1933) was less concerned with nationalism, being a resident of Alexandria in Egypt; his themes ranged from the erotic to the philosophical.

The best known 20th-century Greek poets are George Seferis (1900–71), who won the Nobel Prize for literature in 1963, and Odysseus Elytis (1911–96), who won the same prize in 1979. Seferis drew his inspiration from the Greek myths, whereas Elytis' work is surreal. The most celebrated 20th-century Greek novelist is Nikos Kazantzakis.

See the Books section in the Facts for the Visitor chapter for more information.

Drama

Drama in Greece can be dated back to the contests staged at the Ancient Theatre of Dionysos in Athens during the 6th century BC for the annual Dionysia festival. During one of these competitions, Thespis left the ensemble and took centre stage for a solo performance regarded as the first true dramatic performance. The term 'Thespian' for actor derives from this event.

Aeschylus (c.525–456 BC) is the so-called 'father of tragedy'; his best-known work is the *Oresteia* trilogy. Sophocles (c.496-406 BC) is regarded as the greatest tragedian. He is thought to have written over 100 plays, of which only seven major works survive. These include *Ajax, Antigone, Electra, Trachiniae* and his most famous play, *Oedipus Rex*. His plays dealt mainly with tales from mythology and had complex plots. Sophocles won first prize 18 times at the Dionysia festival, beating Aeschylus in 468 BC, whereupon Aeschylus went off to Sicily in a huff.

Euripides (c.485–406 BC), another famous tragedian, was more popular than either Aeschylus or Sophocles because his plots were considered more exciting. He wrote 80 plays of which 19 are extant (although one, *Rhesus*, is disputed). His most famous works are *Medea, Andromache, Orestias* and *Bacchae*. Aristophanes (c.427–387 BC) wrote comedies – often ribald – which dealt with topical issues. His play *The Wasp* ridicules Athenians who resorted to litigation over trivialities; *The Birds* pokes fun at Athenian gullibility; and *Ploutos* deals with the unfair distribution of wealth.

You might catch a play by the ancient Greek playwrights during the annual Symi festival (see the Symi section in the Central Dodecanese chapter).

SOCIETY & CONDUCT
Traditional Culture

Like other parts of Greece, the Dodecanese are steeped in traditional customs. Name days, weddings and funerals all have great significance. Name days are celebrated instead of birthdays. A person's name day is the feast day of the saint after whom the person is named; on someone's name day an open-house policy is adopted and refreshments are served to well-wishers who stop by to give gifts. Weddings are highly festive occasions, with dancing, feasting and drinking sometimes continuing for days.

Tourism has played a role in the disappearance of some island culture in the

Dodecanese. For many, the lure of the tourist drachma is more important than maintaining traditional values, and the original essence of some places – predominantly beach resorts on islands such as Rhodes and Kos – has been drowned by commercialism. The best place to experience traditional culture is on the farthest flung islands, such as Kasos, Kastellorizo and Lipsi, or in inland mountain villages, such as Olymbos on Karpathos, which has fiercely clung onto its traditions, including dress and communal breadmaking (see Olymbos in the Southern Dodecanese chapter). However, regardless of tourism, every island has its religious and secular festivities, which haven't changed for hundreds of years.

Greeks tend to be more superstitious than other Europeans. Tuesday is considered unlucky because it's the day on which Constantinople fell to the Ottoman Turks. Many Greeks will not sign an important transaction, get married or begin a trip on a Tuesday.

Greeks also believe in the 'evil eye', a superstition prevalent in many Middle Eastern countries. If someone is the victim of the evil eye, then bad luck will befall them. The bad luck is the result of someone's envy, so one should avoid being too complimentary about things of beauty, especially newborn babies. To ward off the evil eye, Greeks often wear a piece of blue glass, resembling an eye, on a chain around their necks.

Dos & Don'ts

The Greeks' reputation for hospitality is not a myth, although it's a bit harder to find these days. In rural areas, Greece is probably the only country in Europe where you may be invited into a stranger's home for coffee, or even a meal. The recipient may feel uneasy if the host is poor, but to offer money is considered offensive. The most acceptable way of saying thank you is through a gift, perhaps to a child in the family. A similar situation arises if you go out for a meal with Greeks; the bill is not shared as in northern European countries, but paid by the host.

When drinking wine, it is the custom to half fill the glass. It is also bad manners to empty the glass, so it must be constantly replenished.

Personal questions are not considered rude in Greece, and if you react as if they are you will be the one causing offence. You will be inundated with queries about your age, salary, marital status etc.

If you go into a *kafeneio*, taverna, or shop, it is the custom to greet the waiters and assistants with *'kalimera'* (good day) or *'kalispera'* (good evening) – likewise if you meet someone in the street.

RELIGION

About 98% of Greeks belong to the Greek Orthodox Church. Most of the remainder are either Roman Catholic, Jewish or Muslim.

Orthodoxy in the Dodecanese

Greek Orthodoxy is a community of Christian churches that came about when the Greek-speaking Eastern section of the Latin-speaking Church of Rome split from Rome in what was known as the Great Schism in 1054. Orthodoxy means 'the right belief' and its adherents do not recognise the jurisdiction of the Catholic Pope. They recognise only the Patriarch of Constantinople as their leader. Other than dogmatic differences and an entrenched sense of separateness from Rome, the Greek Orthodox Church is in many ways similar to the Catholic Church. However, much of the church liturgy is steeped in tradition and conservatism and little has changed since the Schism. Church services are redolent with formality and ceremony and often last up to three hours. Yet at the same time they are informal family affairs, with participants wandering in and out of the service at will, often exchanging small talk and gossip with other churchgoers. This is in stark contrast to the strict observances of behaviour in the Catholic Church yet its more liberal approach to liturgy. Orthodoxy as a popular religion still wields considerable influence in the Dodecanese and the adaptation of the Church to the modern secularised world – including topless and nude bathing – has proved to be problematic.

The Greek Orthodox Church is closely related to the Russian Orthodox Church and together with it forms the third-largest branch of Christianity. Orthodox, meaning 'right belief', was founded in the 4th century by Constantine the Great, who was converted to Christianity by a vision of the Cross.

During Ottoman times membership of the Orthodox Church was one of the most important criteria in defining a Greek, regardless of where he or she lived. The church was the principal upholder of Greek culture and traditions.

Religion is still integral to life in the Dodecanese (see boxed text 'Orthodoxy in the Dodecanese') and the year is centred on the festivals of the church calendar. Most Greeks, when they have a problem, will go into a church and light a candle to the saint they feel is most likely to help them.

Throughout the Dodecanese you will see tiny churches dotted around the countryside. Most have been built by individual families in the name of their selected patron saint as thanksgiving for God's protection.

If you wish to look around a church, you should dress appropriately. Women should wear skirts that reach below the knees, and men should wear long trousers and have their arms covered. Regrettably, many churches are kept locked nowadays, but it's usually easy enough to locate caretakers, who will be happy to open them up for you.

LANGUAGE

Greek is the predominant language spoken in the Dodecanese and is the same as the Greek spoken elsewhere in Greece. The accent is what distinguishes Dodecanese Greek from Greek spoken in other regions of Greece. It tends to be lighter and to display a sing-song lilt – a trait that is particularly noticeable in small villages on the islands of Kos and Rhodes. In Rhodes itself the accent also displays a marked similarity to that of Cyprus. The guttural *ch* (as in the Scottish *loch*) becomes palatalised and is pronounced as *sh*, while the standard Greek *k* is often pronounced as *ch* (as in *cheese*). The dialect of the village of Olymbos in Karpathos is unquestionably Greek, but outsiders find it invariably difficult to understand. Linguists have noted in the Olymbos vernacular marked traces of the ancient Dorian dialect that was spoken in antiquity in the Peloponnese.

Small groups of Turkish speakers exist in Rhodes Old Town and the village of Platanos on Kos, but these are diminishing in number as the older generation dies out. Italian never took hold as an established language in the Dodecanese, despite the Italian government's insistence on its usage as an official language during their tenure from 1912 to 1943. Italian is now only routinely spoken by the older generations who lived through that era.

English is widely taught and spoken and is the preferred language of choice by operators in the tourist industry. In Rhodes' Old and new Towns you will also find people involved in the tourist industry who speak Norwegian, Swedish, Danish and even Finnish.

Facts for the Visitor

The Best

It's tough trying to pick the top 10 favourite things about the Dodecanese. These are personal favourites – the places and activities that the author of this book would like to dedicate a lot more of his time to.

1 Dining on a rooftop at night in Lindos
2 Taking it easy on Telendos
3 Eating fish at a harbourside restaurant in Halki
4 Enjoying the unique spirit of place in the Hora, Patmos
5 Hiking to hidden beaches on Tilos
6 Learning how to windsurf in Kos
7 Reading a book on a beach in Lipsi
8 Skin diving at Ammoöpi beach in Karpathos
9 Strolling the back streets of Rhodes Old Town at night
10 Talking with the locals and sipping ouzo in Kastellorizo

The Worst

The author would be happy not to do the following again:

1 Being caught in one of Tilos' regular power blackouts
2 Dining at tourist restaurants in Rhodes Old Town
3 Having a night out at 'Bar Alley', Kos
4 Spending more than 30 minutes at Faliraki, Rhodes
5 Spending more than an hour at Kardamena, Kos
6 Staying at second-rate accommodation in Nisyros
7 Swimming at Kos Town's overcrowded beaches
8 Showering in Kalymnos' salty tap water
9 Travelling on rust-bucket ferries from the 1950s
10 Visiting the village of Lindos during the day

SUGGESTED ITINERARIES
One Week
Rhodes & the Central Dodecanese With one week at your disposal start your trip in Rhodes and allow at least three days to see this large and wonderfully varied island. Visit the medieval Old Town, take in a beach or two along the east coast and visit the Acropolis of Lindos and its picture postcard village. Forget the day trips to the island of Symi – spend at least one night there and enjoy its relaxed atmosphere and fine food once the day-trippers have gone back to Rhodes. Take a two-day excursion by catamaran to the little-visited and delightfully laid-back islands of Nisyros, with its dormant volcano, and Tilos, with its slow bucolic pace and relaxed, genuine lifestyle.

Two Weeks
Rhodes, the Southern & Central Dodecanese Combine the one-week itinerary with a visit to Karpathos and Kasos for excellent beaches, mountain villages and simple fishing ports. Allow at least four days to see both islands. Take a plane to Kastellorizo, the most remote of the Dodecanese Islands, and spend two days on the small rocky island where the movie *Mediterraneo* was shot. If you can shave a day off your itinerary from elsewhere, spend a night or two on the peaceful island of Halki.

Three Weeks
Rhodes, the Northern, Central & Southern Dodecanese You won't get to see all the Dodecanese comfortably in three weeks, so you'll have to tackle the islands in one of two ways. Perhaps start at Patmos, the island of St John, and visit the scattered islands of the Northern Dodecanese – Lipsi, Arki, Marathi and Agathonisi. Allow a week for this. In the remaining two weeks work your way down to Rhodes via the central islands of Leros and Kalymnos. Take a detour, if possible, to the butterfly-shaped island of Astypalea with its Cycladic hill village and Venetian castle. Then chill out with some fine swimming, sunset-watching and dining in southern Kos. Pick up Nisyros and Tilos along the way to Rhodes and choose from the remaining Southern Dodecanese islands according to taste and time. Alternatively, travel from south to north following the two-week itinerary and then visit at least Kalymnos, Leros and Patmos.

PLANNING
When to Go
The best times to visit the Dodecanese Islands are in late spring, early summer and autumn. Winter is pretty much a dead loss with the exception of Rhodes where winter tourism is becoming quite popular and there is still a fair amount of activity to keep you busy. Most of the remaining tourist infrastructure goes into hibernation from November until the beginning of April – hotels and restaurants are closed and bus and ferry services are either drastically reduced or cancelled altogether.

The cobwebs are dusted off just in time for Easter, when the first tourists start to arrive. Conditions are usually perfect between Easter and mid-June, when the weather is pleasantly warm throughout the islands, but not too hot; beaches and ancient sites are relatively uncrowded; public transport operates on close to full schedules; and accommodation is cheaper and much easier to find.

Mid-June until the end of August is the high season. It's party time on the islands and everything is in full swing. It's also very hot – in July and August the mercury can soar to 40°C (100°F) in the shade. The beaches are crowded, the ancient sites are swarming with tour groups, and in many places accommodation is booked solid.

The season starts to wind down in September, and conditions are ideal once more until the end of October.

Maps
Most tourist offices hand out free maps, but they are often out of date and not particularly accurate. The same applies to the cheap (400 dr to 500 dr) 'tourist maps' sold on every island.

The best maps by far are published by the Greek company, Road Editions. There is a wide range of maps to suit various needs, starting with a 1:500,000 map of *Greece* which includes the Dodecanese. Individual Dodecanese islands currently covered by Road Editions are the 1:100,000 maps of *Kos* and *Rhodes*. Further island maps from the Dodecanese are being released, with

maps to Karpathos & Kasos, Symi, Nisyros & Tilos, Astypalea, Leros & Kalymnos and Patmos either being produced or on the drawing boards.

These maps can be hard to find in the Dodecanese so your best bet is to get them from Road Editions (☎ 01-361 3242, fax 361 1681, ⒠ road@enet.gr), Ippokratous 65 in central Athens, several blocks north from Akadimias. They are reasonably priced at around 1300 dr for a blue island map and around 1900 dr for a larger regional maroon map of mainland Greece.

What to Bring
Sturdy shoes are essential for clambering around ancient sites and wandering around historic towns and villages, which tend to have lots of steps and cobbled streets. Footwear with ankle support is preferable for trekking, although many visitors get by with trainers.

A day-pack is useful for the beach, and for sightseeing or trekking. A compass is essential if you are going to trek in remote areas, as is a whistle, which you can use should you become lost or disoriented. A torch (flashlight) is not only needed if you intend to explore caves, but comes in handy during occasional power cuts. If you like to fill a washbasin or bathtub (a rarity in Greece), bring a universal plug as Greek bathrooms rarely have plugs.

Many island camping grounds have covered areas where tourists without tents can sleep in summer, so you can generally get by with a lightweight sleeping bag and foam bedroll.

You will need only light clothing – preferably cotton – during the summer months. In spring and autumn you'll need a light jumper or jacket in the evening.

In summer, a broad-rimmed sun hat and sunglasses are essential (see 'Environmental Hazards' in the Health section later in this chapter). Sunscreen creams are quite expensive, as are moisturising and cleansing creams.

If you read a lot, it's a good idea to bring along a few disposable paperbacks to read and swap.

RESPONSIBLE TOURISM

Some hoteliers and tourist operators seem to have been irresponsible and gone overboard in the race to over-develop (in certain parts of Kos and Rhodes at least). Thankfully this trend, with one or two notable exceptions, is now beginning to wane a little. There is no reason for travellers to adopt a similar devil-may-care attitude.

Travelling light, green and lean is the way to go – in the Dodecanese as much as anywhere else in Greece. Water is scarce on some islands – notably the smaller ones – so use it sparingly, even in a big hotel. Dispose of rubbish thoughtfully and be seen to dispose of it. Set a good example to travellers *and* islanders. Spread your spending money around. Support all local businesses and artists: their welfare and the future viability of their community depends on you.

TOURIST OFFICES

Tourist information is handled by the Greek National Tourist Organisation, known by the initials GNTO abroad and EOT (Ellinikos Organismos Tourismou) in Greece.

Local Tourist Offices

The EOT's head office (☎ 01-322 3111, e info@ gnto.gr) is at Amerikis 2, Athens 105 64. There are about 25 EOT offices throughout Greece. Most EOT staff speak English, but their level of enthusiasm and helpfulness varies. Some offices, like those in Kos and Rhodes, have loads of useful local information, but most have nothing more than glossy brochures, usually about other parts of the country. Some have absolutely nothing to offer.

In addition to EOT offices, there are also municipal tourist offices. They are often more helpful.

Tourist Offices Abroad

GNTO offices abroad include:

Australia (☎ 02-9241 1663/4/5) 51 Pitt St, Sydney NSW 2000
Austria (☎ 1-512 5317/8) Opernring 8, Vienna A-10105
Belgium (☎ 2-647 5770) 172 Ave Louise Louizalaan, B-1050 Brussels

Canada (☎ 416-968 2220) 1300 Bay St, Toronto, Ontario M5R 3K8
Denmark (☎ 3-325 332) Vester Farimagsgade 1, 1606 Copenhagen
France (☎ 01-42 60 65 75) 3 Ave de l'Opéra, Paris 75001
Germany (☎ 69-237 735) Neue Mainzerstrasse 22, 60311 Frankfurt
(☎ 89-222 035/6) Pacellistrasse 5, W 80333 Munich 2
(☎ 40-454 498) Abteistrasse 33, 20149 Hamburg 13
(☎ 30-217 6262) Wittenbergplatz 3A, 10789 Berlin 30
Israel (☎ 23-517 0501) 5 Shalom Aleichem St, Tel Aviv 61262
Italy (☎ 06-474 4249) Via L Bissolati 78-80, Rome 00187
(☎ 02-860 470) Piazza Diaz 1, 20123 Milan
Japan (☎ 03-350 55 911) Fukuda Building West, 5F 2-11-3 Akasaka, Minato-Ku, Tokyo 107
Netherlands (☎ 020-625 4212/3/4) Leidsestraat 13, Amsterdam NS 1017
Norway (☎ 2-426 501) Ovre Slottsgate 15B, 0157 Oslo 1
Sweden (☎ 8-679 6480) Birger Jarlsgatan 30, Box 5298 S, 10246 Stockholm
Switzerland (☎ 01-221 0105) Loewenstrasse 25, CH 8001-Zürich
UK (☎ 020-7499 4976) 4 Conduit St, London W1R ODJ
USA (☎ 212-421 5777) Olympic Tower, 645 5th Ave, New York, NY 10022
(☎ 312-782 1084) Suite 600, 168 North Michigan Ave, Chicago, Illinois 60601
(☎ 213-626 6696) Suite 2198, 611 West 6th St, Los Angeles, California 92668

Tourist Police

The tourist police work in cooperation with the regular Greek police and EOT. Each tourist police office has at least one member of staff who speaks English. Hotels, restaurants, travel agencies, tourist shops, tourist guides, waiters, taxi drivers and bus drivers all come under the jurisdiction of the tourist police. If you think that you have been ripped off by any of these, report it to the tourist police and they will investigate.

If you need to report a theft or loss of passport, the tourist police will act as interpreters between you and the regular police. The tourist police also fulfil the same functions as the EOT and municipal tourist offices, dispensing maps and brochures, and giving information on transport. If there is no tourist police representative available, such as on the smaller islands of Agathonisi and Arki, you should contact the regular police.

VISAS & DOCUMENTS
Passport
To enter Greece you need a valid passport or, for EU nationals, travel documents (ID cards). You must produce your passport or EU travel documents when you register in a hotel or pension in Greece. You will find that many proprietors will want to keep your passport during your stay. This is not a compulsory requirement: they need it only long enough to take down the details.

Visas
The list of countries whose nationals can stay in Greece for up to three months without a visa include Australia, Canada, all EU countries, Iceland, Israel, Japan, New Zealand, Norway, Switzerland and the USA. Other countries included are Cyprus, Malta, the European principalities of Monaco and San Marino, and most South American countries. This list changes, so contact a Greek embassy for an update. Those not on the list can expect to pay about US$20 for a three-month visa. Additionally, an AIDS test is required for performing artists and students on Greek government scholarships; US test results are not accepted.

Greece may refuse entry to people whose passport indicates that they have visited Turkish-occupied North Cyprus since November 1983. This can be overcome if, upon entering North Cyprus, you ask the immigration officials to stamp a piece of paper (loose-leaf visa) rather than your passport. If you enter North Cyprus from the Greek Republic of Cyprus (only possible for a day visit), an exit stamp is not put into your passport.

Visa Extensions If you want to stay in Greece for longer than three months, apply at a consulate abroad or at least 20 days in advance to the Aliens Bureau (☎ 01-770 5711), Leoforos Alexandras 173 in Athens. Take your passport and four passport photographs along. You may be asked for proof that you can support yourself financially, so keep all your bank exchange slips (or the equivalent from a post office). These slips are not always automatically given – you may have to ask for them. The Aliens Bureau is open 8 am to 1 pm on weekdays. In the Dodecanese apply to the local police authority. You will be given a permit, which will authorise you to stay in the country for a period up to six months.

Most travellers get around this by visiting Bulgaria or Turkey briefly and then re-entering Greece.

Travel Insurance
A travel insurance policy to cover theft, loss and medical problems is a good idea. The policies handled by STA Travel (with offices worldwide) and other student travel organisations are usually good value.

There is a wide variety of policies available; check the small print. Some policies specifically exclude 'dangerous activities' which can include scuba diving, motorcycling, even trekking. Remember that a locally acquired motorcycle licence is not valid under some policies.

You may prefer a policy that pays doctors or hospitals direct rather than you having to pay on the spot and claim later. If you have to claim later make sure you keep all documentation. Some policies ask you to call back (reverse charges) to a centre in your home country where an immediate assessment of your problem is made.

Check that the policy covers ambulances or an emergency flight home.

Driving Licence & Permits
Greece recognises all national driving licences, provided the licence has been held for at least one year. It also recognises an International Driving Permit, which should be obtained before you leave home.

Student & Youth Cards
The most widely recognised (and thus the most useful) form of student ID is the International Student Identity Card (ISIC). Card holders qualify for half-price admission to museums and ancient sites and for discounts

at some budget hotels and hostels. See the boxed text 'Student Cards' for more details.

Aegean Airlines and Cronus Airlines both offer student discounts on domestic flights, but there are no discounts on buses, ferries or trains.

Copies

All important documents (passport data page and visa page, credit cards, travel insurance policy, air/bus/train tickets, driving licence etc) should be photocopied before you leave home. Leave one copy with someone at home and keep another with you, separate from the originals.

It's also a good idea to store details of your vital travel documents in Lonely Planet's free

Student Cards

An ISIC (International Student Identity Card) is a plastic ID-style card displaying your photograph. These cards are widely available from budget travel agencies (you will need to show documents proving you are a student, provide a passport photograph and cough up 2500 dr). In Athens you can get one from the International Student & Youth Travel Service (ISYTS; ☎ 01-323 3767), 2nd floor, Nikis 11.

Some travel agencies in Greece offer discounts on organised tours to students. However, there are no student discounts for travel within Greece (although Olympic Airways gives a 25% discount on domestic flights that are part of an international flight). Turkish Airlines (THY) gives 55% student discounts on its international flights. THY has flights from Athens to İstanbul and İzmir. Most ferries to Cyprus, Israel and Egypt from Piraeus give a 20% student discount and a few services between Greek and Italian ports do so also.

If you are under 26 years but not a student, the Federation of International Youth Travel Organisation (FIYTO) card gives similar discounts. Many budget travel agencies issue FIYTO cards, including London Explorers Club (☎ 020-7792 3770), 33 Princes Square, Bayswater, London W2; and SRS Studenten Reise Service (☎ 030-2 83 30 93), Marienstrasse 23, Berlin.

online Travel Vault in case you lose the photocopies or can't be bothered with them. Your password-protected Travel Vault is accessible online anywhere in the world – create it at www.ekno.lonelyplanet.com.

EMBASSIES & CONSULATES
Greek Embassies & Consulates

The following is a selection of Greek diplomatic missions abroad:

Australia (☎ 02-6273 3011) 9 Turrana St, Yarralumla, Canberra ACT 2600
Canada (☎ 613-238 6271) 76-80 Maclaren St, Ottawa, Ontario K2P OK6
Denmark (☎ 33-11 4533) Borgergade 16, 1300 Copenhagen K
France (☎ 01-47 23 72 28) 17 Rue Auguste Vacquerie, 75116 Paris
Germany (☎ 228-83010) An Der Marienkapelleb 10, 53 179 Bonn
Ireland (☎ 01-676 7254) 1 Upper Pembroke St, Dublin 2
Israel (☎ 03-605 5461) 47 Bodenheimer St, Tel Aviv 62008
Italy (☎ 06-854 9630) Via S Mercadante 36, Rome 00198
Netherlands (☎ 070-363 87 00) Koninginnegracht 37, 2514 AD, Den Hague
New Zealand (☎ 04-473 7775) 5-7 Willeston St, Wellington
Norway (☎ 22-44 2728) Nobels Gate 45, 0244 Oslo 2
South Africa (☎ 12-437 351/2) 995 Pretorius St, Arcadia, Pretoria 0083
Sweden (☎ 08-663 7577) Riddargatan 60, 11457 Stockholm
UK (☎ 020-7229 3850) 1A Holland Park, London W11 3TP
USA (☎ 202-939 5818) 2221 Massachusetts Ave NW, Washington DC 20008

Embassies & Consulates in Greece

All foreign embassies in Greece are in Athens and its suburbs (telephone code 01). They include:

Australia (☎ 645 0404) Dimitriou Soutsou 37, Athens GR-115 21
Bulgaria (☎ 647 8105) Stratigou Kalari 33A, Psyhiko, Athens GR-154 52
Canada (☎ 727 3400) Gennadiou 4, Athens GR-115 21
Cyprus (☎ 723 7883) Irodotou 16, Athens GR-106 75

Egypt (☎ 361 8613) Leoforos Vasilissis Sofias 3, Athens GR-106 71

France (☎ 339 1000) Leoforos Vasilissis Sofias 7, Athens GR-106 71

Germany (☎ 728 5111) Dimitriou 3 & Karaoli, Kolonaki, Athens GR-106 75

Ireland (☎ 723 2771) Leoforos Vasileos Konstantinou 7, Athens GR-106 74

Israel (☎ 671 9530) Marathonodromou 1, Psyhiko, Athens GR-154 52

Italy (☎ 361 7260) Sekeri 2, Athens GR-106 74

Japan (☎ 775 8101) Athens Tower, Leoforos Mesogion 2-4, Athens GR-115 27

Netherlands (☎ 723 9701) Vasileos Konstantinou 5-7, Athens GR-106 74

New Zealand *Consulate* (☎ 771 0112) Xenias 24, Athens GR-115 28

South Africa (☎ 680 6645) Kifisias 60, Maroussi, Athens GR-151 25

Turkey (☎ 724 5915) Vasilissis Georgiou 8, Athens GR-106 74

UK (☎ 723 6211) Ploutarhou 1, Athens GR-106 75

USA (☎ 721 2951, ⓔ consul@global.net) Leoforos Vasilissis Sofias 91, Athens GR-115 21

Foreign consulates in the Dodecanese (telephone code 0241) include:

Denmark (☎ 31 540) Ionos Dragoumi 5a, Rhodes GR-851 00

France (☎ 22 318, fax 22 435) Kritis 7-11, Rhodes GR-851 00

Germany (☎ 63 730) Parados Isodou, Rhodes GR-851 00

Ireland (☎ 22 461) Amerikis, Rhodes GR-851 00

Italy (☎ 27 342) Ippoton, Rhodes GR-851 00

Netherlands (☎ 31 571) Diakou 25, Rhodes GR-851 00

Norway (☎ 27 313) Ierou Lohou 11, Rhodes GR-851 00

Sweden (☎ 31 822, fax 77 758) Averof 9, Rhodes GR-851 00

Turkey (☎ 23 362) Polytehniou 10, Rhodes GR-851 00

UK (☎ 27 306, fax 22 615) Pavlou Mela 3, Rhodes GR-851 00

Generally speaking, your own country's embassy won't be much help in emergencies if the trouble you're in is remotely your own fault. Remember that you are bound by Greek laws. Your embassy will not be sympathetic if you end up in jail after committing a crime locally, even if such actions are legal in your own country.

In genuine emergencies you might get some assistance if you're lucky, but only if other channels have been exhausted. For example, if you need to get home urgently, a free ticket home is exceedingly unlikely – the embassy would expect you to have insurance. If you have all your money and documents stolen, it might assist with getting a new passport, but a loan for onward travel is out of the question.

CUSTOMS

There are no longer duty-free restrictions within the EU. This does not mean, however, that customs checks have been dispensed with – random searches are still made for drugs.

Upon entering the country from outside the EU, customs inspection is usually cursory for foreign tourists. There may be spot checks, but you probably won't have to open your bags. A verbal declaration is usually all that is required.

You may bring the following into Greece duty-free: 200 cigarettes or 50 cigars; 1L of spirits or 2L of wine; 50g of perfume; 250ml of eau de Cologne; one camera (still or video) and film; a pair of binoculars; a portable musical instrument; a portable radio or tape recorder; a typewriter; sports equipment; and dogs and cats (with a veterinary certificate).

Importation of works of art and antiquities is free, but they must be declared on entry, so that they can be re-exported. Import regulations for medicines are strict; if you are taking medication, make sure you get a statement from your doctor before you leave home. It is illegal, for instance, to take codeine into Greece without an accompanying doctor's certificate.

You are allowed to bring an unlimited amount of foreign currency and travellers cheques into Greece. If, however, you intend to leave the country with foreign banknotes in excess of US$1000, you must declare the sum upon entry.

It is strictly forbidden to export antiquities (anything over 100 years old) without an export permit. This crime is second only to drug smuggling in the penalties imposed.

It is an offence to remove even the smallest article from an archaeological site.

The place to apply for an export permit is the Antique Dealers & Private Collections Section, Archaeological Service, Polygnotou 13, Athens.

Vehicles

Cars registered in the EU can be brought into Greece for six months without a carnet; only a green card (international third party insurance) is required. Your vehicle will not be registered in your passport when you enter and you can in theory stay for as long as you like, depending on your nationality and visa regulations. However, in the case of an inquiry by customs, the onus is upon you to prove that you have had the vehicle in the country for less than six months, or you may end up being asked to pay import duties or road taxes. If you have arrived by boat, keep your car ferry ticket stubs safely stored with your other vehicle documents. If you arrived overland, your exit stamp from the neighbouring country should be sufficient proof.

MONEY
Currency

The unit of currency in Greece is the drachma (dr). Coins come in denominations of five, 10, 20, 50 and 100 dr. Banknotes come in 100, 200, 500, 1000, 5000 and 10,000 dr. The euro will replace the drachma in January 2002.

Exchange Rates

country	unit		drachma
Albania	100 lekë	=	261.40 dr
Australia	A$1	=	197.30 dr
Canada	C$1	=	243.00 dr
euro	€1	=	340.75 dr
France	1FF	=	51.95 dr
Germany	DM1	=	174.20 dr
Ireland	IR£1	=	432.70 dr
Italy	L1000	=	175.98 dr
Japan	¥100	=	311.50 dr
Netherlands	fl	=	154.63 dr
New Zealand	NZ$1	=	160.14 dr
United Kingdom	UK£1	=	531.86 dr
United States	US$1	=	367.25 dr

euro currency converter €1 = 340.75dr

Warning It's all but impossible to exchange Turkish lira in Greece. The only place you can change them is at the head office of the National Bank of Greece, Panepistimiou 36, Athens – and it'll give only about 75% of the going international rate.

Exchanging Money

Banks will exchange all major currencies in either cash, travellers cheques or Eurocheques. The best-known travellers cheques in Greece are Thomas Cook and American Express. A passport is required to change travellers cheques, but not cash.

Commission charged on the exchange of banknotes and travellers cheques varies from bank to bank and from branch to branch. It's less for cash than for travellers cheques. For travellers cheques the commission is 350 dr for up to 20,000 dr; 450 dr for amounts between 20,000 dr and 30,000 dr; and a flat rate of 1.5% on amounts over 30,000 dr.

Post offices can exchange banknotes – but not travellers cheques – and charge less commission than banks. Many travel agencies and hotels will also change money and travellers cheques at bank rates, but their commission charges are higher.

If there is a chance that you may apply for a visa extension, make sure you receive, and keep hold of, a bank exchange slip after each transaction.

Cash Nothing beats cash for convenience – or for risk. If you lose it, it's gone for good and very few travel insurers will come to your rescue. Those that will, normally limit the amount to about US$300. It's best to carry no more cash than you need for the next few days, which means working out your likely needs when you change travellers cheques or withdraw cash from an ATM.

It's also a good idea to set aside a small amount of cash, say US$50 or so, as an emergency stash.

Travellers Cheques The main reason to carry travellers cheques rather than cash is the protection they offer against theft. They are, however, losing popularity as more and more travellers opt to put their money in a bank at home and withdraw it at ATMs as they go along.

American Express, Thomas Cook and Visa cheques are widely accepted and have efficient replacement policies. Maintaining a record of the cheque numbers and recording when you use them is vital when it comes to replacing lost cheques. Keep this record separate from the cheques themselves. US dollars are a good currency to use.

ATMs ATMs (automatic teller machines) are to be found in almost every town large enough to support a bank – and certainly in all the tourist areas. If you have MasterCard or Visa/Access, there are plenty of places to withdraw money.

Cirrus and Maestro users can make withdrawals in all major towns and tourist areas.

AFEMs (Automatic Foreign Exchange Machines) are common in major tourist areas. They take all the major European currencies, Australian and US dollars and Japanese yen, and are useful in an emergency.

The islands of Agathonisi, Arki, Marathi, Nisyros, Tilos and Halki did not have ATMs at the time of research of this book. All other Dodecanese islands had at least one machine.

Credit Cards The great advantage of credit cards is that they allow you to pay for major items without carrying around great wads of cash. Credit cards are now an accepted part of the commercial scene just about everywhere in Greece. They can be used to pay for a wide range of goods and services such as upmarket meals and accommodation, car hire and souvenir shopping.

If you are not familiar with the card options, ask your bank to explain the workings and relative merits of the various schemes: cash cards, charge cards and credit cards. Ask whether the card can be replaced in Greece if it is lost or stolen.

The main credit cards are MasterCard, Visa (Access in the UK) and Eurocard, all of which are widely accepted in Greece. They can also be used as cash cards to draw drachma from the ATMs of affiliated Greek

banks in the same way as at home. Daily withdrawal limits are set by the issuing bank. Cash advances are given in local currency only. Credit cards can be used to pay for accommodation in all the smarter hotels. Some C-class hotels will accept credit cards, but D- and E-class hotels rarely do. Most upmarket shops and restaurants accept credit cards.

The main charge cards are American Express and Diner's Club Card, which are widely accepted in tourist areas but unheard of elsewhere.

International Transfers If you run out of money or need more for whatever reason, you can instruct your bank back home to send you a draft. Specify the city and the bank as well as the branch that you want the money sent to. If you have the choice, select a large bank and ask for the international division. Money sent by electronic transfer should reach you within 48 hours.

Security

The safest way of carrying cash and valuables (passport, travellers cheques, credit cards etc) is a favourite topic of travel conversation. The simple answer is that there is no foolproof method. The general principle is to keep things out of sight. The front pouch belt, for example, presents an obvious target for a would-be thief – only marginally less inviting than a fat wallet bulging from your back pocket.

The best place is under your clothes in contact with your skin where, hopefully, you will be aware of an alien hand before it's too late. Most people opt for a money belt, while others prefer a leather pouch hung around the neck. Whichever method you choose, put your valuables in a plastic bag first – otherwise they will get soaked in sweat as you wander around in the heat.

Costs

Greece is still a cheap country by northern European standards, but it is no longer dirt-cheap. A rock-bottom daily budget would be 7000 dr to 8000 dr. This would mean hitching, staying in youth hostels or camping, staying away from bars, and only occasionally eating in restaurants or taking ferries. Allow at least 12,000 dr per day if you want your own room and plan to eat out regularly as well as travelling about and seeing the sights. You will still need to do a fair bit of self-catering. If you really want a holiday – comfortable rooms and restaurants all the way – you will need closer to 20,000 dr per day. These budgets are for individuals; sharing a double room will cost less.

The prices given in this guide are for high season (July 15 to August 20). Outside these dates prices may be 10% to 40% lower. Prices for food and accommodation across the Dodecanese Islands are fairly uniform, with perhaps Rhodes and Kos Towns having the highest overall costs.

Tipping & Bargaining
In restaurants the service charge is included in the bill but it is the custom to leave a small tip. The practice is often just to round off the bill. The same applies for taxis, where a small amount is added.

Bargaining is not as widespread in the Dodecanese as it is further east. Prices in most shops are clearly marked and non-negotiable. The same applies to restaurants and public transport. It is always worth bargaining over the price of hotel rooms or *domatia* (the Greek equivalent of the British B&B, minus the breakfast), especially if you are intending to stay a few days. You may get short shrift in peak season, but prices can drop dramatically in the off season. Souvenir shops and market stalls are other places where your negotiating skills will come in handy. If you feel uncomfortable about haggling, walking away can be just as effective – you can always go back.

Taxes & Refunds
Value Added Tax (VAT), known as FPA in Greece, is added automatically to everything more or less and you won't notice it. There is currently no FPA refund scheme.

POST & COMMUNICATIONS
Post offices *(tahydromia)* are easily identifiable by means of the yellow signs outside.

Regular post boxes are also yellow. The red boxes are for express mail only.

Postal Rates
The postal rate for postcards and airmail letters to destinations within the EU is 180 dr for up to 20g, and 280 dr for up to 50g. To other destinations the rate is 200 dr for up to 20g, and 300 dr for up to 150g. Post within Europe takes five to eight days and to the USA, Australia and New Zealand, nine to 11 days. Some tourist shops sell stamps, but with a 10% surcharge.

Express mail costs an extra 400 dr and should ensure delivery in three days within the EU – use the special red post boxes. Valuables should be sent registered post, which costs an extra 350 dr.

Sending Mail
If you are sending a parcel overseas, do not wrap it until it has been inspected at a post office. On the Dodecanese Islands inspection rarely occurs, but it is better to be prepared than to have to unpack and repack in the post office.

Receiving Mail
You can receive mail at poste restante (general delivery) at any main post office. The service is free of charge, but you are required to show your passport. Ask senders to write your family name in capital letters on the envelope and underline it, and to mark the envelope 'poste restante'. It is a good idea to ask the post office clerk to check under your first name as well if letters you are expecting cannot be located. After one month, uncollected mail is returned to the sender. If you are about to leave a town and expected mail hasn't arrived, ask at the post office to have it forwarded to your next destination, c/o poste restante.

Parcels are not normally delivered in Greece. Instead, they must be collected from the parcel counter of a post office.

Telephone
The Greek telephone service is maintained by the public corporation known as Organismos Tilepikoinonion Ellados, which is

always referred to by the acronym OTE (pronounced O-tay). The system is modern and efficient. Public telephones all use phonecards, which cost 1000 dr for 100 units, 1800 dr for 200 units, 4200 dr for 500 units, and 8200 dr for 1000 units. The 100-unit cards are widely available at *periptera* (street kiosks), corner shops, as well as tourist shops; the others can be bought at OTE offices.

The phones are easy to operate and can be used for local, long distance and international calls. The 'i' at the top left of the push-button dialling panel brings up the operating instructions in English. Don't remove your card before you are told to do so or you will wipe out the remaining credit. Local calls cost one unit per minute.

It is possible to use various national card schemes, such as Telstra Australia's Telecard, to make international calls. You will still need a phonecard to dial the scheme's access number, which will cost you one unit, and the time you spend on the phone is charged at local call rates.

OTE offices are becoming less useful places to make calls as cardphones make ever wider inroads into all the islands. In some cases you can't even make calls at an OTE office.

To call overseas direct from Greece, dial the Greek overseas access code (☎ 00), followed by the country code for the country you are calling, then the local area code (dropping the leading zero if there is one) and then the number. The following table lists some useful country codes and per-minute charges:

country	code	cost per minute
Australia	61	236 dr
France	33	183 dr
Germany	49	183 dr
Ireland	353	183 dr
Italy	39	183 dr
Japan	81	319 dr
Netherlands	31	183 dr
New Zealand	64	319 dr
Turkey	90	183 dr
UK	44	183 dr
USA & Canada	1	236 dr

Useful Phone Numbers

Directory Inquiries	☎ 131
International access code from within Greece	☎ 00
International access code to call Greece	☎ 30
International dialling instructions in English, French and German	☎ 169
International operator	☎ 161
Toll-free 24-hour emergency numbers	
Ambulance	☎ 100
Fire Brigade	☎ 199
Forestry Fire Service	☎ 191
Police	☎ 100
Roadside Assistance (ELPA)	☎ 104
Tourist Police	☎ 171

Off-peak rates are 25% cheaper. They are available to Africa, Europe, the Middle East and India between 10 pm and 6 am; to the Americas between 11 pm and 8 am; and to Asia and Oceania between 8 pm and 5 am. These charges may well drop during 2001 given the advent of competition in the telecommunications scene.

To call Greece, the international access code is ☎ 30.

eKno Communication Service

Lonely Planet's eKno global communication service provides low-cost international calls – for local calls you're usually better off with a local phonecard. eKno also offers free messaging services, email, travel information and an online travel vault, where you can securely store all your important documents.

You can join this service online at www .ekno.lonelyplanet.com, where you will find the local-access numbers for the 24-hour customer-service centre. Once you have joined, always check the eKno Web site for the latest access numbers for each country and updates on new features.

Fax

Most post offices have fax machines, which you can use to send a fax reasonably

Getting Mobile

Greece and the Dodecanese use GSM 900/1800, which is compatible with the rest of Europe and Australia but not with the North American GSM 1900 or the totally different system in Japan. If you have a GSM phone, check with your service provider about using it in the Dodecanese. Be aware that calls to your number will be routed via your home mobile service provider and *you* will pay for the call from your home country to the Dodecanese. This can get very expensive. Calls made by you, however, will be charged at local (ie, Greek) mobile rates.

Using the SMS (short message service) of your mobile phone is one way to avoid high connection costs and will work most of the time in Greece. The pay-as-you-talk service offered by the three mobile service providers in Greece – Panafon, CosmOTE and Telestet – is good if you plan to be in Greece for a while, or visit the country regularly. It typically costs around 25,000 dr for a connection package, which may or may not include around 5000 dr worth of calls. For the Dodecanese, OTEnet has probably the best overall coverage. See any mobile phone supplier in Greece to request a connection package *(paketo syndesis)*. There are a number of these shops near each other in Rhodes New Town or Kos.

From many of the Dodecanese Islands you can pick up Turkish GSM phone networks. This is handy if you are really stuck for coverage, or want to book an onward hotel room in Turkey at Turkish domestic mobile rates, not international call charges from Greece.

---

cheaply. There are also a number of private fax service providers around.

Email & Internet Access

Internet cafes are springing up everywhere in the Dodecanese Islands, and are listed under the Information section for cities and islands where available. The Web site www.netcafeguide.com has up-to-date listings of cybercafes. You may also find public net access in post offices, libraries, hostels, hotels, universities and so on.

The email addresses of hotels and businesses have also been listed where available.

If you plan to bring your laptop computer to the Dodecanese it may be worthwhile taking out a temporary local account. This will cost around US$25 per month and you will be provided with a universal dial-up number, which is charged at very reasonable local rates irrespective of your location, or the location of the nearest Internet server. Forthnet (www.forthnet.gr) are a good service provider and have kept this writer connected to the Net on more than one occasion.

Greek ISPs have reciprocal global Internet roaming arrangements with a number of overseas ISPs. Check with your home provider if they have an arrangement with Greece.

INTERNET RESOURCES

The World Wide Web is a rich resource for travellers. You can research your trip, hunt down bargain air fares, book hotels, check on weather conditions or chat with locals and other travellers about the best places to visit (or avoid!).

There's no better place to start your Web explorations than the Lonely Planet Web site (www.lonelyplanet.com). Here you'll find succinct summaries on travelling to most places on earth, postcards from other travellers and the Thorn Tree bulletin board, where you can ask questions before you go or dispense advice when you get back. You can also find travel news and updates to many of our most popular guidebooks, and the subWWWay section links you to the most useful travel resources elsewhere on the Web.

Predictably enough, there has also been a huge increase in the number of Web sites providing information about Greece, and the Dodecanese specifically. Individual island sites are listed under Internet Resources in the relevant chapters.

The Greek Ministry of Culture has an excellent site at www.culture.gr, with loads of information about museums and ancient sites. You'll find addresses of more specialist Web sites listed throughout the book.

BOOKS

Most books are published in different editions by different publishers in different countries. As a result, a book might be a hardcover rarity in one country while it's readily available in paperback in another. Fortunately, bookshops and libraries search by title or author, so your local bookshop or library is best placed to advise you on the availability of the following recommendations.

Lonely Planet

Lonely Planet's popular guide to *Greece* has comprehensive coverage of mainland Greece as well as the islands. Lonely Planet's *Greek Islands* guide contains information on Athens, the islands and a few select access ports, and the new *Athens* city guide provides comprehensive listings on the capital.

The Lonely Planet Europe series guidebooks, *Mediterranean Europe* and *Western Europe* include coverage of Greece, as does *Europe on a shoestring*. Also available are the regional titles *Corfu & the Ionians*, *Crete* and *Crete Condensed*, which are indispensable if you are including these islands in your itinerary. The handy *Greek Phrasebook* will help enrich your visit.

If this is your first time in Europe, grab a copy of Lonely Planet's *Read this First: Europe* guide for all the ins and outs of planning for an overseas trip.

Katherine Kizilos vividly evokes the country's landscapes, people and politics in her book, *The Olive Grove: Travels in Greece*. She explores the islands and borderlands of her father's homeland, and life in her family's village in the Peloponnese mountains. The book is part of the Journeys travel literature series.

You'll find these titles at major English-language bookshops in Athens. See the Bookshops section later in this chapter.

Travel

English writer Lawrence Durrell, who spent an idyllic childhood on Corfu, is the best known of the 20th-century philhellenes who helped with Greece's struggle for self-determination. His evocative book *Reflections on a Marine Venus* is about Rhodes, where he lived from 1945 to 1947 as a press officer. His coffee-table book *The Greek Islands* is one of the most popular books of its kind. Even if you disagree with Durrell's opinions, you will probably concede that the photographs are superb.

John Ebdon's *Ebdons' Iliad* is a light-hearted description of Rhodes, Kos and Karpathos prior to the onslaught of mass tourism to these islands. William Manus' *This Way to Paradise* is a very readable memoir of almost 40 years spent in the Rhodian village of Lindos, before it became the mecca for mass tourism.

Bus Stop Symi by William Travis is a thoughtful look at life on Symi in the '60s, long before 'day-tripper' became a commercial buzz word and turned Symi's hitherto depressed fortunes around.

People & Society

The Greeks by James Pettifer is a worthwhile read and a remarkably accurate look at contemporary life in Greece from a historical, societal, environmental and ethnographical perspective. *Culture Shock! Greece*, another title in this ever-expanding series, is good for potential long-term visitors to Greece, or for people planning to settle in the country. It is a rather dry guide to customs and etiquette, and it's seen through occasionally tinted, British-made spectacles, but worth a browse.

Patricia Storeace's *Dinner with Persephone* is as much a travelogue as it is a series of sociological observations seen through the eyes of an American woman living in Greece. Women travellers to Greece would find this book of special interest.

Bitter Sea by Faith Warn is a fascinating look at the hidden world of sponge diving on the island of Kalymnos. The author, who is currently a resident on Kalymnos, looks at the history and the practicalities of this dangerous profession and its impact over the years on the social life of this industrious Dodecanese island.

History & Mythology

Mythology was an intrinsic part of life in ancient Greece, and some knowledge of it will enhance your visit. *The Greek Myths* by Robert Graves is regarded as the definitive book on the subject. Maureen O'Sullivan's *An Iconoclast's Guide to the Greek Gods* presents entertaining and accessible versions of the myths.

There are many translations of Homer's *Iliad* and *Odyssey*, which tell the story of the Trojan War and the subsequent adventures of Odysseus. The translations by EV Rieu are among the best.

A Traveller's History of Greece by Timothy Boatswain & Colin Nicholson gives the layperson a good general reference on the historical background of Greece, from Neolithic times to the present day. *Modern Greece: A Short History* by CM Woodhouse is in a similar vein, although it has a right-wing bent. It covers the period from Constantine the Great to 1990.

A Short History of Modern Greece by Richard Clogg is one of the more readable and recent histories of the Greek State, covering Greek events from the last stage of Byzantium from 1204 to 1453 up to Greece in the late '70s. *The Unification of Greece 1770-1923* by Douglas Dakin is a more detailed look at events that surrounded the War of Independence and the ultimate reunification of the Greek State in 1923.

Poetry

Sappho: A New Translation by Mary Bernard is the best translation of this great ancient poet's works.

Collected Poems by George Seferis, *Selected Poems* by Odysseus Elytis and *Collected Poems* by Constantine Cavafy are all excellent translations of the greatest modern Greek poets. *Exile and Return*, the selected poems of Greece's foremost leftist poet, Yiannis Ritsos, are also worth reading for an insight into the political turbulence of the Junta years of 1967–74.

Novels

The most well known and widely read Greek author is the Cretan writer, Nikos Kazantzakis, whose novels are full of drama and larger-than-life characters. His most famous works are *The Last Temptation*, *Zorba the Greek*, *Christ Recrucified* and *Freedom or Death*. The first two have been made into films.

Language & Literature

An excellent overall guide to Modern Greek literature is Linos Politis' *History of Modern Greek Literature*, which covers literary genres from the Cretan Renaissance to postwar poetry and prose.

Serious students of the Greek language should seek out Peter Mackridge's *The Modern Greek Language*, an erudite but thoroughly readable analysis of the finer points of the modern vernacular.

Bookshops

There is a dearth of decent bookshops anywhere in the Dodecanese so stock up in Athens, or at home before you depart. All major towns and tourist resorts have bookshops that sell some foreign-language books, but imported books are expensive – normally two to three times the recommended retail price in the UK and the USA. Many hotels have second-hand books to read or swap.

There are several specialist English-language bookshops in Athens, and shops selling books in French, German and Italian. Eleftheroudakis (☎ 01-331 4180, fax 323 9821, ℮ elebooks@hellasnet.gr), with shops on Panepistimiou and Nikis, has a wide range of Lonely Planet titles.

In the UK, the best bookshop for new and second-hand books about Greece, written in both English and Greek, is the Hellenic Book Service (☎ 020-7267 9499, fax 7267 9498), 91 Fortress Rd, Kentish Town, London NW5 1AG. It stocks almost all of the books recommended here. Zeno's Greek Bookshop (☎ 020-7836 2522), 6 Denmark St, London WC2H 8LP, is another good bookshop stocking a large range of Greece-related titles.

Lonely Planet books can be bought online at www.lonelyplanet.com and many of the other titles recommended can be located and ordered online at amazon.com.

FILMS

Greece is nothing if not photogenic, and countless films have made the most of the country's range of superb locations. The islands do, of course, figure prominently. The delightfully escapist Italian-language film *Mediterraneo* (1991) is set in Kastellorizo (Megisti). Towards the end of WWII a bunch of Italian soldiers are sent to secure and hold the tiny island of Kastellorizo, only to slowly realise that the war is over – for them at least – and that there is more to life than fighting. This is a must-see film if you are heading to the Dodecanese.

Mykonos was the setting for the smash hit *Shirley Valentine*, featuring Pauline Collins in the title role and Tom Conti as her Greek toy boy. While Mykonos is not in the Dodecanese, the film could easily have been set on Patmos or Symi, as the theme of escapism (again) and love (Greek style) are equally valid on any small, photogenically-arresting Greek island in the sun.

Those with longer memories may recall Gregory Peck and David Niven leading the assault on the *Guns of Navarone* back in 1961. It was filmed on the island of Rhodes.

NEWSPAPERS & MAGAZINES

Greeks are great newspaper readers. There are 15 daily newspapers, of which the most widely read are *Ta Nea*, *Kathimerini* and *Eleftheros Typos*.

The main English-language newspapers are the daily (except Monday) *Athens News* (250 dr), which carries Greek and international news; and the weekly *Hellenic Times* (300 dr), with predominantly Greek news. In addition to these, the Athens edition of the *International Herald Tribune* (350 dr) includes an English-language edition of the Greek daily, *Kathimerini*. All are widely available in Athens and at major towns and resorts. The *Athens News* electronic edition is on the Internet at athensnews.dolnet.gr; the site's archives date back to 1995.

Foreign newspapers are also widely available, although only between April and October on smaller islands. You'll find all the British and other major European dailies, as well as international magazines such as *Time*, *Newsweek* and *The Economist*. The papers reach the Dodecanese on the following day. Note that on some islands like Leros, Nisyros, Tilos or Astypalea you won't find too many English-language newspapers. Italian papers tend to dominate.

RADIO & TV

Greece has two state-owned radio channels, ET 1 and ET 2. ET 1 runs three programs; two are devoted to popular music and news, while the third plays mostly classical music. It has a news update in English at 7.30 am Monday to Saturday, and at 9 pm Monday to Friday. It can be heard on 91.6 MHz and 105.8 MHz on the FM band, and 729 KHz on the AM band. ET 2 broadcasts mainly popular music.

Choices on the Dodecanese Islands tend to be limited to the state-owned channels plus a few local stations, but you can pick up re-transmissions of the BBC World Service on Karpathos from transmitters located in Crete. If you fancy a change in music style or language, you can easily tune in to any number of Turkish FM band broadcasts, since all islands are very close to Turkey.

The best short-wave frequencies for picking up the BBC World Service are:

GMT	frequency
3 to 7.30 am	9.41 MHz (31m band)
	6.18 MHz (49m band)
	15.07 MHz (19m band)
7.30 am to 6 pm	12.09 MHz (25m band)
	15.07 MHz (19m band)
6.30 to 11.15 pm	12.09 MHz (25m band)
	9.41 MHz (31m band)
	6.18 MHz (49m band)

As far as Greek TV is concerned, it's a case of quantity rather than quality. There are nine TV channels and various pay-TV channels. All the channels show English and US films and soapies with Greek subtitles. A bit of channel-zapping will normally turn up something in English.

VIDEO SYSTEMS

If you want to record or buy videotapes to play back home, you won't get a picture unless the image registration systems are the same. Greece uses PAL, which is incompatible with the North American and Japanese NTSC system. However, Australia and most of Europe use PAL.

PHOTOGRAPHY & VIDEO
Film & Equipment
Major brands of film are widely available. In Athens, expect to pay about 1600 dr for a 36 exposure roll of Kodak Gold ASA 100, and less for other brands. You'll pay more on the islands, particularly in the more remote areas, when old stock can also be a problem. You'll find all the gear you need in the photography shops of Athens and other major towns and tourist areas.

As elsewhere in the world, developing film is a competitive business. Most places charge around 90 dr per print, plus a 450 dr service charge.

Technical Tips
Lonely Planet's *Travel Photography*, by renowned photographer Richard I'Anson, offers professional, practical tips for improving the quality of your photographs.

Because of the brilliant sunlight in summer, you'll get better results using a polarising lens filter. For optimum results shoot before 10 am and after 4 pm.

Restrictions
Never photograph a military installation or anything else that has a sign forbidding photography. Flash photography is not allowed inside churches, and it's considered taboo to photograph the main altar.

Greeks usually love having their photos taken, but always ask permission first. The same goes for video cameras.

TIME
Greece is two hours ahead of GMT/UTC and three hours ahead on daylight-saving time, which begins on the last Sunday in March, when clocks are put forward one hour. Daylight saving ends on the last Sunday in September.

So, when it is noon in Rhodes it is also noon in İstanbul, 10 am in London, 11 am in Rome, 2 am in San Francisco, 5 am in New York and Toronto, 8 pm in Sydney and 10 pm in Auckland.

ELECTRICITY
Electricity is 220V, 50 cycles. Plugs are the standard continental type with two round pins. All hotel rooms have power points and most camping grounds have supply points. Adaptors for UK, US, or Australian style plugs are not easy to find in the Dodecanese, so bring your own with you. You can usually find them in airport Duty Free shops.

WEIGHTS & MEASURES
Greece uses the metric system. Liquids – especially barrel wine – are sold by weight rather than volume. For example, 959g of wine is equivalent to 1000mL.

Remember that Greeks indicate decimals with commas and thousands with points, like other continental Europeans.

LAUNDRY
Large towns and some islands have laundrettes. They charge from 2000 dr to 2500 dr to wash and dry a load whether you do it yourself or have it service-washed. Hotel and room owners will usually provide you with a washtub. In the Dodecanese, laundrettes can be found on Patmos, Leros, Kos, Karpathos and Rhodes.

TOILETS
Most places in the region have western-style toilets, especially hotels and restaurants that cater for tourists. You'll occasionally come across Asian-style squat toilets in public facilities, older houses and *kafeneia* (usually male-only coffee houses).

Public toilets are rare, except at airports and bus and train stations. Cafes are the best option if you get caught short, but you'll be expected to buy something for the privilege.

One peculiarity of the Greek plumbing system is that it can't handle toilet paper; apparently the pipes are too narrow. Whatever the reason, anything larger than a postage stamp seems to cause a terrible problem – flushing away tampons and sanitary napkins is guaranteed to block the system. Toilet paper etc should be placed in the small bin provided in every toilet.

HEALTH
Travel health depends on your predeparture preparations, your day-to-day health care while travelling and how you handle any medical problem or emergency that does develop. While the list of potential dangers can seem quite frightening, few travellers experience more than upset stomachs.

Predeparture Planning
Health Insurance Refer to Travel Insurance under Visas & Documents earlier in this chapter for information.

Warning Codeine, which is commonly found in headache preparations, is banned in Greece; check labels carefully, or risk prosecution. There are strict regulations applying to the importation of medicines into Greece, so obtain a certificate from your doctor which outlines any medication you may have to carry into the country with you.

Health Preparations Make sure you're healthy before you start travelling. If you are embarking on a long trip make sure your teeth are OK.

If you wear glasses take a spare pair and your prescription.

If you require a particular medication take an adequate supply, as it may not be available locally. Take the prescription or, better still, part of the packaging showing the generic rather than the brand name (which may not be locally available), as it will make getting replacements easier.

Hospital Treatment Citizens of EU countries are covered for free treatment in public hospitals within Greece on presentation of an E111 form. Inquire at your national health service or travel agent in advance. Emergency treatment is free to all nationalities in public hospitals. In an emergency, dial ☎ 166. There is at least one doctor on every island in Greece, and larger islands have hospitals. Pharmacies dispense medicines that are available only on prescription

Medical Kit Check List

Following is a list of items you should consider including in your medical kit – consult your pharmacist for brands available in your country.

- ☐ **Aspirin or paracetamol (acetaminophen in the USA)** – for pain or fever
- ☐ **Antihistamine** – for allergies, eg, hay fever; to ease the itch from insect bites or stings; and to prevent motion sickness
- ☐ **Cold and flu tablets, throat lozenges and nasal decongestant**
- ☐ **Multivitamins** – consider for long trips, when dietary vitamin intake may be inadequate
- ☐ **Antibiotics** – consider including these if you're travelling well off the beaten track; see your doctor, as they must be prescribed, and carry the prescription with you
- ☐ **Loperamide or diphenoxylate** – 'blockers' for diarrhoea
- ☐ **Prochlorperazine or metaclopramide** – for nausea and vomiting
- ☐ **Rehydration mixture** – to prevent dehydration, which may occur, for example, during bouts of diarrhoea; particularly important when travelling with children
- ☐ **Insect repellent, sunscreen, lip balm and eye drops**
- ☐ **Calamine lotion, sting relief spray or aloe vera** – to ease irritation from sunburn and insect bites or stings
- ☐ **Antifungal cream or powder** – for fungal skin infections and thrush
- ☐ **Antiseptic (such as povidone-iodine)** – for cuts and grazes
- ☐ **Bandages, Band-Aids (plasters) and other wound dressings**
- ☐ **Water purification tablets or iodine**
- ☐ **Scissors, tweezers and a thermometer** – note that mercury thermometers are prohibited by airlines

in most European countries, so you can consult a pharmacist for minor ailments.

All this sounds fine, but although medical training is of a high standard in Greece, the health service is badly underfunded and one of the worst in Europe. Hospitals are overcrowded, hygiene is not always what it should be and relatives are expected to bring in food for the patient – which could be a problem for a tourist. Conditions and treatment are better in private hospitals, which are expensive. All this means that a good health-insurance policy is essential.

Immunisations No jabs are required for travel to Greece but, although yellow fever does not occur in Greece, a yellow fever vaccination certificate is required if you are coming from an infected area. There are also a few routine vaccinations that are recommended, namely diphtheria, tetanus, and polio. These should be recorded on an international health certificate, available from your doctor or government health department. Don't leave your vaccinations until the last minute as some require more than one injection.

Basic Rules

Care in what you eat and drink is the most important health rule. Stomach upsets are the most likely travel health problem (between 30% and 50% of travellers experience this in a two-week stay) but the majority of these upsets will be relatively minor. Don't become paranoid; trying the local food is part of the experience of travel, after all.

Food & Water Generally speaking, tap water is safe to drink in Greece and the Dodecanese Islands, however on Kalymnos and Leros the ground water is tainted by marine salinity, making the tap water unpalatable for both drinking and cooking. Mineral water is widely available.

You might experience mild intestinal problems if you're not used to copious amounts of olive oil; however, you'll get used to it and current research says it's good for you.

If you don't vary your diet, are travelling hard and fast and missing meals, or simply lose your appetite, you can soon start to lose weight and place your health at risk. Fruit and vegetables are good sources of vitamins and Greece produces a greater variety of these than almost any other European country. Eat plenty of grains (including rice) and bread. If your diet isn't well balanced or if

your food intake is insufficient, it's a good idea to take vitamin and iron pills.

In hot weather make sure you drink enough – don't rely on feeling thirsty to indicate when you should drink. Not needing to urinate or very dark yellow urine is a danger sign. Always carry a water bottle with you on long trips. Excessive sweating can lead to loss of salt and therefore muscle cramping. Salt tablets are not a good idea as a preventative, but in places where salt is not used much, adding salt to food can help.

Environmental Hazards

Sunburn By far the biggest health risk in Greece comes from the intensity of the sun. You can get sunburnt surprisingly quickly, even through cloud. Using a sunscreen and taking extra care to cover the areas that don't normally see sun helps, as does zinc cream or some other barrier cream for your nose and lips. Calamine lotion is good for mild sunburn. Greeks say that yogurt applied to sunburn is soothing. Protect your eyes with good-quality sunglasses.

Prickly Heat This is an itchy rash caused by excessive perspiration trapped under the skin. It usually strikes people who have just arrived in a hot climate. Keeping cool but bathing often, using a mild talcum powder or even staying under the air-conditioning may help until you acclimatise.

Heat Exhaustion Dehydration or salt deficiency can cause heat exhaustion. Take time to acclimatise to high temperatures, and drink sufficient liquids. Do not do anything too physically demanding.

Salt deficiency is characterised by fatigue, lethargy, headaches, giddiness and muscle cramps. Salt tablets may help, although adding extra salt to your food is better. Vomiting or diarrhoea can deplete your liquid and salt levels.

Heat Stroke This is a serious, sometimes fatal condition that occurs if the body's heat-regulating mechanism breaks down and the body temperature rises to dangerous levels. Long, continuous periods of exposure to high temperatures can leave you vulnerable to heat stroke.

The symptoms are feeling unwell, not sweating very much or at all and a high body temperature (39° to 41°C or 102° to 106°F). Where sweating has ceased, the skin becomes flushed and red. Severe, throbbing headaches and lack of coordination will also occur, and the sufferer may be confused or aggressive. Eventually the victim will become delirious or convulsive. Hospitalisation is essential, but in the interim get victims out of the sun, remove their clothing, cover them with a wet sheet or towel and then fan continually. Give fluids if they are conscious.

Motion Sickness Sea sickness can be a problem. The Aegean is very unpredictable and gets very rough when the *meltemi* wind blows. If you are prone to motion sickness, eat lightly before and during a trip and try to find a place that minimises disturbance – near the wings on aircraft, close to midships on boats, near the centre on buses. Fresh air usually helps; reading and cigarette smoke don't.

Commercial motion-sickness preparations, which can cause drowsiness, have to be taken before the trip commences; when you're feeling sick it's too late. Ginger (available in capsule form) and peppermint (including mint-flavoured sweets) are natural preventatives.

Infectious Diseases

Diarrhoea Simple things like a change of water, food or climate can all cause a mild bout of diarrhoea, but a few rushed toilet trips with no other symptoms are not indicative of a major problem.

Dehydration is the main danger with any form of diarrhoea, particularly in children or the elderly as dehydration can occur quite quickly. Under all circumstances *fluid replacement* (at least equal to the volume being lost) is the most important thing to remember. Weak black tea with a little sugar, soda water, or soft drinks allowed to go flat and diluted 50% with clean water, are all good.

Fungal Infections These types of infections occur with greater frequency in hot weather, and are most likely to occur on the scalp, between the toes or fingers, in the groin and on the body. You can get ringworm (which is a fungal infection, not a worm) from infected animals or by walking on damp areas like shower floors.

To prevent fungal infections wear loose, comfortable clothes, avoid artificial fibres, wash frequently and dry carefully. If you do get an infection, wash the infected area daily with a disinfectant or medicated soap and water, and rinse and dry well. Apply an antifungal cream or powder like tolnaftate. Try to expose the infected area to air or sunlight as much as possible and wash all towels and underwear in hot water as well as changing them often.

Hepatitis This is a general term for inflammation of the liver and is a common disease worldwide. The symptoms are fever, chills, headache, fatigue, feelings of weakness and aches and pains, followed by loss of appetite, nausea, vomiting, abdominal pain, dark urine, light-coloured faeces, and jaundiced (yellow) skin. The whites of the eyes may also turn yellow. **Hepatitis A** is transmitted by contaminated food and drinking water. The disease poses a real threat to the western traveller. You should seek medical advice, but there is not much you can do apart from resting, drinking lots of fluids, eating lightly and avoiding fatty foods. People who have had hepatitis should avoid alcohol for some time after the illness, as the liver needs time to recover. **Hepatitis E** is transmitted in the same way, and can be very serious in pregnant women.

There are almost 300 million chronic carriers of **Hepatitis B** in the world today. It is spread through contact with infected blood, blood products or body fluids; for example, through sexual contact, unsterilised needles and blood transfusions, or contact with blood via small breaks in the skin. Other risky situations include having a shave, tattoo, or having your body pierced with contaminated equipment. The symptoms of type B may be more severe and may lead to long-term problems. **Hepatitis D** is spread in the same way, but the risk is mainly in shared needles.

Hepatitis C can lead to chronic liver disease. The virus is spread by contact with blood and blood products – usually via contaminated transfusions or shared needles – or bodily fluids.

Sexually Transmitted Diseases Sexual contact with an infected sexual partner spreads these diseases. While abstinence is the only 100% preventative, using condoms is also effective. Gonorrhoea, herpes and syphilis are among these diseases; sores, blisters or rashes around the genitals, discharges or pain when urinating are common symptoms. In some STDs, such as wart virus or chlamydia, symptoms may be less marked or not observed at all in women. Syphilis symptoms eventually disappear completely but the disease continues and can cause severe problems in later years. The treatment of gonorrhoea and syphilis is with antibiotics.

There are numerous other sexually transmitted diseases, for most of which effective treatment is available. But there is currently no cure for herpes or AIDS.

HIV/AIDS Infection with the human immunodeficiency virus (HIV) may lead to acquired immune deficiency syndrome (AIDS), which is a fatal disease. Any exposure to blood, blood products or body fluids may put the individual at risk. The disease is often transmitted through sexual contact or dirty needles – vaccinations, acupuncture, tattooing and body piercing can be potentially as dangerous as intravenous drug use.

If you do need an injection, ask to see the syringe unwrapped in front of you, or take a needle and syringe pack with you.

However, fear of HIV infection should never preclude treatment for serious medical conditions.

Cuts, Bites & Stings
Bedbugs & Lice Bedbugs live in various places, but particularly in dirty mattresses and bedding. Spots of blood on bedclothes or on the wall around the bed can be read as a suggestion to find another hotel. Bedbugs leave itchy bites in neat rows. Calamine lotion or sting relief spray may help.

All lice cause itching and discomfort. They make themselves at home in your hair, your clothing or in your pubic hair. You catch lice through direct contact with infected people or by sharing combs, clothing and the like. Powder or shampoo treatment will kill the lice and infected clothing should then be washed in very hot water.

Jelly Fish, Sea Urchins & Weever Fish Watch out for sea urchins around rocky beaches; if you get some of their needles embedded in your skin, olive oil will help to loosen them. If they are not removed they will become infected. Be wary also of jelly fish, particularly during the months of September and October. Although they are not lethal in Greece, their stings can be painful. Dousing in vinegar will deactivate any stingers which have not 'fired'. Calamine lotion, antihistamines and analgesics may reduce the reaction and relieve the pain.

Much more painful than either of these, but thankfully much rarer, is an encounter with the weever fish. It buries itself in the sand of the tidal zone with only its spines protruding, and injects a powerful toxin if trodden on. Soaking your foot in very hot water (which breaks down the poison) should solve the problem. It can cause permanent local paralysis in the worst instance.

Snakes Wear boots, socks and long trousers when walking through undergrowth where snakes may be present. Don't put your hands into holes and crevices, and be careful when collecting firewood.

Snake bites do not cause instantaneous death and antivenenes are usually available. Keep the victim calm and still, wrap the bitten limb tightly, as you would for a sprained ankle, and attach a splint to immobilise it. Then seek medical help, if possible with the dead snake for identification. Don't attempt to catch the snake if there is even a remote possibility of being bitten again. Tourniquets and sucking out the poison are now comprehensively discredited.

euro currency converter €1 = 340.75dr

Ticks You should always check all over your body if you have been walking through a potentially tick-infested area, as ticks can cause skin infections and other more serious diseases. If a tick is found attached, press down around the tick's head with tweezers, grab the head and gently pull upwards. Avoid pulling the rear of the body as this may squeeze the tick's gut contents through the attached mouth parts into the skin, increasing the risk of infection and disease. Smearing chemicals on the tick will not make it let go and is not recommended.

Women's Health

Antibiotic use, synthetic underwear, sweating and contraceptive pills can lead to fungal vaginal infections, especially when travelling in hot climates. Fungal infections are characterised by a rash, itch and discharge and can be treated with a vinegar or lemon-juice douche, or with yogurt. Nystatin, miconazole or clotrimazole pessaries or vaginal cream are the usual treatment. Maintaining good personal hygiene and wearing loose-fitting clothes and cotton underwear may help prevent these infections.

Sexually transmitted diseases are a major cause of vaginal problems. Symptoms include a smelly discharge, painful intercourse and sometimes a burning sensation when urinating. Medical attention should be sought and male sexual partners must also be treated. For more details see the section on Sexually Transmitted Diseases earlier. Besides abstinence, the best thing is to practise safer sex using condoms.

Less Common Diseases

Leishmaniasis This is a group of parasitic diseases transmitted by sandflies, which are found in many parts of the Middle East, Africa, India, Central and South America and the Mediterranean. Cutaneous leishmaniasis affects the skin tissue, causing ulceration and disfigurement, while visceral leishmaniasis affects the internal organs. Seek medical advice, as laboratory testing is required for diagnosis and correct treatment. Avoiding sandfly bites is the best precaution. Bites are usually painless, but itchy

and yet another good reason to cover up and apply repellent.

Lyme Disease This is a tick-transmitted infection which may be acquired throughout North America, Europe and Asia. The illness usually begins with a spreading rash at the site of the tick bite and is accompanied by fever, headache, extreme fatigue, aching joints and muscles, and mild neck stiffness. If untreated, these symptoms usually resolve over several weeks but over subsequent weeks or months disorders of the nervous system, heart and joints may develop. Treatment works best early in the illness. Medical help should be sought.

Rabies This fatal viral infection is found in many countries. Many animals can be infected (such as dogs, cats and bats) and it is their saliva which is infectious. Any bite, scratch or even lick from a warm-blooded, furry animal should be cleaned immediately and thoroughly. Scrub with soap and running water, and then clean with an alcohol or iodine solution. If there is any possibility that the animal is infected, medical help should be sought immediately to prevent the onset of symptoms and death. Even if the animal is not rabid, all bites should be treated seriously as they can become infected or can result in tetanus. A rabies vaccination is now available and should be considered if you are in a high risk category – eg, if you intend to explore caves (bat bites can be dangerous), work with animals, or travel so far off the beaten track that medical help is more than two days away.

Tetanus This potentially fatal disease is found worldwide. It is difficult to treat but is preventable with immunisation.

Typhus Tick typhus can be a problem from April to September in rural areas, particularly where animals congregate. Typhus begins with a fever, chills, headache and muscle pain, followed a few days later by a body rash. There is often a large painful sore at the site of the bite and nearby lymph nodes are swollen and painful. There is no vaccine available. The best way to protect yourself is to check your skin carefully after walking in danger areas such as long grass and scrub. A strong insect repellent can help, and serious walkers in tick areas should consider having their boots and trousers impregnated with benzyl benzoate and dibutylphthalate. (See the Cuts, Bites & Stings section earlier for information about ticks.)

WOMEN TRAVELLERS

Many women travel alone in Greece. The crime rate remains relatively low, and solo travel is probably safer than in most European countries. This does not mean that you should be lulled into complacency; although violent offences are rare, bag snatching and rapes do occur.

The biggest nuisance to foreign women travelling alone are the guys the Greeks have nicknamed *kamaki*. The word means 'fishing trident' and refers to the kamaki's favourite pastime, 'fishing' for foreign women. You'll find them everywhere there are lots of tourists. They are young (for the most part), smooth-talking guys who aren't in the least bit bashful about sidling up to foreign women in the street. They can be very persistent, but they are a hassle rather than a threat.

You'll find that the majority of Greek men treat foreign women with respect, and are genuinely helpful.

GAY & LESBIAN TRAVELLERS

In a country where the church still plays a prominent role in shaping society's views on issues such as sexuality, it should come as no surprise that homosexuality is generally frowned upon. While there is no legislation against homosexual activity, it pays to be discreet and to avoid public displays of togetherness.

This has not prevented the Dodecanese Islands from becoming an extremely popular destination for gay travellers. Mykonos (in the Cyclades) has long been famous for its bars, beaches and general hedonism, but Rhodes and Kos also have their fair share of gay hang-outs.

Information The *Spartacus International Gay Guide*, published by Bruno Gmünder (Berlin), is widely regarded as the leading authority on the gay travel scene. The 1998/99 edition has a wealth of information on gay venues around the islands.

There's also stacks of information on the Internet. Roz Mov at www.geocities.com/WestHollywood/2225/ is a good place to start. It has pages on travel information, gay health, the gay press, organisations, events and legal issues – and links to many more useful sites.

Gayscape's interesting Web site at www.jwpublishing.com/comguidegreece.html has lots of links; and www.gay.gr/gaytourism/ is another site with lots of useful information for the traveller.

Organisations The main gay rights organisation in Greece is the Elladas Omofilofilon Kommunitas (☎ 01-341 0755, fax 883 6942, @ eok@nyx.gr), upstairs at Apostolou Pavlou 31 in the Athens suburb of Thisio.

DISABLED TRAVELLERS

If mobility is a problem, visiting the Dodecanese Islands presents some serious challenges – particularly the smaller islands without airports. The hard fact is that most hotels, ferries, museums and ancient sites are not wheelchair accessible.

If you are determined, then take heart in the knowledge that disabled people do come to the islands for holidays. But the trip needs careful planning, so get as much information as you can before you go. The British-based Royal Association for Disability and Rehabilitation (RADAR) publishes some useful guides such as *Getting There: A Guide to Long Distance Travel for Disabled People* (£5) and *European Holidays & Travel: A Guide for Disabled People* (£2), which provide useful general travel information and give a good overview of facilities available to disabled travellers in Europe.

Contact RADAR (☎ 020-7250 3222, fax 7250 0212, @ radar@radar.org.uk) at 12 City Forum, 250 City Road, London EC1V 8AF. Its Web site is at www.radar.org.uk.

TRAVEL WITH CHILDREN

Greece is a safe and relatively easy place to travel with children. It's especially easy if you're staying by the beach or at a resort hotel. If you're travelling around, the main problem is a shortage of decent playgrounds and recreational facilities.

Don't be afraid to take your children to ancient sites. Many parents are pleasantly surprised by how much their children enjoy them. Young imaginations go into overdrive when let loose somewhere like the Old Town of Rhodes.

Hotels and restaurants are usually very accommodating when it comes to meeting the needs of children, although highchairs are a rarity outside resorts. The service in restaurants is normally very quick, which is great when you've got hungry children on your hands.

Fresh milk is readily available in large towns and tourist areas, but hard to find on the smaller islands. Supermarkets are the best place to look. Formula is available everywhere, as is condensed and heat-treated milk.

Mobility is an issue for parents with very small children. Strollers (pushchairs) aren't much use in Greece unless you're going to spend all your time in one of the few flat spots. They are hopeless on rough stone paths and up steps, and a curse when getting on and off buses and ferries. Backpacks or front pouches are best.

Children under four travel for free on ferries and buses. They pay half fare up to the age of 10 (ferries) and 12 (buses). Full fare applies otherwise. On domestic flights, you'll pay 10% of the fare to have a child under two sitting on your knee. Kids aged two to 12 pay half fare.

USEFUL ORGANISATIONS

ELPA (☎ 01-779 1615), the Greek automobile club, has its headquarters on the ground floor of Athens Tower, Mesogion 2-4, Athens 115 27. ELPA offers reciprocal services to members of national automobile associations on production of a valid membership card. If your vehicle breaks down, dial ☎ 104.

DANGERS & ANNOYANCES
Theft

Crime, especially theft, is low in Greece, but unfortunately it is on the increase. Keep track of your valuables on public transport and at crowded gatherings like markets. The vast majority of thefts from tourists are still committed by other tourists; the biggest danger of theft is probably in dormitory rooms in hostels and at camp sites. So make sure you do not leave valuables unattended in such places. If you are staying in a hotel room, and the windows and door do not lock securely, ask for your valuables to be locked in the hotel safe – hotel proprietors are happy to do this.

Labour Unrest

Labor strikes in the transportation sector (national airline, city bus lines, ferries and taxis) occur with some frequency. Most are announced in advance and are of short duration, but can cause severe disruption to travellers' plans if not allowed for.

LEGAL MATTERS
Consumer Advice

The Consumer Association, 'Quality of Life' exists to help people who are having trouble with any tourism-related service. Free legal advice is available in English, French and German from July 1 to September 30. The main office (☎ 01-330 4444, fax 330 0591, ✉ ekpizo@ath.forthnet.gr) is at Valtetsiou 43-45 in Athens. It's open 9 am to 3 pm Monday to Friday. Membership fees are 20,000 dr for foreigners, plus 5000 dr registration. There is currently no office in the Dodecanese.

Drugs

Greek drug laws are the strictest in Europe. Greek courts make no distinction between possession and pushing. Possession of even a small amount of marijuana is likely to land you in jail.

BUSINESS HOURS

Banks are open 8 am to 2 pm Monday to Thursday, and 8 am to 1.30 pm Friday. Some banks in large towns and cities open between 3.30 and 6.30 pm in the afternoon and on Saturday morning.

Post offices are open 7.30 am to 2 pm Monday to Friday. In the major cities they stay open until 8 pm, and open from 7.30 am to 2 pm on Saturday.

The opening hours of OTE offices (for long distance and overseas telephone calls) vary according to the size of the town. In smaller towns they are usually open 7.30 am to 3 pm daily, in larger towns from 6 am until 11 pm, and 24 hours in major cities like Athens and Thessaloniki.

In summer, shops are open 8 am to 1.30 pm and 5.30 to 8.30 pm Tuesday, Thursday and Friday, and 8 am to 2.30 pm Monday, Wednesday and Saturday. They open 30 minutes later in winter. These times are not always strictly adhered to. Many shops in tourist resorts are open seven days a week.

Periptera are open from early morning until late at night. They sell everything from bus tickets and cigarettes to hard-core pornography.

Opening times of museums and archaeological sites vary from place to place, but most are closed on Monday.

PUBLIC HOLIDAYS & SPECIAL EVENTS

All banks and shops and most museums and ancient sites close on public holidays. National public holidays in Greece are:

New Year's Day	1 January
Epiphany	6 January
First Sunday in Lent	February
Greek Independence Day	25 March
Good Friday	March/April
(Orthodox) Easter Sunday	March/April
Spring Festival/Labour Day	1 May
Feast of the Assumption	15 August
Ohi Day	28 October
Christmas Day	25 December
St Stephen's Day	26 December

The Greek year is a succession of festivals and events, some of which are religious, some cultural, others an excuse for a good knees-up, and some a combination of all three. The following list is by no means exhaustive, but it covers the most important events, both national and regional. If you're in the right place at the right time, you'll certainly be invited to join the revelry.

January

Feast of Agios Vasilios (St Basil) The year kicks off with this festival on 1 January. A church ceremony is followed by gift giving, singing, dancing and feasting; the New Year pie *(vasilopitta)* is sliced and the person who gets the slice containing a coin will supposedly have a lucky year.

Epiphany (the Blessing of the Waters) On 6 January, Christ's baptism by St John is celebrated throughout Greece. Seas, lakes and rivers are blessed and crosses immersed in them. The largest ceremony takes place at Piraeus.

February/March

Carnival The Greek Carnival season is the three weeks before the beginning of Lent. There are many regional variations, but fancy dress, feasting, traditional dancing and general merrymaking prevail. The Patra carnival is the largest and most exuberant, with elaborately decorated chariots parading through the streets.

Shrove Monday (Clean Monday) On the Monday before Ash Wednesday (the first day of Lent), people take to the hills throughout Greece to have picnics and fly kites.

March

Independence Day The anniversary of the hoisting of the Greek flag by Bishop Germanos at Moni Agias Lavras is celebrated on 25 March with parades and dancing. Germanos' act of revolt marked the start of the War of Independence. Independence Day coincides with the **Feast of the Annunciation**, so it is also a religious festival.

March/April

Easter The most important festival in the Greek Orthodox religion. Emphasis is placed on the Resurrection rather than on the Crucifixion, so it is a joyous occasion.

Feast of Agios Georgios (St George) The feast day of St George, Greece's patron saint and patron saint of shepherds, takes place on 23 April or the Tuesday following Easter (whichever comes first).

May

May Day On the first day of May there is a mass exodus from towns to the country. During picnics, wildflowers are gathered and made into wreaths to decorate houses.

Feast of St John the Theologian This major feast in Skala, Patmos takes place on 7 May.

Feast of Agios Konstantinos This feast, in honour of the protector of Kastellorizo, takes place in Kastellorizo Town on 20–21 May.

June

Navy Week This festival celebrates the long relationship between the Greek and the sea, with events in fishing villages and ports throughout the country. Rhodes has a colourful celebration centred on the harbour of Mandraki.

Agii Pantes The feast of All Saints at the Panagia Koumana church on Patmos has free food and drink for 1000 people on 14 June.

Feast of St John the Baptist This feast day on 24 June is widely celebrated. Wreaths made on May Day are kept until the 24th, when they are burned on bonfires.

July

Feast of Profitis Ilias This feast day is celebrated on 20 July at hilltop churches and monasteries dedicated to the prophet.

Feast of Agios Pandeleimonas This main feast on the island of Tilos on 25–26 July takes place at the monastery of the same name in the northwest of the island.

August

Assumption Greeks celebrate Assumption Day (15 August) with family reunions. The whole population seems to be on the move either side of the big day, so it's a good time to avoid public transport.

Feast of Panagia tou Harou The feast takes place on Lipsi on August 22. This is the busiest time of the year for the island.

September

Exaltation of the Cross This is celebrated on 14 September throughout Greece with processions and hymns.

Genisis tis Panagias (the Virgin's Birthday) This day is celebrated on 18 September throughout Greece with religious services and feasting. There is a major feast at the Church of Panagia Tsambika in Rhodes.

October

Celebration of Ossios Hristodoulos There is a presentation of all the bishops of the Dodecanese on Skala Patmos on 21 October.

Feast of Agios Dimitrios (St Dimitris) This feast day is celebrated in Thessaloniki on 26 October with wine drinking and revelry.

Ohi (No) Day Metaxas' refusal to allow Mussolini's troops free passage through Greece in WWII is commemorated on 28 October with remembrance services, military parades, folk dancing and feasting.

November

Feast of Agios Konstantinos Idreos Major feast in Rhodes Town on 14 November in honour of the protector of the island. The service in the church of the Presentation of the Virgin Mary in the suburb of Niohori is attended by all the bishops of the Dodecanese.

December

Feasts of Sts Savas and Nikolaos A double, consecutive feast from 4 to 6 December in Pothia, Kalymnos.

Christmas Day Although not as important as Easter, Christmas is still celebrated with religious services and feasting. Nowadays much 'western' influence is apparent, including Christmas trees, decorations and presents.

Summer Festivals & Performances

There are cultural festivals throughout the Dodecanese in summer. The most important is the Symi Festival (see Symi in the Central Dodecanese chapter for full details) with cultural performances throughout the Dodecanese from June to September.

The nightly *son et lumière* (sound and light show) in Rhodes runs from April to October. Greek folk dances are performed in Rhodes from May to October.

ACTIVITIES
Windsurfing

Windsurfing is the most popular water sport in the Dodecanese. Prasonisi on Rhodes, Afiarti on Karpathos and Marmari/Tingaki on Kos vie for the position of the best windsurfing beach. By all accounts, Afiarti is one of the best places in Greece to learn the sport.

Sailboards are for hire almost everywhere. Hire charges range from 2000 dr to 3000 dr an hour, depending on the gear. If you are a novice, most places that rent out equipment also give lessons.

Water-Skiing

The only islands with water-ski centres are Kos and Rhodes, though there are informal beach sport centres that may offer water ski-ing in addition to all their other activities.

Snorkelling & Diving

Snorkelling is enjoyable just about any-where in the Dodecanese Islands. Especially good places are Ammoöpi on Karpathos, Lipsi, Telendos Islet (near Kalymnos) and anywhere off the coast of Kastellorizo.

Diving is another matter. Any kind of underwater activity using breathing appara-tus is strictly forbidden other than under the supervision of a diving school. This is to protect the many antiquities in the depths of the Aegean. There are diving schools on Rhodes; see the Rhodes chapter for details.

Trekking

The islands are a veritable paradise for trek-kers – at the right time of the year. Trekking is no fun at all in July and August, when the temperatures are constantly up around 40°C. Spring (April to May) is the perfect time.

On small islands it's fun to discover path-ways for yourself. You are unlikely to get into danger as settlements or roads are never far away. You will encounter a variety of paths: *kalderimi* are cobbled or flagstone paths which link settlements and date back to Byzantine times. Sadly, many have been bulldozed to make way for roads.

There are a number of companies run-ning organised treks. One of the biggest is Trekking Hellas (☎ 01-331 0323, fax 323 4548, ℮ info@trekking.gr), Filellinon 7, Athens 105 57 (Syntagma Metro station). You'll find more information at its Web site: www.trekking.gr.

COURSES
Art Workshops

There is a series of art courses run by the Symi Arts Workshop including traditional stencilling and watercolour painting. Fees include accommodation, breakfast, tuition, morning coffee and some mezedes meals and is part of a wider program designed to promote cultural tourism to Symi. See the Symi section in the Central Dodecanese chapter for further details or check out the *Symi Visitor*, distributed free on Symi.

WORK
Permits

EU nationals don't need a work permit, but they need a residency permit if they intend to stay longer than three months. Nationals of other countries are supposed to have a work permit.

Bar & Hostel Work

The bars of the Dodecanese Islands couldn't survive without foreign workers and there are thousands of summer jobs up for grabs every year. The pay is not fantastic, but you get to spend a summer in the islands. April and May are the months to go looking. Hos-tels and travellers' hotels are other places that regularly employ foreign workers.

Summer Harvest

Seasonal harvest work seems to be monop-olised by migrant workers from Albania, and is no longer a viable option for trav-ellers. Grape picking in Rhodes is one area where there may be some seasonal work available for travellers.

Other Work

There are often jobs advertised in the classi-fieds of the English-language newspapers, or you can place an ad yourself. EU nation-als can also make use of the OAED (Organ-ismos Apasholiseos Ergatikou Dynamikou), the Greek National Employment Service, in their search for a job.

ACCOMMODATION

There is a range of accommodation avail-able in Greece to suit every taste and pocket. All places to stay are subject to strict price controls set by the tourist police. By law, a notice must be displayed in every room, which states the category of the room and the price charged in each season.

Accommodation owners may add a 10% surcharge for a stay of less than three nights, but this is not mandatory. A mandatory charge of 20% is levied if an extra bed is put into a room. During July and August, ac-commodation owners will charge the maxi-mum price, but in spring and autumn, prices will drop by up to 20%, and perhaps by even more in winter. These are the times to bring your bargaining skills into action.

Rip-offs rarely occur, but if you suspect you have been exploited, report it to either the tourist police or regular police and they will act swiftly.

Camping

There are only five official camping grounds in the Dodecanese and all are privately run. Very few are open outside the high season (April to October). The Panhellenic Camping Association (☎/fax 01-362 1560), Solonos 102, Athens 106 80, publishes an annual booklet listing all camping grounds and their facilities.

Camping fees are highest from 15 June to the end of August. Most camping grounds charge from 1200 dr to 1500 dr per adult and 600 dr to 800 dr for children aged four to 12. There's no charge for children aged under four. Tent sites cost from 900 dr per night for small tents, and from 1200 dr per night for large tents. Caravan sites start at around 2500 dr.

Between May and mid-September it is warm enough to sleep out under the stars, although you will still need a lightweight sleeping bag to counter the pre-dawn chill. It's a good idea to have a foam pad to lie on and a waterproof cover for your sleeping bag.

Freelance (wild) camping is illegal, but the law is not always strictly enforced. It's more likely to be tolerated on islands that don't have camp sites, but it's wise to ask around before freelance camping anywhere in Greece.

Apartments & Studios

Self-contained family apartments and studios are available in some hotels and domatia. There are also a growing number of purpose-built apartments, especially popular in the Dodecanese, available for either long or short-term rental. Prices vary considerably according to the amenities offered, but usually start at around 10,000 dr for two and can reach as high as 40,000 dr. A studio at this price may well accommodate up to five people. This type of accommodation is pitched squarely at the family market, or at groups of two or three people travelling together and is by far the best deal if you can all share the costs and cater for yourselves.

Domatia

Domatia are the Greek equivalent of the British B&B, minus the breakfast. Domatia once comprised little more than spare rooms in the family home which could be rented out to travellers in summer; nowadays, many are purpose-built appendages to the family house. Some come complete with fully equipped kitchens. Standards of cleanliness are generally high. The decor runs the gamut from cool grey marble floors, coordinated pine furniture, pretty lace curtains and tasteful pictures on the walls, to so much kitsch, you are almost afraid to move in case you break an ornament.

Domatia remain a popular option for budget travellers. They are classified A, B or C. Expect to pay from 4000 dr to 9000 dr for a single, and 6000 dr to 15,000 dr for a double, depending on the class, whether bathrooms are shared or private, the season and how long you plan to stay. Domatia are found on almost every island that has a permanent population. Many domatia are open only between April and October.

From June to September domatia owners are out in force, touting for customers. They meet buses and boats, shouting 'Room, room!', and often carry photographs of their establishment. In peak season, it can prove a mistake not to take up an offer – but be wary of owners who are vague about the location of their accommodation. 'Close to town' can turn out to be way out in the sticks. If you are at all dubious, insist they show you the location on a map.

Hostels

There are a number of so-called youth hostels in Greece, though only the Athens International Youth Hostel is officially affiliated to the Hostelling International (HI) organisation. Other Greek youth hostels may be affiliated to their own Greek youth hostelling association. Either way, the Dodecanese is not represented by any official HI hostels, and any place claiming status as a youth hostel should be carefully checked before making a decision to stay there.

Traditional Settlements

Traditional settlements are old buildings of architectural merit that have been renovated and converted into tourist accommodation. You'll find some in Rhodes Town. Most are equivalent in price to an A- or B-class hotel.

Pensions

Pensions throughout the Dodecanese are virtually indistinguishable from hotels. They are classed A, B or C. An A-class pension is equivalent in amenities and price to a B-class hotel, a B-class pension is equivalent to a C-class hotel, and a C-class pension is equivalent to a D- or E-class hotel.

Hotels

Hotels in the Dodecanese (as in Greece in general) are divided into six categories: deluxe, A, B, C, D and E. Hotels are categorised according to the size of the room, whether or not they have a bar, and the ratio of bathrooms to beds, rather than standards of cleanliness, comfort of the beds and friendliness of staff – all elements which may be of greater relevance to guests.

As one would expect, deluxe, A- and B-class hotels have many amenities, private bathrooms and constant hot water. C-class hotels have a snack bar, private bathrooms with the rooms, but hot water may only be available at certain times of the day. D-class hotels may or may not have snack bars, most rooms will share bathrooms (but there may be some with private bathrooms), and they may have solar-heated water, which means hot water is not guaranteed. E-class places do not have a snack bar, bathrooms are shared and you may have to pay extra for hot water – if it exists at all.

Prices are controlled by the tourist police and the maximum rate that can be charged for a room must be displayed on a board behind the door of each room. The classification is not often much of a guide to price. Rates in D- and E-class hotels are generally comparable with domatia. You can pay anywhere from 10,000 dr to 20,000 dr for a single in

high season in C class and 15,000 dr to 25,000 dr for a double. B-class prices range from 15,000 dr to 25,000 dr for singles, and from 25,000 dr to 35,000 dr for doubles. A-class prices are not much higher.

FOOD

Greek food does not enjoy a reputation as one of the world's great cuisines. Maybe that's because many travellers have experienced Greek cooking only in tourist resorts. The old joke about the Greek woman who, on summer days, shouted to her husband 'Come and eat your lunch before it gets hot' is based on truth.

Until recently, food was invariably served lukewarm, which is how Greeks prefer it. Most restaurants that cater to tourists have now cottoned on to the fact that foreigners expect cooked dishes to be served hot, and improved methods of warming meals (including the dreaded microwave) have made this easier. If your meal is not hot, ask that it be served *zesto*, or order grills, which have to be cooked to order. Greeks are generally fussy about fresh ingredients, and frozen food is rare.

Greeks eat out regularly, regardless of socioeconomic status. Enjoying life is paramount to Greeks and a large part of this enjoyment comes from eating and drinking with friends.

By law, every eating establishment must display a written menu including prices. Bread will automatically be put on your table and usually costs between 100 dr and 200 dr, depending on the restaurant's category.

Where to Eat

Tavernas Traditionally, the taverna is a basic eating place with a rough-and-ready ambience, although some are more upmarket, particularly in Athens, resorts and big towns. All tavernas have a menu, often displayed in the window or on the door, but it's usually not a good guide to what's actually available on the day. You'll be told about the daily specials – or ushered into the kitchen to peer into the pots and point to what you want. This is not merely a privilege for tourists; Greeks also do it because they want to see the taverna's version of the dishes on offer. Some tavernas don't open until 8 pm, and then stay open until the early hours. Some are closed on Sunday.

Greek men are football (soccer) and basketball mad, both as spectators and participants. If you happen to be eating in a taverna on a night when a big match is being televised, expect indifferent service.

Psistaria These places specialise in spit roasts and charcoal-grilled food – usually lamb, pork or chicken.

Restaurants An *estiatorio* (restaurant) is normally more sophisticated than a taverna or psistaria and features damask tablecloths, smartly attired waiters and printed menus at each table with an English translation. Ready-made food is usually displayed in a *bain-marie* and there may also be a charcoal grill.

Ouzeria An *ouzeri* serves ouzo. Greeks believe it is essential to eat when drinking alcohol so, in traditional establishments, your drink will come with a small plate of titbits or *mezedes* (appetisers) – perhaps olives, a slice of feta and some pickled octopus. Ouzeria are becoming trendy and many now offer menus with both appetisers and main courses.

Zaharoplasteia A *zaharoplasteio* (patisserie) sells cakes (both traditional and western), chocolates, biscuits, sweets, coffee, soft drinks and, possibly, bottled alcoholic drinks. They usually have some seating.

Kafeneia These coffee houses are often regarded by foreigners as the last bastion of male chauvinism in Europe. With bare light bulbs, nicotine-stained walls, smoke-laden air, rickety wooden tables and raffia chairs, they are frequented by middle-aged and elderly Greek men in cloth caps who while away their time fiddling with worry beads, playing cards or backgammon, or engaged in heated political discussion.

It was once unheard of for women to enter a kafeneia but in large cities this situation is starting to change.

In rural areas, Greek women are rarely seen inside kafeneia. When a female traveller enters one, she is inevitably treated courteously and with friendship if she manages a few Greek words of greeting. If you feel inhibited about going into a kafeneio, opt for outside seating. You'll feel less intrusive.

Kafeneia originally only served Greek coffee but now most also serve soft drinks, Nescafe and beer. They are generally fairly cheap, with Greek coffee costing about 150 dr and Nescafe with milk 250 dr or less. Most kafeneia are open all day every day, but some close during siesta time (roughly from 3 to 5 pm).

Meals

Breakfast Most Greeks have Greek coffee and perhaps a cake or pastry for breakfast. Budget hotels and pensions offering breakfast generally provide it continental-style (rolls or bread with jam, and tea or coffee), while more upmarket hotels serve breakfast buffets (western- and continental-style). Otherwise, restaurants and cafes serve bread with butter, jam or honey; eggs; and the budget travellers' favourite, *yiaourti* (yogurt) with honey. In tourist areas, many menus offer an 'English' breakfast, which means bacon and eggs.

Lunch This is eaten late – between 1 and 3 pm – and may be either a snack or a complete meal. The main meal can be lunch or dinner – or both. Greeks enjoy eating and often have two large meals a day.

Dinner Greeks also eat dinner late. Many people don't start to think about food until about 9 pm, which is why some restaurants don't even bother to open their doors until after 8 pm. In tourist areas dinner is often served earlier.

A full dinner in Greece begins with appetisers and/or soup, followed by a main course of either ready-made food, grilled meat, or fish. Only very posh restaurants or those pandering to tourists include western-style desserts on the menu. Greeks usually eat cakes and dessert separately in a galaktopoleio or zaharoplasteio.

Greek Specialities

Snacks Favourite Greek snacks include pretzel rings sold by street vendors, *tyropitta* (cheese pie), *bougatsa* (custard-filled pastry), *spanakopitta* (spinach pie) and *sandouits* (sandwiches). Street vendors sell various nuts and dried seeds such as pumpkin for 300 dr to 500 dr a bag.

Mezedes In a simple taverna, possibly only three or four mezedes (appetisers) will be offered – perhaps taramasalata (fish-roe dip), tzatziki (yogurt, cucumber and garlic dip), olives and feta (sheep or goat cheese). Ouzeria and restaurants usually offer a wider selection.

Cold mezedes include *ohtapodi* (octopus), *garides* (shrimps), *kalamaria* (squid), dolmadhes (stuffed vine leaves), *melitzanosalata* (aubergine or eggplant dip) and *mavromatika* (black-eyed beans). Hot mezedes include *keftedes* (meatballs), *fasolia* (white haricot beans), *gigantes* (lima beans), *loukanika* (little sausages), tyropitta, spanakopitta, *bourekaki* (a tiny meat pie), *kolokythakia* (deep-fried zucchini), *melitzana* (deep-fried aubergine) and *saganaki* (fried cheese).

It is quite acceptable to make a full meal of these instead of a main course. Three plates of mezedes are about equivalent in price and quantity to one main course. You can also order a *pikilia* (mixed plate).

Soups Soup is normally eaten as a starter, but can be an economical meal in itself with bread and a salad. *Psarosoupa* is a filling fish soup with vegetables, while *kakavia* (Greek bouillabaisse) is laden with seafood and is more expensive. *Fasoladha* (bean soup) is also a meal in itself. *Avgolemono soupa* (egg and lemon soup) is usually prepared from a chicken stock. If you're into offal, don't miss the traditional Easter soup, *mayiritsa*, at this festive time.

Salads The ubiquitous (and no longer inexpensive) Greek or village salad, *horiatiki salata*, is a side dish for Greeks, but many drachma-conscious tourists make it a main dish. It consists of peppers, onions, olives, tomatoes and feta cheese, sprinkled with oregano and dressed with olive oil and lemon juice. A tomato salad often comes with onions, cucumber and olives, and, with bread, makes a satisfying lunch. In spring, try *radikia salata* (dandelion salad).

Main Dishes The most common main courses are *mousakas* (layers of eggplant or zucchini, minced meat and potatoes topped with cheese sauce and baked), *pastitsio* (baked cheese-topped macaroni and béchamel, with or without minced meat), dolmadhes and *yemista* (stuffed tomatoes or green peppers). Other main courses include *giouvetsi* (casserole of lamb or veal and pasta), *stifado* (meat stewed with onions), *soutzoukakia* (spicy meatballs in tomato sauce) and *salingaria* (snails in oil with herbs). *Melitzanes papoutsakia* is baked eggplant stuffed with meat and tomatoes and topped with cheese, which looks, as its Greek name suggests, like a little shoe. Spicy *loukanika* (sausages) are a good budget choice and come with potatoes or rice. *Arni frikase me maroulia* (lamb fricassee, cooked with lettuce) is usually filling enough for two to share.

Fish is usually sold by weight in restaurants, but is not as cheap nor as widely available as it used to be. Calamari (squid), deep-fried in batter, remains a tasty option for the budget traveller at 1000 dr to 1400 dr for a generous serve. Other reasonably priced fish (about 1000 dr a portion) are *maridhes* (whitebait), sometimes cloaked in onion, pepper and tomato sauce, and *gopes* (similar to sardines). More expensive are *ohtapodi* (octopus), *bakaliaros* (cod), *xifias* (swordfish) and *glossa* (sole). Ascending the price scale further are *synagrida* (snapper) and *barbounia* (red mullet). *Astakos* (lobster) and *karavida* (crayfish) are top of the range at about 10,000 dr per kilogram.

Fish is mostly grilled or fried. More imaginative fish dishes include shrimp casserole and mussel or octopus saganaki (fried with tomato and cheese).

Desserts Greek cakes and puddings include *baklavas* (layers of filo pastry, interwoven with honey and chopped almonds), *loukoumadhes* (puffs or fritters with honey or syrup), *kataïfi* (chopped nuts inside shredded wheat pastry or filo soaked in honey), *rizogalo* (rice pudding), *loukoumi* (Turkish delight), *halva* (made from semolina or sesame seeds) and *pagoto* (ice cream). Tavernas and restaurants usually only have a few of these on the menu. The best places to go for these delights are galaktopoleia or zaharoplasteia.

Dodecanese Specialities

Greek food is not all mousakas and souvlaki, but you will find plenty of it throughout the Dodecanese. A dish to look out for is *makarounes* (handmade macaroni cooked with onions and cheese), which is popular in Karpathos. In Nisyros look out for *pitties* (chickpea and onion patties), in Astypalea every second restaurant seems to be offering *astakos me makaronia* (lobsters with pasta), while on Kalymnos squid cooked a special island way is called *mermizelli*.

On Patmos look out for *ahini* (sea urchins), served as a mezes with a dash of lemon and a glass of ouzo. Even the tiny island of Arki has its own speciality in *pastos*, a kind of salted fish mash. Not to be outdone, Agathonisi in the north has *markakia* (feta cheese fingers rolled in vine leaves with a tangy sauce).

Vegetarian

Greece has few vegetarian restaurants. Unfortunately, many vegetable soups and stews are based on meat stocks. Fried vegetables are safe bets as olive oil is always used – never lard. The Greeks do wonderful things with *anginares* (artichokes). They can be served stuffed, as a salad, as a mezes (particularly with *raki* in Crete) or used as the basis of a vegetarian stew.

Vegetarians who eat eggs can rest assured that an economical omelette can be whipped up anywhere. Salads are cheap, fresh, substantial and nourishing. Other options are yogurt, rice pudding, cheese and spinach pies, and nuts.

Lent, incidentally, is a good time for vegetarians because the meat is missing from many dishes.

Fast Food

Western-style fast food has definitely arrived in Greece in a big way – creperies, hamburger joints and pizza places are to be found in all major towns and resort areas.

However, it's hard to beat eat-on-the-street Greek offerings. Foremost among them are the *yiros* and the souvlaki. The yiros is a giant skewer laden with slabs of seasoned meat which grills slowly as it rotates; the meat is trimmed steadily from the outside. Souvlaki are small individual kebab sticks. Both are served wrapped in pitta bread, with fresh salad and lashings of tzatziki.

Another favourite is *tost*, which is a bread roll cut in half, stuffed with the filling(s) of your choice, buttered on the outside and then flattened in a heavy griddle iron.

Fruit

Greece grows many varieties of fruit. Most visitors will be familiar with *syka* (figs), *rodakina* (peaches), *stafylia* (grapes), *karpouzi* (watermelon), *milo* (apples), *portokalia* (oranges) and *kerasia* (cherries).

Many will not, however, have encountered the *frangosyko* (prickly pear). Also known as the Barbary fig, it is the fruit of the opuntia cactus, recognisable by the thick green spiny pads that form its trunk. The pale orange to deep red fruit are delicious but need to be approached with extreme caution because of the thousands of tiny prickles (invisible to the naked eye) that cover their skin. Never pick one up with your bare hands. They must be peeled before you can eat them. The simplest way to do this is to trim the ends off with a knife and then slit the skin from end to end.

Another fruit that will be new to many people is the *mousmoulo* (loquat). These small orange fruit are among the first of summer, reaching the market in mid-May. The flesh is juicy and pleasantly acidic.

Self-Catering

Eating out in Greece is as much an entertainment as a gastronomic experience, so to self-cater is to sacrifice a lot. But if you are on a low budget you will need to make this sacrifice – for breakfast and lunch at any rate. You'll find that towns and villages of any size have supermarkets, fruit and vegetable stalls and bakeries.

Only in isolated villages and on remote islands is food choice limited. There may only be one all-purpose shop – a *pantopoleio* which will stock meat, vegetables, fruit, bread and tinned foods.

Markets Most larger towns have huge indoor *agora* (food markets) which feature fruit and vegetable stalls, butchers, dairies and delicatessens, all under one roof. They are lively places that are worth visiting for the atmosphere as much as for the shopping. The markets at Kos and Rhodes Towns are good examples.

Smaller towns have a weekly *laïki agora* (street market) with stalls selling local produce.

DRINKS
Nonalcoholic Drinks
Coffee & Tea Greek coffee is the national drink. It is a legacy of Ottoman rule and, until the Turkish invasion of Cyprus in 1974, the Greeks called it Turkish coffee. It is served with the grounds, without milk, in a small cup. Connoisseurs claim there are at least 30 variations of Greek coffee, but most people know only three – *glykos* (sweet), *metrios* (medium) and *sketos* (without sugar).

After Greek coffee, the next most popular coffee is instant and called Nescafe (which it usually is). Ask for 'Nescafe *me ghala*' (me-**ga**-la) if you want it with milk. In summer, Greeks drink Nescafe chilled and shaken, with or without milk and sugar – this version is called *frappé*.

Espresso and filtered coffee, once sold only in trendy cafes, are now also widely available.

Tea is inevitably made with a tea bag, unless you ask for *tsaï tou vounou* (mountain tea) or *faskomilo* (sage tea).

Fruit Juice & Soft Drinks Packaged fruit juices are available everywhere. Fresh orange juice is also widely available, but doesn't come cheap.

The products of all the major soft-drink multinationals are available everywhere in cans and bottles, along with local brands.

Milk Fresh milk can be hard to find on the islands and in remote areas. Elsewhere, you'll have no problem. A litre costs about 350 dr. UHT milk is available almost everywhere, as is condensed milk.

Water Tap water is safe to drink in Greece, although on Kalymnos and Leros it is tainted by sea water so it doesn't taste too good. Most tourists prefer to drink bottled spring water, sold widely in 500mL and 1.5L plastic bottles. If you're happy with tap water, fill a container with it before embarking on ferries, or you'll wind up paying through the nose for bottled water. Sparkling mineral water is available in most supermarkets and is often known by the brand name of Souroti. Otherwise, the nearest is plain soda – fizzy, gassy water and not the soft drink that Americans and Canadians might expect.

Alcoholic Drinks
Beer Beer lovers will find the market dominated by the major northern European breweries. The most popular beers are Amstel and Heineken, both brewed locally under licence. Other beers brewed locally are Henninger, Kaiser, Kronenbourg and Tuborg.

The only local beer is Mythos, launched in 1997 and widely available. It has proved popular with drinkers who find the northern European beers a bit sweet.

Imported lagers, stouts and beers are found in popular tourist spots such as music bars and discos. You might even spot Newcastle Brown, Carlsberg, Guinness and Castlemaine XXXX.

Supermarkets are the cheapest place to buy beer, and bottles are cheaper than cans. A 500mL bottle of Amstel or Mythos costs about 300 dr (including 25 dr deposit on the bottle), while a 500mL can cost 350 dr. Amstel also produces a low-alcohol beer and a bock, which is dark, sweet and strong.

Wine According to mythology, the Greeks invented or discovered wine and have been producing it in Greece on a large scale for more than 3000 years.

The modern wine industry, though, is still very much in its infancy. Until the 1950s, most Greek wines were sold in bulk and were seldom distributed any further afield than the nearest town. It wasn't until industrialisation (and the resulting rapid urban growth) that there was much call for bottled wine. Quality control was unheard of until 1969, when appellation laws were introduced as a precursor to applying for membership of the European Community. Wines have improved significantly since then.

Don't expect Greek wines to taste like French wines. The grape varieties grown in Greece are quite different. Some of the most popular and reasonably priced labels include Rotonda, Kambas, Boutari, Calliga and Lac des Roches, all available in most large supermarkets. Retsina is a resinated white, or occasionally rosé wine with a taste that needs to be acquired. It is great on its own but even better when drunk with a dash of soda water. Liokri and Georgiadis are two brand names to look out for.

Rhodes' KAIR winery produces some of the better local wines at a reasonable price. Try the red Arhondiko, or the white Rodos 2400. The red Cava Emery or Zacosta and white Villare from Emery wines in Embonas in Rhodes are also good choices. Although not a Dodecanese wine, the Golden Samaina, produced in Samos, is a delicately-flavoured, fruity white and this writer's favourite tipple, when it is available.

You usually can't go wrong with draft wine, served in *miso kilo* (half litre) or *kilo* (litre) copper carafes. The wine is cheap, generally good to better and you can have *lefko* (white), *rozay* (rosé) or *kokkino* (red).

Spirits Ouzo is the most popular aperitif in Greece. Distilled from grape stems and flavoured with anise, it is similar to the Middle Eastern *arak*, Turkish *raki* and French Pernod. Clear and colourless, it turns white when water is added. A 700mL bottle of a popular brand like Ouzo 12, Olympic or Sans Rival costs about 1400 dr in supermarkets. In an ouzeri, a glass costs from 350 dr

to 600 dr. It will be served neat, with a separate glass of water to be used for dilution.

The second most popular spirit is Greek brandy, which is dominated by the Metaxa label. Metaxa comes in a wide choice of grades, starting with three star – a high-octane product without much finesse. You can pick up a bottle in a supermarket for about 1500 dr. The quality improves as you go through the grades: five star, seven star, VSOP, Golden Age and finally the top-shelf Grand Olympian Reserve (5600 dr). Other reputable brands include Cambas and Votrys. The speciality from nearby Crete is raki, a fiery clear spirit that is served as a greeting (regardless of the time of day).

If you're travelling off the beaten track, you may come across *tsipouro*. Like ouzo, it's made from grape stems but without the anise. It's an acquired taste, much like Irish poteen – and packs a similar punch. You'll most likely encounter tsipouro in village kafeneia or private homes.

ENTERTAINMENT
Cinemas
Greeks are keen movie-goers and almost every town of consequence has a cinema. English-language films are shown in English with Greek subtitles. Admission ranges from 1000 dr in small-town movie houses to 1800 dr at plush big-city cinemas.

Discos & Music Bars
Discos can be found in big cities and resort areas, though not in the numbers of a decade ago.

Most young Greeks prefer to head for the music bars that have proliferated to fill the void. These bars normally specialise in a particular style of music – Greek, modern rock, '60s rock, techno and, occasionally, jazz.

Theatre
There are no major performances staged in the Dodecanese such as you will find at Epidavros or Athens on the mainland. However, a number of plays are staged during the Symi festival (though all will be in Greek). See Symi in the Central Dodecanese chapter for details of the Symi Festival.

Traditional Music

Most of the live music you hear around the resorts is tame stuff laid on for the tourists. Karpathos, however, has a bit of a reputation for impromptu music sessions taking place in restaurants, or wherever people gather. Either way, the best time to catch island music – either the violin-based *nisiotiki* 'island' music or the lyra-based and Cretan-leaning *karpathiotiki* sort – is at the many *paniyiria* (regional festivals) or weddings, or staged as part of a cultural event like the Symi Festival (see Symi in the Central Dodecanese chapter).

Folk Dancing

The pre-eminent folk dancers in the Dodecanese are from the Nelly Dimoglou Dance Company in Rhodes Old Town (see the Rhodes chapter), which performs during the summer months. Folk dancing is an integral part of all festival celebrations and there is often impromptu folk dancing in tavernas.

SPECTATOR SPORTS

Greeks are mad about football (soccer) and basketball in more or less equal percentages. Although no major teams are based in the Dodecanese, Greeks – young and old alike – will flock to any impromptu or official match, given half a chance.

Rhodes and Kos are the best places for catching a live soccer match from September to May. Matches are played on Sunday. Basketball is best enjoyed on the TV when often whole cafes or bars are taken over by wildly enthusiastic crowds cheering on their own favourite mainland team.

SHOPPING

Greece produces a vast array of handicrafts, and you will see ceramic objects of every shape and size – functional and ornamental – for sale throughout the Dodecanese. The best places for high-quality handmade ceramics are Kos, Rhodes and the islands of Leros and Karpathos. There are a lot of places selling plaster copies of statues, busts, grave stelae and so on.

There are leather goods for sale throughout the Dodecanese; most are made from leather imported from Spain. The best place for buying leather goods is Rhodes Old Town. Bear in mind that the goods may not be as high quality nor as good value as those available in Turkey.

You could join the wealthy tourists who spill off the cruise ships onto Patmos or Rhodes to indulge themselves in the high-class gold jewellery shops there. But although gold is good value in Greece, and designs are of a high quality, it is priced beyond the capacity of most tourists' pockets.

It is illegal to buy, sell, possess or export any antiquities in Greece (see the Customs section earlier in this chapter). However, there are antiques and 'antiques'; a lot of items only a century or two old are regarded as junk, rather than part of the national heritage. These items include handmade furniture and odds and ends from rural areas throughout Greece, ecclesiastical ornaments from churches and items brought back from far-flung lands. Good hunting grounds for this 'junk' are Monastiraki and the flea market in Athens, and the Piraeus market held on Sunday morning.

Getting There & Away

AIR

Most travellers arrive in Greece by air, the cheapest and quickest way to get there.

Airports

There are international airports at Karpathos, Kos and Rhodes but these are for charter operators only. There are additional domestic airports on Leros, Kastellorizo and Kasos.

International scheduled flights to Greece are handled mainly by Athens (including all intercontinental traffic) and Thessaloniki. In summer there are domestic connections provided by three domestic airlines to Astypalea, Leros, Kos, Rhodes and Karpathos. The small airports on Kastellorizo and Kasos are only served by flights to and from Rhodes.

Athens' new Eleftherios Venizelos airport at Spata was due to open in March 2001 after many years of work and anticipation. It

is a far cry from the old, badly rundown airport at Alimos closer to Athens' city centre. Although the new airport is some distance from Athens, passengers should for once have a pleasant experience arriving in and departing from Greece.

Kos' domestic and international charter airport has just about as much air traffic as it can handle comfortably in high season. It is a smallish modern airport, conveniently located in the middle of the island. Visitors to Kalymnos commonly use the airport on Kos to get to their destination on the neighbouring island, using a three times daily local ferry from Kos to Kalymnos.

The domestic and international charter airport on Rhodes has long reached saturation point and facilities and services are generally poor and over-used. Thessaloniki's airport, which also serves the Dodecanese with one flight weekly to Rhodes, is fairly modern and has undergone a facelift in recent years. It is 16km from the city centre.

The small airports at Astypalea, Leros, Kastellorizo and Kasos are usually nothing more than a single small building with minimum facilities. Astypalea is served by a 50-seater aircraft, while the other three airports are served by an 18-seater aircraft.

Airlines

Olympic Airways is no longer Greece's only international airline. Cronus Airlines flies direct from Athens to London, Paris and Rome, and via Thessaloniki to Cologne, Düsseldorf, Frankfurt, Stuttgart and Munich. There is an additional weekly flight from Kavala to Stuttgart.

Olympic Airways The vast majority of domestic flights are handled by Greece's much-maligned national carrier, Olympic Airways, together with its offshoot, Olympic Aviation.

Olympic Airways has offices wherever there are flights, as well as in other major Greek towns. The head office is in Athens

Air Travel Glossary

Alliances Many of the world's leading airlines are now intimately involved with each other, sharing everything from reservations systems and check-in to aircraft and frequent-flyer schemes. Opponents say that alliances restrict competition. Whatever the arguments, there is no doubt that big alliances are the way of the future.

Courier Fares Businesses often need to send urgent documents or freight securely and quickly. Courier companies hire people to accompany the package through customs and, in return, offer a discount ticket which is sometimes a bargain. However, you may have to surrender all your baggage allowance and take only carry-on luggage.

Fares Airlines traditionally offer 1st class (coded F), business class (coded J) and economy class (coded Y) tickets. These days there are so many promotional and discounted fares available that few passengers pay full fare.

Lost Tickets If you lose your airline ticket, an airline will usually treat it like a travellers cheque and, after inquiries, issue you with another one. Legally, however, an airline is entitled to treat it like cash and if you lose it then it's gone forever. Take very good care of your tickets.

Onward Tickets An entry requirement for many countries is that you have a ticket out of the country. If you're unsure of your next move, the easiest solution is to buy the cheapest onward ticket to a neighbouring country or a ticket from a reliable airline which can later be refunded if you do not use it.

Open-Jaw Tickets These are return tickets where you fly out to one place but return from another. If available, this can save you backtracking to your arrival point.

Overbooking Since every flight has some passengers who fail to show up, airlines often book more passengers than they have seats. Usually excess passengers make up for the no-shows, but occasionally somebody gets 'bumped' onto the next available flight. Guess who it is most likely to be? The passengers who check in late. If you do get 'bumped', you are normally offered some form of compensation.

Reconfirmation Some airlines require you to reconfirm your flight at least 72 hours prior to departure. Check your travel documents to see if this is the case

Restrictions Discounted tickets often have various restrictions on them – such as needing to be paid for in advance and incurring a penalty to be altered or cancelled. Others are restrictions on the minimum and maximum period you must be away.

Round-the-World Tickets RTW tickets give you a limited period (usually a year) in which to circumnavigate the globe. You can go anywhere the carrying airlines go, as long as you don't backtrack. The number of stopovers or total number of separate flights is decided before you set off and they usually cost a bit more than a basic return flight.

Ticketless Travel Airlines are gradually waking up to the realisation that paper tickets are unnecessary encumbrances. On simple one-way or return trips, reservations details can be held on computer and the passenger merely shows ID to claim their seat.

Transferred Tickets Airline tickets cannot be transferred from one person to another. Travellers sometimes try to sell the return half of their ticket, but officials can ask you to prove that you are the person named on the ticket. On an international flight, tickets are compared with passports.

(☎ 01-966 6666) at Leoforos Syngrou 96. You can call reservations inquiries on ☎ 0801 44 444, or check out the Web site www.olympic-airways.gr.

The free-baggage allowance on domestic flights is 15kg. However, this does not apply when the domestic flight is part of an international journey. The international free-baggage allowance of 20kg is then extended to the domestic sector. This allowance applies to all tickets for domestic travel sold and issued outside Greece. Olympic offers a 25% student discount on domestic flights, but only if the flight is part of an international journey.

Olympic lost its monopoly on domestic routes in 1993. It took a while for any serious opposition to emerge, but there are now two established competitors travelling to the Dodecanese and newcomers are likely to appear in the future.

Cronus Airlines Cronus is a popular company new to the local scene. It flies Athens-Rhodes-Athens once daily and offers feeder links to Thessaloniki as well as eight European destinations. The head office (☎ 01-994 4444, ℯ info@cronus.gr) is in Athens at Leoforos Vouliagmenis 517.

Cronus offers discounts for students and for travellers aged over 60, and special rates for advance purchase. Its Web site (www .cronus.gr) has more information on routes and fares.

Aegean Airlines Aegean is the latest addition to the line-up. It flies from Athens to Rhodes and offers feeder links for passengers from Rhodes to a further six domestic destinations. The fleet is very modern and utilises jet aircraft on all routes and the service by all accounts is excellent. Passenger feedback suggests that Aegean will be giving the current competitors a solid run for their money.

The head office is in Athens (☎ 01-998 2888) at Leoforos Vouliagmenis 572.

Buying Tickets

If you're flying to Greece from outside Europe, the plane ticket will probably be the most expensive item in your travel budget, and buying it can be an intimidating business. There will be a multitude of airlines and travel agencies hoping to separate you from your money, so take time to research the options. Start early – some of the cheapest tickets must be bought months in advance, and popular flights sell out early.

Discounted tickets fall into two categories – official and unofficial. Official discount schemes include advance-purchase tickets, budget fares, Apex, Super-Apex and a few other variations on the theme. These tickets can be bought from travel agencies or direct from the airline. They often have restrictions (advance purchase is the usual one). There may also be restrictions on the period you have to be away, such as a minimum of 14 days and a maximum of one year.

Unofficial tickets are simply discounted tickets the airlines release through selected travel agencies.

Return tickets can often be cheaper than a one-way ticket. Generally, you can find discounted tickets at prices as low as, or even lower than, Apex or budget tickets. Phone around travel agencies for bargains.

If you are buying a ticket to fly out of Greece, Athens is one of the major centres in Europe for budget air fares.

Always remember to reconfirm your onward or return bookings by the specified time – usually 72 hours before departure on international flights. If you don't, there's a risk you'll turn up at the airport, only to find that you've missed your flight because it was rescheduled, or the airline has given the seat to someone else.

Charter Flights

Charter flight tickets are for seats left vacant on flights which have been block-booked by package companies. Tickets are cheap but conditions apply on charter flights to Greece. A ticket must be accompanied by an accommodation booking. This is normally circumvented by travel agencies issuing accommodation vouchers, which are not meant to be used – even if the hotel named on the voucher actually exists. The law requiring accommodation bookings was introduced in the 1980s to prevent budget travellers flying to Greece on cheap flights and sleeping rough on beaches or in parks. It hasn't worked.

There used to be a catch for travellers taking charter flights that involved any overnight visit to Turkey. If you flew to Greece with a return ticket on a charter flight, you had to forfeit the return portion if you visited Turkey. Greece was one of several popular charter destination countries that decided to band together to discourage tourists from leaving the destination country during the duration of the ticket. The countries involved wanted to ensure people didn't flit off somewhere else to spend their tourist cash. The result was that some travellers fronting up at the airport for their return charter flight with a Turkish stamp in their passport were forced to buy another ticket. However, this law has since been abolished, and overnight excursions to Turkey are no longer a concern for charter flight travellers.

Charter flight tickets are valid for up to four weeks, and usually have a minimum-stay requirement of at least three days. Sometimes it's worth buying a charter return, even if you want to stay longer than four weeks. The tickets can be so cheap you can afford to throw away the return portion.

The travel section of major newspapers is the place to look for cheap charter deals. More information on charter flights is given later in this chapter under specific point-of-origin headings.

Travel Agencies

Many of the larger travel agencies use the travel pages of national newspapers and magazines to promote their special deals. Before you make a decision, there are a number of questions you need to ask about the ticket. Find out the airline, the route, the duration of the journey, the stopovers allowed, any restrictions on the ticket and – above all – the price. Also make sure you ask whether the fare quoted includes all taxes and other possible inclusions.

You may discover when you start ringing around that those impossibly cheap flights,

charter or otherwise, are not available, but the agency just happens to know of another one that 'costs a bit more'. Or the agent may claim to have the last two seats available for Greece for the whole of July, which they will hold for a maximum of two hours only. Don't panic – keep ringing around.

If you are flying to Greece from the USA, South-East Asia or the UK, you will probably find the cheapest flights are being advertised by obscure agencies whose names haven't yet reached the telephone directory – the proverbial bucket shops. Many such firms are honest and solvent, but there are a few rogues who will take your money and disappear, only to reopen elsewhere a month or two later under a new name. If you feel suspicious about a firm, don't give them all the money at once – leave a small deposit and pay the balance when you get the ticket. If they insist on cash in advance, go somewhere else or be prepared to take a big risk. Once you have booked the flight with the agency, ring the airline to check you have a confirmed booking.

It can be easier on the nerves to pay a bit more for the security of a better-known travel agency. Firms such as STA Travel (with offices worldwide), Council Travel in the USA or Travel CUTS in Canada offer good prices to Europe (including Greece), and are unlikely to disappear overnight.

The fares quoted in this book are intended as a guide only. They are approximate and are based on the rates advertised by travel agencies at the time of writing.

Travel Insurance

The kind of cover you get depends on your insurance and type of ticket, so ask both your insurer and your ticket-issuing agency to explain where you stand. Ticket loss is usually covered.

Buy travel insurance as early as possible. If you buy it just before you fly, you may find you're not covered for such problems as delays caused by industrial action. Make sure you have a separate record of all your ticket details – preferably a photocopy.

Paying for your ticket by credit card sometimes provides limited travel insurance, and you may be able to reclaim the payment if the operator doesn't deliver. In the UK, for instance, credit card providers are required by law to reimburse consumers if a company goes into liquidation and the amount in contention is more than UK£100. Some credit cards are also linked to frequent flyer point schemes. Make sure you get your full allocation by using your card to pay for your ticket.

Travellers with Special Needs

If you've broken a leg, require a special diet, are travelling in a wheelchair, are taking a baby, or have some other special need, let the airline staff know as soon as possible – preferably when booking your ticket. Check that your request has been registered when you reconfirm your booking (at least 72 hours before departure) and again when you check in at the airport.

Children under two years of age travel for 10% of the standard fare (or free on some airlines) as long as they don't occupy a seat. But they do not get a baggage allowance. 'Skycots' should be provided by the airline if requested in advance. These will take a child weighing up to about 10kg. Olympic Airways charges half-fare for accompanied children aged between two and 12 years, while most other airlines charge two-thirds.

Departure Tax

There is an airport tax of 6800 dr on all international departures from Greece. This is paid when you buy your ticket, not at the airport.

The domestic airport tax of 3400 dr is paid when you purchase your ticket.

Connections to the Dodecanese

If you are flying into Greece with Olympic Airways your domestic Dodecanese connection will be seamlessly built in to your ticketing. Olympic Airways gives you the most destination choices in the Dodecanese.

Olympic Airways runs a busy schedule to the region, particularly in summer. It offers flights from Athens to Leros, Astypalea, Kos, Rhodes and Karpathos and feeder links from Rhodes to Kastellorizo and Kasos.

There's an additional weekly flight between Thessaloniki and Rhodes. Olympic's competitors offer cheaper fares on some of the more popular routes, so check around.

Cronus Airlines and Aegean Airlines offer flights from Athens to Rhodes only, though Aegean Airlines does offer a summer-only service from Thessaloniki to Rhodes. Tickets for these airlines can be arranged through your travel agency or bought on the spot at Athens or Thessaloniki airports.

In spite of the number of flights, demand far exceeds supply and it can be hard to find a seat during July and August. Early bookings are recommended. Flight schedules are greatly reduced in winter.

The UK

British Airways, Olympic Airways and Virgin Atlantic operate daily flights between London and Athens. Pricing is very competitive, with all three offering return tickets for around UK£200 in high season, plus tax. These prices are for mid-week departures; you will pay about UK£40 more for weekend departures.

There are connecting flights to Athens from Edinburgh, Glasgow and Manchester.

The Greek newcomer, Cronus Airlines (☎ 020-7580 3500), flies the London-Athens route five times a week for £210, and offers connections to Thessaloniki on the same fare. Olympic Airways has daily direct London-Thessaloniki flights. Most scheduled flights leave from Heathrow.

The cheapest scheduled flights are with no-frills specialist EasyJet (☎ 0870 6 000 000), which has two Luton-Athens flights daily. One-way fares range from UK£89 to UK£139 in high season, and from a bargain UK£39 to UK£69 at other times. Its Web site is at www.easyjet.com.

There are numerous charter flights between the UK and Greece. Typical London-Athens charter fares are UK£79/129 one way/return in the low season and UK£99/189 in the high season. These prices are for advance bookings, but even in high season it's possible to pick up last-minute deals for as little as UK£59/99. Many travel agencies offer charter flights to the islands as well as to Athens. Most island destinations cost about UK£109/209 in high season. Charter flights to Greece also fly from Birmingham, Cardiff, Glasgow, Luton, Manchester and Newcastle. Contact the Air Travel Advisory Bureau (☎ 020-7636 5000) for information about current charter flight bargains, or try its Web site www.atab.co.uk.

London is Europe's major centre for discounted fares. Some of the most reputable agencies selling discount tickets are:

Usit Campus (☎ 020-7730 3402) 52 Grosvenor Gardens, London SW1
Web site: www.usitcampus.co.uk
Council Travel (☎ 020-7287 3337) 28A Poland St, London W1V 3DB
Web site: www.counciltravel.com
STA Travel (☎ 020-7361 6161) 86 Old Brompton Rd, London SW7
Web site: www.statravel.co.uk
Trailfinders (☎ 020-7937 5400) 215 Kensington High St, London W8

Listings publications such as *Time Out*, the Sunday papers, the *Evening Standard* and *Exchange & Mart* carry advertisements for cheap fares. The *Yellow Pages* is worth scanning for travel agents' ads. Also look out for the free magazines and newspapers widely available in London, especially *TNT*, *Footloose*, *Southern Cross* and *LAM* – you can pick them up outside the main train and tube stations.

Some travel agencies specialise in flights for students aged under 30 and travellers aged under 26 (you need an ISIC card or an official youth card). Whatever your age, you should be able to find something to suit your budget.

Most British travel agencies are registered with ABTA (Association of British Travel Agents). If you have paid for your flight through an ABTA-registered agent who then goes out of business, ABTA will guarantee a refund or an alternative. If an agency is registered with ABTA, its advertisements will usually say so.

If you're flying from Athens to the UK, budget fares start at 25,000 dr to London or 30,000 dr to Manchester, plus airport tax.

The USA

The North Atlantic is the world's busiest long-haul air corridor, and the flight options to Europe – including Greece – are bewildering.

Microsoft's popular Expedia.com Web site at www.expedia.msn.com gives a good overview of the possibilities. Other sites worth checking out are ITN (www.itn.net) and Travelocity (www.travelocity.com).

The *New York Times*, *LA Times*, *Chicago Tribune* and *San Francisco Chronicle Examiner* all publish weekly travel sections in which you'll find any number of advertisements for travel agencies. Council Travel (www.counciltravel.com) and STA Travel (www.statravel.com) have offices in major cities nationwide.

New York has the most direct flights to Athens. Olympic Airways has at least one flight a day, and Delta Airlines has three a week. Apex fares range from US$960 to US$1600, depending on the season and how long you want to stay away.

Boston is the only other east coast city with flights to Athens (via Manchester) – three times weekly with Olympic Airways. Fares are the same as for flights from New York.

There are no direct flights to Athens from the west coast. There are, however, connecting flights to Athens from many US cities, either linking with Olympic Airways in New York or flying with one of the European national airlines to their home country, and then on to Athens. These connections usually involve a stopover of three or four hours.

One-way fares can be very cheap on a stand-by basis. Airhitch (☎ 212-864 2000) specialises in this. It can get you to Europe one way for US$159 from the east coast and US$239 from the west coast, plus tax. Its Web site is at www.airhitch.org.

Courier flights are another possibility. The International Association of Air Travel Couriers (☎ 561-582 8320, fax 582 1581) has flights from six US cities to a range of European capitals – but not Athens. Check out its Web site at www.courier.org.

If you're travelling from Athens to the USA, the travel agencies around Syntagma offer the following one-way fares (prices do not include airport tax): Atlanta 110,000 dr, Chicago 110,000 dr, Los Angeles 125,000 dr and New York 85,000 dr.

Canada
Olympic Airways has four flights weekly from Toronto to Athens via Montreal. There are no direct flights from Vancouver, but there are connecting flights via Toronto, Amsterdam, Frankfurt and London on Canadian Airlines, KLM, Lufthansa and British Airways.

Travel CUTS (☎ 1-888-838 CUTS) has offices in all major cities and is a good place to ask about cheap deals. You should be able to get to Athens from Toronto and Montreal for about C$1150 or from Vancouver for C$1500. The *Toronto Globe & Mail*, the *Toronto Star*, the *Montreal Gazette* and the *Vancouver Sun* all carry advertisements for cheap tickets.

For courier flights originating in Canada, contact FB On Board Courier Services in Montreal (☎ 514-631 2677). They can get you to London for C$575 return.

At the time of writing, budget travel agencies in Athens were advertising flights to Toronto for 105,000 dr and to Montreal for 100,000 dr, plus airport tax.

Australia
Olympic Airways has two flights a week from Sydney and Melbourne to Athens. Return fares are normally priced from about A$1699 in low season to A$2199 in high season.

Thai International and Singapore Airlines also have convenient connections to Athens, as well as a reputation for good service. If you're planning on doing a bit of flying around Europe, it's worth checking around for special deals from the major European airlines. British Airways and Lufthansa are a couple of likely candidates with good European networks.

Two of Australia's major dealers in cheap fares are STA Travel and Flight Centres International. The Sunday tabloid newspapers and the travel sections of the *Sydney Morning Herald* and *The Age* in Melbourne are a good place to look for cheap flights.

AXIS Travel Centre (☎ 08-8331 3222, fax 8364 2922, e axistravel@msn.com.au) in Adelaide offers special deals to Athens with Gulf Air and Egypt Air, starting at A$1399 return in low season. These fares include free hotel accommodation if no immediate connection to Athens is available.

A one-way ticket from Athens to Sydney or Melbourne in Australia costs about 180,000 dr, plus airport tax.

New Zealand
There are no direct flights from New Zealand to Athens. However, there are connecting flights via Sydney, Melbourne, Bangkok and Singapore on Olympic Airways, United Airlines, Qantas Airways, Thai Airways and Singapore Airlines.

Continental Europe
Athens is linked to every major city in Europe by either Olympic Airways or the flag carrier of each country.

If you're travelling from Athens to Europe, budget fares to a host of European cities are widely advertised by the travel agencies around Syntagma. Following are some typical one-way fares (not including airport tax):

destination	one-way fare
Amsterdam	57,500 dr
Copenhagen	59,500 dr
Frankfurt	55,000 dr
Geneva	54,000 dr
Hamburg	52,000 dr
Madrid	73,000 dr
Milan	48,000 dr
Munich	55,000 dr
Paris	55,500 dr
Rome	42,000 dr
Zürich	53,500 dr

London is the discount capital of Europe, but Amsterdam, Frankfurt, Berlin and Paris are also major centres for cheap airfares.

France Air France (☎ 0802 802 802) and Olympic Airways (☎ 01 44 94 58 58) have at least four Paris-Athens flights daily between them. Expect to pay from 2950FF to

3300FF in high season, dropping to about 2100FF at other times. Cronus Airlines (☎ 01 47 42 56 77) flies the same route four times weekly. Olympic Airways also has three flights weekly to Athens from Marseille.

Charter flights are much cheaper. You'll pay around 2000FF in high season for a return flight from Paris to Athens, and 2050FF to Rhodes or Santorini. The fare to Athens drops to 1500FF in low season. Reliable travel agencies include:

Air Sud (☎ 01 40 41 66 66) 18 Rue du Pont-Neuf, 75001 Paris
Atsaro (☎ 01 42 60 98 98) 9 Rue de l'Echelle, 75001 Paris
Bleu Blanc (☎ 01 40 21 31 31) 53 Avenue de la République, 75011 Paris
Héliades (☎ 01 53 27 28 21) 24-27 Rue Bas-froi, 75011 Paris
La Grèce Autrement (☎ 01 44 41 69 95) 72 Boulevard Saint Michel, 75006 Paris
Nouvelles Frontières (☎ 08 03 33 33) 87 Boulevard de Grenelle, 75015 Paris
Planète Havas (☎ 01 53 29 40 00) 26 Avenue de l'Opéra, 75001 Paris

Germany Atlas Reisewelt, with offices throughout Germany, is a good place to start checking prices.

In Berlin, Alternativ Tours (☎ 030-8 81 20 89), Wilmersdorfer Strasse 94, has discounted fares to just about anywhere in the world. SRS Studenten Reise Service (☎ 030-28 59 82 64), at Marienstrasse 23 near Friedrichstrasse station, offers special student (under 35) and youth (under 26) fares. Travel agencies offering unpublished cheap flights advertise in *Zitty*, Berlin's fortnightly entertainment magazine.

In Frankfurt, try SRID Reisen (☎ 069-43 01 91), Berger Strasse 118.

The Netherlands Reliable travel agencies in Amsterdam include:

Budget Air (☎ 020-627 12 51) Rokin 34
Malibu Travel (☎ 020-626 32 20, @ postbus@ pointtopoint.demon.nl) Prinsengracht 230
NBBS Reizen (☎ 020-624 09 89) Rokin 66

Turkey
Olympic Airways and Turkish Airlines share the İstanbul-Athens route, with at least one

daily flight each. The full fare is US$250 one way. Olympic Airways also flies twice weekly between İstanbul and Thessaloniki (US$200). Students qualify for a 50% discount on both routes.

There are no direct flights from Ankara to Athens; all flights go via İstanbul.

Cyprus
Olympic Airways and Cyprus Airways share the Cyprus-Greece routes. Both airlines have three flights daily from Larnaka to Athens, and there are five flights weekly to Thessaloniki. Cyprus Airways also flies from Pafos to Athens once a week in winter, and twice a week in summer.

Travel agencies in Athens charge around 50,000 dr one way to Larnaka and Pafos, or 83,000 dr return.

SEA
Ferry
For most people, travel throughout the Dodecanese will mean island-hopping. Every island has a ferry service of some sort, although in winter, services to some of the smaller islands are fairly skeletal. Services start to pick up again from April onwards, and by July and August there are a fair number of services moving up and down the Dodecanese chain. Ferries come in all shapes and sizes, from the large ferries that work the major routes to the small, ageing open ferries that chug around the backwaters.

The sinking of the *Express Samena* off the island of Naxos in October 2000 has resulted in a shake-up of the Greek shipping industry. Many boats were recalled pending safety checks and many older boats may ultimately be scrapped.

Routes The hub of Greece's ferry network is Piraeus, the port of Athens. Large ferries leave here daily for the Dodecanese Islands. The main access route includes the islands of Patmos, Leros, Kalymnos, Kos and Rhodes with less frequent stops in Lipsi, Nisyros, Symi and Tilos. A second and longer route to Rhodes goes via Milos, Agios Nikolaos and Sitia (both in Crete), Kasos, Karpathos and Halki.

Astypalea in the far west of the Dodecanese chain is less frequently linked to Piraeus and the other Dodecanese islands via a circuitous route that includes Paros, Naxos and Amorgos. Both these routes are served by two main ferry lines DANE Seaways and G&A Ferries.

A further weekly service connects Rhodes with Thessaloniki, while small Chios-based car ferries connect the northern Dodecanese islands with Samos and Chios.

Schedules Timetables change from year to year and season to season, and ferries are subject to delays and cancellations at short notice due to bad weather, strikes or boats simply conking out. No timetable is infallible, but the comprehensive weekly list of departures from Piraeus put out by the EOT in Athens is as accurate as humanly possible. The people to go to for the most up-to-date ferry information are the local port police *(limenarhio)*, whose offices are usually on or near the quayside.

You'll find all the latest information about ferry routes, schedules and services on the Internet. For the best overview and useful links to just about all the shipping

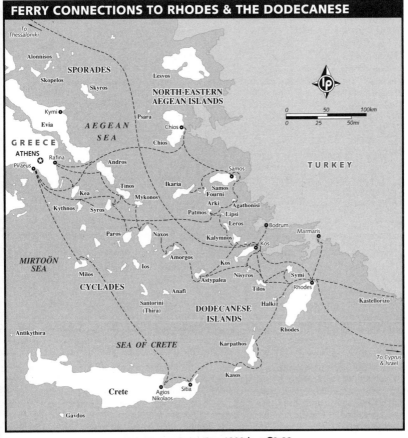

FERRY CONNECTIONS TO RHODES & THE DODECANESE

Ferry Connections to the Dodecanese

origin	destination	duration	price	frequency
Agios Nikolaos (Crete)	Diafani (Karpathos)	6¾ hours	3600 dr	3 weekly
Agios Nikolaos (Crete)	Halki	9½ hours	3800 dr	2 weekly
Agios Nikolaos (Crete)	Kasos	4½ hours	3200 dr	3 weekly
Agios Nikolaos (Crete)	Pigadia (Karpathos)	6 hours	3600 dr	3 weekly
Agios Nikolaos (Crete)	Rhodes	11 hours	6100 dr	3 weekly
Milos	Diafani (Karpathos)	14¾ hours	6400 dr	3 weekly
Milos	Halki	17 hours	6100 dr	2 weekly
Milos	Kasos	12 hours	5800 dr	3 weekly
Milos	Pigadia (Karpathos)	13½ hours	6400 dr	3 weekly
Milos	Rhodes	18½ hours	8300 dr	3 weekly
Piraeus	Astypalea	12 hours	6700 dr	5 weekly
Piraeus	Diafani (Karpathos)	20 hours	7800 dr	3 weekly
Piraeus	Halki	21½ hours	9300 dr	2 weekly
Piraeus	Kalymnos	10 hours	6600 dr	daily
Piraeus	Kasos	17 hours	7800 dr	3 weekly
Piraeus	Kos	15¼ hours	7100 dr	daily
Piraeus	Leros	11 hours	6300 dr	9 weekly
Piraeus	Lipsi	10 hours	8900 dr	1 weekly
Piraeus	Nisyros	15¾ hours	7370 dr	3 weekly
Piraeus	Patmos	9 hours	6700 dr	10 weekly
Piraeus	Pigadia (Karpathos)	16 hours	7500 dr	3 weekly
Piraeus	Rhodes	17½ hours	8500 dr	daily
Piraeus	Symi	14 hours	9200 dr	4 weekly
Piraeus	Tilos	17 hours	7400 dr	2 weekly
Pythagorio (Samos)	Agathonisi	1¼ hours	1450 dr	4 weekly
Pythagorio (Samos)	Kalymnos	7¼ hours	3200 dr	1 weekly
Pythagorio (Samos)	Leros	5 hours	2500 dr	1 weekly
Pythagorio (Samos)	Lipsi	4 hours	1800 dr	5 weekly
Pythagorio (Samos)	Patmos	3 hours	1750 dr	4 weekly
Pythagorio (Samos)	Rhodes	8½ hours	6400 dr	1 weekly
Sitia (Crete)	Diafani (Karpathos)	7½ hours	3600 dr	3 weekly
Sitia (Crete)	Halki	7½ hours	3800 dr	2 weekly
Sitia (Crete)	Kasos	2½ hours	2500 dr	3 weekly
Sitia (Crete)	Pigadia (Karpathos)	6 hours	3600 dr	3 weekly
Sitia (Crete)	Rhodes	9¼ hours	5800 dr	3 weekly
Thessaloniki	Kos	19½ hours	12,200 dr	1 weekly
Thessaloniki	Rhodes	23½ hours	14,800 dr	1 weekly
Vathy (Samos)	Kos	4 hours	3400 dr	1 weekly

companies serving Greece see the Web sites www.ferries.gr or gtpnet.gr.

Throughout the year there is at least one ferry a day from Piraeus to the major islands in the Dodecanese, and during the high season (from June to mid-September) there are usually more services. Ferries sailing from the Dodecanese to the Cyclades, however, are another matter, and if you're going to travel in this way you'll need to plan carefully, otherwise you may end up having to backtrack to Piraeus. Connections to the islands of the North Eastern Aegean are also a bit thin on the ground, so you will need to build in some elasticity to your itinerary if you plan to cross to another island group.

Travelling time can vary considerably from one ferry to another, depending on the ship and the route it takes. For example, the Piraeus-Rhodes trip can take between 14 and 18 hours. Before buying your ticket, check how many stops the boat is going to make, and its estimated arrival time. Note that the local F/B *Nisos Kalymnos* is considerably slower than the larger boats operated by DANE and G&A Ferries.

Island hoppers are not going to be helped much by the big ferries on the north–south run as they nearly always depart at inconvenient times – usually between midnight and 5 am. Heading north from Rhodes is much better, as departures from and to other major islands are between 2 and 10 pm.

Costs Prices are fixed by the government, and are determined by the distance travelled rather than by the facilities of a particular boat. There can be big differences in the size, comfort and facilities of boats offering rival services on a given route, but the fares will be the same. The small differences in price you may find at ticket agencies are the result of some agents sacrificing part of their designated commission to qualify as a 'discount service'. The discount is seldom more than 50 dr.

Classes The large ferries usually have four classes: 1st class has air-con cabins and a posh lounge and restaurant; 2nd class has smaller cabins and sometimes a separate lounge; tourist class is in a shared four-berth cabin; and 3rd (deck) class gives you access to a room with 'airline' seats, a restaurant, a lounge/bar and, of course, the deck.

Deck class remains an economical way to travel, while a 1st-class ticket can cost almost as much as flying on some routes. Children under four travel for free, while children between four and 10 pay half-fare. Full fares apply for children over 10. Unless you state otherwise when purchasing a ticket, you will automatically be given deck class. Prices quoted in this book are for deck class, as this is what most tourists choose.

Ticket Purchase Ferries are prone to delays and cancellations in bad weather, so it's best not to buy a ticket until it has been confirmed that the ferry is operating. If you need to reserve a car space, you may need to pay in advance. If the service is cancelled, you can transfer your ticket to the next available service with that company.

Agencies selling tickets line the waterfront of most ports, but rarely is there one that sells tickets for every boat, and often an agency is reluctant to give you information about a boat they do not sell tickets for. This means you have to check the timetables displayed outside each agency to find out which ferry is next to depart – or ask the port police. In high season, a number of boats may be due at a port at around the same time, so it is not beyond the realms of possibility that you might get on the wrong boat. The crucial thing to look out for is the name of the boat; this will be printed on your ticket, and in large English letters on the side of the vessel.

If for some reason you haven't purchased a ticket from an agency, makeshift ticket tables are put up beside a ferry about an hour before departure. Tickets can sometimes be purchased on board the ship after it has sailed, though this practice is officially frowned upon, as it is harder to keep records of passengers and overbookings can occur. If you are waiting at the quayside for a delayed ferry, don't lose patience and wander off. Ferry boats, once they turn up, can demonstrate amazing alacrity – blink and you may miss the boat.

Mainland Ports
Only two mainland ports serve the Dodecanese directly. Piraeus is the main port with daily sailings in summer. Thessaloniki is the other port, with one service a week, in summer only.

Other Island Groups
The Dodecanese are generally poorly linked to other Aegean island groups. One service links Rhodes via Astypalea with the Central Cyclades group twice a week, with four services a week in high season linking

the Dodecanese with Amorgos, Naxos and Paros. These services drop to twice weekly or less out of season. Northwards, the only reliable link is with the slow and small F/B *Nisos Kalymnos* that links the Dodecanese with Samos, or with the even smaller boats run by Miniotis Lines that link Patmos and Agathonisi with Samos and Chios. Crete is linked to the Dodecanese via the thrice-weekly service offered by LANE Lines. Their two sizeable boats run from Rhodes to Sitia and Agios Nikolaos in Crete via Halki, Karpathos and Kasos.

Cyprus & Israel

Two companies ply the route between the Israeli port of Haifa and Rhodes via Lemesos in Cyprus. The boats continue on to Piraeus either directly or via Santorini and Mykonos. They then make the return journey to Cyprus and Israel. However, these boats cannot be used to travel from other Greek ports to Rhodes.

During July and August, Salamis Lines' F/B *Nisos Kypros* leaves Haifa at 8 pm on Sunday and Lemesos at 4 pm on Monday, reaching Rhodes at noon on Tuesday. For the rest of the year, the boat leaves Haifa at 8 pm on Monday. Bookings in Haifa are handled by Rosenfeld Shipping (☎ 04-861 3670, fax 853 3264), 104 Ha'Atzmaut St, and in Lemesos by Salamis Tours (☎ 05-355 555, fax 364 410), Salamis House, 28 October Ave.

Poseidon Lines operates a similar service throughout the year. Either the F/B *Sea Harmony* or F/B *Sea Serenade* sails from Haifa at 8 pm on Thursday and Lemesos at 1 pm on Friday, arriving in Rhodes at 9 am on Saturday. Bookings in Haifa are handled by Caspi Travel (☎ 04-867 4444, fax 866 1958), 76 Ha'Atzmaut St.

Both lines have different fare structures, with Salamis Lines having cheaper fares, but an older ferry. High-season deck-class fares from Haifa to Rhodes are US$91 (Poseidon Lines) and US$62 (Salamis Lines); from Lemesos to Rhodes they are US$58 (Poseidon) and US$39 (Salamis Lines). An aircraft style seat is an extra US$10 while a bed in the cheapest cabin is an extra US$30.

Poseidon Lines (☎ 05-745 666, fax 745 666) is at 124 Franklin Roosevelt St, Lemesos, while Salamis Lines (☎ 05-355 555, fax 364 410) can be contacted at Salamis Tours, PO Box 351, Lemesos. Information about both companies' schedules can be obtained from Viamare Travel Ltd (☎ 020-7431 4560, fax 7431 5456, [e] ferries@ viamare.com) at 2 Sumatra Rd, London NW6 1PU in the UK.

Sailing details and current ticket prices for both companies can be viewed on the Internet at www.greekislands.gr/Poseidon and www.viamare.com/Salamis/.

Departure tax from Lemesos is CY£15 to CY£18 when leaving by sea, however it's normally included in the cost of your ferry ticket.

Turkey

There are five regular ferry services between Turkey's Aegean coast and the Greek Islands. Tickets for all ferries to Turkey must be bought a day in advance. You will almost certainly be asked to turn in your passport the night before the trip, but don't worry – you'll get it back the next day before you board the boat. Port tax for departures to Turkey is 3000 dr.

See the relevant sections under individual island entries for more information about the following services.

Rhodes to Marmaris The once regular ferry service to Marmaris now only runs on demand. Check with travel agencies in Rhodes Town to see if there are any boats going. There are, however, daily hydrofoils to Marmaris (weather permitting) from April to October for 10,000/14,000 dr one way/return plus Turkish port tax.

Chios to Çeşme There are daily Chios-Çeşme boats from July to September, dropping steadily back to one boat a week in winter. Tickets cost 15,000/20,000 dr one wayreturn, including port taxes.

Kos to Bodrum There are daily ferries in summer from Kos to Bodrum (ancient Halicarnassus) in Turkey. Boats leave at 8.30 am

Day Trips to Turkey

There is nothing quite like a day trip to make a vacation seem just that bit more exciting. It's even more fun if it takes you to another country and positively mind-blowing to know that you can hop over to another continent between breakfast and dinner. Turkey, Greece's giant neighbour to the East, is visible from most of the Dodecanese's 18 inhabited islands and taking a day trip is a popular outing for visitors. It is also a lucrative one for the operators of the hydrofoils and caïques that make the relatively short runs across to the Asian mainland.

Although relations between Turkey and Greece are occasionally strained (see 'The Imia Incident' in Facts about Rhodes & the Dodecanese), things are usually cordial and friendly, and travellers come and go unhindered. A day trip to Turkey requires a little bit of planning, but it's generally a breeze. Firstly it's not cheap: trips can cost around 14,000 dr return plus another US$10 for Turkish port taxes. You'll have to make your booking the day before, as your passport details must be processed by immigration police. You will not need a Turkish visa for a single day trip, but you will if you decide to extend your stay. Though there used to be a law that made longer stays in Turkey difficult for charter flight ticket holders, it has now been abolished, meaning that restrictions on overnight stays are no longer a concern.

If you plan to do some heavy shopping in Turkey, bear in mind that Greek customs may be interested in those leather jackets or Turkish carpets you bought for a bargain, and they may sting you for import duty. Finally, spend all those loose millions of Turkish lira in your pocket before you go back to Greece: it is difficult to change them into drachma.

See the Gateway Ports chapter later for more information.

and return at 4 pm. The one hour journey costs 13,000 dr return, including port taxes.

Lesvos to Ayvalık There are up to five boats per week travelling this route in the high season. Tickets cost 16,000/21,000 dr one way/return.

Samos to Kuşadası There are two boats daily to Kuşadası (for Ephesus) from Samos in summer, dropping to one or two boats weekly in winter. Tickets cost 10,000/11,000 dr one way/return plus 5000 dr Greek port tax and US$10 Turkish port tax.

Italy

There are ferries to Greece from the Italian ports of Ancona, Bari, Brindisi, Trieste and Venice. These ferries are usually superior in quality to those plying the Greek domestic routes and in some cases are like mini cruise ships. A number of ferries have partially open 'campervan decks' where you can park your campervan and use it to sleep and live in for the duration of the voyage.

The ferries can get very crowded in the summer months. If you want to take a vehicle across it's a good idea to make a reservation. In the UK, reservations can be made on almost all of these ferries at Viamare Travel Ltd (☎ 020-7431 4560, fax 7431 5456, @ ferries@viamare.com), 2 Sumatra Rd, London NW6 IPU.

The following ferry services are for high season (July and August), and prices are for one-way deck class. Deck class on these services means exactly that. If you want a reclining, aircraft-type seat, you'll be up for another 10% to 15% on top of the listed fares. Most companies offer discounts ranging from 30% to 50% for return travel. Prices are about 30% less in the low season.

Ancona to Patra This route has become increasingly popular in recent years. There can be up to three boats daily in summer, and at least one a day year-round.

Superfast Ferries (☎ 071-20 28 05, fax 20 21 19, @ info.anconaport@superfast.com) provides the fastest, most convenient, and also the most expensive service. It has boats daily (20 hours, L131,000). Minoan Lines (☎ 071-20 17 08) has ferries to Patra (20 hours, L126,000) via Igoumenitsa (15 hours) daily except Tuesday. ANEK Lines (☎ 071-20 59 99) runs two direct boats weekly (24 hours, L120,000) and three via Igoumenitsa (34 hours). Blue Star Ferries (formerly Strintzis Lines; ☎ 071-20 10 68) sails direct

Ferry Travel

Ferry travel around the Dodecanese can be absolute chaos in high season. No matter how many passengers are already on the ferry, more will be crammed on. Bewildered, black-shrouded grannies are steered through the crowd by teenage grandchildren, children get separated from parents, people stumble over backpacks, dogs get excited and bark – and everyone rushes to grab a seat. As well as birds in cages and cats in baskets there is almost always at least one truck of livestock on board – usually sheep, goats or cattle, vociferously making their presence known.

Greeks travelling deck class usually make a beeline for the indoor lounge/snack bar, while tourists make for the deck where they can sunbathe. Some ferry companies have allegedly attempted to capitalise on this natural division by telling backpackers and non-Greeks that they are barred from the deck-class saloon and indoor-seating area, directing them instead to the sun deck. There is no such thing as 'deck only' class on domestic ferries, although there is on international ferries.

You'll need strong nerves and lungs to withstand the lounge/snack bar, though. You can reckon on at least two TVs turned up full blast, tuned to different channels and crackling furiously from interference. A couple of other people will have ghetto blasters pumping out heavy metal, and everyone will be engaged in loud conversation. Smoke-laden air adds the final touch to this delightful ambience. Unlike other public transport in Greece, smoking is rarely prohibited on ferries.

On overnight trips, backpackers usually sleep on deck in their sleeping bags – you can also roll out your bag between the 'airline' seats. If you don't have a sleeping bag, claim an 'airline' seat as soon as you board. Leave your luggage on it – as long as you don't leave any valuables in it. The noise on board usually dies down around midnight so you should be able to snatch a few hours of sleep.

The food sold at ferry snack bars ranges from mediocre to inedible, and the choice is limited to packets of biscuits, sandwiches, very greasy pizzas and cheese pies. Most large ferries also have a self-service restaurant where the food is OK and reasonably priced, with main courses starting at around 1800 dr. If you are budgeting, have special dietary requirements, or are at all fussy about what you eat, take food with you.

to Patra (23 hours, L92,000) three times weekly, twice via Igoumenitsa and Corfu.

All ferry operators in Ancona have booths at the *stazione marittima* (ferry terminal) off Piazza Candy, where you can pick up timetables and price lists and make bookings.

Bari to Corfu, Igoumenitsa & Patra
Superfast Ferries (☎ 080-52 11 416) operates daily to Patra (15 hours, L86,500) via Igoumenitsa (9½ hours, L80,000), while Marlines (☎ 080-52 31 824) runs daily boats to Igoumenitsa (12 hours, L87,000). Ventouris

(☎ 080-521 7118) goes to Igoumenitsa (13½ hours, L77,000) via Corfu.

Brindisi to Corfu, Igoumenitsa & Patra
The route from Brindisi to Patra (18 hours) via Corfu (nine hours) and Igoumenitsa (10 hours) is the cheapest and most popular of the various Adriatic crossings. There can be up to five boats daily in high season.

Companies operating ferries from Brindisi are: Adriatica di Navigazione (☎ 0831-52 38 25), at Corso Garibaldi 85-87, and on the 1st floor of the stazione marittima, where you must go to check in; Five Star Lines (☎ 0831-52 48 69), represented by Angela Gioia Agenzia Marittima, Via F Consiglio 55; Fragline (☎ 0831-59 01 96), Corso Garibaldi 88; Hellenic Mediterranean Lines (☎ 0831-52 85 31), Corso Garibaldi 8; and Med Link Lines (☎ 0831-52 76 67), represented by Discovery Shipping, Corso Garibaldi 49.

Adriatica and Hellenic Mediterranean are the most expensive at around L91,000 for deck-class passage to Corfu (7½ hours), Igoumenitsa (nine hours) or Patra (15½ hours), but they are the best. They are also the only lines that accept Eurail passes. You will still have to pay port tax and a high-season loading in summer – usually about L15,000. If you want to use your Eurail pass, it is important to reserve some weeks in advance, particularly in summer. Even with a booking, you must still go to the Adriatica or Hellenic Mediterranean embarkation office in the stazione marittima to have your ticket checked.

The cheapest crossing is with Five Star Lines, which charges L56,000 to either Igoumenitsa (7½ hours) or Patra (15½ hours). Med Link charges L70,000 to Igoumenitsa and L75,000 to Patra, while Fragline charges L76,800 to Corfu and Igoumenitsa. Fares for cars range from L65,500 to L120,000 in the high season, depending on the line.

From 1 July to 19 September, Italian Ferries (☎ 0831-59 03 05), Corso Garibaldi 96, operates a daily high-speed catamaran to Corfu (3¼ hours, L160,000), leaving Brindisi at 2 pm. The service continues to Paxi (4¾ hours, L200,000 dr).

Brindisi to Kefallonia & Zakynthos

Hellenic Mediterranean Lines has daily services to the port of Sami on Kefallonia from late June to early September. The trip takes 15 hours and costs L110,000 for deck class. Med Link also stops occasionally at Sami on its Brindisi-Patra run during July and August.

Hellenic Mediterranean Lines stops at Zakynthos (17 hours, L110,000) two or three times weekly in July and August.

Trieste to Patra ANEK Lines (☎ 40-30 28 88), Stazione Marittima di Trieste, has three boats weekly to Patra travelling via Igoumenitsa. The trip takes 37 hours and costs L106,000 for deck class.

Venice to Patra This route is becoming almost as popular as the Ancona-Patra route, given Venice's even closer proximity to major population centres in northern Europe. Sailings to Patra involve two nights on board. Minoan Lines (☎ 41-27 12 345), Magazzino 17, Santa Marta, has boats from Venice to Patra (35 hours, L132,000). All services go via Corfu and Igoumenitsa, and from mid-May until late September there are two boats weekly to Kefallonia.

LAND
Greek Mainland/Athens

Bus If you arrive in Thessaloniki from neighbouring countries you can head directly to Rhodes either via the twice-weekly flights or the once-weekly ferry. Alternatively, you can take the bus down to Athens and pick up a ferry from Piraeus.

The trip to Athens takes 7½ hours and costs 8000 dr one way. There are departures at 12, 7.45, 9.30 and 10.30 am, 12, 1.30, 3, 4.30, 6, 9.30 and 11 pm. The Thessaloniki-Athens bus terminal (☎ 03-510 834) is opposite the train station at Monastiriou 65 in Thessaloniki.

In Athens, the terminal (☎ 01-514 8856) is at Kifisou 100, somewhat inconveniently located on the west side of Athens. You will need to take a taxi from this terminal (3000 dr) to get to the port of Piraeus.

Train The same principle as the bus applies to the train, except that some trains go as far as Piraeus port, which may be more convenient for ferry travellers. However, from the Athens train stations you can also now take the metro all the way to Piraeus port.

There are about 12 departures daily from Thessaloniki to Athens/Piraeus. Of these, five are Inter City services, which are infinitely more preferable to the slow, regular services. An Inter City train does the Thessaloniki-Athens run in about six hours, compared to

7½ hours for the regular train. The 7 am departure (IC53) from Thessaloniki to Athens is the most convenient train in order to meet up with a same-day ferry connection to the Dodecanese. It arrives in Athens at 1 pm.

A one-way fare from Thessaloniki to Athens on the regular train is 3720 dr, while a one-way Inter City ticket costs 8250 dr – over twice as much. For further details call Thessaloniki train station (☎ 031-517 517), or Athens' Stathmos Larisis train station (☎ 01-823 7741).

Car & Motorcycle If you are bringing your own transport with you, you can either drive/ride to Thessaloniki and pick up the weekly car ferry to Rhodes, or drive/ride down to Athens. The road network from Thessaloniki to Athens is good and is gradually being improved to bring it up to motorway quality. You could drive from Thessaloniki to Athens (514 km) comfortably in about six hours. Allow an extra hour at least to get from the outskirts of Athens to the port of Piraeus.

If you are bringing your car or motorcycle from Italy it's better to disembark at Patra on the West Peloponnese, not Igoumenitsa in Epirus. From Patra it is only 218km along a fast coastal toll-highway and it's easily done in under three hours. Allow seven to eight hours if coming from Igoumenitsa. If heading for Piraeus, you can short-circuit much of the Athens traffic by heading directly to Piraeus from Skaramangas, on the Bay of Elefsina west of Athens. Obtain a local map and use it carefully.

Western Europe

Overland travel between Western Europe and Greece is almost a thing of the past. Air fares are so cheap that land transport cannot compete. Travelling from the UK to Greece through Europe means crossing various borders, so check whether any visas are required before setting out.

Travelling by car or motorcycle is still a good option, particularly when you consider that you can take a car ferry from Venice and sail all the way to the Peloponnese in Greece in only 33 hours.

Bus There are no bus services to Greece from the UK, nor from anywhere else in northern Europe. Bus companies can no longer compete with cheap air fares.

Train Unless you have a Eurail pass or are aged under 26 and eligible for a discounted fare, travelling to Greece by train is prohibitively expensive. For example, the full one-way/return fare from London to Athens is UK£265/521, including the Eurostar service from London to Paris.

Greece is part of the Eurail network. Eurail passes can only be bought by residents of non-European countries and are supposed to be purchased before arriving in Europe. They can, however, be bought in Europe as long as your passport proves that you've been there for less than six months. In London, head for the Rail Europe Travel Centre (☎ 08705 848 848), 179 Piccadilly, W1. Sample fares include UK£461 for an adult Eurail Flexipass, which permits 10 days 1st-class travel in two months, and UK£323 for the equivalent youth pass.

If you are starting your European travels in Greece, you can buy your Eurail pass from the Hellenic Railways Organisation offices at Karolou 1 and Filellinon 17 in Athens, and at the train station in Patra and Thessaloniki.

Greece is also part of the InterRail Pass system, but the pass for those aged over 26 is not valid in France, Italy and Switzerland – rendering it useless if you want to get to Greece. InterRail Youth Passes for those under 26 are divided into zones. A Global Pass (all zones) costs UK£259 and is valid for a month. You need to be under 26 on the first day of travel and to have lived in Europe for at least six months.

A good Internet site for all rail fares is www.raileurope.com.

Car & Motorcycle Before the troubles in the former Yugoslavia began, most motorists driving from the UK to Greece opted for the direct route: Oostende, Brussels, Salzburg and then down the Yugoslav highway through Zagreb, Belgrade and Skopje and crossing the border to Evzoni.

It is theoretically still possible, now that the border between Croatia and Serbia is open, but it is a long, hard haul and not really recommended.

These days most people drive to an Italian port and get on a ferry to Greece. Your options are to take a ferry from Trieste, Venice, Ancona, Bari or Brindisi to Corfu, Igoumenitsa, Kefallonia, Zakynthos or Patra. From Venice to Igoumenitsa (the first port of call in Greece) is 29 hours sailing, while from Brindisi to Igoumenitsa it is only eight hours.

However, weigh up the disadvantages of high fuel costs, autostrada tolls and at least one night's accommodation in Italy against the higher cost of a Venice-Greece ferry ride and you may find you are better off going for the longer sea voyage. For further information see the Sea section earlier in this chapter.

Purchase-Repurchase Schemes It is hardly worth hiring a car to drive to Greece all the way from Western Europe since you can hire a car in Greece. However, if you are resident outside the European Union and you plan to make an extended visit to Greece, or include other countries as part of your itinerary then it may be in your interest to look at the Purchase-Repurchase schemes to meet your transport needs.

Basically you lease a brand-new car for the duration of your stay at rates considerably below daily rental rates. The two major players are Peugeot and Renault, both French car manufacturers. This means in effect that you need to pick up your car in France, or for an extra premium from another designated European city.

You can then drive your car to more or less anywhere in Europe (including Greece of course) and return to a nominated French or European city of your choice (but not Athens). It takes no more than 10 minutes to complete the so-called 'repurchase' formalities. The most efficient way to get to Greece is to pick up your car (at no extra cost) from either Geneva or Nice airports and drive it to Venice or Ancona (1½ days) and take a ferry to Greece from there.

For further details on this excellent scheme contact the following agents:

France: Peugeot (☎ 01 49 04 81 56, fax 01 49 04 82 50); Renault (☎ 01 40 40 32 32, fax 01 42 41 83 47)
Australia: Peugeot (☎ 02-9976 3000, fax 9905 5874), Web site: www.driveaway.com.au; Renault (☎ 02-9299 3344, ☎ 9262 4590)
Canada: Peugeot (☎ 514-735 3083, fax 342 8801), Web site: www.europauto.qc.ca; Renault (☎ 450-461 1149, fax 461 0207)
New Zealand: Peugeot (☎ 09-914 9100, fax 379 4111); Renault (☎ 09-525 8800, fax 525 8818)
South Africa: Peugeot (☎ 011-458 1600, fax 455 2818); Renault (☎ 011-325 2345, fax 325 2840)
USA: Peugeot (toll-free ☎ 1800 572 9655, fax 201-934 7501), Web site: www.auto-france.com; (☎ 1800 223 1516, fax 212-246 1458), Web site: www.europebycar.com; (☎ 914 825 3000, fax 835 5449), Web site: www.kemwel.com; Renault (☎ 1800 221 1052, fax 212-725 5375)

Albania

Bus There is a daily OSE bus between Athens and Tirana (12,600 dr) via Ioannina and Gjirokastër. The bus departs from Athens (Larisis train station) at 7 pm, arriving in Tirana the following day at 5 pm. It leaves Ioannina at 7.30 am and passes through Gjirokastër at 10.30 am. On the return trip, the bus departs from Tirana at 7 am. There are buses from Thessaloniki to Korça (Korytsa in Greek) at 8 am daily. The fare is 6600 dr.

Car & Motorcycle There are two crossing points between Greece and Albania. The main one is at Kakavia, 60km north-west of Ioannina. The closest town on the Albanian side is Gjirokastër.

The alternative crossing is at Krystallopigi, north-west of Kastoria. Kapshtica is the closest town on the Albanian side.

Former Yugoslav Republic of Macedonia

Train Thessaloniki-Skopje trains (three hours, 4200 dr, two daily) cross the border between Idomeni and Gevgelija. They leave Thessaloniki at 6 am and 5.30 pm. Both trains continue to the Serbian capital of Belgrade (12 hours, 11,500 dr). The

5.30 pm service goes all the way to Budapest (21 hours, 20,000 dr).

Car & Motorcycle There are three border crossings between Greece and FYROM. The one at Evzoni, 68km north of Thessaloniki, is the main highway to Skopje, which continues to Belgrade. Another border crossing is at Niki, 16km north of Florina, while there is a third, little used crossing at Doïrani, 70km north of Thessaloniki.

Bulgaria
Bus The OSE operates two Athens-Sofia buses (15 hours, 13,400 dr) daily except Monday, leaving at 7 am and 5 pm. It also operates Thessaloniki-Sofia buses (7½ hours, 5600 dr, three daily).

Train There is an Athens-Sofia train daily (18 hours, 10,330 dr) via Thessaloniki (nine hours, 6700 dr).

Car & Motorcycle The Bulgarian border crossing is at Promahonas, 145km northeast of Thessaloniki and 50km from Serres. This crossing can get very busy and there are usually long lines of trucks waiting to cross in either direction.

Turkey
Bus The Hellenic Railways Organisation (OSE) operates Athens-İstanbul buses (22 hours) daily except Wednesday, leaving the Peloponnese train station in Athens at 7 pm and travelling via Thessaloniki and Alexandroupolis. One-way fares are 21,800 dr from Athens, 14,300 dr from Thessaloniki and 5600 dr from Alexandroupolis. Students qualify for a 15% discount and children under 12 travel for half-fare.

Buses from İstanbul to Athens leave the Anadolu Terminal (Anatolia Terminal) at the Topkapı bus station *(otogar)* at 10 am daily except Sunday.

Train There are daily trains between Athens and İstanbul (19,000 dr) via Thessaloniki (13,000 dr) and Alexandroupolis (6350 dr). The service is incredibly slow and the train gets uncomfortably crowded. There are often delays at the border and the journey can take much longer than the supposed 22 hours.

Car & Motorcycle If you're travelling between Greece and Turkey by private vehicle, the crossing points are at Kipi, 43km north-east of Alexandroupolis, and at Kastanies, 139km north-east of Alexandroupolis. Kipi is more convenient if you're heading for İstanbul, but the route through Kastanies goes via the fascinating towns of Soufli and Didymotiho in Greece, and Edirne (ancient Adrianoupolis) in Turkey. However, the border post at Kastanies is only open from 9 am to 1 pm.

ORGANISED TOURS
A lot of UK companies specialise in package holidays to the Dodecanese. Among the better ones are Laskarina Holidays (☎ 01629-824 884, fax 822 205 🅴 info@laskarina.co.uk) at St Mary's Gate, Wirksworth, Matlock, Derbyshire DE4 4DQ. Laskarina deals in self-catering holidays in tasteful studios and apartments and has some of the best accommodation in the Dodecanese.

Greece Direct (☎ 020-8785 4000), at Oxford House, 182 Upper Richmond Rd, Putney, London SW15 2 SH, offer villas, apartments and restored houses on Rhodes and Halki.

Getting Around

It is easy enough to get around the Dodecanese Islands, both from island to island and around each of the islands, thanks to a reasonably well-developed public transport system. On larger islands like Rhodes and Kos, there are excellent bus systems linking the farthest points on the islands with the main town, while smaller islands may have just a minibus or two. Only two islands with a road system do not have a bus system at all.

All islands have at least one or two taxis and one island even has a system whereby you share a taxi with other passengers for the price of a bus fare. Taxi boats are a useful way to get from a port to a remote beach or settlement and there are also local inter-island caïques to ferry passengers to and fro.

Having your own car is a great bonus though it can get expensive shipping it from island to island. For an extended stay there is nothing quite like having your own wheels and it may actually be cheaper in the long run. Consider leasing a new car from Europe and using that as your main transport (see under Land in the Getting There & Away chapter).

Seven of the Dodecanese islands have airports, five of which have direct flights to and from Athens or Thessaloniki. Inter-island flights are limited to a few scheduled services out of Rhodes.

Bear in mind that schedules and ticket prices listed throughout this book are given as a guide only. Check locally once you are on the ground and be prepared for some changes. You'll also find lots of travel information on the Internet. A useful general site is www.ellada.com, which has lots of links and includes airline timetables.

AIR
Inter-Island Flights
Olympic Airways link Rhodes with Karpathos, Kasos and Kastellorizo with daily flights in high season. Aegean Airlines links Rhodes with Iraklio in Crete four times a week in summer.

Domestic Departure Tax
The airport tax for domestic flights is 3400 dr, paid as part of the ticket. The only sector where the departure tax is not payable is for the short flight between Kasos and Karpathos. All prices quoted in this book include this tax.

BOAT
Inter-Island Boat
In addition to the large ferries that ply between the large mainland ports and island groups, there are smaller boats which link islands within a group, and occasionally link an island in one group with an island in another. In the past these boats were always caïques – sturdy old fishing boats – but gradually these are being replaced by new purpose-built boats, which are usually called express or excursion boats.

In the case of the Dodecanese these ferries operate primarily out of Patmos: to Lipsi, Arki and Marathi; between Leros and Kalymnos; between Kos and Nisyros; and there is even a car ferry service between Kalymnos and Kos. Tickets tend to cost somewhat more than those for the large ferries, but the boats are very useful if you're island-hopping.

A Kalymnos-based boat, F/B *Nisos Kalymnos,* does an almost continuous run up and down the Dodecanese, linking the islands of Agathonisi, Arki and Kastellorizo with the rest of the chain as well as providing a twice weekly service to and from Astypalea.

Hydrofoil
Hydrofoils offer a faster alternative to ferries on some routes, particularly to islands close to the mainland – they take half the time, but cost twice as much. They do not take cars or motorbikes. Most routes operate only during high season, and according to demand, and all are prone to cancellations if the sea is rough. The ride can be bumpy at the best of times. Hydrofoils are also beginning to show their age and construction quality with many of them beginning to fray (literally) on the

interior and looking rather battered on the exterior. For about the same price passengers can take the much better catamaran.

The biggest operator is Kyriacoulis Flying Dolphins, which connects all the islands of the Dodecanese with the exception of Kasos, Karpathos and Kastellorizo. Further links take passengers up to Samos, Fourni and Ikaria.

Tickets cannot be bought on board hydrofoils – you must buy them in advance from an agent. You will be allocated a seat number if it is full, or you can sit where you like at slack times.

Caïques & Boats & Coves

While for the most part you will be moving around the Dodecanese on large ferry boats, catamarans and hydrofoils, you will, from time to time, be relying on smaller caïques (*kaïkia* in Greek) to get to and from remoter beaches and even between islands. While these sturdy former fishing boats are often solid and safe, and distances are not usually far, you should bear a few things in mind.

If you are not a swimmer, know where the life jackets are stored. Don't get on a caïque if it doesn't have life jackets. Seat yourself in the shade. Getting a tan may be important, but half an hour in the Aegean sun with the additional reflected glare of the sea may be just enough to burn you to toast before you know it.

Some caïques link islands like Patmos with satellite islands like Arki and Marathi and this is the only way to get there. This particular trip can get very choppy in the open waters east of Patmos. Take anti-nausea tablets if you are likely to be affected.

You may take the opportunity to hire a motorboat and take yourself off to your own private cove. These boats are often underpowered, so don't venture too far out to sea. The Aegean Sea can develop a nasty swell once you are away from the protection of the little bays. Make sure you have spare fuel on board; you could be stranded (it has happened to this author). Bear in mind that petrol costs are usually *in addition* to the hire charges. Account for that in your budget and happy sailing!

Catamaran

High-speed catamarans have rapidly become an important part of the island travel scene. They are just as fast as the hydrofoils – if not faster – and much more comfortable. They are also much less prone to cancellation in rough weather.

In the Dodecanese there are only two players: the Rhodes-based *Dodekanisos Express* connects all islands except Kasos, Karpathos and Kastellorizo – though that may change in future. The Tilos-based *Sea Star* connects Tilos with Rhodes and Nisyros daily. Both vessels enjoy an extremely high engineering and comfort level, are airconditioned, mainly nonsmoking and run at convenient times up and down the Dodecanese Islands. They are a much better alternative to the hydrofoils.

Taxi Boat

Most islands have taxi boats – small speedboats that operate like taxis, transporting people to places that are difficult to get to by land. Some owners charge a set price for each person, others charge a flat rate for the boat, and this cost is divided by the number of passengers. Either way, prices are usually quite reasonable.

Yacht

Despite the disparaging remarks among backpackers, yachting is *the* way to see the Greek Islands. Nothing beats the peace and serenity of sailing the open sea, and the freedom of being able to visit remote and uninhabited islands.

The free EOT booklet *Sailing the Greek Seas*, although long overdue for an update, contains lots of information about weather conditions, weather bulletins, entry and exit regulations, entry and exit ports and guidebooks for yachties. You can pick up the booklet at any GNTO/EOT office either abroad or in Greece. The Internet is the place to look for the latest information. The Hellenic Yachting Server site, www-na.biznet.com.gr/sail, has general information on sailing around the islands and some useful links.

The sailing season lasts from April until October. The best time to go depends on

The Cost of the Catamaran

The following passenger fares are for one-way trips on the *Dodekanisos Express*, based in Rhodes. Prices are listed in Greek drachma.

Children's fares are 50% of the adult fare. A small motor vehicle costs just over twice the price of an adult passenger fare. Motorbikes (up to 250cc) cost 42% of the adult passenger fare.

PORT	Rhodes	Halki	Symi	Tilos	Nisyros	Kos	Kalymnos	Leros	Lipsi	Patmos
Rhodes	-	3700	3100	5500	5600	6800	8500	9300	10,100	10,700
Halki	3700	-	N/A	3700	6000	6600	8200	8800	N/A	N/A
Symi	3100	N/A	-	N/A	N/A	5000	6900	8700	8500	9900
Tilos	5500	3700	N/A	-	3000	3800	5300	6000	N/A	7500
Nisyros	5600	6000	N/A	3000	-	3500	3400	4800	N/A	5800
Kos	6800	6600	5000	3800	3500	-	2800	4100	4000	5400
Kalymnos	8500	8200	6900	5300	3400	2800	-	3600	3600	4900
Leros	9300	8800	8700	6000	4800	4100	3600	-	2600	3100
Lipsi	10,100	N/A	8500	N/A	N/A	4000	3600	2600	-	2300
Patmos	10,700	N/A	9900	7500	5800	5400	4900	3100	2300	-

where you are going. The most popular time is between July and September, which ties in with the high season for tourism in general. Unfortunately, it also happens to be the time of year when the *meltemi* is at its strongest. The meltemi is a northerly wind that affects the Aegean throughout summer. It starts off as a mild wind in May and June, and strengthens as the weather hots up – often blowing from a clear blue sky. In August and September, it can blow at gale force for days on end.

If your budget won't cover buying a yacht there are several other options open to you. You can hire a bare boat (a yacht without a crew) if two crew members have a sailing certificate. Prices start at US$1300 per week for a 28-footer that will sleep six. You can also hire a skipper for an extra US$100 per day.

Most of the hire companies are based in and around Athens. They include:

Aegean Tourism (☎ 01-346 6229, fax 342 2121, [e] aegeantours@ibm.net) Kadmias 8, Athens
Alpha Yachting (☎ 01-968 0486, fax 968 0488, [e] mano@otenet.gr) Poseidonos 67, Glyfada
Ghiolman Yachts & Travel (☎ 01-323 3696, fax 322 3251, [e] ghiolman@ghiolman.com) Filellinon 7, Athens
Hellenic Charters (☎/fax 01-988 5592, [e] hctsa@ath.forthnet.gr) Poseidonos 66, Alimos

Kostis Yachting (☎ 01-895 0657, fax 895 0995) Epaminonda 61, Glyfada
Web site: www.kostis-yachting.com
Vernicos Yachts (☎ 01-985 0122, fax 985 0120) Poseidonos 11, Alimos
Web site: www.vernicos.gr

The EOT can provide addresses to many more yacht charter companies in Greece.

BUS

Buses are the mainstay of Greece's public transport system. Fares are fixed by the government, and are very reasonable by European standards.

Island Buses

Only two islands, Kos and Rhodes, have a system resembling the KTEL co-operative of the mainland. Both these islands are covered extensively by a good system of buses, though some of the remoter mountain villages have services designed to get villagers to market and back, rather than tourists to the villages and back to the main town.

Larger towns usually have a central, covered bus station with seating, waiting rooms, toilets, and a snack bar selling pies, cakes and coffee. In small towns and villages, the 'bus station' may be no more than a bus stop outside a *kafeneio* (coffee house) or taverna which doubles as a booking office.

On islands where the capital is inland rather than a port, buses normally meet the boats. Some of the more remote islands, such as Kasos and Agathonisi, have not yet acquired a bus, but most have some sort of motorised transport – even if it is only a bone-shaking, three-wheeled truck. Kastellorizo has one 18-seater minibus that only ferries people to and from the airport. The mini islands of Arki and Marathi do not even have a road system, so buses are nonexistent there.

CAR & MOTORCYCLE

Many of the islands are plenty big enough to warrant having your own vehicle. With the exception perhaps of Agathonisi, Arki, Marathi, Kastellorizo and Kasos, all the other Dodecanese islands have decent road networks, and having a car – whether it be a hire car or your own vehicle – can be a major benefit.

The main advantage is if you plan to island hop to at least six or more islands. In this case, the fact that you do not have to load and unload your luggage each time you take a ferry or catamaran, is a major time and energy saver. If you are driving a campervan, you are of course carrying your home with you and you will save considerably on accommodation costs.

In 2000 the process of ferrying a car or motorbike up and down the Dodecanese was made a lot easier by the introduction of a six-car-carrying catamaran, the *Dodekanisos Express*, based in Rhodes. Not only are departure and arrival times more convenient than the ferries, but loading and unloading time is reduced by 150%. This makes the transition from one island to another fast and hassle-free.

The cost of transporting a car by catamaran is about twice the price of the catamaran passenger ticket. See the boxed text 'The cost of the catamaran' for a listing of passenger tariffs.

Roads have improved enormously in recent years, particularly on the larger, more visited islands like Rhodes and Kos, and even lowly Tilos where a new, smooth sealed highway runs from the north of the

island to the south. While a growing number of people do bring their own vehicle or motorbike from Europe, there are plenty of places to hire both cars and motorcycles.

The greatest cost will be incurred in getting to the Dodecanese. Patmos or Rhodes are logical starting points, though you could in practice start at Kasos or Karpathos (some people do), via the three times weekly service from Piraeus, via Milos and Crete. The average cost of shipping your car to Patmos or Rhodes is 24,000 dr compared to 22,000 dr to ship it to Kasos or Karpathos. The charge for a large motorbike is about the same as the price of a 3rd-class passenger ticket.

You can, of course, exit Greece to Turkey via Rhodes, though this is expensive and subject to demand. See the Getting There & Away section of the Rhodes chapter on the ins and outs and costs of this option.

Petrol in Greece is on a par with Europe and cheaper than some countries, notably Italy. On the islands, prices are pretty similar across the board, with the possible exception of remote villages where you may have to buy petrol by the plastic container.

See the Documents section in the Facts for the Visitor chapter for information on licence requirements.

See the Useful Organisations section in the Facts for the Visitor chapter for information about the Greek automobile club (ELPA).

Road Rules

In Greece, as throughout Continental Europe, you drive on the right and overtake on the left. Outside built-up areas, traffic on a main road has right of way at intersections. In towns, vehicles coming from the right have right of way. Seat belts must be worn in front seats, and in back seats if the car is fitted with them.

Children under 12 years of age are not allowed in the front seat. It is compulsory to carry a first-aid kit, fire extinguisher and warning triangle, and it is forbidden to carry cans of petrol. Helmets are compulsory for motorcyclists if the motorbike is 50cc or more.

Outside residential areas the speed limit is 120km/h on highways, 90km/h on other roads and 50km/h in built-up areas. The speed limit for motorbikes up to 100cc is 70km/h and for larger motorbikes, 90km/h.

Drivers exceeding the speed limit by 20% are liable for a fine of 20,000 dr; and by 40%, 50,000 dr. Other offences and fines include:

illegal overtaking – 100,000 dr
going through a red light – 100,000 dr
driving without a seat belt – 50,000 dr
motorcyclist not wearing a helmet – 50,000 dr
wrong way down one-way street – 50,000 dr
illegal parking – 10,000 dr

Be warned that the police have also cracked down on drink-driving laws – at last. A blood-alcohol content of 0.05% is liable to incur a fine of 50,000 dr, and over 0.08% is a criminal offence.

The police can issue traffic fines, but payment cannot be made on the spot – you will be told where to pay.

If you are involved in an accident and no-one is hurt, the police will not be required to write a report, but it is advisable to go to a nearby police station and explain what happened. A police report may be required for insurance purposes. If an accident involves injury, a driver who does not stop and does not inform the police may face a prison sentence.

Rhodes Town has a vigilant network of parking inspectors who readily slap out fines of 5000 dr for parking offences. Buy your parking ticket from the streetside dispenser and display it on your dashboard to avoid a fine.

Warning If you are planning to use a motorcycle or moped, check that your travel insurance covers you for injury resulting from a motorbike accident. Many insurance companies don't offer this cover; so check the fine print!

Not too many motorbike and scooter rental outlets provide helmets as part of the deal. Greeks may prefer not to wear protection, or to protect their elbows instead, but don't take the risk yourself. Insist on a helmet or move on.

Rental

Car Most of the big multinational car hire companies have branches throughout the Dodecanese. High-season weekly rates with unlimited mileage start at about 110,000 dr for the smallest models, such as a 900cc Fiat Panda. The rate drops to about 90,000 dr per week in winter. The VAT of 13% must be added to these prices. Then there are the optional extras, such as a collision damage waiver of 3300 dr per day (more for larger models), without which you will be liable for the first 1,500,000 dr of the repair bill (much more for larger models). Other costs include a theft waiver of at least 1000 dr per day and personal accident insurance. It all adds up to an expensive exercise. Some companies offer much cheaper pre-booked and prepaid rates.

The many local companies are normally more open to negotiation, especially if business is slow. Their advertised rates are about 25% cheaper than those offered by the multinationals. Smaller islands may have only one car hire outlet.

To take a hire car onto a ferry, you will need advance written authorisation from the hire company. Unless you pay with a credit card, most hire companies will require a minimum deposit of 20,000 dr per day.

The minimum driving age in Greece is 18 years, but most car hire firms require you to be at least 23, although some will rent to 21-year-olds.

See the Getting Around sections of cities and islands for details of places to rent cars.

Motorcycle Mopeds and motorcycles are available for hire wherever there are tourists to rent them. In many cases their maintenance has been minimal, so check the machine thoroughly before you hire it – especially the brakes; you'll need them!

Motorbikes are a cheap way to travel around. Rates range from 2500 dr to 4000 dr per day for a moped or 50cc motorbike to 6000 dr per day for a 250cc motorbike. Out of season these prices drop considerably, so use your bargaining skills. By October it is sometimes possible to hire a moped for as little as 1500 dr per day.

The islands can be a dangerous place for novices. Dozens of tourists have accidents every year on occasionally steep and poorly maintained roads. Most motorbike hirers include third party insurance in the price, but it is wise to check this. This insurance will not include medical expenses.

LOCAL TRANSPORT
To/From the Airports

Olympic Airways operates buses to a few domestic airports (see individual entries in the appropriate chapters). Where the service exists, buses leave the airline office about 1½ hours before departure. In many places, the only way to get to the airport is by taxi.

Check-in is an hour before departure for domestic flights. Transport to and from Greek international airports is covered in the Getting Around section of the relevant city.

Taxi

Taxis are widely available in the Dodecanese, except on very small or remote islands. They are reasonably priced by European standards, especially if three or four people share costs.

City cabs are metered. Flagfall is 200 dr, followed by 62 dr per kilometre (120 dr per kilometre outside town). These rates double between midnight and 5 am. Additional costs (on top of the per-kilometre rate) are 300 dr from an airport, 150 dr from a bus, port or train station, and 55 dr for each piece of luggage. Grey rural taxis do not have meters, so you should always settle on a price before you get in.

Island taxis on the whole work off fixed tariffs and these are posted at the main taxi rank. Where known we have included these tariffs as part of the Getting Around sections in each chapter.

Bus

Most Greek towns are small enough to get around on foot. The only places where you may need to use local buses are Athens, Kos Town and Rhodes Town. You usually buy tickets at kiosks or small shops, or occasionally on board.

BICYCLE

Cycling has not caught on in Greece on the whole, which isn't surprising considering the hilly terrain of mainland Greece. Tourists are beginning to cycle in Greece, but you'll need strong leg muscles.

Of all the Dodecanese islands, Kos is the only one that has developed a cyclist scene, with hire bikes being very popular for excursions around the north-east sector of the island. However, cycling for the independent traveller is not difficult in the Dodecanese and transporting a bike from island to island is very easy and is free on ferries. A small charge applies on the catamaran.

You can hire bicycles in most tourist places, but they are not as widely available as cars and motorbikes. Prices range from 1000 dr to 3000 dr per day, depending on the type and age of the bike.

HITCHING

Hitching is never entirely safe in any country in the world, and we don't recommend it. Travellers who decide to hitch should understand that they are taking a small but potentially serious risk. People who do choose to hitch will be safer if they travel in pairs and should let someone know where they are planning to go. Greece has a reputation for being a relatively safe place for women to hitch, but it is still unwise to do it alone. It's better for women to hitch with a companion, preferably a male one.

Notwithstanding, hitching *is* a fairly common mode of transport on the Dodecanese Islands and is practised as much by locals as by travellers. The usual method of calling for a ride is to outstretch a downturned palm and to gesture by moving the hand up and down, not by jerking a thumb at a driver. If you have a car it is considered common courtesy to give a lift to locals. If you are hitching, do it with a smile on your face and keep your baggage to a minimum.

WALKING

Unless you have come to Greece just to lie on a beach, the chances are you will do quite a bit of walking. You don't have to be a trekker to start clocking up the kilometres.

The narrow, stepped streets of many towns and villages can only be explored on foot, and visiting the archaeological sites involves a fair amount of legwork.

On each of the Dodecanese islands there are some excellent opportunities for walking. See the individual destination chapters for the full story.

See also the What to Bring, Health and Trekking sections in the Facts for the Visitor chapter for more information about walking.

ORGANISED TOURS

Tours are worth considering only if your time is very limited, in which case you'll find countless companies vying for your money. However, in some cases, such as Pserimos off the island of Kalymnos, tours are the only way you will get to see certain places. Some of the more remote island beaches can only be reached by day trips on caïques. See the respective destination chapters for more information.

Gateway Ports

Athens & Piraeus

The greater majority of travellers heading to the Dodecanese will be passing through Athens and Piraeus. While you can avoid Athens all together by heading straight to Piraeus, the following brief section will help you navigate what can at first sight seem a very confusing pair of cities.

ATHENS Αθήνα
☎ 01 • postcode 102 00 (Omonia), 103 00 (Syntagma) • pop 3.7 million

Athens seems a disorienting and noisy city to new arrivals at first and many choose not to linger, preferring instead to head straight for the beaches of the Aegean or the Dodecanese Islands. This is a pity because Athens grows on you and is a city with an enormous wealth of history. Its ancient sites and museums deserve a few days of your time and unlike many tourist resorts on the islands, Athens never shuts down. The capital of Greece is now gearing up to host the Olympic Games in 2004, so expect gradual and even radical improvements to the infrastructure of the city. Unless you are flying to the Dodecanese directly, or taking a ferry from Thessaloniki or the Turkish or Cypriot ports, you will inevitably pass through the capital on your way to your destination. Take time out and enjoy!

Orientation

Although Athens is a huge, sprawling city, nearly everything of interest to travellers is located within a small area bounded by Omonia Square (Plateia Omonias) to the north, Monastiraki Square to the west, Syntagma Square to the east and the Plaka district to the south. The city's two major landmarks, the Acropolis and Lykavittos Hill, can be seen from just about everywhere in this area. Syntagma is the heart of modern Athens; it's flanked by luxury hotels, banks and fast-food outlets and dominated by the old royal palace, home of the Greek

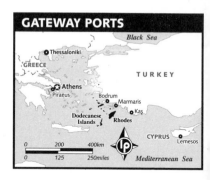

GATEWAY PORTS

parliament since 1935. The Plaka is the old quarter of Athens and probably the most attractive part of the city. The two train stations are about 1km north-west of Omonia Square, and only five minutes' walk away from each other. Larisis Metro station links the adjoining station with central Athens and Piraeus via the Athens Metro.

Information

Tourist Offices The main EOT tourist office (☎ 331 0561, fax 325 2895, ℮ gnto@eexi.gr) is close to Syntagma at Amerikis 2. It has a useful free map of Athens, which has most of the places of interest clearly marked and also shows the trolleybus routes. It also has information about public transport prices and schedules from Athens, including ferry departures from Piraeus. The office is open 9 am to 7 pm Monday to Friday, and 9.30 am to 2 pm Saturday.

Money Most of the major banks have branches around Syntagma, open 8 am to 2 pm Monday to Thursday, and 8 am to 1.30 pm Friday. The National Bank of Greece on Stadiou has an automatic exchange machine. Most banks now have ATMs.

American Express (☎ 324 4975), Ermou 2, Syntagma, is open 8.30 am to 4 pm Monday to Friday, and 8.30 am to 1.30 pm Saturday.

Eurochange (☎ 322 0155) has an office at Karageorgi Servias 4, Syntagma, open

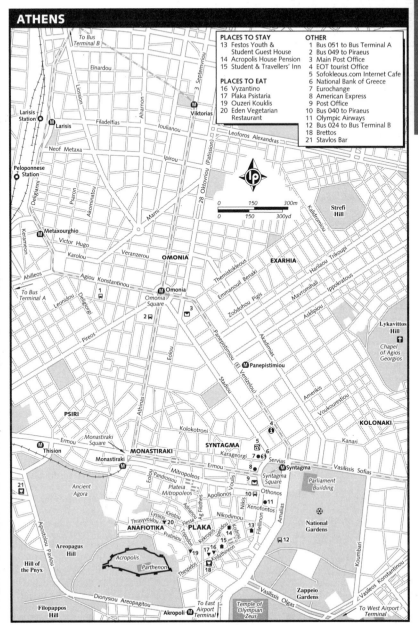

ATHENS

PLACES TO STAY
13 Festos Youth &
   Student Guest House
14 Acropolis House Pension
15 Student & Travellers' Inn

PLACES TO EAT
16 Vyzantino
17 Plaka Psistaria
19 Ouzeri Kouklis
20 Eden Vegetarian
   Restaurant

OTHER
1 Bus 051 to Bus Terminal A
2 Bus 049 to Piraeus
3 Main Post Office
4 EOT tourist Office
5 Sofokleous.com Internet Cafe
6 National Bank of Greece
7 Eurochange
8 American Express
9 Post Office
10 Bus 040 to Piraeus
11 Olympic Airways
12 Bus 024 to Bus Terminal B
18 Brettos
21 Stavlos Bar

euro currency converter 1000dr = €2.93

8.30 am to 8 pm Monday to Friday, 9.30 am to 4 pm Saturday, and 10 am to 4 pm Sunday. Eurochange changes Thomas Cook travellers' cheques without commission.

There are banks, currency exchange machines and ATMs at Athens' new airport.

Post & Communications The main post office is at Eolou 100, Omonia. Unless specified otherwise, poste restante mail will be sent here. If you're staying in Plaka, it's best to get mail sent to the post office on Syntagma Square. Both are open 7.30 am to 8 pm Monday to Friday, 7.30 am to 2 pm Saturday, and 9 am to 1.30 pm Sunday. There are card phones aplenty all over Athens and kiosks also have card-accepting phones. Few phones (if any) accept coins any more.

The handiest Internet cafe to Syntagma Square is the Sofokleous.com Internet Cafe at Stadiou 5, behind the Flocafé. It's open 10 am to 10 pm Monday to Saturday, and 1 pm to 9 pm Sunday.

Dangers & Annoyances

The most common cause for complaint in the past has been airport taxi drivers who routinely ripped-off unsuspecting tourists in rides from the old airport terminals to central Athens. Whether the practice will continue at the new airport remains to be seen, but travellers should be very wary and keep an eagle eye on the meter at all times.

Lone males should be aware of 'bar scams' whereby you are invited to a bar by a 'friendly Athenian' (usually a tout for the bar). You are joined by more friendly, female Athenians and drinks are produced all round. The trick is *you* pick up the tab (or else!) and it is usually a big one. Avoid this scam at all costs.

Things to See & Do

No trip to Athens would be complete without a wander up to the Acropolis, the most important ancient monument in the western world. Crowned by the Parthenon, it stands sentinel over Athens, visible from almost everywhere within the city. The buildings now gracing the Acropolis were commissioned by Pericles during the golden age of

Athens in the 5th century BC. Inspiring as these monuments are, they are but faded remnants of Pericles' city, with its colossal buildings, lavishly coloured and gilded, and its gargantuan bronze and marble statues.

The Acropolis archaeological site (☎ 321 0219) is open 8 am to 6.30 pm daily in summer, and 8.30 am to 4.30 pm Monday to Friday and 8 am to 3 pm Saturday to Sunday in winter. It costs 2000/1000 dr for adults/students.

Places to Stay

There is a wide variety of places to stay in Athens from grunge to top class international. Hostels and small hotels in the Plaka area are probably the best overall choice since the Plaka is pretty, pleasant, close to the Syntagma Square metro station and close to the major sites. Here are a few places in and close to Plaka.

The *Student & Travellers' Inn* (☎ 324 4808, fax 321 0065, **e** students-inn@ ath.forthnet.gr, Kydathineon 16) is hard to look past. It's a well run place with spotless rooms. The dormitories are particularly good value with beds in triple/quad rooms for 4500/4000 dr. Rooms with bunk beds are 3500 dr and singles/doubles are 7500/9500 dr. All rooms share communal bathrooms. The place stays open all year, and rooms are heated in winter.

Festos Youth & Student Guest House (☎ 323 2455, **e** consolas@hol.gr, Filellinon 18) is a popular place with travellers despite being on one of the noisiest streets in Athens. It has dorm beds priced from 3000 dr to 3500 dr, but tends to cram beds into the rooms in summer. There are a couple of doubles for 7500 dr. A popular feature is the bar on the 1st floor, which also serves meals, including several vegetarian options.

Plaka also has some good mid-range accommodation. *Acropolis House Pension* (☎ 322 2344, fax 322 6241, Kodrou 6-8) is a beautifully preserved 19th-century house. Singles/doubles with shared bathroom are 12,800/15,300 dr, or 15,000/18,000 dr with private bathroom. There's a 20% discount for stays of more than two days. All rooms have central heating.

Places to Eat

For most people, Plaka is the place to be. It's hard to beat the atmosphere of dining out beneath the floodlit Acropolis. You do, however, pay for the privilege – particularly at the outdoor restaurants around the square on Kydathineon.

The best of this bunch is *Vyzantino*, which has reasonable prices and is popular with Greek family groups. One of the best deals in the Plaka is the nearby *Plaka Psistaria (Kydathineon 28)*, with a range of gyros and souvlaki to eat in or take away.

Ouzeri Kouklis (Tripodon 14) is an old-style place with an oak-beamed ceiling, marble tables and wicker chairs. It serves only *mezedes* (appetisers), which are brought round on a large tray for you to take your pick. They include flaming sausages – ignited at your table – and cuttlefish for 1200 dr, as well as the usual dips for 600 dr. The whole selection, enough for four hungry people, costs 9800 dr.

Vegetarian restaurants are thin on the ground in Athens. *Eden Vegetarian Restaurant (Lysiou 12)* has been around for years, substituting soya products for meat in tasty vegetarian versions of mousakas (1700 dr) and other Greek favourites.

Entertainment

English-language listings appear daily in the *Kathimerini* supplement that accompanies the *International Herald Tribune*, while Friday's edition of the *Athens News* carries a 16-page entertainment guide.

Welcome to Athens is a quarterly magazine free from the tourist office, which has details of theatre, dance, classical music concerts and art exhibitions.

Athens has a good selection of pubs and bars bound to satisfy all tastes. There are the inevitable English and Irish themed bars full of expats as well as some fun local bars and a growing number of German style beer halls.

Brettos (☎ 323 2110, Kydathineon 41) is a delightful little family-run business right in the heart of Plaka. Shots of Brettos brand spirits (ouzo, brandy and many more) cost 500 dr, while Brettos wine sells at 600 dr per tumbler. Cold beers are 700 dr. It's open 10 am to midnight daily.

Stavlos (☎ 345 2502, Iraklidon 10) occupies an amazing old rabbit warren of a building and plays mainly alternative British music, with more mellow sounds in the cafe/brasserie outside. Large beers cost 1600 dr, spirits are 2000 dr and cocktails 2500 dr. It's open 11 am to 5 am.

Getting There & Away

Air Athens' new Eleftherios Venizelos airport, 21km west of the city, was due to open in March 2001 and early accounts indicate that it's a massive improvement on the old airports at Alimos, on Athens' eastern foreshore. The only disadvantage is the greater distance from central Athens and the lack, as yet, of a Metro link.

The Olympic Airways head office (☎ 966 6666, or ☎ 0801-44 444 for calls within Greece) is at Syngrou 96, but the office at Filellinon 13, near Syntagma, is generally more convenient.

Bus Athens has two main intercity bus stations. The EOT gives out comprehensive schedules for both with departure times, journey durations and fares.

Terminal A is north-west of Omonia at Kifisou 100 and has departures to the Peloponnese, the Ionian Islands and western Greece. To get there, take bus No 051 from the junction of Zinonos and Menandrou, near Omonia. This service runs every 15 minutes from 5 am to midnight.

Terminal B is north of Omonia off Liosion and has departures to central and northern Greece as well as to Evia. To get there, take bus No 024 from outside the main gate of the National Gardens on Amalias. Liosion 260 is where you should get off the bus. Turn right onto Gousiou and you'll see the terminal at the end of the road.

Buses travelling to Rafina and Lavrio leave from the Mavromateon terminal at the junction of Leoforos Alexandras and 28 Oktovriou-Patision.

Train Athens has two train stations, located about 200m apart on Deligianni, which is about 1km north-west of Omonia. Trains to the Peloponnese leave from the Peloponnese station, while trains to the north, as well as international trains, leave from Larisis station. You can travel between Syntagma Square and the train stations by catching the metro to/from the nearby Larisis metro station (250 dr), with intermediate stops on Panepistimiou and at Omonia Square.

Ferry The ports of Piraeus (10km) and Rafina (30km) serve Athens with ferry services to the Aegean Islands. Ferries to the Dodecanese leave from Piraeus.

Getting Around

Metro The first phase of the metro extension program began in November 1999. This added two new lines and 21 new stations to the old Kifisia-Piraeus line. Maps showing all the new destinations are available in the new Metro stations.

Ticket prices are 150 dr for most journeys, including Monastiraki-Piraeus. There are ticket machines and ticket booths at all stations, and validating machines at platform entrances.

Bus & Trolleybus You probably won't need to use the normal blue-and-white suburban buses. They run every 15 minutes from 5 am to midnight. Important routes are listed on the free EOT map. The map also marks the routes of the yellow trolleybuses, which also run from 5 am to midnight.

There are special buses that operate 24 hours a day to Piraeus. Bus No 040 leaves from the corner of Syntagma and Filellinon, and No 049 leaves from the Omonia end of Athinas. They run every 20 minutes from 6 am to midnight, and then hourly.

All these services cost a flat rate of 130 dr. Tickets can be bought from ticket kiosks and *periptera* (street kiosks). They must be validated when you board a bus.

Taxi Athenian taxis are yellow. The flag fall is 200 dr, with a 160 dr surcharge from ports and train and bus stations, and 300 dr from the airport. After that, the day rate (tariff 1 on the meter) is 66 dr per kilometre. The

rate doubles between midnight and 5 am (tariff 2 on the meter).

Baggage is charged at the rate of 55 dr per item over 10kg. The minimum fare is 500 dr, which covers most journeys in central Athens.

To hail a taxi, stand on a pavement and shout your destination as they pass. If a taxi is going your way the driver may stop, even if there are already passengers inside. This does not mean the fare will be shared: each person will be charged the fare shown on the meter.

PIRAEUS Πειραιάϖ
☎ 01 • postcode 185 01 • pop 171,000
Piraeus (pir-ay-**ahs**) is the port of Athens, the main port of Greece and one of the major ports of the Mediterranean.

Piraeus has been the port of Athens since classical times, when the two were linked by defensive walls. Nowadays, Athens has expanded sufficiently to meld imperceptibly into Piraeus. The road linking the two passes through a grey, urban sprawl of factories, warehouses and concrete apartment blocks. The streets are every bit as traffic-clogged as Athens, and behind the veneer of banks and shipping offices most of Piraeus is pretty seedy. The only reason to come here is to catch a ferry or hydrofoil.

Orientation
Piraeus is 10km south-west of central Athens. The largest of its three harbours is the Great Harbour (Megas Limin) on the western side of the Piraeus Peninsula. All ferries leave from here, as well as hydrofoil and catamaran services to Aegina and the Cyclades. There are dozens of shipping agents around the harbour, as well as banks and a post office. Zea Marina (Limin Zeas), on the other side of the peninsula, is the main port for hydrofoils to the Saronic Gulf Islands (except Aegina). East of here is the picturesque, small harbour, Mikrolimano.

The metro line from Athens terminates at the north-eastern corner of the Great Harbour on Akti Kalimassioti. Most ferry departure points are a short walk from here. A left turn out of the metro station leads after 250m to Plateia Karaïskaki, which is the terminus for buses to the airport.

Information
Tourist Offices The EOT office (☎ 452 2586) overlooking the harbour at Zea Marina is fairly useless. For the record, it's open 8 am to 3 pm Monday to Friday. The telephone number of Piraeus' port police is ☎ 412 2501.

Money Many places change money at the Great Harbour, including virtually all the ticket and travel agencies. The Emboriki Bank, just north of Plateia Themistokleous on the corner of Antistaseos and Makras Stoas, has a 24-hour automatic exchange machine. The National Bank of Greece has a Great Harbour branch at the corner of Antistaseos and Tsamadou, and another branch above the maritime museum at Zea Marina.

Post & Communications The main post office is on the corner of Tsamadou and Filonos, just north of Plateia Themistokleous. It's open 7.30 am to 8 pm Monday to Friday and 7.30 am to 2 pm Saturday. The OTE is just north of here at Karaoli 19 and is open 24 hours.

You can check your email at the Surf Internet Café at Platanos 3, just off Iroön Polytehniou. It's open 8 am to 9 pm Monday to Friday and 8 am to 3 pm Saturday.

Places to Stay
There's no reason to stay at any of the shabby, cheap hotels around Great Harbour when Athens is so close. If you're desperate, the C-class *Hotel Delfini (☎ 412 9779, Leoharous 7)* has singles/doubles for 7000/10,000 dr with private bathroom. Make sure you don't get taken there by one of the touts who hang around the port or you will pay the official prices of 14,000/16,000 dr.

Places to Eat
Great Harbour There are dozens of cafes, restaurants and fast-food places along the waterfront. The tiny *Restaurant I Folia (Akti Poseidonos)*, opposite Plateia Karaïskaki, is a rough and ready place that has a bowl of

gigantes beans for 800 dr, calamari for 1100 dr and mousakas for 1000 dr.

If you want to stock up on supplies before your ferry trip to the Dodecanese, head for the area just inland from Poseidonos. You'll find fresh fruit and vegetables at the market, open 8 am to 8 pm Monday to Friday, and 8 am to 4 pm Saturday.

Getting There & Away
Bus There are two 24-hour bus services between central Athens and Piraeus. Bus No 049 runs from Omonia to the Great Harbour, and bus No 040 runs from Syntagma to the tip of the Piraeus Peninsula. This is the service to catch for Zea Marina – get off at the Hotel Savoy on Iroön Polytehniou, but make sure you leave plenty of time as the trip can take over an hour in bad traffic. The fare is 120 dr on each service.

Buses to the airport leave from the southwestern corner of Plateia Karaïskaki. The fare is 250 dr, or 500 dr from 11.30 pm to 6 am. There are no intercity buses to or from Piraeus.

Metro The metro is the fastest and easiest way of getting from the Great Harbour to central Athens and the train stations. The expanded network now takes in suburbs to the west and the east, and is slowly being extended. The station is at the northern end of Akti Kalimassioti.

Train Railway services to the Peloponnese actually start and terminate at Piraeus, although most schedules don't mention it. There are about 15 trains a day to Athens and beyond – a reasonable option if you want to stay close to the stations.

Getting Around
Local bus Nos 904 and 905 run between the Great Harbour and Zea Marina. They leave from the bus stop beside the metro at Great Harbour, and drop you by the maritime museum at Zea Marina.

Getting to the Dodecanese
Ferry Ferries to the Dodecanese all leave from the southern end of the Great Harbour,

along Akti Miaouli. The departure point is a good 15 minutes walk from the train station and about 10 minutes from the metro station. The departure quay is prominently signposted from Akti Miaouli.

While many agencies sell tickets for destinations in the Dodecanese, the main ferry agents are G&A Ferries (☎ 419 9100, fax 419 9016), on the corner of Akti Kondyli and Etolikou, halfway between the train station and the metro station; and DANE Sealines (☎ 01-429 3240, fax 429 3493) on Akti Miaouli, right opposite the Dodecanese ferry departure quay.

For the latest departure information, pick up a weekly ferry schedule from the tourist office in Athens, or look at the posted departure schedules at the port police office on the harbour. Also see the Ferry section in the Getting There & Away chapter for more information.

Northern Greece

Travellers to the Dodecanese can save themselves the 520km haul from Thessaloniki to Piraeus by utilising this northern port to sail to Rhodes, or a number of islands in the North Dodecanese. The drawback is that there is only one sailing a week.

THESSALONIKI Θεσσαλονίκη
☎ 031 • postcode 541 00 • pop 750,000
Thessaloniki, also known as Salonica, is Greece's second-largest city. It's a bustling, sophisticated place with good restaurants and a busy nightlife. It was once the second city of Byzantium, and there are some magnificent Byzantine churches, as well as a scattering of Roman ruins.

Orientation
Thessaloniki is laid out on a grid system. The main thoroughfares – Tsimiski, Egnatia and Agiou Dimitriou – run parallel to Nikis, on the waterfront. Plateia Eleftherias and Plateia Aristotelous, both on Nikis, are the main squares. The city's most famous landmark is the White Tower (no longer white) at the eastern end of Nikis. The train station

is on Monastiriou, the westerly continuation of Egnatia beyond Plateia Dimokratias, and the airport is 16km to the south-east. The old Turkish quarter is north of Athinas.

Information
Tourist Office The EOT (☎ 271 888, 263 112), Plateia Aristotelous 8, is open 8.30 am to 8 pm Monday to Friday and 8.30 am to 2 pm Saturday.

Money Most banks around town are equipped with ATMs. There is an automatic exchange machine and an ATM at the train station. American Express (☎ 269 521) is at Tsimiski 19.

Midas Exchange, at the western end of Tsimiski, close to the Ladadika district, is handy for people using the ferry terminal. It's open from 8.30 am to 8.30 pm Monday to Friday, 8.30 am to 2 pm Saturday and 9 am to 1.30 pm Sunday.

Post & Communications The main post office is at Aristotelous 26. It's open 7.30 am to 8 pm Monday to Friday, 7.30 am to 2.15 pm Saturday and 9 am to 1.30 pm Sunday. The OTE is at Karolou Dil 27 and is open 24 hours a day.

The most convenient Internet cafe is Globus Internet Cafe (☎ 232 901), near the Roman Agora at Amynta 12. However, it is closed from mid-July to mid-August.

Emergency A first aid centre (☎ 530 530) is at Navarhou Koundourioti 6. The tourist police office (☎ 554 871) is on the 5th floor at Dodekanisou 4, and is open from 7.30 am to 11 pm daily all year round. The telephone number of Thessaloniki's port police is ☎ 531 504.

Places to Stay
The *GYHA hostel* (☎ 225 946, fax 262 208, Alex Svolou 44) has dorm beds for 2000 dr. The dorms are open all day.

The best budget hotel in town is the friendly, family-run *Hotel Acropol* (☎ 536 170, Tantalidou 4), close to the central police station. The clean singles/doubles with shared bathroom are listed at 7000/8000 dr, but most of the time it charges a bargain 6000 dr per room. *Hotel Atlantis (☎ 540 131, Egnatia 14)* has tiny but clean rooms with shared bathroom for 6500/9600 dr.

Hotel Atlas (☎ 537 046, Egnatia 40) has rooms with shared bathroom for 9000/12,000 dr and good doubles with bathrooms for 14,000 dr. Be warned that the rooms at the front get a lot of traffic noise. Just around the corner from the Atlas is the quiet *Hotel Averof (☎ 538 498, Leontos Sofou 24)*. Pleasant rooms with shared bathroom are 7000/10,000 dr.

Note that rooms can be hard to find during the international trade fair in September.

Places to Eat

Hryso Pagoni (☎ 265 338, Alex Svolou 40) is right opposite the youth hostel. It's simple and clean, and popular with locals. Ready-made food goes for around 1100 dr a serve; the restaurant is best known for its roast chicken.

A place full of local colour is the lively *O Loutros Fish Taverna (☎ 228 895, Komninon 15)*, which occupies an old Turkish hammam near the flower market. Most dishes cost from 2000 dr to 3000 dr.

Getting There & Away

Air There are at least 13 flights a day to Athens – seven with Olympic Airways (22,000 dr), four with Cronus (19,400 dr) and two with Aegean Airlines (20,400 dr).

Bus There are numerous bus terminals, most of them near the train station. Frequent buses for Athens leave from Monastiriou 65 and 67, opposite the train station; buses for Alexandroupolis leave from Koloniari 17 behind the train station; buses for Volos leave from Anageniseos 22. Kavala buses leave from Langada 59, on the main road north out of Thessaloniki.

Train There are 12 trains a day to Athens and five to Alexandroupolis. All international trains from Athens and from Eastern Europe stop at Thessaloniki. You can get more information from the OSE office at Aristotelous 18 or from the train station.

Getting Around

To/From the Airport Thessaloniki's airport is 16km south-east of town. You can get there on public bus No 78, which leaves from in front of the train station and stops in front of the ferry terminal. It costs 140 dr. A taxi to or from the airport costs around 2500 dr.

Bus There is a flat fare of 100 dr on city buses, paid either to a conductor at the rear door or to coin-operated machines on driver-only buses.

Getting to the Dodecanese

Air There is one direct weekly flight with Olympic Airways (30,000 dr) to Rhodes

---

The Ouzeri

An *ouzeri* (pl. *ouzeria*) is a type of small taverna where you eat from various plates of *mezedes* (tasty tidbits) and drink small bottles of *tsipouro* or ouzo. Tsipouro is similar to ouzo, but stronger. You can dilute it with water if you prefer it weaker, or if you want it to last a little longer. When you have finished one round of mezedes or tsipouro, you order another until you are full or can't stand up – whichever comes first. The ouzeri is a familiar sight in most port towns in Greece. It came about as a result of the exchange of populations in 1923, when Greeks and Turks were forced to swap homelands. Most of the Greeks who came to the ports were seafarers who would gather on the harbour at lunchtime to drink tsipouro accompanied by various mezedes. As this eating and drinking routine flourished, demand for more and more varied mezedes grew and so did the repertoire of the ouzeria. The port of Thessaloniki has some excellent ouzeria. Seek out the *Ladadika* district a couple of blocks north of the ferry terminal. In this restored warehouse district you will find small ouzeria, tavernas and bars. It's an ideal spot for a pre-voyage splurge before you head out to the Dodecanese.

---

and one with Aegean Airlines (29,000 dr). Both operate only in summer.

Ferry DANE Sealines operates one ferry a week to Rhodes (23½ hours, 14,800 dr), via Samos and Kos, throughout the year.

You can get to the Dodecanese indirectly via the islands of the north-eastern Aegean. There's a Sunday ferry to Chios (18 hours, 8300 dr) via Limnos (eight hours, 5300 dr) and Lesvos (13 hours, 8300 dr) year round. From there you can take a local ferry with Miniotis Lines to Samos or Ikaria and a connecting ferry or hydrofoil to Agathonisi and Patmos in the northern Dodecanese.

Karaharisis Travel & Shipping Agency (☎ 524 544, fax 532 289), on Navarhou Koundourioti 8, handles tickets.

Turkey

Travellers working their way round the main Turkish sights can and frequently do enter Greece via one of three ports facing the Dodecanese Islands. Currently only one of these ports allows drivers to ship their vehicle across and even that is subject to demand. The following section will give you some idea of what to expect at each of the ports.

BODRUM
☎ 252 • postcode 48400 • pop 30,000
Don your designer sunglasses, stuff tissues in your wallet and stroll through the dazzling white laneways of this postcard perfect, yachting town. After dark Bodrum has a thumping nightlife. Come morning, revellers hide in the restaurants lining the bays. But this town has more than hedonistic pursuits; formerly Halicarnassus, Bodrum is the site of the Mausoleum, the monumental tomb of King Mausolus and one of the Seven Wonders of the World. However, little remains of the Mausoleum, which was probably damaged by an earthquake and finished off by the Knights of St John.

Orientation & Information
Bodrum lines two bays divided by the castle-topped peninsula. Below the castle lies the centre of town where you'll find the tourist office (☎ 316 1091) on Oniki Eylül (İskele) Meydanı, and Adliye Camii (Courthouse Mosque). Cevat Şakir Caddesi runs from Adliye Camii 500m inland to the bus station *(otogar)*; along this street are the post office and several banks. Head north of Adliye Camii up Türkkuyusu Sokak where you'll find the Neşe-i Muhabbet Internet Cafe and much of the accommodation; more is behind Cumhuriyet Caddesi around the east bay.

Places to Stay
Some villages on the peninsula, such as Bitez Yalısı and Ortakent Yalısı, have camp sites.

Head up Türkkuyusu Sokak to the friendly *Şenlik Pansiyon (☎ 316 6382, Türkkuyusu Sokak 115)*, charging US$7/12 for singles/doubles. Behind, at the family-run *Sedan (☎ 316 0355, Türkkuyusu Sokak 121)*, you'll pay a few dollars more for the bonuses of car spaces and a large garden.

Closer to the action (read: dust out the earplugs), *Durak Villa (☎ 316 4053, Rasathane Sokak 16)* has clean rooms and superb terrace views for US$8/15 with breakfast. It's behind Cumhuriyet Caddesi. Nearby *Evin Pansiyon (☎ 316 1312, Ortanca Sokak 7)* charges a bit more for its rooms (with balconies).

Gurup Otel (☎ 316 1140, Karantina Sokak 3) charges US$15 per person, with breakfast and balconies overlooking the marina; check there's hot water.

Places to Eat
Between the cane-chair-swamped eateries along Cumhuriyet Caddesi you'll find a few gems. Up the western end, the cheapest feed is the *Meshur Karadeniz Börek ve Pide Salonu (Cumhuriyet Caddesi 96)*. Up the other end, the unpretentious *Berk Balık Restaurant (Kumbahçe Parki Karsısı)* is well worth the US$6 to US$8 you'll pay for a superb meal; it's packed with locals. About halfway along, *Cafe Penguen*, right by the water, has pricey but delicious breakfasts.

In the grid of small market streets just east of the Adliye Camii are several restaurants. One of the best is *Kardeşler Restaurant (Yeni Çarşi 6 Sokak 10)*, with tasty meat dishes for about US$5; beer costs US$1.

Getting There & Around

Bodrum is a well connected town. Some bus services include: Izmir (four hours, US$12), Selçuk (three hours, US$5.50) and Marmaris (three hours, US$6). Catch the Havas bus (US$4) from the bus station to the Milas airport.

Getting to the Dodecanese

Boats go to Kos (Istanköy) frequently in summer for US$16 one way, US$20 same-day return and US$30 open return; these prices include port taxes. In summer there are also boats to Rhodes.

MARMARIS

☎ 252 • postcode 48700 • pop 18,000

Primed for the package holiday set, Marmaris has decent food, innumerable souvenirs and lascivious living after dark. If you're after something else it's time to move on – this bustling town has limited offerings. Still, it's a pretty setting, the best spot to head to Rhodes (Rodos) and a good place to pick up a boat or gulet (a Turkish wooden yacht) trip.

Orientation & Information

Marmaris has a small castle overlooking the town centre. Barbaros Caddesi, with its many restaurants, curls south, around the castle and heads east to Netsel marina. İskele Meydanı (the main square) and the tourist office (☎ 412 1035) are just north of the castle. Haci Mustafa Sokak (or Bar Street) runs east from İskele Meydanı; the bazaar spreads northwards. Beside Netsel marina is the homely Marmaris Internet Cafe-Bar.

The bus station is 1.5km north-east of the town centre, on the way to Muğla.

Places to Stay

About 1km east of Marmaris is the Günlücek Reserve and basic **Dimet Camping** (☎ 412 5601).

The quaint **Yılmaz Pansiyon** (☎ 412 3754, Kalti Mahallesi, 7 Sokak No 33) is just inland from the little park near the Turkish Airlines office on Atatürk Caddesi. Doubles/triples cost US$9/13. **Interyouth Hostel** (☎ 412 3687, e interyouth@ turk.net, Tepe Mahallesi, 42 Sokak No 45), in the bazaar, is spartan but clean and charges US$4.50 for dorm beds, and US$6/12 for singles/doubles. In the same price range the **Imbat Otel** (☎ 412 1413) and **Otel Karaaslan** (☎ 412 1867), close by the tourist office, have sea view balconies but can be noisy.

Places to Eat

Head to the open-air restaurants along 51 Sokak (the street with the post office). Try **Marmaris Lokantasi** for a US$4 feed or the better (and pricier) **Yeni Liman Restaurant** on Ismetpasa Caddesi around the corner.

South of the castle along Barbaros Caddesi, posh restaurants come from the same bland mould; **Birtat Restaurant** is popular. Squeezed in between these restaurants, quaint **Barış Cafe** will let you enjoy the same views for half the price.

Getting There & Around

To get to the bus station, catch a *dolmus* (minibus) outside the Tansas shopping centre, north of the Atatürk statue; arriving in town you may get dropped here instead of the bus station.

Marmaris has frequent direct bus services to towns throughout the region, including Antalya (seven hours, US$12), Bodrum (three hours, US$6), Köyceg (one hour, US$3), Datça (1¾ hours, US$4) and Bozburun (1½ hours, US$2).

Getting to the Dodecanese

Small car ferries run to Rhodes daily in summer (less frequently in the off-season) for US$35 one way, US$40 same-day return, or US$70 open return; these fares include port taxes. Ask the tourist office for details.

KAŞ

☎ 242 • postcode 07580 • pop 5000

Kaş is a small town on the far south-western tip of Turkey just a few kilometres from the island of Kastellorizo (Meis in Turkish). Known by the Greeks as Andifellos, Kaş has a picturesque quayside square, a big Friday market, Lycian stone sarcophagi and rock-cut tombs in the cliffs above the town. All in all, it's a fine laid-back place and the first port coming from the east where you can cross over to Greece.

Orientation & Information

The bus station is 400m north-west of the main square and marina. The tourist office (☎ 836 1238) is on the main square. The post office and Net-House Internet Cafe are a short walk north.

Places to Stay

Kaş Camping *(☎ 836 1050)*, in an olive grove 1km west of town past the theatre, has tent sites and simple bungalows.

There are a lot of pension-pushers at the bus station. Yenicami Caddesi, just south of the bus station, has lots of standard clean places charging US$10/15 for singles/doubles with breakfast. Try **Ani Motel** *(☎ 836 1791)* or **Melisa** *(☎ 836 1068)*. **Ay Pansiyon** *(☎ 836 1562)*, near the mosque, has sea views from its front rooms. For more comfort and services, try the two-star **Hotel Kayahan** *(☎ 836 3577,* e *hotelkayahan@superonline .com)*, north-east of Küçük Çakıl Plaj. Rooms with wonderful sea views cost US$20/35, with breakfast.

Places to Eat

Corner Café, at the post office end of Ibrahim Serin Caddesi, serves juices or a vegetable omelette for US$1.50, and yogurt with fruit and honey for US$2. **Eris**, behind the tourist office, is a favourite as much for its setting as for its food. Also quite popular is **Smiley's Restaurant** next door, where pizza and mains cost US$4. **Bahçe Restaurant**, farther inland, is even better.

Getting There & Away

Regular buses go from the bus station to towns like Kalkan (35 minutes, US$1.50), Demre (one hour, US$2.50), Patara (one hour, US$3), Fethiye (2½ hours, US$4.50), Antalya (four hours, US$5) and İstanbul (12 hours, US$25).

Getting to the Dodecanese

There are daily caïques in summer to the port of Kastellorizo (Megisti). The trip takes just under an hour (US$30 one way).

Cyprus

Travellers from Israel often stop off in Cyprus and start their Greek island hopping holiday in the Dodecanese. The first port of call is Rhodes to which there are twice-weekly ferries from Cyprus. Lemesos is the only Cypriot port with ferry services to Greece. Note that it is not possible to exit Cyprus to Turkey and then re-enter Greece via one of the Turkish Aegean ports (see Visas in the Facts for the Visitor chapter for more information on travel between Cyprus and Greece).

LEMESOS Λεμεσόϖ

☎ 05 • postcode 3000 • pop 151,200

Brash, bold and carrying the reputation as the city that never sleeps, Lemesos (still sometimes known as Limassol) is Cyprus' second-largest city and is the main passenger and cargo port. It is the only port with passenger ferry connections to both Israel and Greece. At first sight the city has a rough workaday appearance. The seafront is functional and somewhat tatty in parts, but it is a city with soul and its Old City is undergoing a gentrification of sorts with a growing number of fine restaurants and bars. The tourist centre, stretching 12km east of Lemesos is, in contrast, a riotous confusion of bars and restaurants.

Orientation

Lemesos' Old City is fairly compact but the New City now extends for some distance along the seafront, encompassing the main tourist centre. Buses and taxis all arrive within a short distance of each other in the Old City, though the New Port where all ships and ferries dock is about 3km to the west of the Old City.

Information

Tourist Offices The Cyprus Tourism Organisation (CTO) has offices at the ferry terminal (☎ 343 868), at Spyrou Araouzou 15 (☎ 362 756, fax 746 596), and in the tourist centre at Georgiou 1, 22a (☎ 323 211, fax 313 451). Opening times are 8.15 am to

euro currency converter €1 = 340.75dr

2.30 pm, and 4 to 6.15 pm daily except Tuesday and Friday during the summer months from June to August. Times outside of summer are subject to change.

Money You can change money upon arrival at the New Port, but there is a scattering of banks around the centre of the Old City, some equipped with ATMs for cash withdrawals. The Bank of Cyprus on Agiou Andrea is probably the most convenient for visitors to the Old City, while there are numerous banks scattered along the main street in the tourist centre.

Post & Communications The main post office is centrally located in the Old City, one block north of the pedestrian zone. Poste restante mail is held here also.

The city sports at least four Internet cafes though the most convenient for travellers in the Old City is CyberNet (e cafeinfo@ zenon.logos.cy.net) at Eleftherias 79, a couple of blocks behind the CTO. On weekdays it doesn't open until 1 pm. Another Old City Internet cafe is Explorer on Agias Zonis. Both charge around CY£2 per hour.

Emergency For an ambulance, police or the fire service, call ☎ 199. For night pharmacy assistance call ☎ 1415. The police station is on the corner of Griva Digeni and Omirou on the Lefkosia road.

Places to Stay
The cheapest hotels are clustered in the Old City, to the east of the castle. A reasonable one with large, clean rooms is the *Luxor Guest House* (☎ 362 265, Agiou Andreou 101), which charges CY£6 per person, without breakfast.

A couple of decent two-star hotels near the Old City are the *Continental Hotel* (☎ 362 530, fax 373 030, Spyrou Araouzou 137) on the waterfront, which has very pleasant singles/doubles with bathroom for CY£15/25, including breakfast. Still within walking distance of the Old City is the two-star *Eastland Hotel* (☎ 377 000, fax 359 600, Droushiotis 23) which offers reasonable rooms for CY£17/28.

Places to Eat
The most convenient place to dine is in the Old City near the castle and museum, where there is a clutch of decent restaurants.

For a lunchtime snack or cold beer make for the gaudily coloured *Richard & Berengaria Café* on the Castle Square. A couple of doors to the left is the less gaudy *Cafe Antique*, popular with evening coffee- and brandy-drinkers. Farther along the same street, *To Frourio* (☎ 359 332, Tsanakali 18) is a restaurant tavern housed in an 18th-century building serving up excellent meat and vegetarian mezedes; it's closed Sunday.

Getting There & Away
Air The Cyprus Airways office (☎ 373 787) is at Leoforos Makariou 203, a 20-minute walk north-east of the main CTO office. Lemesos is more or less equidistant from Pafos and Larnaka airports. Service or private taxis are the only way to reach either airport.

Bus Kemek has frequent daily services to Lefkosia (CY£1.50) and Pafos (CY£1.50) from the corner of Enoseos and Eirinis Sts, north of the castle. From here there is also a weekday bus at noon to Agros (CY£1.50) in the Troödos Mountains.

Kallenos goes to Larnaka (CY£1.70) from the old port or from outside the CTO. The Kyriakos/Karydas service-taxi company has a minibus to Platres (CY£1.50) at 11.30 am Monday to Saturday, from its office.

Service Taxi Close to the CTO at Spyrou Araouzou 65, Acropolis Taxis (☎ 366 766) has taxis every half-hour to Lefkosia (CY£3), Larnaka (CY£2.60) and Pafos (CY£2.30). Kyriakos/Karydas (☎ 364 114), at Thessalonikis 21, travels the same routes.

Getting to the Dodecanese
Ferry services to Greece depart from Lemesos, which is served by two ferry companies. On the outward run to Piraeus, boats call in at Rhodes. On the inward run from Piraeus, Salamis Lines calls in at Patmos and Rhodes. These services also link Israel with Greece. See the Getting There & Away chapter for details.

Rhodes Ρόδος

Rhodes (**ro**-dos in Greek), the largest by far of the Dodecanese with a total population of 98,181, is the number one package tour destination of the group. With 300 days of sunshine a year, and an east coast of virtually uninterrupted beaches, it fulfils the two prerequisites of the sun-starved British, Scandinavians and Germans who flock there.

But beaches and sunshine are not its only attributes. Rhodes is a beautiful island with unspoilt villages nestled in the foothills of its mountains. The landscape varies from arid and rocky around the coast to lush and forested in the interior.

The Unesco World Heritage-listed Old Town of Rhodes is the largest inhabited medieval town in Europe, and its mighty fortifications are the finest surviving example of defensive architecture of the time.

HISTORY & MYTHOLOGY

As is the case elsewhere in Greece, the early history of Rhodes is interwoven with mythology. The sun god Helios chose Rhodes as his bride and bestowed upon her light, warmth and vegetation. Their son, Cercafos, had three sons, Camiros, Ialysos and Lindos, who each founded the cities that were named after them.

The city of Rhodes itself was founded in 408 BC, the cities of Kamiros, Ialysos and Lindos consolidated their powers for mutual protection and expansion by co-founding a new unified city in the north of the island, where the main advantage was access to five natural harbours. The architect Hippodamos, who came to be regarded as the father of town planning, designed the city. The result was one of the most harmonious cities of antiquity, with wide, straight streets connecting its four distinct parts: the acropolis, agora, harbour and residential quarter.

For a fuller history of the town of Rhodes, see the History section in the Facts about Rhodes & the Dodecanese chapter earlier in this book.

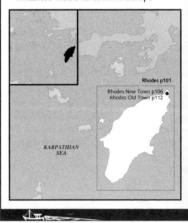

GETTING THERE & AWAY

All the addresses listed in this section are in Rhodes City (area code 0241).

Air

Domestic Olympic Airways has at least five flights daily to Athens (24,900 dr), two

RHODES

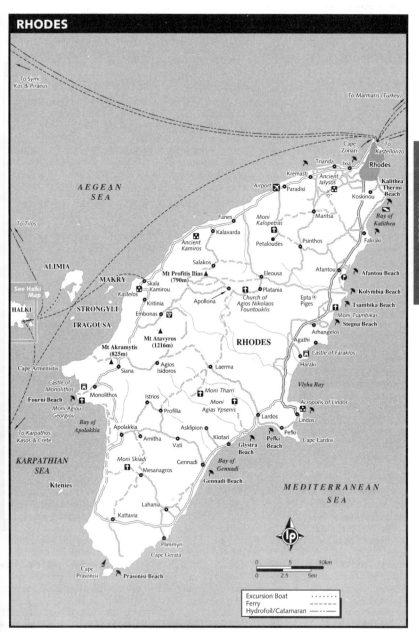

To Symi,
Kos & Piraeus

To Marmaris (Turkey)

Cape
Zonari

To
Kastellorizo

Trianda   Ixia

Rhodes

Kremasti

Kalithea
Thermi
Beach

AEGEAN
SEA

Airport   Paradisi

Ancient
Ialysos

Koskinou

To Tilos

Fanes

Moni
Kalopetras

Maritsa

Bay of
Kalithea

ALIMIA

Kalavarda

Petaloudes

Psinthos

Faliraki

MAKRY

Ancient
Kamiros

Salakos

See Halki
Map

Mt Profitis Ilias
(790m)

Eleousa

Afantou

Afantou Beach

HALKI

STRONGYLI

Skala
Kamirou

Kastelos

Platania

Epta
Piges

Kolymbia Beach

TRAGOUSA

Kritinia

Church of
Agios Nikolaos
Fountouklis

Apollona

Moni Tsambikas

Tsambika Beach

Embonas

Stegna Beach

Mt Akramytis
(825m)

Mt Atavyros
(1216m)

RHODES

Arhangelos

Agathi

Cape Armenistis

Siana

Agios
Isidoros

Laerma

Castle of Faraklos

Haraki

Castle of
Monolithos

Vlyha Bay

Fourni Beach

Monolithos

Istrios

Moni Tharri

Acropolis of Lindos

Moni Agiou
Georgiou

Profilia

Moni
Agias Ypsenis

Lardos

Lindos

To Karpathos,
Kasos & Crete

Bay of
Apolakkia

Apolakkia

Asklipion

Kiotari

Pefki

Cape Lardos

Arnitha

Vati

Glystra
Beach

Pefki
Beach

KARPATHIAN
SEA

Moni Skiadi

Gennadi

Bay of
Gennadi

MEDITERRANEAN
SEA

Ktenies

Mesanagros

Gennadi Beach

Lahania

Kattavia

Plimmyri

Cape Gerata

0   5   10km

0   2.5   5mi

Cape
Prasonisi

Prasonisi Beach

Excursion Boat   ·········
Ferry   ---------
Hydrofoil/Catamaran —·—·—·—

euro currency converter 1000dr = €2.93

daily to Karpathos (12,800 dr), one daily to Kastellorizo (10,900 dr), five weekly to Santorini (22,900 dr), four weekly to Iraklio (21,900 dr), three weekly to Kasos (13,400 dr), and two weekly to Thessaloniki (31,900 dr) and Mykonos (22,900 dr). The Olympic Airways office (☎ 24 571, fax 21 992) is at Ierou Lohou 9, Rhodes Town.

Both Aegean and Cronus Airlines offer cheaper options. Aegean Airlines has four flights daily to Athens, one week to Thessaloniki and one a week to Iraklio. Cronus Airlines has daily flights to Athens; its timetables can be viewed on its Web site at www.cronus.gr.

Aegean Airlines (☎ 24 166, fax 24 431) is located at Ethelondon Dodekanision 20, while Cronus (☎ 25 444, fax 28 468, e info@cronus.gr) is at 25 Martiou 5. Both offices are in Rhodes Town.

International The Rhodes' Diagoras International Airport (☎ 83 401), 16km southwest of Rhodes City near Paradisi, receives no scheduled international flights. However, it's the destination of many charter flights throughout the year.

Generally, the airport is now rather ill-equipped to handle the large volume of annual traffic. Delays and technical malfunctions with departure/arrival announcements are common and ground facilities for departing and arriving passengers are very basic. Though there are ATMs, exchange bureaus and car rental offices, shopping (other than duty free) and dining facilities are near to non-existent.

Ferry
Domestic Rhodes is the main port of the Dodecanese and offers a complex array of routes and departures.

The EOT and the municipal tourist office in Rhodes City can provide you with schedules. The following table lists scheduled domestic ferries from Rhodes to other islands in the Dodecanese in high season. See the Getting There & Away chapter for connections to other island groups. Further details and inter-island links can be found under each island entry.

destination	duration	price	frequency
Astypalea	10 hours	5000 dr	2 weekly
Halki	1½ hours	1900 dr	2 weekly
Kalymnos	5½ hours	4300 dr	1 daily
Karpathos	3½ hours	4400 dr	3 weekly
Kasos	5 hours	5200 dr	3 weekly
Kastellorizo	3½ hours	4000 dr	2 weekly
Kos	3½ hours	3400 dr	1 daily
Leros	7½ hours	4700 dr	1 daily
Lipsi	9½ hours	5100 dr	1 weekly
Nisyros	3¾ hours	2800 dr	3 weekly
Patmos	8½ hours	5400 dr	1 daily
Symi	2 hours	1600 dr	1 daily
Tilos	2½ hours	2800 dr	4 weekly

International Poseidon Lines and Salamis Lines both stop at Rhodes en route from Piraeus to Cyprus (Lemesos/Limassol) and Israel (Haifa). From Rhodes to Cyprus takes 15 hours (22,000 dr), with a further 11 hours to Haifa (36,000 dr). The boats leave from the large ferry quay to the north-east of Rhodes' Old Town on Tuesday and Friday. See the introductory Getting There & Away chapter and the Piraeus section of the Gateway Ports chapter for more information. You can buy tickets from Kydon Agency (☎ 23 000, fax 32 741) at Ethelondon Dodekanision 14, in the New Town, or Kouros Travel (☎ 24 377, 22 400), Karpathou 34.

There are no longer any scheduled car ferry services to and from Marmaris in Turkey and Rhodes. Travellers with a vehicle may have to wait for up to four days for an unscheduled crossing to be arranged. A ferry will be dispatched from Marmaris to pick up passengers with a vehicle only if there is also a vehicle to be transported from Marmaris. The crossing takes 2½ hours.

If you still plan to cross to Turkey, be prepared to wait. Contact Triton Holidays (see Travel Agencies in the Rhodes Town section) upon arrival to arrange a crossing.

The following fares applied in 2000 for crossings to Marmaris in Turkey: passenger (16,000 dr), motorbike (30,000 dr), car (60,000 dr), minibus/jeep (80,000 dr), campervan (100,000 dr). Greek port taxes are an additional 3000 dr. Turkish port taxes are US$10 per person and US$3 per vehicle. Immigration and customs are on the quay.

Hydrofoil

Domestic Kyriacoulis Hydrofoils (☎ 24 000, fax 20 272), on the quay at Plateia Neoriou 6, operates the following services from Rhodes in high season:

destination	duration	price	frequency
Astypalea	5½ hours	9500 dr	1 weekly
Kalymnos	3½ hours	8200 dr	1 weekly
Kos	2 hours	6500 dr	2 daily
Leros	3½ hours	8950 dr	3 weekly
Nisyros	2¼ hours	5400 dr	1 weekly
Patmos	3½ hours	10,300 dr	3 weekly
Symi	1 hour	2950 dr	2 weekly
Tilos	1¼ hours	5350 dr	2 weekly

Tickets are available from Triton Holidays (See Travel Agencies). There is an additional daily hydrofoil, *Aegli*, to and from Gialos on Symi. It is run and owned by the island of Symi and costs 3000/6000 dr single/return.

International Daily hydrofoils to Marmaris (one hour, weather permitting) run from April to October. Fares are currently cheaper than ferries at 10,000/14,000 dr one way/return (plus US$10 Turkish port tax, payable in Turkey). You can buy tickets from Triton Holidays, to whom you must submit your passport on the day before your journey. This is currently the only scheduled transport option to get to and from Turkey.

Catamaran

The *Dodekanisos Express* catamaran starts its daily run up the Dodecanese at around 8.30 am each day. This fast, sleek craft stops at Kos, Kalymnos and Leros daily with stops at other times in Symi (once weekly), Halki (twice weekly), Tilos (three times weekly), Nisyros (twice weekly), Lipsi (three times weekly) and Patmos (six times weekly).

The air-conditioned *Dodekanisos Express*, new in 2000, carries up to six cars, a few motorbikes and around 300 passengers. It can make the journey from Rhodes to Patmos in just over 4½ hours. For details of fares, see the boxed text 'The cost of the catamaran' in the Getting Around chapter.

Tickets may be bought at Skevos Travel (☎ 22 461, fax 22 354) at Amerikis 11, or from the offices of Dodekanisos Naftiliaki (☎ 70 590, fax 70 591, e sofia@12ne.gr) at Afstralias 3, in the New Town.

The ultramodern Tilos-owned *Sea Star* leaves Rhodes each morning at 9 am for Tilos (55 minutes, 5500 dr) and Nisyros (5600 dr). The Tilos round-trip costs 9000 dr, and to Nisyros, with a stop in Tilos, it costs 11,000 dr. This makes a perfect day trip from Rhodes. See Triton Holidays for tickets.

Caïque

The *Nikos Express* and the *Nisos Halki* operate between Halki and Skala Kamirou. From Monday to Saturday, one caïque leaves Halki at 6 am (to connect with the 7.15 am bus from Skala Kamirou to Rhodes); the return trip leaves Skala Kamirou at 2.30 pm. On Sunday, it leaves Halki at 9 am and Skala Kamirou at 4 pm. The fare is 2000 dr.

To get to Skala Kamirou from Rhodes Town, take the 1.15 pm Monolithos bus from the west side bus station (1100 dr). There are no connecting buses on Sunday morning. A taxi to or from Rhodes Town will cost around 10,000 dr.

Excursion Boat

There are excursion boats to Symi (4000 dr return) every day in summer, leaving Mandraki Harbour at 9 am and returning at 6 pm. You can buy tickets at most travel agencies, but it is better to buy them at the harbour, where you can check out the boats, and bargain. Look for shade and the size and condition of the boat, as these vary greatly. You can buy an open return if you want to stay on Symi.

GETTING AROUND
To/From the Airport

Each day 21 buses travel between the airport and Rhodes Town's west side bus station (400 dr). The first leaves Rhodes Town at 6 am and the last at 11 pm; the first leaves the airport at 5.55 am and the last at 11.45 pm.

Bus

Rhodes Town has two bus stations. From the east side bus station on Plateia Rimini there are 18 buses daily to Faliraki (450 dr),

RHODES

10 to Lindos (1000 dr), eight to Kolymbia (600 dr), five to Gennadi (1200 dr) via Lardos, and three to Psinthos (500 dr).

From the west side station next to the New Market there are 16 buses daily to Kalithea Thermi (400 dr), 11 to Koskinou (400 dr), five to Salakos (850 dr), and one to Ancient Kamiros (1000 dr), Monolithos (1400 dr) via Skala Kamirou, and Embonas (1250 dr). The EOT and municipal tourist office give out schedules.

Urban buses cost 230 dr for each trip if you buy your ticket from a kiosk, or 250 dr if you pay on board.

Car & Motorcycle

There are numerous car and motorcycle rental outlets in Rhodes' New Town. Shop around and bargain because the competition is fierce.

If you fancy a bike with style, rent a Harley Davidson from Rent a Harley (☎/fax 74 925) at 28 Oktovriou 80 in the New Town. Daily rates start at 22,000 dr per day for an XLM Sportster 883 to 38,000 dr for an FHR Road King.

Taxi

Rhodes Town's main taxi rank is east of Plateia Rimini. There are two zones on the island for taxi meters: zone one is Rhodes Town and zone two (slightly higher) is everywhere else. Rates are a little higher between midnight and 6 am. Sample fares are: the airport (2700 dr), Filerimos (2200 dr), Petaloudes (4000 dr), Ancient Kamiros (6500 dr), Lindos (7000 dr) and Monolithos (9000 dr). For taxis call ☎ 64 712, 64 734, 64 778 or 27 666. Rip-offs are rare but if you think you have been ripped off take the taxi number and go to the tourist police.

Bicycle

The Bicycle Centre (☎ 28 315), Griva 39, Rhodes Town, has three-speed bikes for 800 dr and mountain bikes for 1200 dr.

Excursion Boat

Excursion boats to Lindos (5000 dr return) travel every day in summer, leaving Mandraki Harbour at 9 am and returning at 6 pm.

You might like to buy a one-way ticket and return by bus or taxi.

The superfast catamaran *Sea Star* runs a daily round trip excursion to Tilos (9000 dr) and Nisyros (11,000 dr) as well as a regular one-way service. See also Getting There & Away – Catamaran in this section.

Rhodes Town

☎ 0241 • postcode 851 00 • pop 43,500
The heart of Rhodes is the Old Town, enclosed within massive walls. Avoid the worst of the tourist hordes by starting your exploration early in the morning. But at any time of the day, away from the main thoroughfares and squares, you will find deserted labyrinthine alleyways (see the Rhodes Old Town special section for more information). Much of the New Town to the north is a monument to package tourism, but it does have several places of interest to visitors.

ORIENTATION

The Old Town is a mesh of Byzantine, Turkish and Latin architecture with quiet, twisting alleyways punctuated by lively squares. Sokratous, which runs east to west, and its easterly continuation Aristotelous, are the Old Town's bustling main commercial thoroughfares. The Old Town's two main squares are also along here: Plateia Evreon Martyron, with an attractive fountain, at the eastern end of Aristotelous; and Plateia Ippokratous, with the distinctive Castellania fountain, at the eastern end of Sokratous. Acquainting yourself with these two squares will help with orientation, but getting lost is almost inevitable and part of the fun of exploring the place. Farther north, parallel to Sokratous, is Ipoton (Avenue of the Knights), which was the main medieval thoroughfare.

The commercial harbour, for international ferries and large inter-island ferries, is east of the Old Town. Excursion boats, small ferries, hydrofoils and private yachts use Mandraki Harbour, farther north. When you buy a ticket check where the ferry is leaving from.

In Mandraki, two bronze deer (the stag and doe) on stone pillars mark the supposed site of the Colossus of Rhodes. Mandraki's grandiose public buildings are relics of Mussolini's era. The main square of the New Town is Plateia Rimini, just north of the Old Town. The tourist offices, bus stations and main taxi rank are on or near this square.

Most of the Old Town is off limits to motorists, with carparks on the periphery.

Maps

The Road Editions 1:100,000 *Rhodes* map is the best commercially available map of Rhodes and costs 1300 dr. Look for it in New Town street kiosks. The free *Greece – Rhodes* map from the EOT has a good map of the town of Rhodes as well as a general and clear map of the whole island.

INFORMATION
Tourist Offices

The EOT tourist office (☎ 23 255, fax 26 955, ℮ eot-rodos@otenet.gr), on the corner of Makariou and Papagou, supplies brochures and maps of the city, and will help in finding accommodation. Opening times are from 7.30 am to 3 pm Monday to Friday. In summer the same service is provided by Rhodes' municipal tourist office (☎ 35 945), Plateia Rimini. Opening times are 8 am to 8 pm Monday to Saturday and 8 am to noon on Sunday; it's closed in winter.

From either of these you can pick up the *Rodos News*, a free English-language newspaper that could prove useful.

Money

The main National Bank of Greece and the Alpha Credit Bank are on Plateia Kyprou. In the Old Town there is a National Bank of Greece on Plateia Mousiou, and a Commercial Bank of Greece nearby. All have ATMs. Opening times are 8 am to 2 pm Monday to Thursday, and 8 am to 1.30 pm Friday. Arriving ferry passengers should note that there is a convenient Commercial Bank ATM near the port police office at the harbour gates.

In the New Town the National Bank exchange bureau on Papanikolaou is open from 8 am to 2 pm (1.30 pm on Friday).

American Express (☎ 21 010, fax 74 025) is represented by Rhodos Tours, at Ammohostou 29.

RHODES

The Colossus of Rhodes

Whether the famous Colossus of Rhodes, one of the Seven Wonders of the World, ever existed has not been proven, since there are no remains and no tangible evidence other than the reports of ancient travellers. The statue was apparently commissioned by Demetrios 1 Poliorketes in 305 BC after he finally capitulated to Rhodian defiance following his long and ultimately failed siege of Rhodes in that same year (see History in the Facts about Rhodes & the Dodecanese chapter). The bronze statue was built over 12 years (294–282 BC) and when completed stood 32m high. What is not clear is where this gargantuan statue actually stood. Popular medieval belief has it astride the harbour at Mandraki (as depicted on today's T-shirts and tourist trinkets), but it is highly unlikely that this is the case and it is also said to be technically unfeasible.

An earthquake in either 225 or 226 BC toppled the statue, most likely on land, where the remains laid undisturbed for 880 years. In AD 654 invading Saracens had the remains broken up and sold for scrap to a Jewish merchant in Edessa (in modern-day Turkey). The story goes that the remains were then moved to Syria, taking almost 1000 camels to convey them.

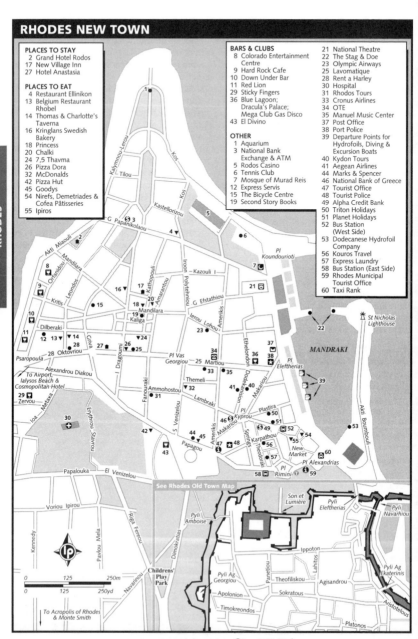

RHODES NEW TOWN

PLACES TO STAY
2 Grand Hotel Rodos
17 New Village Inn
27 Hotel Anastasia

PLACES TO EAT
4 Restaurant Ellinikon
13 Belgium Restaurant Rhobel
14 Thomas & Charlotte's Taverna
16 Kringlans Swedish Bakery
18 Princess
20 Chalki
24 7,5 Thavma
26 Pizza Dora
32 McDonalds
42 Pizza Hut
45 Goodys
54 Nirefs, Demetriades & Cofea Pâtisseries
55 Ipiros

BARS & CLUBS
8 Colorado Entertainment Centre
9 Hard Rock Cafe
10 Down Under Bar
11 Red Lion
29 Sticky Fingers
36 Blue Lagoon; Dracula's Palace; Mega Club Gas Disco
43 El Divino

OTHER
1 Aquarium
3 National Bank Exchange & ATM
5 Rodos Casino
6 Tennis Club
7 Mosque of Murad Reis
12 Express Servis
15 The Bicycle Centre
19 Second Story Books

21 National Theatre
22 The Stag & Doe
23 Olympic Airways
25 Lavomatique
28 Rent a Harley
30 Hospital
31 Rhodos Tours
33 Cronus Airlines
34 OTE
35 Manuel Music Center
37 Post Office
38 Port Police
39 Departure Points for Hydrofoils, Diving & Excursion Boats
40 Kydon Tours
41 Aegean Airlines
44 Marks & Spencer
46 National Bank of Greece
47 Tourist Office
48 Tourist Police
49 Alpha Credit Bank
50 Triton Holidays
51 Planet Holidays
52 Bus Station (West Side)
53 Dodecanese Hydrofoil Company
56 Kouros Travel
57 Express Laundry
58 Bus Station (East Side)
59 Rhodes Municipal Tourist Office
60 Taxi Rank

RHODES

euro currency converter €1 = 340.75dr

Post & Communications
The main post office is on Mandraki. Opening times are 7.30 am to 8 pm Monday to Friday. The Old Town sub post office is open seven days. The OTE at Amerikis 91 is open 7 am to 11pm daily.

Rhodes has two Internet cafes: Rock Style Internet Cafe (☎ 27 502, ℮ info@ rockstyle.gr), Dimokratias 7, just south of the Old Town; and Mango Cafe Bar (☎ 24 877, ℮ karelas@hotmail.com), Plateia Dorieos 3, in the Old Town. Access costs around 1200 dr per hour at both of them.

Internet Resources
Rhodes is well supported by Web resources, and sites come and go. A couple you might try starting with are www.rodorama.gr and www.rodos.com. Both are general information sources and have links to other sites. The EOT runs its own rather dry and limited Web site at www.ando.gr/eot.

Triton Holidays (see Travel Agencies following) runs its own site www.tritondmc.gr and has good travel-related information.

Travel Agencies
Castellania Travel Service (☎ 75 860, fax 75 861, ℮ castell@otenet.gr), on Plateia Ippokratous in the Old Town, specialises in youth and student fares, and is one of the best places for low-cost air tickets.

Triton Holidays (☎ 21 657, fax 31 625, ℮ info@tritondmc.gr), at Plastira 9 in the New Town, is a good, helpful travel agency for all kinds of tickets. It offers a wide range of tours and provides specialist advice on any of the islands and Turkey.

Bookshops
Second Story Books, at Amarandou 24 in the New Town, has a broad selection of second-hand foreign-language books.

Laundry
Rhodes has two self-service laundrettes: Lavomatique, 28 Oktovriou 32, and Express Servis, Dilberaki 97 (off Orfanidou). Both charge around 1000 dr a load. Express Laundry, at Kosta Palama 5, does service washes for 1000 dr.

Toilets
There are clean public toilets at Plateia Rimini not far from the entrance to the Son et Lumière show ground.

Luggage Storage
You can store luggage at Planet Holidays (☎ 35 722), Gallias 6, for 800 dr for four hours and 1200 dr for one day. You can negotiate a price for a longer period.

Medical Services
Rhodes' general hospital (☎ 80 000) is on Papalouka, just north-west of the Old Town. For emergency first aid and the ambulance service, call ☎ 25 555 or ☎ 22 222.

Emergency
The tourist police (☎ 27 423) are next door to the EOT on Karpathou and are open 24 hours daily.

NEW TOWN
Rhodes' New Town has developed north, west and south of the Old Town. The northern section, with its west side and east side beaches, is where the tourists all tend to congregate. It is a busy area and hosts a predominance of Scandinavian visitors. The abundance of cheap alcohol outlets with signs in Finnish, Swedish and Norwegian and multilingual restaurant menus testify to the northern New Town's popularity as a resort in itself.

It's not bad as a centre, and there are enough leafy, tree-shaded streets and grand old buildings to make up for the appearance of boxy and generally characterless hotels. The beaches are very handy and quite reasonable, though their proximity to a major population centre may make some people prefer to seek bathing – and space – elsewhere. The beaches can get rather crowded at times, especially the ones on the more protected east side.

THINGS TO SEE & DO
The **Acropolis of Rhodes**, south-west of the Old Town on Monte Smith, was the site of the ancient Hellenistic city of Rhodes. The hill is named after the English admiral Sir

RHODES

Sydney Smith, who watched for Napoleon's fleet from here in 1802. It has superb views.

The site's restored 2nd-century stadium once staged competitions in preparation for the Olympic Games. The adjacent theatre is a reconstruction of one used for lectures by the Rhodes School of Rhetoric. Steps above here lead to the **Temple of Pythian Apollo**, with four re-erected columns. The unenclosed site can be reached on city bus No 5.

North of Mandraki, at the eastern end of G Papanikolaou, is the graceful **Mosque of Murad Reis**. In its grounds are a Turkish cemetery and the Villa Cleobolus, where Lawrence Durrell lived in the 1940s, writing Reflections on a Marine Venus.

The **aquarium** is housed in a red and cream Italianate building at the island's northernmost point. Opening times are 9 am to 9 pm daily. Admission is 600 dr.

The town **beach** begins north of Mandraki and continues around the island's northernmost point and down the west side of the New Town. The best spot is on the northernmost point, where it's not as crowded.

ACTIVITIES
Scuba Diving
Two diving schools operate out of Mandraki: the Waterhoppers Diving Centre (☎/fax 38 146, mobile ☎ 09-3296 3173, 🄴 water-hoppers@rodos.com), Perikleous 29; and Dive Med Centre (☎ 33 654). Both offer a range of courses, including a One Day Try Dive for 13,500 dr. You can get information either from the Waterhoppers boat MV *Kouros*, or Dive Med Centre's boats *Phoenix* and *Free Spirit* at Mandraki. Kalithea Thermi is the only site around Rhodes where diving is permitted.

Yachting
You can hire yachts at the YAR Maritime Centre (☎ 22 927, fax 23 393), Vyronos 1. For more yachting information, contact the Rodos Yacht Club (☎ 23 287).

Windsurfing
Pro Horizon (☎ 95 819), just west of town at Ialyssos Beach, Ixia, rents out boards. There are many other rental outlets around

Safety Guidelines for Diving

Before embarking on a scuba diving, skin diving or snorkelling trip, carefully consider the following points to ensure a safe and enjoyable experience:

• Possess a current diving certification card from a recognised scuba diving instructional agency (if scuba diving).

• Be sure you are healthy and feel comfortable diving.

• Obtain reliable information about physical and environmental conditions at the dive site (eg, from a reputable local dive operation).

• Be aware of local laws, regulations and etiquette about marine life and the environment.

• Dive only at sites within your realm of experience; if available, engage the services of a competent, professionally trained dive instructor or dive master, especially if you need to refresh rusty skills.

• Be aware that underwater conditions vary significantly from one region, or even site, to another. Seasonal changes can significantly alter any site and dive conditions. These differences influence the way divers dress for a dive and what diving techniques they use.

• Ask about the environmental characteristics that can affect your diving and how local trained divers deal with these considerations.

the coast. The Fun & Action Windsurfing School at Faliraki offers expert tuition. See the Faliraki section for further details.

Tennis
Many large hotels have tennis courts open to nonguests. Rhodes Tennis Club (☎ 25 705) is on the waterfront north of Mandraki. Open from 1 to 9 pm, it costs 2400/3200 dr per hour for a concrete/clay court. Equipment hire costs an extra 500 dr per person.

Childrens' Play Park
There is a decent play park for children with swings and things in a quiet and shady corner of town, two minutes from the Amboise Gate. It's great for frazzled parents who need a breather.

Greek Dancing Lessons

The Nelly Dimoglou Dance Company (☎ 20 157, 29 085), at the Folk Dance Theatre on Andronikou, gives lessons. Dance performances are given at 9.30 pm on Monday, Wednesday and Friday. Entrance costs 3500 dr for an individual, and 2500 dr if you are part of a group. (See also Entertainment in the Rhodes Old Town special section.)

SPECIAL EVENTS

Throughout the year there are any number of events taking place. The following are the more predictable and regular events. Check with the local EOT office for further details.

March 7 – Unification of the Dodecanese with Greece
March 25 – National Day
May (towards the end) – Flower Festival
June 28 to July 5 – Nautical Week
September 27 – Tourism Day
October 28 – National 'Ohi' Day Celebration

Various additional cultural events including concerts, modern and traditional music performances, dances and art exhibitions are organised by the Municipality of Rhodes (☎ 29 678). These take place from July to September and are announced in late May. See the EOT office for full details.

PLACES TO STAY – BUDGET

For accommodation suggestions in the Old Town, see the special section later in this chapter. As far as the New Town goes, hotels are generally modern and characterless, but there are notable exceptions. *Hotel Anastasia* (☎ 28 007, fax 21 815, **e** *nikas2@ otenet.gr, 28 Oktovriou 46*), in a former Italian mansion, is set back from the road, and is very quiet. The rooms with high ceilings and tiled floors are spotless; doubles/triples are 14,500/18,000 dr with breakfast. The hotel has a lovely, shady garden – home to two large tortoises and two cats. The owners enjoy helping guests plan their itineraries.

New Village Inn (☎/fax 34 937, **e** *new villageinn@rho.forthnet.gr, Konstantopedos 10*) is a Greek-American owned inn on a very quiet street. The tastefully furnished

single/double rooms, with orthopaedic mattresses on stone-based beds, refrigerator and fan, cost 8000/12,000 dr. The traditional stone-walled courtyard is festooned with plants.

PLACES TO STAY – MID-RANGE TO TOP END

The pricey *Grand Hotel Rhodes* (☎ 26 284, fax 35 589) on Akti Miaouli is open all year and has a bar, restaurant and swimming pools. Single/double rooms with either a pleasant garden or sea view are 26,500/ 39,000; buffet breakfast is included.

At Ixia, the A-class *Cosmopolitan Hotel* (☎ 25 281, fax 32 823) on Iraklidon St has rooms for 16,400/27,000 dr. The deluxe *Rodos Palace* (☎ 25 222, fax 25 350), on Trianton Ave in Ixia, is a vast place with loads of amenities. Prices start at 39,400/ 54,100 dr for singles/doubles, but there are plenty of other options right up to the royal suite at 350,000 dr per night.

You can get discounts of up to 30% on the more expensive hotels if you book through Triton Holidays (see Travel Agencies).

PLACES TO EAT – BUDGET

Although not quite as atmospheric as the Old Town, eating in the New Town has its moments. You will eat well and generally cheaper if you choose your restaurant carefully. There are plenty of fast food places, and hole-in-wall souvlaki stands. The New Market has a good selection of eateries and the atmosphere at night is both busy and convivial.

Practically hidden away from passing trade is the down to earth and mildly idiosyncratic *Chalki* (☎ 33 198, Kathopouli 30) where you can choose from an enticing display of mezedes and down them with excellent draft wine. Prices are average.

The Swedish-influenced diner, *7,5 Thavma* (☎ 39 805, Dilperaki 15), is surprisingly cheap. Greek and Swedish dishes alternate on an inventive menu.

Thomas & Charlotte's Taverna (☎ 73 557, Georgiou Leondos 8) serves a selection of Greek and Scandinavian dishes. One tasty dish is *kleftiko* (the thieves' dish), a slow-cooked mixture of meat and vegetables which is served wrapped in greaseproof paper.

For a quick and cheap roast meat dinner, **Ipiros** is the best of the *psistarias* in the New Market. A huge helping of succulent spit-roast lamb, Greek salad and soft drink costs 3000 dr.

For breakfast, the **Kringlans Swedish Bakery** (☎ 39 090, Dragoumi 14) serves up sandwiches and pastries that are out of this world. This place is even open on Sunday morning.

STELLA HELLANDER

Cheap and cheerful: when it comes to a tipple, you can't go wrong with draft wine.

PLACES TO EAT – MID-RANGE & TOP END

Three-course meals with wine at the following places will cost around 9000 dr. **Restaurant Ellinikon** (☎ 28 111, G Papanikolaou 6) excels in traditional Greek fare. The *stifado* is highly recommended, but leave room for the luscious iced caramel which often features as dessert of the day. **Belgium Restaurant Rhobel** (Georgiou Leondos 13-15) specialises in steaks but, for something a bit different, the 'rabbit cooked in the traditional way' (with dried fruit) is commendable.

Metaxy Mas (☎ 73 456, Klavdiou Pepper) is a little way out of the New Town on 'ouzeri strip' overlooking a beach area on the south side. This little ouzeri caters mainly to Greeks and is excellent for various seafood-based mezedes. It's open evenings only. Metaxy Mas is best reached by a 10-minute taxi ride from the Old Town.

Princess (☎ 20 068, Mandilara 26) is a classy place offering Mediterranean dishes from Greece, Spain, Italy and the Middle East. It's great for that special, romantic night out.

Cafes

Feverish touting reaches its acme at the people-watching patisseries with names like **Nirefs**, **Demetriades** and **Cofea** bordering the New Market. Nevertheless, they're convivial meeting places. Coffee and cake costs around 2000 dr.

A lively cafe strip that's worth a visit is along S Venizelou.

Fast Food

Pizza Hut on Papagou is easy to find and so is **Goodys**, 100m or so east along the same street. **McDonalds**, on S Venizelou, is housed in an old Italian mansion restored in 2000 at a cost of some 350,000,000 dr. Even so, the burgers still cost the same as everywhere else.

Good, tasty and cheap sandwiches and pizza can be had at **Pizza Dora** (☎ 21 972, I Dragoumi 31), which is handy for guests at Hotel Anastasia (See Places to Stay).

Self-Catering

If you're self-catering, there is a small **supermarket** on Evripidou. There are many supermarkets in the New Town, and fruit and vegetable stalls in the New Market.

ENTERTAINMENT

The New Town has a plethora of discos and bars – over 600 at last count and rising. The two main areas are Top Street (Alexandrou Diakou) and the Street of Bars (Orfanidou), where a cacophony of western music blares from every establishment. For a wild night of dancing on the bar top, make for **Down Under Bar** (Orfanidou 35). If you prefer somewhere more subdued, try the **Red Lion** (Orfanidou 9), with the relaxed atmosphere of a British pub. Proprietors Ron and Vasilis will gladly answer questions about Rhodes for the price of a drink. Yet another **Hard Rock Cafe** (Orfanidou 29) can be enjoyed in the same strip as the above pubs.

The most amazing of the theme music bars is **Blue Lagoon** (25 Martiou 2), where you can indulge your tropical island fantasies amid a shipwreck and lagoon, watched over by a live parrot, three turtles and a waxwork pirate who must have escaped from the adjoining *Dracula's Palace* – Rhodes' answer to Madame Tussaud's Chamber of Horrors. Above the bar is *Mega Club Gas Disco*.

For live rock and roll, try *Sticky Fingers (Zervou 6)*. It's open on Friday and Saturday evening only.

The *Colorado Entertainment Centre (☎ 75 120, Akti Miaouli & Orfanidou 57)* was the 'in' place when this book was researched. Consisting of three clubs in one – the Dancing Club, the Heaven Night Club and another venue where the *QF Band* plays live – there is more than enough fun for a week in this enormous palace of hype. For what is currently on, see the Web site (www.coloradoclub.gr).

El Divino (Alexandrou Diakou 5) is the place to sit and have a relaxed beer or a cocktail. Overlooking the long strip of cafes along S Venizelou, El Divino is the biggest and hippest of the lot and is mostly popular with Greeks.

There are classical music recitals at the *National Theatre (☎ 29 678)*, and the *Pallas Cinema (☎ 24 475, Dimokratias 13)* screens a wide range of current release movies from 3 to 8 pm. See their current showings at www.cinemapallas.gr.

SHOPPING

Good buys in Rhodes' Old Town are gold and silver jewellery, leather goods and ceramics. However, leather goods are cheaper in Turkey. Look around and be discriminating – it's quite acceptable to haggle.

For good quality Greek music (not 'Zorba the Greek does Syrtaki' tourist music), go to the Manuel Music Center (☎ 28 266) at 25 Martiou 10-13. All the latest and more Greek albums are on sale. There's a decent Marks & Spencer outlet on Papagou, should you be down on your Y-fronts or frillies.

GETTING AROUND

Local buses leave from Mandraki. Bus No 2 goes to Analipsi, No 3 to Rodini, No 4 to Agios Dimitrios and No 5 to Monte Smith. You can buy tickets at the kiosk on the Mandraki harbourfront.

RHODES

PAUL HELLANDER

The view towards the harbour from the top of the Rhodes Old Town Clock Tower is spectacular.

RHODES OLD TOWN

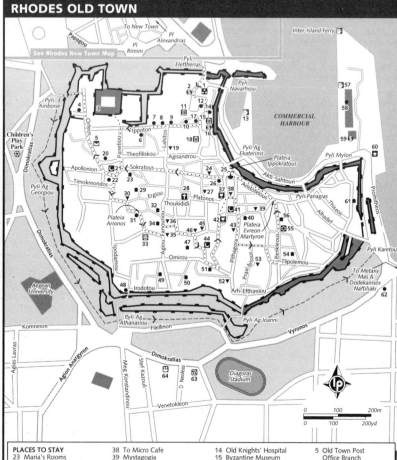

PLACES TO STAY
23 Maria's Rooms
29 Mike and Mama's Pension
32 Marco Polo Mansion
34 Pension Olympos
40 Hotel Via Via
47 Mango Rooms & Café Bar
49 Pink Elephant
50 Pension Andreas
51 Pension Minos
54 Kamiros Rooms to Let
56 Hotel Spot
61 Hotel Cava d'Oro

PLACES TO EAT
19 Myrovolos
24 Alexis Restaurant
27 Pizza da Spillo
30 Diafani Garden Restaurant
35 Nisyros
36 Cleo's Italian Restaurant

38 To Micro Cafe
39 Mystagogia
43 Taverna Kostas
45 Synaxaria
46 Araliki
52 Andonis
53 L'Auberge Bistrot

THINGS TO SEE
1 Temple of Aphrodite
3 Palace of the Grand Masters
4 Entrance to Moat #2
6 Inn of Spain
7 Inn of Provence
8 Chapelle Française
9 Inn of France
10 Palace of Villiers de l'Île Adam
11 Museum of Decorative Arts
12 Inn of Auvergne

14 Old Knights' Hospital
15 Byzantine Museum
17 Inn of the Order of the Tongue of Italy
18 Archaeological Museum
20 Clock Tower
21 Süleymaniye Mosque
22 Ottoman Library
25 Castellania Fountain
28 Agios Spyridon Church (Kavakli Mosque)
31 Mustafa Pasha Baths (Hammam)
41 Ibrahim Pasha Mosque
44 Recep Pasha Mosque
48 Entrance to Moat
55 Kahal Shalom Synagogue

OTHER
2 Commercial Bank of Greece & ATM

5 Old Town Post Office Branch
13 Departure Point for F/B Nisos Kalymnos & Dodekanisos Express Catamaran
16 National Bank of Greece
26 Castellania Travel
33 Nelly Dimoglou Folk Dance Theatre
37 Resalto Club
42 Kafe Besara
57 Departure Point for Boats to Turkey
58 Customs Office
59 Commercial Bank ATM
60 Port Police
62 YAR Maritime Centre
63 Rock Style Internet Cafe
64 Pallas Cinema

---

euro currency converter €1 = 340.75dr

Rhodes Old Town

GEORGE TSAFOS

STELLA HELLANDER

JUDI WILLOUGHBY

Title Page: Strong Ottoman influences distinguish Rhodes' Turkish Quarter. (Photographer: Stella Hellander)

Top: Moonlight sets the mood outside Rhodes' city fortifications.

Far left: A local craftswoman hard at work

Left: A tiled image from the Byzantine era, Old Rhodes Town

The Old Town of Rhodes makes a visit to the island of Rhodes and indeed the whole of the Dodecanese a memorable experience. Few places in Europe – with competition perhaps only from Carcassonne in France and Ávila in Spain – match Rhodes' Old Town in atmosphere, architecture and style. Jerusalem also draws comparisons: it is quite possible that the Knights of St John, expelled from the Holy City in the 13th century, may have designed the Old Town based on their experiences in their original home.

The key to enjoying Rhodes' Old Town is to give it time and to wander at will, appreciating the subtle textures and elements that make up what is today the largest permanently-inhabited medieval town in the world. Its massive outer walls, counterpoised by narrow, cobblestone interior alleyways overhung with flying buttresses, weave an intricate pattern that is at first totally disorienting. However, you can't get lost. At some point you will once more chance upon the outer wall and regain your sense of direction. Entering the Pyli Ambouaz (Amboise Gate) at night, you could be forgiven for believing that you have been momentarily transported back in time. But then the glitter, bustle and sheer exuberance of the commercial centre, with its countless tavernas and shops, remind you that this is a town that lives life to the full in the 21st century.

What we see today is essentially the legacy of more recent interventions, which can be viewed as positive or negative. The Italians, who reigned in Rhodes from 1912 to 1943, restored large sections of the Old Town and to their credit did a good job overall. Successive Greek governments have maintained the preservation impetus by limiting the unfettered encroachment of the modern world into the Old Town.

GEORGE TSAFOS

Right: From a darkened archway, visitors emerge into the grand old Avenue of the Knights.

The Kollakio

The Kollakio, known during the reign of the Knights of St John as the Collachium, occupies the northernmost quadrant of the Old Town. Encompassing the headquarters of the Grand Master and the main residential street of the privileged few Knights, the Kollakio was essentially a town within a town. The Knights could be sequestered here in relative comfort away from the crowded, everyday life of the inhabitants of the lower town, known collectively as the Hora, where the local Rhodians lived. In theory, the Kollakio was to provide a safe haven for the rulers to retire to if the outer walls of the larger town were breached. In practice it was an enclave of privilege, ritual and relative opulence for the foreign masters. Here they could practise their avowed moral code of chastity, poverty and obedience away from the rigours – and temptations – of life outside their exclusive precinct. The original walls of the Kollakio extended as far south as Theofiliskou and Agisandrou streets and to the west as far as Orfeos St. Little remains of the original walls, though some sections are now being excavated along the western sector between Panetiou and Orfeos streets.

The Palace of the Grand Masters

Dominating the Kollakio, if not the whole of the Old Town, is the magnificent 14th-century Palace of the Grand Masters. It was almost completely destroyed in the gunpowder explosion of 1856. However the ever resourceful and imaginative Italians rebuilt it in accordance with medieval descriptions and engravings. They subsequently 'restored' it to its appearance when the Knights abandoned it in 1523 and the results have been mixed, to say the least. Admittedly the palace looks better 'restored' than left a ruin (in much the same way that Evan's Knossos in Crete looks better) but it must be viewed in that light: that it is essentially an artificial edifice. If the exterior fails to totally convince, then the interior clearly bewilders. The Italian

PAUL HELLANDER

Left: The Palace of the Grand Masters: more a celebration of Italian Fascist excess than a carefully restored homage to the Knights

The Knights of St John

The Knights of St John were a religious order of the church of Rome founded in Amalfi in the 11th century. They went to Jerusalem initially to minister to the pilgrims who arrived there, but soon extended their duties to tending the poor and sick of the Holy Land. Over the years they became increasingly militant, joining forces with the Knights Templars and the Teutonic Knights of St Mary in battles against infidels.

The Knights of St John were expelled from the Holy Land with the fall of Jerusalem. They went first to Cyprus and then, in 1309, to Rhodes. Through some wheeling and dealing with the island's ruling Genoese admiral, Viguolo de Viguoli, they became the possessors of Rhodes, transforming it into a mighty bulwark that stood at the easternmost point of the Christian west, safeguarding it from the Muslim infidels of the east. The knights withstood Muslim offensives in 1444 and 1480, but in 1522 Sultan Süleyman the Magnificent staged a massive attack with 200,000 troops. After a long siege the 600 knights, with 1000 mercenaries and 6000 Rhodians, surrendered – hunger, disease and death having taken their toll.

architects lent free reign to their vision of a rejuvenated Fascist palace, with sweeping marble staircases, vaulted rooms, antique furniture pieces and state rooms decked out in plundered Hellenistic mosaics from Kos.

The extravagance and arbitrary architectural restoration is explained by the fact that the building was intended to be the Aegean palace of both Mussolini and King Victor Emmanuel III, rather than an accurate representation for the benefit of future history and archaeology students. The irony is that neither Mussolini nor King Victor Emmanuel III ever took up residency and so this wonderful white elephant remains today as a reminder of both Italian zeal and excess. A visit to Rhodes would nonetheless not be complete without a look in at this rather startling building and its curiously renovated interior.

The palace is now a museum (☎ 23 359) and is open 8.30 am to 3 pm Tuesday to Sunday; admission is 1200 dr.

The Palace Exhibitions

The entry fee to the Palace is worth it for the access to the two permanent exhibitions that are housed in opposite ground floor sections abutting the inner courtyard. The **Ancient Rhodes – 2400 years** exhibition was opened in 1993 as part of celebrations of the 2400th anniversary of the foundation of the city of Rhodes in 408–407 BC. This exhibition, housed over two storeys, displays finds from excavations since 1948.

The 12 rooms exhaustively depict the history of Rhodes with a wide array of displays. Foremost are the clay head of the sun god Helios (150–100 BC); a Rhodian house, replete with a Hellenistic floor mosaic of a New Comedy mask; finds from bronze workshops in which statues were cast using the *cire perdue* (lost wax) technique, pioneered by the Cretans in pre-classical times; recreations of various supposed versions of the Colossus of Rhodes; and *katadesmi* (sheets of lead with incised inscriptions, commonly curses), which were placed in the graves of people who met violent deaths.

The **Rhodes From the 4th century to its Capture by the Turks (1522)** exhibition in the ground floor of the Palace (to your left as you enter) comprehensively covers Rhodes from the Christian era to its capture by Süleyman the Magnificent. The similarly extensive displays cover life not only in the Town of Rhodes, but on the island of Rhodes in general. It aims to cover aspects of everyday life with rooms thematically assigned to represent: religion; economy – farming, handicrafts, commerce and coinage; domestic life – diet, clothing, leisure, entertainment, social welfare and burial rituals; defence and administration; and cultural life and worship.

The Street of the Knights

The imposing cobblestone Avenue of the Knights (Ippoton) is where the Knights of St John lived. The Knights were divided into seven 'tongues' or languages, according to their place of origin – England, France, Germany, Italy, Aragon, Auvergne and Provence – each responsible for protecting a section of the bastion. The Grand Master, who was in charge, lived in the palace, and each tongue was under the auspices of a bailiff. The Knights were divided into soldiers, chaplains and ministers to the sick.

To this day the street exudes a noble and forbidding aura, despite modern offices now occupying most of the inns. Its lofty buildings stretch in a 600m-long unbroken wall of honey-coloured stone blocks, and its flat facade is punctuated by huge doorways and arched windows. The inns reflect the Gothic styles of architecture of the Knights' countries of origin. They form a harmonious whole in their bastion-like structure, but on closer inspection each possesses graceful and individual embellishments.

First on the right, at the eastern end of the Avenue of the Knights, is the **Inn of the Order of the Tongue of Italy** (1519); next to it is the **Palace of Villiers de l'Île Adam**. After Sultan Süleyman had taken the city, it was Villiers de l'Île who had the humiliating task of arranging the Knights' departure from the island. Next along is the **Inn of France**, the most ornate and distinctive of all the inns. On the opposite side of the street is a wrought-iron gate in front of a Turkish garden.

GEORGE TSAFOS

Left: Avenue of the Knights: the long unbroken wall is only interrupted by huge doorways and multiple arched windows.

Back on the right side is the **Chapelle Française** (Chapel of the Tongue of France), embellished with a statue of the Virgin and Child. Next door is the residence of the Chaplain of the Tongue of France. Across the alleyway is the **Inn of Provence**, with four coats of arms forming the shape of a cross, and opposite is the **Inn of Spain.**

The Museums

The **archaeological museum** (☎ 27 657), on Plateia Mousiou, is housed in the 15th-century Knights' hospital. Its most famous exhibit is the exquisite Parian marble statuette, the *Aphrodite of Rhodes,* a 1st century BC adaptation of a Hellenistic statue.

Less charming to most people is the 4th century BC *Aphrodite of Thalassia* in the next room. However, writer Lawrence Durrell was so enamoured of this statue that he named his book *Reflections on a Marine Venus* after it. Also in this room is the 2nd century BC marble *Head of Helios*, found near the Palace of the Grand Masters where a Temple of Helios once stood. The museum is open 8.30 am to 3 pm Tuesday to Sunday; admission is 800 dr.

Across the square is the 11th-century Church of the Virgin of the Castle. It was enlarged by the Knights and became their cathedral. It is now the **Byzantine Museum**, with Christian artworks. It is open 8.30 am to 3 pm Tuesday to Sunday; admission is 500 dr.

Farther north, on the opposite side of the square, the **Museum of the Decorative Arts** houses a collection of artefacts from around the Dodecanese. Opening times are 8.30 am to 3 pm Tuesday to Sunday; admission is 600 dr.

Other Sites

On Plateia Symis, there are the remains of a 3rd century BC **Temple of Aphrodite**, one of the few ancient ruins in the Old Town. It was discovered by the Italians and covers a broad area in Plateia Symis. It is fenced off so all you can see are the remains of columns and a fairly easily identifiable floor plan of the temple.

GEORGE TSAFOS

Right: The atmospheric Church of the Virgin of the Castle now houses the Byzantine Museum.

The Turkish Quarter

The Turkish Quarter, also known as the Hora, has many Ottoman lega-
cies. This large area constitutes the heartland of Rhodes Old Town and
offers the visitor some of the most atmospheric browsing and strolling.
It is here that the long swathe of tourist trinket outlets ply their trade,
primarily along the sloping Sokratous St, which becomes Aristotelous at
its eastern termination and which eventually ends in Plateia Evreon Martyron. Immediately south of Sokratous is a jumbled warren of narrow alleyways, full of houses, more small shops, boutique restaurants and some
of the more atmospheric lodgings in the Old Town. Agiou Fanouriou is
a busy and picturesque secondary side street replete with flying buttresses linking two sides of the street and disorienting kinks and turns. It
runs south and at right angles to Sokratous and neatly cuts the Turkish
Quarter in two. Dive into Agiou Fanouriou and be prepared to get lost
for half an hour or so.

Süleymaniye Mosque

The newly renovated, pink-domed **Süleymaniye Mosque** at the top of
Sokratous is the most important mosque in Rhodes Old Town. It was built
in 1522 to commemorate the Ottoman victory against the Knights of St
John, then rebuilt with an imposing dome in 1808. Its once tall minaret
was thought to be in danger of collapsing and was taken down for safety
reasons. A truncated stub is all that remains today. Because of ongoing
renovations the mosque is not yet open to the public, but once fully restored it is expected to be open for services and prayers by the small
Muslim community in Rhodes.

Ottoman Library

Opposite the Süleymaniye Mosque is the **Turkish Library** where many
Islamic manuscripts are kept. It was founded in 1794 by Turkish Rhodian
Ahmed Hasuf and houses a small collection of Persian and Arabic manuscripts and a collection of Korans hand-written on parchment. Two of the
parchments, worth around 130 million drachmas, went walkabout in 1990
and turned up four years later at an art auction in London. They were
happily restored to the library in due course.

The library is open to the public from 9.30 am to 4 pm Monday to Saturday and entry is free.

The Hammam

The 18th-century **Mustafa Pasha Baths** (the Hammam) on Plateia Arionos
was built around 1764 and is one of the few purpose-built Turkish era buildings in the Old Town. The building was restored in the late 1990s and is
supposed to be open for public use, but more often than not it is closed, as
it maintains unpredictable opening hours. If you do manage to get in (entry
500 dr), note that bathing is segregated. Men use the larger domed hall and
women the smaller annexes. You will also have to bring all your own
bathing paraphernalia, as this hammam is very much a bathe-yourself place
unlike the counterparts in Turkey today.

Minor Mosques

The Ottomans were, on the whole, fairly practical when it came to mosque building. Other than the custom-built Süleymaniye Mosque, the others were commissioned by recycling Christian churches. This meant, in principle, adding a minaret and refurbishing the interior. A number of these mosques can be spotted in and around the Turkish Quarter including the **Kavakli Mosque**, which is now once more the **church of Agios Spyridon**. The **Ibrahim Pasha Mosque**, dating from 1531, is still used on occasion for Islamic services pending full restoration of the Süleymaniye Mosque and is one of the better surviving examples of an Ottoman-era mosque. Also built from recycled church materials is the **Recep Pasha Mosque** nearby, built in 1588.

The Jewish Quarter

The Jewish Quarter of the Old Town is an almost forgotten sector of Rhodes. Life continues here at an unhurried pace and local residents live almost oblivious to the hubbub of the Turkish commercial sector no more than a few blocks away to the north-west. This area of quiet streets and sometimes dilapidated houses was once home to a thriving Jewish community that had lived in peace and harmony with the Ottomans for hundreds of years. Descendants of Sephardic Jews from Spain, the Jewish community here spoke Ladino and numbered over 2000 souls at the height of their prosperity.

When the Nazi Germans arrived in 1944, the greater majority of Jewish residents were sent off to concentration camps in Germany and Eastern Europe. Less than 200 returned to Rhodes. The *Rodesli*, as they and their descendants call themselves, now number less than a hundred and are probably in terminal decline, as the community can no longer support a rabbi for their synagogue (see Kahal Shalom Synagogue following). Nonetheless, a stroll around these timeless streets – the closer to the southern wall, the more timeless the atmosphere becomes – is a breath of fresh air after the relative hype of Sokratous and Orfeos streets.

Top: The minaret of Ibrahim Pasha mosque
Right: For a change of pace and some peace and quiet, retreat to the Old Town's uncrowded backblocks.

Kahal Shalom Synagogue

The **Kahal Shalom Synagogue** on Dossaïdou is the only operating synagogue in Rhodes. Jews still worship here and it is usually open in the morning. However, the synagogue can only operate when a rabbi is found and dispatched from Jewish communities elsewhere in Greece.

There is a commemorative plaque inside the mosque to the many members of the area's large Jewish population who were sent to Auschwitz during the Nazi occupation. A small one-room museum at the rear of the synagogue serves as a kind of resource focal point for the now widely scattered Rodesli Jewish Diaspora, the majority of whom are now in the United States.

Close by is Plateia Martyron Evreon (Square of the Jewish Martyrs) named in honour of the Jews who were forcibly deported from Rhodes.

The Town Walls & Moat

The enormous and seemingly impregnable walls stretching some 4km around the land side of the Old Town are what give Rhodes its special atmosphere. The current configuration of the walls and their intervening moat were built and strengthened by the Knights of St John during their 200-year tenure on the island in anticipation of Ottoman attacks, which eventually materialised in 1522. The thick (12m), sloping walls repulsed the concerted attacks by Süleyman the Magnificent and it is thought that only treachery rather than superior Ottoman force led to the eventual capture and surrender of Rhodes. More than just walls, the whole defence perimeter is a complex array of fortifications, towers, bastions, moats and gates.

Seven gates (*pyles* – singular *pyli*) allowed entry into the walled city. The most important of these was the **Pyli Ambouaz**, named after Grand Master Emery d'Amboise (1505–12). This heavily-guarded gate gave direct access to the Kollakio and the Palace of the Grand Masters. Moving anticlockwise, **Pyli Agiou Georgiou**, now closed to public entry, is on the west side of the walls. Next along, **Agiou Athanasiou** and **Pyli Agiou Ioanni** both gave outlet to the outside world on the south side of the walls and today serve as public and local

STELLA HELLANDER

Left: Combine some exercise and a close-up view of the Old Town's imposing defences on the moat walking tour.

vehicle access points. This latter gate is also known as the **Koskinou Gate** (after the village of the same name south of Rhodes), though its reference to Agios Ioannis is to **John the Baptist** whose relief features on the portal of the gate.

It's a long run around the southern ramparts to **Pyli Karetou,** another vehicular access point today which leads out onto Akantia harbour. The minuscule **Pyli Mylon** (Windmill Gate), almost hidden and opposite the passenger ferry terminal is for pedestrians only, while cruise-ship passengers and new arrivals at the passenger harbour will commonly enter the Old Town by the **Pyli Panagias**. The **Pyli Agias Ekaterinis** is the main (pedestrian only) entry point from the commercial harbour and drops visitors right smack bang into the middle of activity at **Plateia Ippokratous**.

Pyli Navarhiou (Arsenal Gate) is at the far north-eastern corner of the walls; nearby is **Pyli Eleftherias**, which was created by the Italians in 1912.

Moat Walking Tour

A walk along the beautifully renovated and landscaped **medieval moat** from Pyli Eleftherias to Pyli Karetou will give visitors a chance to appreciate the immensity of the defence system. Allow at least an hour for a leisurely stroll. Strategically positioned towers, each manned by a different 'tongue' of the Grand Knights, protected the walls from assault and along the southern section of the walls you will notice the double walls, giving added protection from would-be besiegers on the land side.

Access to the moats is available at two other gates, other than the entry and exit points. The most obvious is the signposted entry by **Pyli Agiou Antoniou,** inside the walls just after Pyli Ambouaz. The second is less obvious and is via an underground tunnel, signposted off Irodotou on the south side of the Old Town.

You can take a guided walk at 2.45 pm on Tuesday and Saturday (1200 dr). Starting at the courtyard of the Palace of the Grand Masters, the walk takes in the western reaches of the walls and goes as far as Pyli Agiou Ioanni (Koskinou).

Right: People-watching is a favourite pastime in Plateia Ippokratous.

PAUL HELLANDER

Walking Tour

There are myriad permutations in which you can walk around the Old Town and generally get lost, only to emerge later in some familiar territory. That is half the fun. Walk through the narrow back streets of the Turkish and Jewish Quarters (the Hora) and you can feel as though you have been transported back in time to another world – the Middle Ages in fact. This feeling is even more accentuated in the evening with wonderful and perfectly safe-wanders through the dimly-lit inner neighbourhoods.

The following Old Town tour will take about an hour to simply walk. Allow a minimum of half a day if you plan to visit all the sights along the way. Most of the sights are described earlier in this section.

Start walking from **Pyli Eleftherias** (Freedom Gate) on the north side of the Old Town. It was created in 1924 by the Italians, who believed that *they* were the liberators of Rhodes, and is now one of three gates open to vehicular traffic. You will enter **Plateia Symis** and come across the relatively late-discovered, and rather incongruous 3rd century BC remains of the **Temple of Aphrodite**. Continuing south into the Old Town you will come upon **Plateia Argyrokastrou**, dominated by the imposing **Inn of Auvergne** which was built in 1507 by Grand Master Guy de Blanchfort. Opposite is the **Old Knights' Hospital**, built by Grand Master Roger de Pins in 1457.

A cluster of museums offer the option to bone up on Rhodian culture before continuing your walk. The **Byzantine Museum** has an eclectic collection of ecclesiastical art from the smaller churches of Rhodes Old Town as well as outlying and harder-to-reach churches and monasteries around Rhodes. The **Decorative Arts Museum** on Plateia Argyrokastrou has a compelling display of folk art, ceramics and costumes, while the rather lacklustre **Archaeological Museum**, on the corner of Ippoton (the Knight's Street) may tempt the keenest archaeology fan. It is the turn right into Ippoton that is the most impressive feature of this segment of the walk. This stark, commerce-free street running uphill and east-west is a delight to stroll

STELLA HELLANDER

Left: A quick visit to the Clock Tower is a pleasant diversion on the Old Town walking tour.

along, if you don't mind the clusters of camera-wielding Japanese, American and Italian tour groups. Admire the facades of the grandiose **Inns** that once belonged to the various Knights' contingents and note the distinctive coats of arms that identify the various nationalities.

A visit to the **Palace of the Grand Masters** at the western end of Ippoton can easily take a half-day of your time, so perhaps leave it for another occasion. Turn left onto Panetiou following the remains of the walls of the original **Kollakio** and head for the now visible **Clock Tower** and **Süleymaniye Mosque**. A quick visit to the Clock Tower will take no more than 15 minutes and you will be served a free drink for the cost of the entrance fee.

Duck into the now narrow streets of the Turkish Quarter past the 1793 **Ottoman Library** and down Ippodamou. A sign to the Municipal Baths will shortly divert you left to Plateia Arionos and the **Mustafa Pasha Baths**, or public baths. Nowadays, this place is more than likely to be closed, ostensibly 'for repairs'. Following a zigzagging track taking you past the **Nelly Dimoglou Folk Dance Theatre** along Andronikou, you come out at the southern end of Agiou Fanouriou. Turn left here onto **Plateia Dorieos** with its cafes, Internet access, **Recep Pasha Mosque** and ornamental fountain.

Squeeze through a narrow entrance at the southern side of Plateia Dorieos and turn left along Omirou for 100m or so. Turn sharply left onto the narrow Sofokleous (blink and you will miss the turn), through Plateia Sofokleous, past cafes and bars, to the **Ibrahim Pasha Mosque**. Double back, one block over, along Pythagora, taking yet another impossibly narrow side street that links Pythagora with Perikleous, now in the **Jewish Quarter**. The **Kahal Shalom Synagogue** is better approached from the east side. Proceed down to **Plateia Evreon Martyron** and pause by the **Seahorse Fountain** before the longish haul through the centre of the **commercial district** threaded by Aristotelous and Sokratous streets.

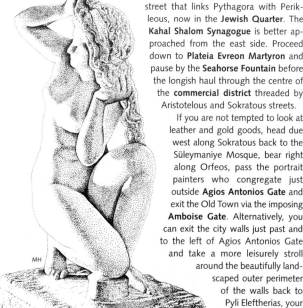

If you are not tempted to look at leather and gold goods, head due west along Sokratous back to the Süleymaniye Mosque, bear right along Orfeos, pass the portrait painters who congregate just outside **Agios Antonios Gate** and exit the Old Town via the imposing **Amboise Gate**. Alternatively, you can exit the city walls just past and to the left of Agios Antonios Gate and take a more leisurely stroll around the beautifully landscaped outer perimeter of the walls back to Pyli Eleftherias, your starting point.

Right: A trip to the Archaeology Museum wouldn't be complete without a visit to the *Aphrodite of Rhodes*.

MH

Places to Stay

There is no better way of soaking up the atmosphere of the Old Town than finding a base right in the middle of the action. With a wide range of hotels and pensions on offer, this medieval district has plenty to choose from, whether you're after a budget pension or historic mansion.

Budget

The comfortable **Mike and Mama's Pension** (☎ 25 359, Menekleous 28) has singles/doubles for 6000/7000 dr. **Mango Rooms** (☎/fax 24 877, [e] karelas@ hotmail.com, Plateia Dorieos 3) has clean, nicely furnished doubles/triples with bathroom, refrigerator, TV and fan for 12,000/15,000 dr.

Hotel Via Via (☎/fax 77 027, [e] viavia@rho.forthnet.gr, Lisipou 2), just off Pythagora, has pristine, tastefully furnished doubles/triples with telephone, fan and fridge for 16,000/20,000 dr. The hotel is open all year.

Pension Minos (☎ 31 813, Omirou 5) has spotless, spacious rooms for 8000/10,000 dr and a roof garden with views of the Old Town. The exceptionally friendly **Pension Andreas** (☎ 34 156, fax 74 285, [e] andreasch@ otenet.gr, Omirou 28D) has clean, pleasant rooms with private bathrooms for 10,000/14,000 dr, and a terrace bar with terrific views. **Kamiros Rooms to Let** (☎ 33 545, Tavriskou 27 and Ikarou 26) is a characterful place (in two separate buildings) with immaculate rooms for 10,000/12,000 dr with bathrooms.

Maria's Rooms (☎ 20 730, Menekleous 147), off Sokratous, has pleasantly furnished doubles for 8000/9000 dr with shared/private bathroom. **Hotel Spot** (☎/fax 34 737, [e] spothot@otenet.gr, Perikleous 21) has exceptionally clean, pleasant singles/doubles for 10,000/12,000 dr with bathroom and ceiling fan. There is also a small book exchange, left luggage facilities and Internet access for guests. The **Pink Elephant** (☎/fax 22 469, Irodotou 42) has doubles/triples with bathroom for 12,000/14,000 dr and doubles without for 10,000 dr. Despite the name, the hotel's attractive decor is blue and white.

Pension Olympos (☎/fax 33 567, Agiou Fanouriou 56) has pleasant singles/doubles for 12,000/16,000 dr with bathroom, television, TV and fridge. It has an attractive little courtyard. If you call beforehand you can be picked up at the airport.

Mid-Range to Top End

Fans of Michael Palin's Pole to Pole TV adventure will remember the **Hotel Cava D'Oro** (☎ 36 980, Kistiniou 15) at the eastern end of the Old Town. Michael Palin stayed in one of the very tasteful old stone rooms in an 800-year-old building. Double/triple rooms with air-conditioning, TV and telephone go for a reasonable 13,000/20,000 dr. This place is accessible by taxi, which is handy if you have lots of luggage.

Featured in glossy European architecture and design magazines is the quietly plush **Marco Polo Mansion** (☎/fax 25 562, [e] marcopolomansion@ hotmail.com, Agiou Fanouriou 40-42), run by owner Efi Dede. This cool and shady lodging is an old-fashioned Anatolian inn decorated in rich Ottoman-era colours. Beds are four poster and are wrapped in rich red drapes. The main hall is done out in traditional Ottoman decor. Rates are between 30,500 dr and 44,000 dr for two people.

Places to Eat

GEORGE TSAFOS

Enthusiastic touting and displays of tacky photographs of food seem to be the order of the day at many of the restaurants in Rhodes Old Town, with the enthusiasm of the touts not always reflected in the quality of the food. Most tout-dominated eateries tend to be within shouting distance of Sokratous and the two squares of Plateia Ippokratous and Plateia Evreon Martyron. If you want to find less touristy places, you'll probably have to hit the back streets.

Budget

Myrovolos (☎ *38 693, Lahitos 13)* is a welcome antidote to Rhodes' tacky tourist restaurants. 'Tourists are welcome here, but we do nothing to attract them,' says the owner. Nothing, that is, except serve some of the most imaginative and reasonably priced dishes in town. These include chicken stuffed with cheese, cuttlefish stuffed with feta and spicy pork.

Taverna Kostas (☎ *26 217, Pythagora 62)* is good value with souvlaki for 1800 dr and swordfish for 2500 dr. The ***Diafani Garden Restaurant*** (☎ *26 053, Plateia Arionos)*, opposite the Turkish bath, serves gratifying, reasonably priced dishes, 'cooked from the heart', as the owner says. It is open for lunch and dinner.

The atmospheric ***Araliki*** (☎ *73 708, Aristofanous 45)* serves creative mezedes while almost next door the ***Synaxaria*** (☎ *36 562, Aristofanous 47)* offers traditional fare with specialities such as cuttlefish with spinach (1700 dr) and lamb fricassée (1900 dr).

The Italian chef at ***Pizza da Spillo*** (*Apellou 41)* conjures up a variety of mouthwatering pizzas. If your feet are killing you after hours of walking the Old Town's pebbled thoroughfares, a pleasant option for a break is ***To Micro Cafe*** (*Evripidou 13-15)*, near the Castellania fountain, which serves coffee and snacks in a tranquil walled garden.

Andonis, on Pythagora at the southern end of the Old Town, is a totally budget and low key souvlaki and grill joint. Few tourists make it up here and this place is mainly dominated by locals.

Top: Fun-loving tourists flock to the cafes on Plateia Ippokratous.

Mid-Range & Top End

Alexis Restaurant *(☎ 29 347, Sokratous 18)* is a first-rate seafood restaurant but is pretty pricey. There is an extensive French wine list and a range of mouthwatering seafood. Bank on a budget between 20,000 dr and 30,000 dr for a seafood meal with wine for two.

If you crave something other than Greek food, **L'Auberge Bistrot** *(☎ 34 292, Praxitelous 21)* serves terrific French/Mediterranean cuisine. The pepper steak and mushroom quiche are highly recommended. A Côte du Rhône rouge costs 3950 dr, while a very decent 1L draft wine will cost 1900 dr. It is open from 7.30 pm to midnight daily.

Cleo's Italian Restaurant *(☎ 28 415, Agiou Fanouriou 17)* is a sophisticated place with a cool, elegant interior and a quiet courtyard. Set menus cost around 4000 dr. **Nisyros** *(☎ 31 741, Agiou Fanouriou 45-47)* is a beautiful and tastefully decorated restaurant with impeccable service and a wide range of Greek dishes. Dining is in a leafy, secluded courtyard and it's open evenings only.

Mystagogia *(☎ 32 981, Themistokleous 5)* opened in late 1999 to considerable local acclaim, drawing its charm as much from the open fireplace for winter dining as its carefully cooked dishes. *Mystagogia* means 'initiation into mystic rites' and this little eatery is great for an initiation into some subtly Greek food away from the touts and plastic offerings only a few hundred metres away.

Entertainment

The **son et lumière** *(☎ 21 922)*, staged in the grounds of the Palace of the Grand Masters, depicts the Turkish siege of Rhodes and is superior to most other efforts. The entrance is on Plateia Rimini and admission is 1200 dr. A noticeboard outside gives the times for performances.

The **Nelly Dimoglou Folk Dance Company** gives first-rate performances at the **Theatre** *(☎ 29 085, 20 157)* on Andronikou, at 9.20 pm nightly except Saturday from May to October. Admission is 3500 dr.

Kafe Besara *(☎ 30 363, Sofokleous 11-12)* is Aussie owned, and one of the Old Town's liveliest bars. Live music is played three evenings a week in summer. The **Mango Cafe Bar** *(Plateia Dorieos 3)* claims to have the cheapest drinks in the Old Town as well as Internet access and is the preferred haunt of local expats, scuba divers and diehard travellers.

The **Resalto Club** *(Plateia Damagitou)* is a Greek music centre featuring live music every night except Tuesday and Wednesday. The repertoire ranges from *entehno* (artistic compositional) to *laïko* (popular) to *rembetiko* (blues). The club opens from 11 pm. Entry is free but beer costs 2000 dr, cocktails 3000 dr and a bottle of French champagne 40,000 dr.

East Coast

The East Coast is home to most of the island's best beaches and as a consequence most of its package accommodation and related tourist facilities are concentrated here. Facilities range from the high class to the frankly garish, while beaches vary from wide and very popular to small and homely. If you like the rough and tumble of the various shades of package tourism, big beaches, adventure sports, a heavy nightlife and doing little but succumbing to the pleasures of eating, drinking and being merry, the East Coast is definitely for you. If you like your island vacation to be more subtle and quiet, keep on going until you get to Southern Rhodes.

It's a fairly long haul on a scooter or underpowered motorbike from Rhodes Town to Lindos – the furthest extent of the beaches described here. Consider a day excursion from Mandraki, in Rhodes Town, to the beach of your choice rather than making the long journey by road just for a swim. With the exception of perhaps Stegna Beach, all beaches can be reached by local buses.

This busy stretch of coast can be tackled two ways. If you are in a hurry to go south, take the inland route from Rhodes Town. If you just plan to make a short day trip loop along the coast, take the coastal road. Note that finding either of these roads from Rhodes Town can be a hit and miss affair. Use your local map judiciously, or you may find yourself heading in the wrong direction.

Getting There & Away

Regular hourly buses link Rhodes Town with destinations up to Faliraki. Buses run two-hourly or so from Faliraki to Lindos. The last bus back from Faliraki is at 10.30 pm.

KOSKINOU TO VLYHA BEACH
Koskinou

Koskinou is a small dormitory village 9km from Rhodes Town. It is famous for its hohlaki courtyards and ornate doorways, and it is also something of an artists' retreat with several having set up home here. You can easily detour to Koskinou from either the inland highway or the coastal road.

A selection of restaurants has made Koskinou a popular night-time destination for Rhodian diners. One of its best-kept culinary secrets is *Giannis Restaurant (☎ 0241-63 547)*. The cosy taverna, set in a narrow paved alleyway in the back streets, is open only in the evenings; it's small, intimate and an absolute delight. Try Symi prawns, suckling pig, or baby pumpkin among its wide range of tasty dishes. Easily reached by taxi from Rhodes Town, Giannis Restaurant is a hit.

Kallithea

Kallithea is the nearest beach to Rhodes Town and is consequently very popular and busy. Kallithea is a rather odd former spa resort that was, in fact, built by the Italians. It consists of a couple of narrow sandy beaches, a rocky headland and the crumbling buildings of the art deco former resort. It is slowly being renovated, but it's all a bit messy at the moment. There is good swimming in the shallow protected water and it's a good family beach with ample facilities. The Rhodes scuba diving fraternity is based here so you will be sharing water space with black-clad frogpersons.

There are buses travelling every 30 minutes or so to and from Rhodes Town and Kallithea (450 dr).

Faliraki

Faliraki, 10km south of Koskinou, is ostensibly the island's premier resort and comes complete with high-rise hotels, fast-food joints and bars. There is very little that can be said in favour of the place if you don't like noise, kitsch, bad taste and excess. Its reputation for sleaze and booze is only matched by that of Kardamena on the island of Kos.

The northern end of Faliraki is given over to expensive, high rise and – it must be said – rather well-appointed luxury hotels. Unless you are on a package, or have chosen to mix it with the package beach-goers on their public beaches, you are unlikely to be staying here. For the independent traveller it is also rather impersonal and overbearing.

RHODES

The main resort of Faliraki essentially consists of one main restaurant and bar strip running at right angles to the beach and a series of spaces devoted to extreme and bumpy activities. Here you can bungie jump, skysurf, rocket, ride the Octopussy, or go-kart to your heart's content and still have time to do the donut ring, the big banana, windsurf for an hour or so *and* pack in a game of five-a-side soccer before it's time to crack your first Bacardi Breezer. That's Faliraki for you. The Fun & Action Windsurfing School is one place you may care to check out. You'll find them on the main beach.

If you get into trouble after all this contact the tourist police on ☎ 23 329, seek first aid on ☎ 85 555, or order an ambulance on ☎ 22 222.

Faliraki Beach Faliraki Beach is the waterfront beach of the eponymous and decidedly tacky resort. The wide, sandy beach is generally fine though much space is given over to water sports and 'extreme' activities. The beach is always crowded, but you will find a quiet spot somewhere – eventually. To the north of Faliraki village is a long sandy beach that fronts a stretch of luxury tourist hotels. It is used mainly by hotel guests, though it is open to all visitors. If you want to bathe starkers, just head to the southern end.

There are buses about every 30 minutes to and from Rhodes Town and Faliraki (450 dr).

Places to Stay For the budget traveller, there's *Faliraki Camping (☎ 0241-85 358)*, which has a restaurant, bar, minimarket and swimming pool. The bus stop is located close to the beach.

Most accommodation is monopolised by package tour companies, but a pleasant option for independent travellers is the Greek-American owned *Cannon Bar Pension (☎ 0241-85 596)* on Poseidon St in Faliraki, where doubles/triples with bathrooms cost 10,000/12,000 dr.

There are two decent upmarket hotels in Faliraki village, very close to the beach. The *Faliraki Beach Hotel (☎ 0241-85 301, fax 85 675)* and the *Apollo Beach*

Hotel (☎ 0241-85 513, fax 85 823) will charge you around 20,000 dr for a well appointed and reasonably quiet double room.

Places to Eat Dining in Faliraki is basically hit and miss. If you are serious about eating here, you might as well have a curry at the *Faliraki Raj (☎ 0241-86 986, Lindou)* opposite the church. It makes a spicy change from mousakas. Also near the church is *La Strada Ristorante (☎ 0241-85 878, Lindou)*, which offers up crispy wood-oven pizzas, and over 100 imaginative variations of pasta, fish and meat.

Entertainment For high-octane, home-style entertainment, stick around. If you are hankering after a decent pint and some good Gaelic *craic*, look no further than *Kelly's Irish Bar* for Guinness & Caffreys ales and an assortment of other draft beers served with the occasional burst of live music. Kelly's is opposite the Apollo Beach Hotel.

Scottspeople can sip on a pint of Mc-Ewans or draft Tennants and watch Billy Connolly videos at *The Tartan Arms*, the only Scottish pub in Rhodes. Regular imbibers can drink two of their fancy for the price of one between 7.30 and 9.30 pm at the *Camel Bar* on the main street.

If you are looking for Greek entertainment, don't come to Faliraki.

Traganou, Afandou & Kolymbia Beaches

These three beaches constitute a long uninterrupted stretch of sand from a headland just south of Faliraki to Cape Vagia, some 8km to the south. It is a surprisingly undeveloped part of the coast and there are large stretches of underpopulated sand and pebble to be enjoyed by bathers seeking space. Perhaps the overall openness of the three beaches is the reason for their lack of mass popularity. Umbrella and beach lounger rentals are few and far between, as are cafes and restaurants. The exception to this very low-key beach scene is to be found at the southern end of Kolymbia Beach, which has something that better resembles a resort atmosphere.

Fourni Beach on Rhodes' west coast, a protected haven for sun-lovers seeking some peace and quiet

A typical Greek nosh-up

Dodecanesian handicrafts

Valley of the Butterflies, Rhodes

The stunning Castle of Monolithos perches atop a sheer 240m rock on Rhodes' west coast.

Wild and windy, Rhodes' Prasonisi beach can be a hazard for swimmers, but pure joy for windsurfers.

The Acropolis of Rhodes, gone to rack and ruin

It's a goat's life on Rhodes' west coast.

God works in mysterious ways.

Golfers can play a round or two at the well-equipped Rhodes Golf Club (☎ 51 255) at Afandou Bay, 18km from Rhodes Town. Green fees for casual visitors are 6000 dr a day or 32,000 dr for a week (seven rounds maximum). Clubs can be hired for between 2000 dr and 4000 dr a round, plus a further 500 dr for a buggy.

There are more or less hourly buses to and from Afandou Beach and Rhodes Town (450 dr) and nine buses daily to and from Kolymbia (650 dr).

Tsambika Beach

Tsambika Beach is a very large, very wide and very sandy beach sited in its own cove under the watchful eye of the monastery of the same name, the **Moni Panagias Tsambikas**. Tsambika beach has a reputation as a 'fun beach'. There is something for everyone – from the usual plethora of rental umbrellas and loungers to water sports, restaurants, showers, ample parking and, thankfully for some, no large resort complexes. You may find restaurants with occasional live music and possibly even Greek dancing lessons. Duck into *Zorba's Taverna* to see if anything is on.

The best section of the beach is the northern end, past the large rock. Boats can be rented for 4000 dr for 30 minutes, pedal boats for 2500 dr and canoes cost 1000 dr for an hour.

There is one bus daily from Rhodes Town to Tsambika Beach (650 dr) at 9 am, which returns to Rhodes Town at 4 pm.

Moni Panagias Tsambikas

A steep road (signposted from the main highway south of Faliraki) leads in 1.5km to Moni Tsambikas, from where there are terrific views. It is a place of pilgrimage for childless women. On 18 September, the monastery's festival day, they climb up to it on their knees and pray to conceive.

Stegna Beach

Stegna Beach is a fairly narrow, 500m stretch of coarse sand and pebble backed by a disproportionate amount of building development in the form of holiday homes and domatia. The beach and sea don't have a good reputation among local Rhodians and most keep away – the suspicion being that the water quality is less than pristine. In fairness, it is a fairly low-key place and superficially pleasant enough, but if you have come this far down under your own steam, you are perhaps better advised to head for the next beach. There are no direct buses to Stegna Beach.

Arhangelos

Arhangelos, 4km farther on and inland from Stegna Beach, is a large agricultural village with a tradition of carpet weaving and handmade goatskin boot production. Both local industries are being overtaken by tourism as the major money-earner.

Agathi Beach

Agathi Beach is perhaps the best beach on this stretch for those looking for the right combination of solitude, sand and water quality, facilities, and the sense of being on an island beach. Agathi Beach is nestled between two sandstone headlands on the northern side of Haraki village. It is sandy, just wide enough to give you a sense of space and enjoys clean, aquamarine water. There are three beach *snack bars* (the middle one is the best one), beach showers, rental umbrellas, loungers and 'donut rings' if you like to be dragged at high speed behind a motorboat and then unceremoniously dumped into the water.

There are two buses daily from Rhodes Town to Haraki (750 dr) from where it is a 1.5km walk to Agathi Beach. To save yourself some sandal leather, ask the bus driver to drop you off at the Agathi Beach turn-off before you reach Haraki.

The **Castle of Faraklos** above Agathi was a prison for recalcitrant knights and the island's last stronghold to fall to the Turks.

Vlyha Beach

Vlyha Beach is the last major beach before Lindos and is appreciated by bathers who don't like the Lindos Beach crowds. It is at the southern end of a long, 10km stretch of open beach and is home to a couple of

RHODES

rather large resort hotels. Still, it is sandy, clean and undeniably popular with all the expected facilities of a major beach.

There are two buses daily (1000 dr) to Vlyha from Rhodes Town, but only one bus back at the inconvenient time of 10 am.

LINDOS Λίνδος
☎ 0244 • postcode 851 07 • pop 900

Lindos (lin-dhos) village, 47km from Rhodes, lies below the Acropolis and is a showpiece of dazzling white 17th-century houses, many with courtyards with black and white *hohlakia* (pebble mosaic) floors. The village is unquestionably pretty and atmospheric but its charm is severely put to the test between 10 am and 4 pm daily when literally thousands of day-trippers swamp this hapless settlement. Studiously *avoid* Lindos between these times. Come earlier (from 8 to 10 am), or in the evening when Lindos has once more returned to some semblance of normality.

Its attraction is its location, draped across the shoulder of the all-dominating **Acropolis**, with views on both sides of the village down to crystal clear water. Its beautiful, old traditional houses were once the dwellings of wealthy admirals. Many have been bought and restored by foreign celebrities, including – so rumour has it – Roger Waters of Pink Floyd. To fully appreciate Lindos, take some time exploring the labyrinthine alleyways, as the main thoroughfares are lined with tourist shops and cafes.

The 15th-century **Church of Agia Panagia**, on Acropolis, is festooned with 18th-century frescoes.

Orientation
Lindos' narrow approach road, usually clogged with arriving and departing pedestrians, ends in the busy Main Square (Plateia Eleftherias) dominated and shaded by a large plane tree. The bus stop, taxi rank and tourist information office are in the square. Just before the square a road turns sharply to the left and leads down to Lindos' main beach.

Drivers should get in early to find a parking spot, or leave the car on the main road away from Lindos village. There is parking along the approach road as well as on the Lindos Beach road. A better option is to park on the southern side of the village at a largely underused and enormous parking lot. Continue south past the Lindos village turn-off to reach it.

From the main square onwards Lindos is totally pedestrianised. A donkey station is 50m along on the right as you enter the village. Donkeys are used to ferry people to and from the Acropolis.

Information
Tourist Offices The municipal tourist information office (☎ 31 900, fax 31 288) on Plateia Eleftherias has some stylised maps of Lindos village and is open 7.30 am to 9 pm daily. Pallas Travel (☎ 31 494, fax 31 595) and Lindos Sun Tours (☎ 31 333) on Acropolis have room-letting services. The latter also rents out cars and motorcycles.

Money The Commercial Bank of Greece, with ATM, is by the donkey station. The National Bank of Greece is on the street opposite the Church of Agia Panagia.

Post & Communications Turn right at the donkey terminus for the post office. There is no OTE, but there are cardphones on Plateia Eleftherias, the main beach and the Acropolis.

Kafeneio Internet Cafe (☎ 32 116, [e] lindosinternetcafe@yahoo.com), near the post office, is open from 9 to 1.30 am. Access costs 1000 dr per 30 minutes. The Lindianet Internet Cafe (☎ 32 142, [e] lindianet@lindianet.gr) is open from 10 am to midnight (4 to 9 pm in winter) and charges 500 dr per 20 minutes (minimum). It is near the China Town restaurant (see Places to Eat).

Mobile phone users will pick up all three Greek GSM mobile service providers.

Internet Resources The useful Web site www.lindianet.gr has a good range of traveller information on Lindos itself.

Travel Agencies A fair number of travel agencies in Lindos offer the full gamut of services from room-finding to car hire. Interestingly, a number offer cheap one-way flights back to the UK using unused seats on charter flights out of Rhodes airport. Pallas Travel (☎ 31 494, fax 31 595) and Savaïdis Travel (☎ 31 347, 31 451, ⓔ info@savaidis-travel.gr), both on Rodou, are reputable agencies.

Bookshops The privately owned Lindos Lending Library, on Acropolis, is well stocked with English books and has a selection of Italian, German and French titles.

Laundry The Lindos Lending Library on Acropolis also has a laundrette (2500 dr per load) which is, oddly enough, its main business.

Dangers & Annoyances Getting to the Acropolis of Lindos between 11 am and 3 pm can be a serious trial, with thousands of people trying to do the same thing at the same time. The winding path up to the entrance is narrow, progress can be painfully slow and the waiting time to get in through the narrow Acropolis entrance to the ticket booth can be anywhere between 10 and 30 minutes. Go early or late, if you want to get in without a hassle.

The Acropolis of Lindos

Lindos is the most famous of the Dodecanese's ancient cities, receiving 500,000 visitors a year. It was an important Doric settlement because of its excellent vantage point and good harbour. It was first established around 2000 BC and is overlaid with a conglomeration of Byzantine, Frankish and Turkish remains.

After the founding of the city of Rhodes, Lindos declined in commercial importance, but remained an important place of worship. The ubiquitous St Paul landed here en route to Rome. The Byzantine fortress was strengthened by the knights, and also used by the Turks.

The Acropolis of Lindos is spectacularly perched atop a 116m-high rock. It's about a 10-minute climb to the well signposted entrance gate. Once inside, a flight of steps leads to a large square. On the left (facing the next flight of steps) is a *trireme* (warship) hewn out of the rock by the sculptor Pythocretes. A statue of Hagesandros, priest of Poseidon, originally stood on the deck

RHODES

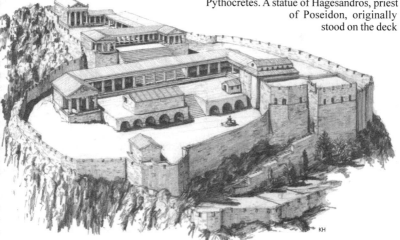

The imposing Acropolis of Lindos as it would have been some 4000 years ago

of the ship. At the top of the steps ahead, you enter the acropolis by a vaulted corridor. At the other end, turn sharply left through an enclosed room to reach a row of storerooms on the right. The stairway on the right leads to the remains of a 20-columned **Hellenistic stoa** (200 BC). The Byzantine **Church of Agios Ioannis** is to the right of this stairway. The wide stairway behind the stoa leads to a 5th century BC propylaeum, beyond which is the 4th-century **Temple to Athena**, the site's most important ancient ruin. Athena was worshipped on Lindos as early as the 10th century BC; this temple has replaced earlier ones on the site. From its far side there are splendid views of Lindos village and its beach.

Donkey rides to the acropolis cost 1000 dr one way. The site is open 8 am to 6.30 pm Tuesday to Sunday and 12.30 pm to 6.30 pm Monday. Admission is 1200 dr.

Beaches

Lindos' **Main Beach**, featured on all the pretty Lindos postcards, is to the north of the village. With its three lines of beach umbrellas and loungers, its protected sandy cove and generally clean-looking water, the beach is popular – and nearly always crowded. There is a range of beach restaurants, none of which can be seriously recommended, and it's all very twee and touristy.

St Paul's Beach on the southern side of Lindos is ostensibly where Paul landed in AD 58 to evangelise the Rhodians. This quieter, sandy cove is much smaller and almost cut off from the sea by an impossibly narrow opening which is said to have miraculously opened up when St Paul was looking for a place to land.

Places to Stay

Accommodation is generally expensive and reservations are essential in summer. Pickings are not huge, though you will always find somewhere if you look around or ask at the Tourist Information Office.

Fedra Rooms to Rent (☎ 31 286), along the street opposite the Church of Agia Panagia, has doubles/triples for 8000/10,000 dr with bathroom. *Pension Electra (☎ 31 266)*,

along the road leading to Lindos Beach, has a roof terrace with superb views and a beautiful shady garden; doubles with shared bathroom cost 14,000 dr, and double/triple studios cost 14,000/16,000 dr. To get there, follow the signs to the Acropolis but don't turn right at Restaurant Aphrodite – carry on towards the beach. *Pension Katholiki (☎ 31 445)*, next door, has six double rooms with private bathroom for 16,000 dr.

Places to Eat

Dining in Lindos is best enjoyed at night, once the day-trippers have gone home. Lindos makes a big (and justifiable deal) out of its rooftop dining scene – impossible during the day thanks to the merciless sun, but very enjoyable and atmospheric at night.

A moonlight meat meal for two with a bottle of Rhodian wine will cost around 9000 dr. There are *many* choices in Lindos.

Mavrikos (☎ 31 232), on the main square, has been around since 1933 and serves up tried and tested dishes at a reasonable price. *The Kalypso (☎ 31 669)* is set in one of Lindos' historic buildings and is open for lunch and dinner. Try either sausages in mustard, chicken in coconut sauce, rabbit stew in red wine or a vegetarian platter of spring rolls, mushrooms and vegetables of the day – all for under 2000 dr a dish. For a special treat order lamb *horiatiko* (lamb cooked village-style in a brick oven) the day before; it costs around 2000 dr per person.

Cyprus Taverna (☎ 31 539), on the stairs leading up to the Acropolis, serves Cypriot food such as *afelia* and *sheftalia*, or large mezes meals (7000 dr for two people). It's open from 11 am to 3 pm and 6 to 11 pm.

Taverna Dionysos (☎ 31 810), in the middle of Lindos towards the Acropolis, is one of many places you can dine al fresco on the roof – magic during the full moon. The food is average in quality, but large on servings (around 2000 dr for a main dish). It is open for lunch and dinner, but dinner is definitely the best time to dine.

Maria's Taverna (☎ 31 375) is a neat, smart restaurant that is open for dinner only and has a wide selection of meat- and fish-based dishes. Nearby, *China Town (☎ 31*

RHODES

983) has a cool, green garden and offers up a wide range of Chinese-Malay dishes if you fancy a change from the omnipresent Greek cuisine.

El Greco Cafe is good for a quick coffee and apple pie, or ice cream and crepes.

Entertainment
There is no shortage of watering holes in Lindos – most of them noisy and raucous. If you really like to drink in peace and quiet look for the *Captain's House Bar*, the only place in Lindos where they play exclusively classical music for guests. Housed in an old, earthquake-proof house belonging to the Ganotakis family and built in the 17th century, you can sip a cool gin and tonic (900 dr) in a small, hohlakia-paved courtyard and relax to Mozart or Vivaldi.

The *Museum Bar* on the other hand is the place to go to watch live sports over a beer or five. Housed in the former museum, the bar is classy and subtle despite the plasma TV screens.

Getting There & Around
Buses to and from Rhodes Town run more or less hourly from 8.30 am (1100 dr) with a further eight buses daily linking Lindos with Pefkos (300 dr) farther south. The last bus back to Rhodes is at about 7 pm.

Excursion caïques run daily from Rhodes Town. Dependence on the bus or the caïque service, however, will not allow you to dine at night in Lindos.

A free shuttle bus service ferries visitors to and from the main through road and the main square in Lindos.

Given the almost certain pedestrian crush to get up to the Lindos Acropolis, the 1000 dr you spend on a donkey ride up the quicker back route may well be pocket money wisely invested.

West Coast

Western Rhodes is more green and forested than the east coast, but its exposure to the windy Aegean, as opposed to the quieter Mediterranean on the east coast, means that the sea tends to be rough. The beaches here are mostly of pebbles or stones. It is here that Rhodes' tourist industry originally took off. The coast from Rhodes Town as far as the airport is an almost contiguous resort strip consisting of the suburb resorts of Ixia, Trianda and Kremasti. The coast is home to two of Rhodes' more important archaeological sites and visitors to the Petaloudes Valley will pass this way en route. Rhodes airport is just outside the village of Paradisi, which despite being next to the airport, has retained some of the feel of a traditional village.

IXIA TO MONOLITHOS
The beach scene at **Ixia**, the starting point of this strip of coast, is surprisingly good, despite its proximity to Rhodes New Town. The water can be startlingly blue and though more prone to northerly winds, this beach is very popular. From Ixia, large hotel complexes and many restaurants line the road, and a constant throng of tourists walk, lilos in tow, to and from the beaches. The whole area is geared to the package tour industry and doesn't offer a lot in the way of a 'travellers scene' as such.

It's difficult to know where the overgrown coastal village of **Trianda** (8.5km from Rhodes Town) begins and ends. A sign to **Ialysos Beach** at the northern end of Trianda will lead you to an extended beach resort running almost up to the perimeter fence of the airport near the village of Kremasti. While it's unfair to criticise the whole scene, it is equally hard to say much in favour of it all. The bars, hotels, restaurants and even accommodation are all dominated by short-term foreign holidaymakers and while there is undoubtedly plenty to do, eat and drink, it's all very watered-down and un-Greek and not unlike 'tourist resorts' throughout the whole Mediterranean region.

The scene is noticeably different south of the airport where a quiet, almost rural complacency takes over. Perhaps the sight of the rather ugly Rhodes power station south of **Paradisi** has something to do with it. Either way, beach annexes become fewer and restaurant pickings thinner as you head down the next 35km or so of unremarkable coast to **Skala Kamirou**, the next break of any substance along this coast after the airport.

Ancient Ialysos Αρχαία Ιαλυσός

The coast is home to two archaeological sites and both are the regular targets of tour buses and individual travellers alike. Like Lindos, **Ialysos** (ee-al-ee-**sos**), 10km from Rhodes, is a hotchpotch of Doric, Byzantine and medieval remains. The Doric city was built on **Filerimos Hill**, which was an excellent vantage point, attracting successive invaders. The only ancient remains are the foundations of a 3rd century BC temple and a restored 4th century BC fountain. Also at the site are the restored **Monastery of Our Lady** and the **Chapel of Agios Georgios**.

The ruined fortress was used by Süleyman the Magnificent during his siege of Rhodes Town. The site is open 8 am to 7 pm Tuesday to Sunday. Admission is 800 dr.

While you are up here you may care to detour 500m to the large **Cross of Filerimos** south along the tree-lined path of the **Stations of the Cross**, both built by the Italians. This enormous cement cross overlooks the plain to the south and is visible from a great distance. At night the cross is illuminated and can be seen from far out to sea. A winding and extremely narrow staircase takes you up to the arms of the cross. Time your climb up carefully as there is only room for one-way traffic and some people will have to backtrack if there is a crowd in the cross. Entry is free.

No buses go to Ancient Ialysos. The airport bus stops at Trianda, on the coast. Ialysos is 5km inland from here. You will spot many people walking up along the main road from Trianda. While this is undoubtedly very admirable and healthy, it is also a *long* and tiring walk and the road is not all that suitable for pedestrians as it is used by a constant stream of tour buses and cars. You are better advised to share a cab.

Ancient Kamiros Αρχαία Κάμειρος

The extensive ruins of the Doric city of Kamiros (**ka**-mee-ros) stand on a hillside above the west coast, 34km from Rhodes

Town. The ancient city, known for its figs, oil and wine, reached the height of its powers in the 6th century BC. By the 4th century BC, it had been superseded by Rhodes. Most of the city was destroyed by earthquakes in 226 BC and 142 BC, but the layout is easily discernible.

From the entrance, walk straight ahead and down the steps. The semicircular rostrum on the right is where officials made speeches to the public. Opposite are the remains of a **Doric temple** with one standing column. The area next to it, with a row of intact columns, was probably where the public watched the priests performing rites in the temple. From here, you can ascend the wide stairway to the ancient city's main street. Opposite the top of the stairs is one of the best preserved of the **Hellenistic houses** which lined the street.

Walk along the street, ascend three flights of steps, and continue straight ahead to the ruins of the 3rd-century **great stoa**, which had a 206m portico supported by two rows of Doric columns. It was built on top of a huge 6th-century cistern which supplied the houses with rainwater through an advanced drainage system. Behind the stoa, at the city's highest point, stood the **Temple to Athena**, with terrific views inland.

All in all, Ancient Kamiros is a relatively impressive site, certainly more so than Ancient Ialysos, which pales in comparison. It is similar in feel and layout to the **Sanctuary of the Great Gods** on the island of Samothraki, though any historical connection ends here.

The site is open 8 am to 7 pm Tuesday to Sunday. Admission is 800 dr. Buses from Rhodes Town to Kamiros stop on the coast road, 1km from the site.

Skala Kamirou to Monolithos

Skala Kamirou, 13.5km south of Ancient Kamiros, is a fairly unremarkable place sporting a few market gardens, a scattering of tavernas and a petrol station. More importantly, it serves as the access port for travellers heading to and from the island of Halki (see the Southern Dodecanese chapter). Buses to/from Rhodes stop on the main road from where it is a 300m walk to the little harbour to catch the daily caïque at 2 pm. Travellers to Halki with cars can leave them in a carpark next to the harbour.

Shortly after Skala Kamirou, make a detour right to visit the ruins of the 16th-century **Castle of Kritinia**, known locally as Kastellos, 1.5km along a narrow winding road. This small but impressively-sited fortification was built within strategic beacon-sight of a similar castle on Halki, which you can make out on a clear day. The visibility of one castle by the other is a detail that was no doubt carefully considered by the builders of both structures.

From the castle the road now winds up and inland towards the village of Kritinia, passing a **folkloric museum** to the left of the main road which skirts the village itself. The highway winds slowly southwards with occasional good views through the trees to Halki to the west, while the bald hulk of **Mt Atavyros** (1216m) looms to the east.

About 4km south of Kritinia you may choose to cut inland and make a visit to the **wineries** in the village of **Embonas**, 5km away. Touted as an authentic mountain village, Embonas is nonetheless a busy working village deriving much of its income from the cultivation of grapes and production of wine and from the many tourists who purchase, or drink the rather excellent drop. The **Emery Winery** (☎ 0246-29 111) is on the north side of the village. Here you can enjoy free wine tasting until 3 pm on weekdays.

If you have both the time and the inclination, it is recommended that you make a clockwise loop of Mt Atavyros from Embonas, passing through many vineyards and smallholdings until you reach the totally untouristy village of **Agios Isidoros**, 17km from Embonas. From here you can head out through thick pine forest and rolling hills along unsealed but driveable roads to the villages of either **Laerma**, or **Profilia** (see also Southern Rhodes). If you choose to return to the coastal road, a further 6.5km will bring you back to the main north-south highway.

It is another 9km to **Siana**, a picturesque village below Mt Akramytis (823m), famous for its honey and *souma*, a local firewater. The village of **Monolithos**, 5km beyond Siana, has the spectacularly-sited **Castle of Monolithos** perched on a sheer 240m rock – the 'monolith'. Follow the signs to the west of Monolithos to reach the castle, which at first glimpse looks totally impregnable. Lower down the road you will find a small carpark and access path to the castle itself. Like the Castle of Kritinia, the Castle of Monolithos is in beacon-sight of the castle on Halki, which is visible to the north-west.

Before returning to Monolithos village you can drive down a very winding, 6km road from just below the castle to **Fourni Beach**, perhaps the last protected beach along this southern shoreline. This quiet swimming locale is a series of fine gravelly coves with some shade from trees backing the beaches, but no facilities other than a seasonal cantina. You have to leave the way you came in, as there is no ongoing exit route.

Places to Stay & Eat

There is little accommodation choice along this stretch of coast, but if you want to stay somewhere, *Hotel Thomas* (☎ 0246-61 291, fax 28 834) at Monolithos has doubles for around 10,000 dr.

There are at least three places to eat at Skala Kamirou, but the most convenient spot to have lunch while waiting for your caïque to Halki is at the *Althemeni Restaurant* (☎ 0246-31 303) on the harbourfront, which touts itself as a fish restaurant – hardly surprising for a fishing port.

In Monolithos and overlooking the turnoff to the castle is the *Panorama Restaurant*. It's reasonable, though it can get busy if a tour bus pulls in. Move on if it looks like the crowds have arrived.

Central Rhodes

Central Rhodes is an area of little traffic and even less public transport, forested mountains, quiet mountain villages, the odd Byzantine church or two and home to the fastest disappearing tourist attraction in Rhodes – black- and red-winged butterflies.

You will need your own transport to get around and most of the places described here can be seen on a long, but leisurely day trip from Rhodes Town.

PETALOUDES Πεταλούδες

Petaloudes (pe-ta-**lou**-dhez), or Valley of the Butterflies, is unfortunately one of the 'must sees' on the package tour itinerary. This quiet, forested valley is reached along a 6km turn-off from the west coast road, 2.5km south of Paradisi.

The so-called 'butterflies' *(Callimorpha quadripunctarea)* are in fact strikingly coloured moths with red and black mottled wings that are lured to this gorge of rustic footbridges, streams and pools by the scent of the resin exuded by the styrax trees. However, when it is at rest the striking coloured patterns are not visible. This in turn tempts tourists to make a noise in order to make the moths fly. But this is potentially their undoing. By resting they are reserving energy for their reproductive cycle. Without sufficient rest they cannot reproduce adequately.

This chronic and unjustifiable noise pollution is causing a drastic seasonal reduction in the numbers of these splendid insects. Instead of strictly limiting access to the park, authorities have simply increased entry fees, which has done nothing more than bolster the coffers of the local authorities.

The best thing you can do for Rhodes' 'butterflies' is to leave them alone and avoid the Petaloudes site. If you feel you must see moths attempting to rest and witness ignorant visitors doing their best to disturb them, then Petaloudes is open 8.30 am to 6.30 pm daily from 1 May to 30 September. Admission is 750 dr. There are buses to Petaloudes from Rhodes Town.

AROUND PETALOUDES

From Petaloudes a winding cross-island road leads first to the 18th-century **Moni Kalopetras**, built by Alexander Ypsilandis, the grandfather of the Greek freedom fighter. A small snack bar here sells soft drinks and *loukoumades*. This same road leads

across the central mountain spine of roads through a rather dry landscape full of olive trees to the pretty village of **Psinthos**, which makes for a very pleasant lunch break.

A great restaurant in Psinthos is the *Pigi Fasouli Estiatorio (☎ 0241-500 071)*. Tables are set out under cool plane trees next to running water and while it is fine to dine here at any time, Sunday lunch when the place is buzzing is optimal. Main meat dishes are all under 2000 dr. Follow the signs from the main square.

Also in Psinthos, *Artemidis Restaurant & Rooms (☎ 0246-51735)* has a swimming pool and double rooms above the restaurant for 10,000 dr. The restaurant serves tasty traditional Greek fare.

From Psinthos you can choose to loop back to Rhodes Town (22km) via a fast but undistinguished direct route passing through **Kalythies**, or to head farther south and pick up the very pretty cross-island route from **Kolymbia** to **Salakos**.

MT PROFITIS ILIAS & SALAKOS
Ορος Προφήτης Ηλίας & Σάλακος

This route to Mt Profitis Ilias (pro-**fee**-tis ee-**lee**-as) and Salakos (**sah**-la-kos) across the north central highlands of Rhodes is perhaps the most scenic of all the day-trip drives or rides you can conveniently make out of Rhodes Town. It can be tackled from either the west or the east coast of Rhodes, though if coming from Psinthos it is more logical to tackle it from east to west.

The route begins in practice at a signposted turn-off near Kolymbia. Shortly after the Kolymbia junction you may decide to stop briefly to visit **Epta Piges** (seven springs), a cool shady valley with running water and…seven springs. This is a popular tourist attraction in its own right and you can hardly miss the fleet of tour buses parked precariously on the main road indicating the entrance.

If you are on a motorbike, or in a car, follow the steep road up to the left for several hundred metres until you reach the main area. Tour bus visitors walk up from the main road. If you're hungry, you'll find that there's a taverna here that serves lunch.

If you head up and inland you will next come to the small villages of **Arhipoli** and **Eleousa**, once used by the Italians as hill stations. In shady and pleasant Eleousa you can hardly miss the abandoned **summer mansion** of the former Italian governor, while at the western end of the village you will pass an enormous art deco **ornamental pool**. The road now begins climbing through a landscape that becomes more and more forested. Around 2km from Eleousa you will pass the small Byzantine **Church of Agios Nikolaos Fountouklis**. It's nothing really special, as the presumably once bright frescoes are now very grubby, but it makes a good picnic spot and there are tables, chairs and spring water.

It is another 6km through a winding, pine-shrouded road to the 'summit' of **Mt Profitis Ilias** (780m), indicated by a curiously out of place **alpine lodge**, once a resort hotel used by Italians prior to 1948. The summit of the mountain itself – the third highest in Rhodes – is actually out of bounds, as it's used by the military as a radar facility. While the surrounding lush greenery is pleasantly cool and refreshing, views down to the plains to the north are frustratingly elusive. In fact, you have to park and walk in order to enjoy the splendid views. The road this far is not unpleasantly steep, but cyclists should allow plenty of time and be reasonably fit, since the approach to the summit is fairly long.

Downhill from here and another 12km of winding and cruising will bring you to the village of **Salakos**, less than 3km directly north of the summit that you have just left. If you are on foot you can walk down on an established track that begins near the easy-to-find **Moni Profiti Ilia**. It will take you about 45 minutes to make the trek down to Salakos.

The village is a cheery place, with a small square and fountain and several cafes for coffee or cold beers. Salakos is also the home of the locally produced and bottled *Nymfi Spring Water*.

If you want to stay overnight, the ***Hotel Nymfi*** (☎ *0246-22 206)* has double rooms for 10,000 dr. Make sure you give this hotel

a call first since its opening times are not always predictable.

From Salakos it is now only another 9.5km downhill to the west coast village of **Kalavarda**.

Southern Rhodes

The long lonely stretches of coastline from Lindos down to the southern tip of Rhodes at Prasonisi becomes the domain of the independent traveller. High-rise hotels give way to small rural villages, shingled dune-backed beaches, monasteries and churches with impressive frescoes and at least one settlement that looks as if nothing has changed for the last 100 years.

Public transport in this southern sector is reduced to thrice-weekly bus services and the greatest amount of traffic is generated by hire car drivers determined not to leave a corner of the island unexplored. This is a Rhodes a world away from the sometimes excessive north. It is a great base for a week or so, but to appreciate it you will need two or four wheels of your own.

LINDOS TO GENNADI

Immediately south of Lindos (**lin**-dhos) is the last package resort of any kind. The village of **Pefki** is developing fairly quickly, but it is spread out enough to allow the visitor some sense of space. Pre-booked package accommodation is the norm here, most of it being the self-catering studio type. Restaurants and related tourist services are developing steadily, Pefki still has a somewhat slow, family destination feel to it. It's a good alternative base to Lindos, without the crushing crowds.

Lardos is a pleasant village 6km west of Lindos and 2km inland from Lardos Beach. It pulls in a fair slice of the passing tourist trade and there is even a well-equipped Internet Cafe. From the west side of Lardos a turn right leads in 4km to **Moni Agias Ypsenis** (Monastery of Our Lady) through hilly, green countryside.

The well-watered village of **Laerma** is around 12km north-west of Lardos, and the approach road from Lardos is deceptively fast. Drivers and riders should take care on this route. Just a couple of kilometres before Laerma, the wide fast road suddenly gives way, without warning, to its original state – a narrow winding rural road.

From Laerma it's another 4km (signposted) to the beautifully sited 9th-century **Moni Tharri**, the island's first monastery, which has recently been re-established as a monastic community. It contains some fine 13th-century frescoes.

From Laerma you can return the same way to Lardos or take an unsealed, picturesque rural road to **Profilia** (10km) where you can pick up the trans-island highway after 3.5km. The road is quite driveable (with care) in a conventional vehicle, but this whole area is the recreational playground of the Rhodes 4WD set, to put things in some perspective.

Heading south from Lardos, try not to miss the almost hidden **Glystra Beach**, 4km south along the coast road. This diminutive bay would have to be one of the best swimming spots along the whole eastern coastline of Rhodes.

A further 4.5km south you will come to the turn-off for **Asklipion**, an unspoilt village with the ruins of yet another castle with fine views over the Rhodes hinterland and a wide river plain immediately to the south. Asklipion is also home to the 11th-century **Church of Kimisis Theotokou** with surprisingly good and even unusual frescoes. More akin to the Troödos Mountains church frescoes in Cyprus, the biblical scenes are intensely didactic, presented in a series of panels, almost like a cartoon.

Finally, there is a developing resort of sorts at **Kiotari**, 4km before the next major port of call at **Gennadi**. Kiotari is a rather strung-out settlement with no real centre as such. It consists of at least a couple of luxury hotel complexes and a considerable number of Germanic-influenced beach tavernas. The beach is quite exposed and gravelly, but offshore the normal pattern of smooth, silky water is broken by a series of rocky outcrops, which punctuate a coastline that is otherwise unremarkable.

GENNADI Γεννάδι
☎ 0244 • postcode 851 09 • pop 400

Gennadi (ye-**nah**-dhi), 13km south of Lardos, is an attractive, largely untouched agricultural village masquerading as a holiday centre. For independent travellers it is probably the best base for a protracted stay in the south. The village itself is a patchwork of narrow streets and whitewashed houses set back several hundred metres from the beach.

Information & Orientation
To reach the centre of Gennadi take the second turn-off after the main junction with the trans-island highway to Vati and Apolakkia. To reach the beach enclave turn left. Here you will find a few restaurants and a broad, pebbly beach with pristine, clear water.

Gennadi's main square is about 200m up from the coastal road. The village's main street runs parallel to the coastal road; the shops and a couple of restaurants are along here. The post office is two blocks south of the main street. The Agios Andonios supermarket near the church sells foreign-language newspapers.

The police (☎ 43 222) are at the far northern end of the village (follow the main street all the way) and there is a doctor's surgery (☎ 43 233) on the main highway just south of the main crossroads.

Places to Stay
Effie's Dream Apartments (☎ 43 410, fax 43 437, e dreams@srh.forthnet.gr), right by a large mulberry tree and spring at the northern end of the village, has modern, spotlessly clean studios with lovely rural and sea vistas from the communal balcony. Doubles/triples cost 10,000/14,000 dr. The friendly Greek-Australian owners will meet you if you call ahead. Look for the direction signs along the main street.

Tina's Studios (☎ 43 204), off the main street, has modern double studios available for 10,000 dr. The spacious *Betty Studios & Apartments* (☎ 43 020), on the main street, offers double/triple studios for 8600/10,000 dr and also has four-person apartments for 11,800 dr.

Places to Eat

You can eat either at the beach or in Gennadi itself. Of the beach eateries, there is honestly little difference between them as far as quality or price is concerned. All have beach views and serve up filling, moderately priced food. *Klimis* (☎ 43 263) is in the middle and *Restaurant Andonis* (☎ 43 300) and *Thalassa* (☎ 43 202) are at the northern end of the little restaurant strip.

In Gennadi and along the main street (which is closed off at night) you will find *I Kouzina tis Mamas* (☎ 43 547) which, apart from pizza and spaghetti, also has a wide range of Greek grills. *Effie's Dream Cafe Bar*, below the apartments (see Places to Stay earlier), serves drinks and tasty snacks in a tranquil setting.

Getting There & Around

Oasis (☎ 43 196) rents out cars starting from 12,500 dr per day for a Fiat Seicento to 21,000 dr for a small jeep. Better deals can be had for three days.

Motorbikes and bicycles can be rented from Explorer (☎ 43 062) and Dimitris (☎ 43 064). Pedal power will cost you around 2000 dr per day while a motorbike costs anywhere between 4500 dr and 10,000 dr.

GENNADI TO PRASONISI

From Gennadi, an almost uninterrupted beach of pebbles, shingle and sand dunes extends down to Plimmyri, 13km south. Along the way, make sure to detour to the village of Lahania, 10.5km south of Gennadi, a small unassuming settlement that is home to a surprisingly large expat population. They are mainly Germans who arrived here after being lured by free or cheap rent back in the '80s and who have stayed on indefinitely. Since that time they have turned the village into some kind of artistic centre for jaded northern Europeans, with ateliers and art shops. The pretty village square, with its ducks and springs, is oddly located at the southern end of the village itself. Turn left just as you reach the beginning of the village to get there. One of the main attractions for visitors is to eat here at one of the most pleasant restaurants in the south.

In Lahania a popular Sunday outing is the *Taverna Platanos* (☎ 46 027), where you can dine on the tiny village square amidst running water and a seemingly permanent gaggle of ducks. The food is wholesome village fare and is filling and reasonably cheap.

From Lahania you can detour a further 8.5km to the lonely, whitewashed village of Mesanagros, standing sentinel on an isolated plateau and surrounded by bare silent hills. The population of Mesanagros has been severely depleted over the years and now only a few older souls linger on. This place is the total antithesis of a tourist village, with barely one kafeneio to provide sustenance. From Mesanagros an unsealed road leads 11.5km over the ridgetops to the west through dry canyons and rutted hillscapes – more reminiscent of the US badlands than Greece – to Arnitha.

The Bay of Plimmyri, 8.5km south of Lahania is reached by a signposted turn. This is about as much isolation as you will get. The large sandy and pebbled bay has but one small taverna, a small boat harbour and not much else other than lots of space stretching ever southwards towards Cape Gerata.

Kattavia is Rhodes' most southerly village and is over 100km from Rhodes Town. Follow the caravan of rental cars and jeeps heading for the last leg south to Rhodes' own Land's End, the island of Prasonisi.

MONOLITHOS TO PRASONISI

Rhodes' south-west coast doesn't see as many visitors as other parts of the island. It is lonely and exposed and has only recently acquired a sealed road, completing the network around this southern quadrant of the island. Forest fires in recent years have devastated many of the hillsides facing west and there is a general end-of-the-world feeling about the whole region.

From Monolithos (mo-**no**-lith-os) it is another 10km to the south's second largest village of Apolakkia. This is a sleepy rural town well-used by through-travellers making the southern loop which, at Apolakkia, barrels east across the island to meet up with Gennadi (17.5km) on the east coast. From this cross-island link you can make an easy loop to visit the inland villages of **Istrios**, **Profilia** and **Arnitha**, which are as far removed from mass tourism as you can get in Rhodes. A picturesque and reasonable unsealed road links Profilia with **Laerma** and the Moni Tharri, 13km north-east (see Lindos to Gennadi earlier).

From Arnitha a very winding, unsealed road leads to Mesanagros (see Gennadi to Prasonisi earlier) across and through the rough 'badlands' of the southern interior. The road is slow, but driveable in a conventional car, and the views back towards Arnitha from near the top of the mountain pass are stunning. This is probably the most impressive way to approach Mesanagros, which appears like an oasis after the brown dust and sandstone canyons of the previous half an hour of travel. Low-powered scooters or motorbikes would be best advised not to tackle this stretch of road, as it can be quite taxing and steep in parts.

It is only 16km from Apolakkia to Kattavia, but there is scant little to command your attention as you skirt the bleak southwest coast with its fire-scarred hillsides on one side and the open sea on the other. A diversion to the 18th-century **Moni Skiadi** might be in order before continuing along the loop. It's a serene place with terrific views down to the coast, and there is free basic accommodation for visitors.

Back on the coastal road, only the little offshore island of **Ktenies** to the west distracts the eye before the well-paved highway swings inland and meets the turn-off to Prasonisi at Kattavia.

PRASONISI

The fast sealed road leads through a heavily militarised tank training ground, so resist the temptation to take your rental jeep off-road and go exploring.

The island of Prasonisi (pra-soh-**ni**-si) used to be linked to Rhodes via a narrow sand spit until early 1999. Rising waters (perhaps an ominous by-product of global warming) effectively isolated the island from the Rhodian mainland. It is no longer possible to get to the rocky island which still sports a rough track leading to a light-

house, a throwback to the days when 4WD drivers would come here. The narrow channel is now prone to dangerous currents and you should not attempt to swim across the deceptively short distance. At least one person has drowned while making the attempt.

Most visitors are content to drive their Suzukis as far south along the beach as possible and take a leisurely swim, or paddle on whichever side of the spit is least affected by the wind. Prasonisi is a popular windsurfing spot and accommodation can be found at either Prasonisi itself (on the mainland), or back in Kattavia.

Places to Stay & Eat

Studios Platanos (☎ 0244-46 027), run by Soula and Manolis who also run the Taverna Platanos, has four double/triple studios to rent for 9000/10,000 dr. Each studio has a fridge, kitchenette and air-conditioning.

Faros Taverna (☎ 0244-91 030), as well as serving food to windsurfers at Prasonisi, has double rooms for 10,000 dr. **Oasis Taverna** (☎ 0244-91 031) has 17 double rooms for 15,000 dr, including breakfast.

Many people simply pitch a tent on the surrounding land in Prasonisi, though there are no formal facilities.

There are two reliable dining options in Prasonisi. The Swiss-run **Faros Taverna** (☎ 0244-91 030) is decent, while across the road the newer and brasher **Oasis** has a largish eating area with good views across the beach to Prasonisi itself.

GETTING THERE & AROUND

Six buses a week venture this far south and they are not designed for day visitors. The bus leaves the southern villages of Mesanagros, Lahania and Kattavia between 7 and 8 am on Tuesday, Thursday and Saturday and returns from Rhodes Town at 2.30 pm.

From Apolakkia, Profilia, Istrios and Arnitha the bus leaves at a similar time on Monday, Wednesday and Friday, returning from Rhodes Town at 2.30 pm.

The best way to get around is by hired car or motorbike. A small jeep may be a better option, if you plan to drive some of the unsealed roads described previously.

Southern Dodecanese

Halki Χάλκη

☎ 0246 • postcode 851 10 • pop 330

Halki is a small rocky island just 16km off the west coast of Rhodes. Like many small islands in the Dodecanese it has suffered the deprivations of a failed economy (sponge diving), a chronic lack of water and a subsequent population depletion due to migration. Many Halkiots now live in Tarpon Springs, Florida where they have established a buoyant sponge-fishing community. Still, Halki has undergone a rejuvenation in recent years thanks to rather select visitors who come to Halki on discreet villa and studio rental vacations from the UK.

This has all meant that Halki has a rather genteel feel to it these days and conservative Brits from the Home Counties seem to outnumber local islanders in the height of summer. Former residents are also coming back in appreciable numbers with cash in hand to renovate ancestral homes that had long fallen into disrepair. Individual travellers, while certainly not discouraged, may have to plan well ahead to secure accommodation since there is little that is not pre-booked by the villa/studio set.

Halki is unquestionably pretty and a great place for a short break. Because it is just that little bit too far from Rhodes it does not get the day tripper crowds that northern neighbour Symi does. In practice, you *can* make an easy day trip from Rhodes courtesy of the twice-weekly catamaran service, or the twice-weekly ferry service that links Rhodes and Crete.

History

Halki has been inhabited continuously since Neolithic times and this is evident in fragments of obsidium and ceramics found in the castle overlooking the former inland capital of Horio. Halki appeared in Athens tax records from the 5th century BC and in-

Highlights

- The quiet reserved and peaceful port of Emborios in Halki, with some of the best villa accommodation in the Dodecanese

- Ammoöpi Beach in Karpathos, boasting the top swimming and skin diving spots in the islands

- Olymbos, a remote Karpathian mountain village where women still wear traditional dress and locals speak a language akin to that spoken by Homer

- The tiny, almost forgotten island of Kasos, with a colourful port, slow lifestyle and friendly engaging people

- Kastellorizo, the beginning or end of Europe, a tiny rock in the sun, Greece's farthest outpost and the location for the cult film *Mediterraneo*

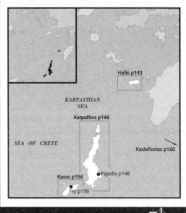

Halki p143
KARPATHIAN SEA
Karpathos p146
SEA OF CRETE
Kastellorizo p160
Kasos p156 • Pigadia p148
Fry p158

SOUTHERN DODECANESE

scriptions from Knidos in the 4th century BC prove that Halki was already existing as an autonomous state. In around 287 BC Halki was taken over by Rhodes and became a dependency of the city state of Kamiros. In the Hellenistic era a large and important fort was built on the site of the current 15th-century castle ruins and Horio's sea annexe, Emborios, flourished as a trading port until pirate invasions in the 7th century AD. After this time the port was essentially abandoned. Emborios was only re-settled in the 19th Century when sponge fishing became the prime source of income for islanders. When this industry collapsed due to sponge blight in the 1950s, the population dropped from around 2000 inhabitants to the 330 or so who remain today. Tourism is now the island's mainstay.

Getting There & Away

Ferry Halki's ferry connections are not ideal. The main link is the 'lifeline' service provided by the F/B *Vitsentzos Kornaros* and the F/B *Ierapetra* of LANE Lines of Crete, which includes Halki on its long, twice-weekly 'milk run' from Rhodes to Piraeus via Crete and Milos.

The following table will give you an overview of services in high season.

destination	duration	price	frequency
Crete (Sitia)	7½ hours	3800 dr	2 weekly
Karpathos			
(Pigadia)	3 hours	2000 dr	2 weekly
Kasos	4¾ hours	3300 dr	2 weekly
Milos	17 hours	6100 dr	2 weekly
Piraeus	21½ hours	9300 dr	2 weekly
Rhodes	2 hours	1900 dr	2 weekly

Note that there are two ports in Karpathos served by LANE – Diafani in the north and the main port of Pigadia in the south of the island. In Crete, LANE also serves two ports – Sitia in eastern Crete and Agios Nikolaos farther west.

Hydrofoil One lone hydrofoil a week connects Halki with Rhodes (1¼ hours, 3600 dr), Tilos (3¼ hours, 5650 dr) and Kalymnos (4½ hours, 7700 dr). Check locally for current departure days.

Catamaran The Rhodes-based *Dodekanisos Express* catamaran calls into Halki twice a week on its run up the Dodecanese to Patmos. The days are usually Wednesday and Sunday. From Halki the departure north

is at 9.55 am and back to Rhodes at 7.40 pm. The Sunday service usually only operates in August and the first week of September. This is a good way to make a day trip to Halki from Rhodes. See the table in the Getting Around chapter for ticket prices.

Caïque A couple of caïques, the *Nikos Express* and the *Nisos Halki*, operate between Halki and Skala Kamirou on Rhodes. From Monday to Saturday, one caïque leaves Halki at 6 am (to connect with the 7.15 am bus from Skala Kamirou to Rhodes); the return trip leaves Skala Kamirou at 2.30 pm. On Sunday, it leaves Halki at 9 am and Skala Kamirou at 4 pm. The fare is 2000 dr.

To get to Skala Kamirou from Rhodes Town, take the 1.15 pm Monolithos bus from the west side bus station (1100 dr). There are no connecting buses on Sunday morning. A taxi to or from Rhodes Town will cost around 10,000 dr. If you want one to meet you at Skala Kamirou, you will have to book it from Halki. See the Rhodes chapter for details of taxi phone numbers.

Getting Around

While it is feasible to bring your own car to Halki on one of the two caïques, there is no real need to. The road network is basically confined to two paved roads: one linking the port of Emborios with the monastery of Agios Ioannis (Moni Agiou Ioanni) and the other with the small beach and occasionally working petrol pump at Kania. Either way you will not be allowed to leave the car on the waterfront so you will have to park at the back end of Emborios. Motorbikes might be a better option, but in reality, no-one on Halki wants to encourage vehicles on the island. Consider leaving your motorised transport at the islanders' car park at Skala Kamirou port.

There are no buses or taxis on the island, but there are water taxis to the main beaches and the island of Alimnia. Better bring a stout pair of walking shoes.

EMBORIOS Εμπορειοσ

The attractive port town of Emborios resembles Gialos on Symi, but on a smaller scale. The port is draped around a horseshoe bay and former sea captains' mansions – some renovated, others still in a state of disrepair – rise up around the bay in a colourful architectural display.

All the island's facilities are here or near here and this will be your base for the duration of your stay on the island. Like Kastellorizo, Halki is the kind of place where you will be on nodding terms with all your fellow-vacationers within 24 hours.

Orientation

The quay is in the middle of the harbour. There is one road out of Emborios, grandly named Tarpon Springs Boulevard for the ex-Halkiots in Florida who financed its construction. It passes Podamos, the island's only sandy beach and goes as far as the Moni Agiou Ioanni.

The only map of any value is the *Halki – Island of Peace and Friendship* map available for around 500 dr in any local store. It is an old Italian-era map that shows the is-land contours fairly accurately, though not the current paved road system. It shows the old foot tracks, but has no scale or compass bearings. Walkers may find the map helpful, but should use it with some caution.

Information

There is no official tourist office on Halki. However, there are two travel agencies that may be able to help with any queries you may have. Halki Tours (☎/fax 45 281) and Zifos Tour (☎/fax 45 082) act primarily as representatives for Laskarina and Direct Greece, the two major travel companies with a presence on the island, but also sell ferry, hydrofoil and catamaran tickets. They are close to each other just back from the main square.

Oddly, given the nature of the island's main clientele, there is no bank and no ATM on Halki. The nearest bank or ATM is on Rhodes. However, the travel agencies will exchange money.

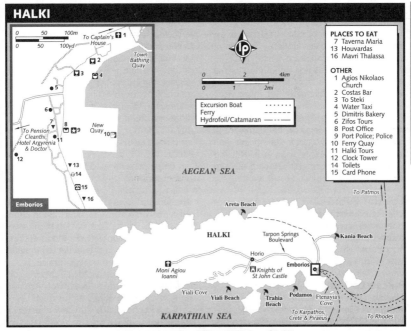

HALKI

PLACES TO EAT
7 Taverna Maria
13 Houvardas
16 Mavri Thalassa

OTHER
1 Agios Nikolaos Church
2 Costas Bar
3 To Steki
4 Water Taxi
5 Dimitris Bakery
6 Zifos Tours
8 Post Office
9 Port Police; Police
10 Ferry Quay
11 Halki Tours
12 Clock Tower
14 Toilets
15 Card Phone

Excursion Boat ....
Ferry ____
Hydrofoil/Catamaran ----

AEGEAN SEA

To Patmos

Areta Beach

HALKI
Horio
Tarpon Springs Boulevard
Kania Beach

Moni Agiou Ioanni
Knights of St John Castle
Emborios

Yiali Cove
Yiali Beach
Trahia Beach
Podamos
Ptenayia Cove

To Karpathos, Crete & Piraeus
To Rhodes

KARPATHIAN SEA

SOUTHERN DODECANESE

There is a post office on the main square, but no OTE office. There are two or three cardphones along the waterfront. Mobile phone users will pick up all three Greek GSM mobile phone service providers. There is, as yet, no public Internet access facility in Halki.

The Web site at www.greekjourneys .com/halki/ is a fairly well-supplied source for information on the island, from accommodation to restaurants.

You'll find some clean and presentable public toilets on the harbourfront.

If you need medical services, there's a small rural clinic near the school on Tarpon Springs Boulevard. Call ☎ 45 206 for a duty doctor.

The port police (☎ 45 220) and the regular police (☎ 45 213) share the same building on the harbourfront.

Things to See

The impressive stone **clock tower** at the southern side of the harbour is a gift (like the main Tarpon Springs Boulevard) from the Halkiots of Florida. While the clock tower may look good, don't rely on it for the time. Each of the four faces is stuck on a different hour of the day.

The **Church of Agios Nikolaos** has the tallest belfry in the Dodecanese and boasts a particularly well-made and impressive **hohlaki courtyard** on the east side.

What is perhaps most enjoyable in Emborios is just wandering the back streets and admiring the newly-restored houses and **mansions**, as well as looking at how badly they once were when you compare them to the unrenovated shells that still remain.

Special Events

The Symi Festival hosts a few events in Halki over a week or so towards the end of August and beginning of September. See the Central Dodecanese chapter for full details on this annual cultural festival.

Places to Stay

The most pleasant place to stay – if you can get in – is **Captain's House** (☎ 45 201, mobile 01-723 1919), a beautiful 19th-century mansion with period furniture and a tranquil tree-shaded garden. Owned by a retired Greek sea captain Alex Sakellaridis and his British wife Christine, it is on the northern side of the harbour, about a 10-minute walk from the ferry quay. Doubles with bathroom are 10,000 dr. Book well in advance.

Pension Kleanthi (☎ 45 334), on the road to Podamos Beach, has some modern double rooms with bathroom for 10,000 dr. **Argyrenia Rooms** (☎ 45 205), at the junction with the road to Kania beach, is another independent accommodation option. It offers presentable double rooms for around 11,000 dr.

The former sponge factory on the southern side of the harbour is now the **Hotel Halki** (☎ 45 208, fax 47 208). It is the only hotel on the island. Reasonable single/double rooms go for 12,000/15,000 dr.

Places to Eat

There are several good eateries in Emborios and a few are listed here. A decent meal with wine will cost on average around 3500 dr.

Starting at the southern end of the harbour, the black-and-yellow painted **Mavri Thalassa** (☎ 45 021) is well regarded by locals and offers good fish dishes. **Houvardas** (☎ 45 377) is the next along, with portions as generous as the restaurant name (houvardas in Greek means 'open-handed').

Taverna Maria (☎ 45 262), just behind the post office, but with tables spilling out onto the main square, is a family restaurant with good mayirefta (ready-made food) dishes.

Newly opened in late 2000, **Taverna Ftenayia** (mobile ☎ 09-4599 8333) on Ftenayia Cove is a 15-minute walk south of Emborios over the hill to the next bay. Open lunch and dinnertime, this waterside taverna does mezes (appetisers) like hot chilli mussels (1100 dr), red peppers stuffed with feta cheese (1100 dr) and excellent dolmades (1300 dr) that even the locals praise.

Dimitris Bakery, back in Emborios, is the local bread store. A couple of waterfront shops stock basic goods and a fresh vegetable **market** takes place near the clock tower once or twice a week.

GEORGE TSAFOS

Take a step back in time in Olymbos village.

GEORGE TSAFOS

PAUL HELLANDER

Catching a gust in Makrygialos Bay, Karpathos

Fishermen flock to Bouka harbour in Kasos.

ROSEMARY HALL

The tiny island of Kastellorizo attracts its fair share of Aussies, yachties and lost souls...

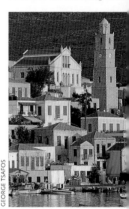

Halki: see the crumbling old...

Mesohori enjoys spectacular views of Karpathos' rugged coastline.

...and the glistening new!

Traditions die hard on Kasos.

With five sandy beaches, Lefkos is a sun-worshipper's paradise.

Entertainment
Locals and tourists gravitate between *Kostas* at the northern end of the harbour, where you can sup Mythos beer, play pool and gossip; and *To Steki* nearer the quay, where you can do much of the same and still see familiar faces.

AROUND HALKI
Beaches
Though Halki is not blessed with many accessible beaches, swimming is guaranteed in clean pristine water wherever you go. **Podamos** is the closest and the best beach. It is a 15-minute walk from Emborios in the direction of Horio. It is long and sandy though a bit on the narrow side. There is one cantina and one restaurant. **Ftenayia Cove** (see also Places to Eat) is another nearby option, though there is no sand as such. Swimming is from the rocks. A brisk 25-minute walk north along a paved road will bring you to the small pebbly beach at **Kania**, which attracts a few dedicated bathers.

Taxi boats will take you to beaches farther afield such as **Areta** on the north coast or **Trahia** and **Yiali** on the south coast. The latter two, while nearer and reachable on foot in an hour or so, are rather exposed and offer no shade, while Areta is probably the best of the three and can also be reached by the adventurous via a cross-island track in about two hours.

Walks
The easiest and most obvious is the 35-minute uphill walk to **Horio**, the abandoned, once pirate-proof inland capital of Halki, which at its peak supported 3000 souls. The walk is along a paved road all the way, though you can shave off a few hundred metres on the last leg by cutting left up an unpaved road. Other than a small community centre and one or two renovated private houses the only real sign of life is the **church**. From here a path leads in another 10 minutes or so to a ruined **Knights of St John castle** that affords superb views across to Rhodes and back down to Emborios.

You can continue your walk across the island along a barren and hot road to **Moni**
Agiou Ioanni at the far western end of Halki and a two-hour walk from Horio. There are no monks here now, but the shepherd-cum-caretaker, Dimitris, lives here with his family. Free beds are available for visitors, but you must take your own food and water.

The easy 25-minute walk to **Kania** (see also Beaches) is a good pre-dinner stroll uphill, then downhill past small farm holdings and rocky fields. From just past an aluminium shed about halfway along the paved road a rough track heads north-west and over the escarpment to **Areta Beach**. This is not an easy walk and you will want the aforementioned map of the island that will at least show you the basic routes. Allow a half day for this walk.

Alimnia Island
Excursions to the beaches on Halki's largish satellite island are very popular though they can be rather expensive at around 7000 dr including a BBQ lunch. There is an abandoned village – the whole island was depopulated in the 1960s – at the head of a long and wide bay. The bay was used to shelter Italian submarines during WWII and you can still see remnants of the submarine pens. Most visitors head for one of the two little beaches to stake out a claim for the day, though if you felt energetic you could follow a rough track inland and northwards to the crumbling remains of an old **castle**.

Karpathos
Κάρπαθος

☎ 0245 • postcode 857 00 • pop 5323
If ever there was a Greek island that combined the right proportions of size, attractiveness, remoteness, water activities and general good feel, that island might just be the elongated island of Karpathos (**kar**-pah-thos), midway between Crete and Rhodes.

Karpathos has rugged mountains, some of the best beaches in the Aegean and unspoilt villages, and despite having charter flights from northern Europe, it has not, so far, succumbed to the worst excesses of mass tourism. It takes just that bit of extra effort to get there. The island is traversed by a north-south mountain range. For hundreds of years the north and south parts of the island were isolated from one another and so they developed independently. It is even thought that the northerners and southerners have different ethnic origins. The northern village of Olymbos is of endless fascination to ethnologists for the age-old customs of its inhabitants.

History

Karpathos has a relatively uneventful history. The island was known in antiquity as 'Porfyris' (purple), named after dye manufactured here and used on the clothes of ancient kings. The island supported four ancient cities – Vrykous, Posidion, Arkesia and Nisyros – but Karpathos features rarely in ancient texts. Pirates made their home here prior to the arrival of the Venetians in the Middle Ages (1306–1540) under whose tutelage the island remained until taken over by the Ottomans. Even then, the Ottomans cared little for their possession and basically left the islanders to their own devices. Unlike almost all other Dodecanese islands, it was never under the auspices of the Knights of St John. Karpathos is a wealthy island, receiving more money from emigrants living abroad (mostly in the USA) than any other Greek island. Returned emigrants, many from New Jersey, now live in the villages of southern central Karpathos.

Getting There & Away

Air There are four flights weekly to and from Athens (27,900 dr), up to two flights daily to Rhodes (13,400 dr) and two weekly to Kasos (3500 dr). The Olympic Airways office (☎ 22 150/057) is on the central square in Pigadia. The airport is 18km south-west of Pigadia, at the southern tip of the island.

Ferry Karpathos shares the same essentially limited ferry services as its neighbours, Halki and Kasos. The F/B *Vitsentzos Kornaros* and the F/B *Ierapetra*, include

Karpathos on their thrice-weekly runs from Rhodes to Piraeus.

The following table will give you an overview of services in high season.

destination	duration	price	frequency
Crete (Sitia)	7½ hours	3600 dr	3 weekly
Halki	3 hours	2000 dr	2 weekly
Kasos	1½ hours	1800 dr	2 weekly
Milos	13 hours	6400 dr	3 weekly
Piraeus	20 hours	7800 dr	3 weekly
Rhodes	4 hours	4200 dr	2 weekly

Two ports in Karpathos are served by LANE – Diafani in the north and the main port of Pigadia in the south of the island. In this table, the sailing times are given for Pigadia.

Getting Around
To/From the Airport There is no airport bus to the airport. Travellers must take a taxi (around 2500 dr) or seek independent transport.

Bus Pigadia is the transport hub of the island. A schedule is posted at the bus terminal. There are three buses daily to Ammoöpi (300 dr), Pyles (380 dr) via Aperi (300 dr), Volada (300 dr) and Othos (300 dr); two daily to Finiki (380 dr) via Menetes (300 dr) and Arkasa (380 dr); and buses to Lefkos on Monday and Thursday. There is no bus between Pigadia and Olymbos or Diafani.

The bus station is one block up from the waterfront on Dimokratias.

Car, Motorcycle & Bicycle Gatoulis Car Hire (☎ 22 747, fax 22 814), on the east side of the road to Aperi, hires out cars, motorcycles and bicycles. Possi Travel (see Travel Agencies) also arranges car and motorcycle hire.

Driving or biking in the south is generally good, with paved if occasionally winding roads linking all major centres. The road from Aperi to Spoa on the east coast is unpaved, but quite driveable. The branch road to Kyra Panagia Beach is paved for the last section and is used by many cars and bikes to access the beach.

Taxi Pigadia's taxi rank (☎ 22 705) is on Dimokratias, near the bus station. A detailed price list is displayed. Taxi prices around the south are reasonable, sample fares from Pigadia are: the airport (2500 dr), Ammoöpi (1500 dr) Arkasa (3000), Pyles (3000 dr) and Kyra Panagia (5000 dr).

If you want to head out onto the dirt beyond Spoa, you will pay for it. A taxi from Pigadia to Olymbos is a steep 19,000 dr and 20,000 dr to Diafani.

Excursion Boat In summer there are daily excursion boats from Pigadia to Diafani for 5000 dr return. There are also frequent boats to the beaches of Kyra Panagia and Apella for 3000 dr. Tickets can be bought from Karpathos Travel in Pigadia.

PIGADIA Πηγάδια
• pop 1300
Pigadia (pi-**gha**-dhi-ya) is the island's capital and main port. It's a modern town, pleasant enough, but without any eminent buildings or sites. It is built on the edge of Vrondi Bay, a 4km-long sandy beach where you can rent water sports equipment. On the beach are the remains of the early Christian basilica of Agia Fotini.

Orientation
From the quay, turn right and take the left fork onto Apodimon Karpathou, Pigadia's main thoroughfare, which leads to the central square of Plateia 5 Oktovriou.

The excellent 1:75,000 Freytag & Berndt map of *Karpathos & Kasos* is the best political map of Karpathos, while the 1:100,000 *Karpathos Tourist Map* by Karto Atelier has both an accurate relief map of the island and a street plan of Pigadia. Both maps are available in Pigadia.

Information
Tourist Offices Pigadia has no EOT, but there is a potentially useful local Tourist Information Office (☎ 23 835, fax 23 836) in a kiosk in the middle of the harbourfront. It offers general information, sells maps and recommends some, but not all accommodation; most of its recommendations are in the

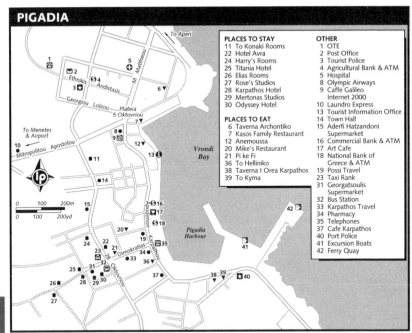

PIGADIA

To Aperi

To Menetes & Airport

Vrondi Bay

Pigadia Harbour

0 100 200m
0 100 200yd

PLACES TO STAY	OTHER
11 To Konaki Rooms	1 OTE
22 Hotel Avra	2 Post Office
24 Harry's Rooms	3 Tourist Police
25 Titania Hotel	4 Agricultural Bank & ATM
26 Elias Rooms	5 Hospital
27 Rose's Studios	8 Olympic Airways
28 Karpathos Hotel	9 Caffe Galileo
29 Mertonas Studios	Internet 2000
30 Odyssey Hotel	10 Laundro Express
	13 Tourist Information Office
PLACES TO EAT	14 Town Hall
6 Taverna Archontiko	15 Aderfi Hatzandoni
7 Kasos Family Restaurant	Supermarket
12 Anemoussa	16 Commercial Bank & ATM
20 Mike's Restaurant	17 Art Cafe
21 Pi ke Fi	18 National Bank of
36 To Helliniko	Greece & ATM
38 Taverna I Orea Karpathos	19 Possi Travel
39 To Kyma	23 Taxi Rank
	31 Georgatsoulis
	Supermarket
	32 Bus Station
	33 Karpathos Travel
	34 Pharmacy
	35 Telephones
	37 Cafe Karpathos
	40 Port Police
	41 Excursion Boats
	42 Ferry Quay

mid-range to more expensive category. It is open 10 am to 3 pm and 7 to 9 pm daily from April to October (closed the rest of the year).

Money The National Bank of Greece, with an ATM, is on Apodimon Karpathou. There are further ATMs at the Agricultural Bank near the post office and at the Commercial Bank on the harbourfront.

Most travel agencies will also exchange money with little or no commission.

Post & Communications The post office (☎ 22 219) and OTE (☎ 22 321) are on Ethnikis Andistasis on the north side of Pigadia. There are plenty of card phones, with a cluster found at the beginning of Dimokratias near the National Bank. Mobile phone users will have no trouble picking up any of Greece's three GSM mobile services.

Caffe Galileo Internet 2000 (☎ 23 606, e caffegal@otenet.gr), on Apodimon Karpathou, has Internet access for 500 dr for 15 minutes or 1500 dr an hour. It is open from 8.30 am to 3 am daily.

Travel Agencies One helpful travel agency is Karpathos Travel (☎ 22 148, fax 22 754, e karpathos_travel@hellasnet.gr), on Dimokratias; its guided walks around the island cost around 5000 dr. Another is Possi Travel (☎ 22 235, fax 22 252, e possitvl@ hotmail.com) on the harbourfront. Both are open 9 am to 1 pm and 5.30 to 9 pm, Monday to Saturday.

Laundry There's a laundrette, Laundro Express, on Mitropolitou Apostolou. It is open from 8 am to 1.30 pm and 5.30 to 8 pm Monday to Friday, and from 8 am to 2 pm on Saturday.

Medical Services The local hospital (☎ 22 228) is on the southern side of Pigadia not far from the tourist police. There is a pharmacy on Apodimon Karpathou.

SOUTHERN DODECANESE

Emergency The tourist police (☎ 22 212) are on Ethnikis Andistasis. The port police (☎ 22 227) are next to the ferry quay.

Special Events
The Symi Festival hosts a few events in Karpathos over one weekend in late August. See the Symi chapter for full details on this annual cultural festival.

Places to Stay – Budget
There's plenty of accommodation available and owners meet the boats. The E-class *Hotel Avra* (☎ 22 388, 28 Oktovriou) has comfortable doubles/triples with private bathrooms for 7000/8000 dr, and doubles with shared bathroom for 6000 dr. *Harry's Rooms* (☎ 22 188), just off 28 Oktovriou, has spotless singles/doubles for 4500/6500 dr. Farther along, *To Konaki Rooms* (☎ 22 908, 28 Oktovriou) has very pleasant doubles for 7000 dr with bathroom.

The immaculate and cosy *Elias Rooms* (☎ 22 446, e eliasrooms@hotmail.com) is in a quiet part of town with great views. Single/double/triple rooms – some in traditional Karpathiot style – with bathroom are 4000/6000/8000 dr. The owner, Elias Hatzigorgiou, is friendly and helpful and is a mine of local information. Farther up the hill, *Rose's Studios* (☎/fax 22 284) has well-kept double studios with bathroom and kitchen for 7500 dr. Doubles with large well equipped communal kitchen and bathrooms cost 4000 dr.

The C-class *Karpathos Hotel* (☎ 22 347) has light, airy rooms for 7000/7500 dr with bathroom.

Places to Stay – Mid-Range
Opposite the Karpathos Hotel, the C-class *Titania Hotel* (☎ 22 144, fax 23 307) has spacious, pleasant rooms for 9900/11,600 dr. *Mertonas Studios* (☎ 22 622, fax 23 283) around the corner has lovely, tastefully furnished studios, managed by the warm and friendly Eva Angelou. The rates for doubles/triples are 8000/9000 dr, and four-person studios are 14,000 dr.

Close by are the very tasteful studio apartments of *Odyssey Hotel* (☎ 23 246, fax 23 762). Each studio has a kitchenette, phone, TV, fridge, room safe and balconies, and fans are available on demand. Rates are a very reasonable 12,000/14,000 dr for two/three persons. For 18,000 dr you can get a top floor penthouse suite for up to six persons *and* get a great view.

Places to Eat
Pigadia is well supplied with good restaurants and most are centred on the two crescents of the harbour. Steer clear of the 'picture menu' establishments – they tend to be bland and over-priced. Give the following a look-in as they are somewhat better. The cafes are nearly all clustered around the centre of the harbour. Most cafes offer breakfast as well as coffees, drinks and snacks.

Starting away from the harbourfront, *Mike's Restaurant* (☎ 22 727, Apodimon Karpathou) is excellent. A meal of lamb stew, Greek salad and retsina costs 3000 dr. Try also the fish soup and wide range of cheap mayirefta dishes. It's open evenings only. *To Helliniko*, on Apodimon Karpathou, has a pleasant outdoor terrace and a tasteful interior. The Karpathian *stifado* (a rich meat stew in tomato sauce with baby onions) is particularly commendable. For the best gyros in town and the cheapest fast food, stop by *Pi ke Fi* just down from the taxi stand and bus stop.

Starting at the southern end of the quay, *Taverna I Orea Karpathos* (☎ 22 501) serves a wide range of traditional Karpathian dishes and reputedly the best *makarounes* (macaroni with onions and cheese) in Pigadia. Close by, *To Kyma* (☎ 22 496) is known for its fish dishes. Both these places are open for lunch and dinner, and prices are mid-range.

The *Anemoussa* (☎ 22 164) is a fairly pricey but worthwhile Italian restaurant on the north side of the harbour, while the *Kasos Family Restaurant* (☎ 22 842) is a simple home-cooking eatery that's open all year. Rooftop dining is at its best at the nearby *Taverna Archontiko* (☎ 22 531), which serves green pepper chicken for 2100 dr and pepper steak for 3300 dr. It's open evenings only.

SOUTHERN DODECANESE

There are two supermarkets worth knowing about. The *Georgatsoulis Supermarket* opposite the taxi stand and the *Aderfi Hatzandoni Supermarket* on 28 Oktovriou are the biggest in Pigadia.

Entertainment
The *Cafe Karpathos*, at the beginning of Apodimon Karpathou, is a great place to meet locals, expats and tourists. The cafe serves good coffee and tasty sandwiches. The *Art Cafe* is a trendy hangout on the harbourfront where you can sup on Krombacher draft beer in big glasses.

SOUTHERN KARPATHOS
Ammoöpi Αμμοοπή
If you are seeking sun and sand and some of the best and clearest water in the whole Aegean, head for Ammoöpi (ammo-oh-**pee**), 8km south of Pigadia. This is *the* place on the island to enjoy eating, sleeping, drinking, swimming and snorkelling to the maximum. Ammoöpi means 'sand hole', named for the rock with a hole in it lying just offshore at the southern end of the resort. It's a scattered settlement without any real centre. The approach road winds down from the main airport road and fizzles out at a series of sand coves, all of which have some restaurants, places to stay and car parking.

Golden Beach is the main (and best) cove where most restaurants are clustered; it's as good a place as any to head for. **Votsalakia** is a narrower pebble beach nearby and usually a little quieter than the other beaches. Snorkelling is particularly good at Ammoöpi, especially if you head to the base of the sandstone cliffs where shoals of multi-coloured fish gather over the underwater rocks.

Accommodation is usually of the studio type, with self-contained units for two or more people. There are enough eating places to visit a different one daily for over a week, but nightlife is of the dinner-for-two, cocktail-on-the-balcony variety, with the occasional live Greek music evening to liven things up.

Windsurfing Diehard windsurfers in the know head for the broad **Bay of Afiarti**, a fur-

ther 8km south of Ammoöpi, to enjoy some world class windsurfing. The large bay supports a few windsurfing centres and caters for advanced surfers at the northern end and beginners in the sheltered **Makrygialos Bay Lagoon** at the southern end next to the airport. While most surfers come on package tours from Germany, casual 'blow-ins' are more than welcome. One particularly good outfit is the Karpathos 2001 Surf Centre (☎ 91 063, fax 91 062, **e** Chris.Schill@ windsurfen-karpathos.com) at Devil's Bay, where equipment hire can work out at less than 11,000 dr for a half-day high-speed surfing session.

Places to Stay Ammoöpi is a scattered place without any easily identifiable landmarks, so ask the bus or taxi driver to drop you off at whichever establishment you decide to check. The cheapest place is *Ammoöpi Beach Rooms (☎ 81 723)*, at the northern end of town, where spotless, simply furnished doubles cost 4500 dr.

Farther back along the main road, *Hotel Sophia (☎/fax 81 078)*, behind the Blue Sea Hotel, has doubles/triples for 12,000/15,000 dr. Nearby, *Votsalakia Rooms & Restaurant (☎/fax 81 004)* has attractively furnished doubles for 8000 dr. *Four Seasons Studios (☎/fax 71 116, **e** fourseasons@hellasnet.gr)*, still farther back along the road, has equally commendable doubles with bathroom for 8000 dr. *Blue Sea Hotel (☎ 81 036, fax 81 095, **e** huguette@hellasnet.gr)* has 27 comfortable double rooms for 14,000 dr with fridge and ceiling fan, and hosts a 'Karpathos Night' every Wednesday evening.

Kastelia Bay Hotel (☎ 81 678) has light, airy singles/doubles for 12,000/14,000 dr. A little way along the approach road to Ammoöpi a sign points to the hotel. For seekers of total quiet and a relaxed self-catering approach, look no further than *Vardes (☎ 81 111, fax 81 112)*, a small block of very tasteful, spacious and airy studios set back against the hillside. These studios have TV and telephone and go for around 16,000 dr for two people.

Places to Eat For obvious reasons the beachside restaurants are preferred by most visitors, though there is a scattering of eating places higher up the hill which may be more convenient for visitors staying nearby.

At the far northern end of Ammoöpi and right on the beach is the ***Ammoopi Taverna (☎ 81 138)***, which serves decent enough food, though service tends to be a bit abrupt and brusque. Things are mellower on 'Greek Night' once a week when local Greeks come to dine and dance. Prices are mid-range.

The ***Four Seasons Restaurant (☎ 71 116)*** back up the hill serves delicious Greek dishes and freshly baked brown bread. Prices are cheap to mid-range.

There are a number of ***minimarkets*** at Ammoöpi, but all tend to be on the expensive side. It is better to get your supplies from Pigadia.

Getting There & Around There are four buses daily to and from Pigadia. From Ammoöpi departures to Pigadia are at 9.50 and 10.30 am, 4.30 and 6 pm daily. There are no services on Sunday.

Trust Rent a Car (☎ 81 060, fax 81 121, e votsalakia@yahoo.co.uk), behind the Votsalakia Cafe Bar, and Ammoöpi Rent a Car (☎ 81 115, fax 81 171) both rent out cars, motorbikes and jeeps at Ammoöpi. Rates start at around 10,000 dr per day for a Fiat Panda.

Menetes Μενετές

Menetes (me-ne-**tes**) is perched on a sheer cliff 8km above Pigadia. It's a picturesque, unspoilt village with pastel-coloured neoclassical houses lining its main street. Behind the main street are narrow, stepped alleyways that wind between more modest whitewashed dwellings. This is the real centre in this part of the island and most people with businesses in Ammoöpi live here. The village has a little **museum** on the right as you come from Pigadia. The owner of Taverna Manolis will open it up for you.

Menetes has only one place to stay: the ***domatia*** of friendly Greek-American Mike Rigas *(☎ 81 269/55)*, in a traditional Karpathian house with a garden brimming with trees and flowers. Doubles/triples with bathroom are 4900/5900 dr. As you approach

from Pigadia, the rooms are 150m down a cement road veering off to the right.

In Menetes ***Taverna Manolis (☎ 81 103)*** dishes up generous helpings of grilled meat. ***Fiesta Dionysos (☎ 81 269)*** specialises in local dishes, including omelettes made with artichokes and Karpathian sausages. ***I Gonia tou Nikou (☎ 81 215)***, next door to Taverna Manolis, has daily special mayirefta dishes. All three places are very economical.

Arkasa & Finiki Αρκάσα & Φοινίκι

Arkasa (ar-**ka**-sa) is 9km farther on from Menetes and is approached along a winding road that passes through a sometimes bleak and barren landscape. The initial disappointment at the starkness of the land gives way to relief as the white cubed houses of Arkasa come into view during the last two kilometres, and the road quickly dips into what is becoming a lively and active low-key holiday resort. Arkasa itself straddles a ravine and the centre of the village can be reached (preferably on foot as the streets get very narrow) via the first right turn you come to.

The resort area is blessed with the pretty beach of **Agios Nikolaos**, which is where most of the accommodation is concentrated. The 150m-long beach is broad and sandy and protected by rocks at either end. There are fresh water showers, but no natural shade. Beach umbrellas and loungers can be rented. The sea is very clean, but can get choppy when the wind is up, which can be quite often. To reach Agios Nikolaos Beach take the first major left as you come into Arkasa from Menetes.

If you continue along the main road you will find a turn-off to the left, just before the ravine. This leads 500m to the remains of the 5th-century **Basilica of Agia Sofia**. Two chapels stand amid mosaic fragments and columns. From here a path leads up to the site of **Paleokastro**, a Mycenaean settlement now marked by the existence of some remaining Cyclopean walls.

The serene fishing village of Finiki (fi-**ni**-ki) lies 2km north of Arkasa. There is no decent swimming here, but it is a pretty diversion while on your way north. The excellent dining options here are even worth

SOUTHERN DODECANESE

the drive from Pigadia at night. The little sculpture at the harbour commemorates the heroism of seven local fishers during WWII – locals will tell you the story.

Places to Stay *Pension Philoxenia (☎ 61 341)*, on the left before the T-junction, has clean doubles for 6500 dr. *Eleni Rooms (☎ 61 248)*, on the left along the road to Finiki, has attractive double apartments for 10,000 dr.

On Agios Nikolaos Beach, *Glaros Studios (☎ 61 015)* has very tasteful double studios for between 15,000 dr and 17,000 dr. Done out in Karpathiot style, they have raised sofa-style beds, enjoy a cool sea breeze and have large terraces with sunbeds. The similarly priced *Seaside Studios (☎ 61 421)*, about 100m back from the beach, are smaller and set in a lush garden.

In Arkasa the moderately luxurious B-Class *Hotel Arkesia (☎ 61 290, fax 61 307)*, set up on the hill on the Menetes road, has very comfortable double/triple rooms with TV, minibar and telephone for 17,000/ 20,500 dr including breakfast. There's also a swimming pool.

Fay's Paradise (☎ 61 308), near Finiki's harbour, has lovely double studios for 10,000 dr. *Finiki View Hotel (☎ 61 309/ 400)*, on the right as you come from Arkasa, has spacious doubles for 12,000 dr and a swimming pool and bar.

Pine Tree Restaurant (see Places to Eat) offers free camping under the protection of 40 cool and shady pine trees, or if you don't have a tent, comfortable double rooms for 8500 dr, or cosy kitchenette-equipped and bougainvillea-draped studios for 10,000 dr.

Places to Eat Glaros Studios (see Places to Stay) also runs the unassuming and convenient *Glaros Restaurant*, which is the only beach dining in Arkasa. The menu is basic with staples like mousakas (1400 dr) or souvlaki (1300 dr) on offer and occasional specials like shrimps and mussels with spaghetti (3700 dr). On the northern side of Arkasa, past the ravine, turn right at the junction to find two local eateries, the cheap *Petalouda (☎ 61 065)* and the *O Paradisos*.

The latter opens after 5 pm only and specialises in seafood.

Locals come from all over the island to eat the fresh fish at *Dimitrios Fisherman's Taverna (☎ 61 294)* in Finiki. Owner Dimitris fishes his own catch and offers, among other delicious dishes, a well-priced fish platter for 5000 dr.

About 4km north of Finiki is the settlement known as Adia. Here you will find the prominently signposted *Pine Tree Restaurant (mobile ☎ 09-77 36 9948)*, a peaceful oasis under the pine trees overlooking the sea. Owner Nikos Papanikolaou cooks all his food in an outdoor wood oven. Try his homemade bread, makarounes and stifado. Fruit of the season is complimentary. Sleep off the retsina in a huge guest hammock after lunch or dinner.

Lefkos Λεύκος

Lefkos (**lef**-kos), 13km north of Finiki, and 2km from the coast road, is a sun-lover's paradise with five sandy beaches and a burgeoning resort centred around a little fishing quay. In reality only one beach really earns the moniker of 'superb' and that is the central **Golden Sands Beach**, with its curving, tree-shaded strand. The other beaches are somewhat more open and exposed, but don't get as crowded as Golden Sands can.

In summer Lefkos gets busy, but at other times it still has a rugged, off-the-beaten-track feel about it. It's a good base with facilities such as restaurants, accommodation, car and bike hire, and one or two minimarkets for self-caterers. It's also about the farthest north you will comfortably get to (and back) on a hired scooter from Pigadia or Ammoöpi. So, unless you have extra fuel provisions with you, this is basically the end of the line for you.

Local boat owners sometimes take visitors to the islet of Sokastro where there is a ruined castle. Another diversion from the beaches is the ancient catacombs, reached by walking inland and turning left at Imeri Rooms.

Places to Stay & Eat *Imeri Rooms (☎ 71 375)*, owned by a friendly elderly couple, is in a peaceful rural setting halfway between the turn-off to Lefkos at Agios Georgios and the beaches. Sparkling doubles/triples cost 7500/8500 dr with bathroom. Inquire at Small Paradise Taverna & Rooms, farther down the road, about its *Sunset Studios* (☎ 71 171) which overlook Golden Sands. Immaculate rooms cost 8000/9000 dr.

Golden Sands Studios (☎ 71 175, fax 71 219), almost on Golden Sands Beach, offers bright double/triple studios with well-equipped kitchens for 9000/12,000 dr. *Zorba's Rooms* (☎ 71 252), close to the quay, are equally pleasant with double studios for 11,000 dr.

Small Paradise Taverna serves tasty local dishes and fresh seafood on a vine-shaded terrace.

Getting There & Around There are two buses weekly to Lefkos. A taxi costs 7000 dr from Pigadia, or 8000 dr from the airport. Telephone the rooms' proprietors ahead and they may be able to arrange a lift from Pigadia or the airport, providing you intend staying with them, of course! Hitching is dicey as there is not much traffic.

Lefkos Rent A Car (☎/fax 71 057) is a reliable outlet with very competitive prices. The English-speaking owner will deliver vehicles free of charge to anywhere in southern Karpathos.

East Coast Beaches

The fine beaches of **Ahata**, **Kato Lakos**, **Kyra Panagia** and **Apella** can be reached along dirt roads off the east coast road, but are most easily reached by excursion boat from Pigadia. Of the four beaches, the vehicle road to Kyra Panagia is probably the most driver/rider friendly; the access roads to the other three are just a shade too rough in parts.

These east side beaches are more protected from the prevailing north-westerly winds and, because they are so easily accessible by daily caïques, they are more popular with travellers based in and around Pigadia. The impressive pine-clad beach at Apella tends to be the one most commonly featured in the travel posters advertising Karpathos.

Day excursions are offered by two or three operators and differ slightly in format. They don't necessarily take in all beaches, so choose carefully. The price (3000 dr) is about the same all round and for an extra 2000 dr you can partake of a BBQ put on by the caïque owner.

Places to Stay & Eat Kyra Panagia has the only good accommodation and tavernas. On Kyra Panagia Beach the *Akropolis* (☎ 31 503) has double rooms for 12,000 dr, studios accommodating two people for 15,000 dr, and a restaurant.

The *No 1 Taverna* does a mean fish soup (3300 dr) as well as mousakas (1600 dr) and grilled octopus (2400 dr), while *Cafe Minas Kostis* serves up cheap chicken souvlakia (450 dr), omelettes (900 dr) and Greek salads (9900 dr).

Mesohori & Spoa

Μεσοχώρι & Σπόα

Mesohori, 4km beyond the turn-off for Lefkos, is a pretty village of whitewashed houses and stepped streets. While the place is not really geared for hoards of travellers, there is some basic accommodation available, a restaurant or two and some friendly curious faces to greet your arrival.

Driving or biking around these parts is a pleasure since the winding, well-surfaced highway dips and bobs its way through one of the most heavily forested regions of Karpathos. About 1km from Spoa, shortly after the forest cover comes to an end, an unsealed track branches south back to Pigadia (21.5km) via Mertonas (7.5km) and Volada (13.5km).

Spoa village, 1.5km farther along past this junction, is at the beginning of the 17km dirt road to Olymbos. The road to Olymbos can be driven with care, but there is no petrol until the port of Diafani a farther 6km beyond Olymbos. Whitewashed Spoa is untouristed, with only the truly curious, or travellers in rental jeeps about to make the road trip to Olymbos. The village sits high on a ledge overlooking the east coast. **Agios Nikolaos Beach** is reached by a rough 2.5km track.

SOUTHERN DODECANESE

Mountain Villages

Aperi, **Volada**, **Othos** and **Pyles**, the well watered mountain villages to the north of Pigadia, are largely unaffected by tourism. None has any accommodation, but all have tavernas and *kafeneia* (coffee houses). Aperi was the island's capital from 1700 until 1892. Its ostentatious houses were built by wealthy returning emigrants from the USA. Like Aperi, Volada has an air of prosperity.

The villages are better seen on a leisurely driving or biking loop starting from **Vrondi Bay** just north of Pigadia. The roads are a bit steep in parts so you will need a bike or scooter with some guts. Two riders on a measly 50cc bike might find the going slow. The villages are not tourist traps, and don't offer the assortment of shops, boutiques and postcard stalls that you might find in other 'traditional mountain villages'. Cars registered in New Jersey can often be seen tooling around the twisting bends. This is a testament to the fact that these villages are retirement and vacation suburbs for hard-working Karpathiots who have done, or are still doing their time in the USA and who come here to relax, not to entertain tourists.

Othos (altitude 510m) is the island's highest village. It has a small ethnographic museum. From Othos the road winds downhill to Pyles, a gorgeous village of twisting, stepped streets, pastel houses and citrus groves. It clings to the slopes of **Mt Kali Limni** (1215m), the Dodecanese's second-highest peak.

NORTHERN KARPATHOS
Olymbos & Diafani
Ολυμπος & Διαφάνι

The highlight of a visit to the north is the traditional village of Olymbos (population 340), best approached for dramatic effect from the Spoa Rd. Viewed from here, Olymbos coyly appears through a fold in the dramatically stark and rocky mountains and is visible to the sea only from the steep and almost inaccessible west coast. Olymbos clings to the ridge of barren Mt Profitis Ilias (716m), 4km above its sea annexe and port, Diafani. While Olymbos is no doubt impressive from afar, closer inspection reveals

that the blight of cement has replaced much of its traditional stone and the end effect is less than appealing.

The whole village is nonetheless a living museum. Women wear bright, embroidered skirts, waistcoats and headscarves, and goatskin boots. The interiors of the houses are decorated with embroidered cloth and their facades feature brightly painted, ornate plaster reliefs. The inhabitants speak in a vernacular which contains some Doric words, and the houses have wooden locks of a kind described by Homer. Olymbos is a matrilineal society – a family's property passes down from the mother to the first-born daughter. The women still grind corn in windmills and bake bread in outdoor communal ovens. Old-timer shoemaker Nikolaos Kanakis still hand-makes traditional shoes and boots in his musty cobbler's shop along the main street.

Olymbos, alas, is no longer a pristine backwater caught in a time warp. Nowadays hordes of tourists come to gape, and tourist shops are appearing everywhere. However, the town is still a fascinating place, and accommodation and food are inexpensive.

Diafani is Karpathos' small northern port. It's a backwater kind of place and very slow. Nonetheless it draws a daily parade of visitors who come on one of the two morning caïques from Pigadia, visit Olymbos, and can usually be found in mid-afternoon lolling around the cafes and pebbly beaches that abut the harbour while waiting for their caïque to take them back to Pigadia. Once they have departed, Diafani reverts back to its languid atmosphere and the streets belong once more to the locals and the handful of travellers who choose to stay on here.

There's no post office or bank, but Orfanos Travel Holidays (☎ 51 410, fax 51 316), owned by helpful English-speaking Nikos, has currency exchange and offers Internet access. There's no OTE but there are cardphones.

Unleaded and leaded petrol is only available in large plastic containers from the Theodora Protopappa store on a side street up from the harbour.

SOUTHERN DODECANESE

Places to Stay Just off the main street in Olymbos, the clean, simply furnished single/double rooms at **Pension Olymbos** (☎ 51 252) cost 4000/6000 dr. Just beyond the bus turnaround, **Mike's Rooms** (☎ 51 304) cost 7000 dr a double.

Hotel Aphrodite (☎ 51 307/454), near the central square, has immaculate doubles for 10,000 dr with bathroom. The views are among the best in Olymbos. Breakfast is included.

There's an unofficial, well-watered **camp site** at Vananda Beach, 30 minutes' walk (signposted) north of Diafani. **Hrysi Akti** (☎ 51 215), opposite the quay in Diafani, has doubles with bathroom, TV and fridge for 10,000 dr. **Nikos Hotel** (☎ 51 289, fax 51 316), just back from the waterfront, has comfortable singles/doubles for 6000/8000 dr with bathroom and breakfast included. The hotel is owned by Nikos of Orfanos Travel. **Balaskas Hotel** (☎ 51 320), set back about 150m from the seafront, has pleasant doubles for 9000 dr with bathroom.

Places to Eat Makarounes are served at all the restaurants in Olymbos. You'll eat well at **Olymbos Taverna** (☎ 51 252), below Pension Olymbos; at **Mike's Taverna** (☎ 51 304), directly below his rooms; and also at **Parthenonas Restaurant** (☎ 51 367), on the central square.

For a good view and top-rate loukoumades and makarounes the **Samiotiko '1769'** (☎ 51 272) is a little cafe-restaurant on the main street. A meal of makarounes, salad and a beer at any of the above places will cost around 2500 dr.

In Diafani the **Chrysi Akti Taverna** (☎ 51 215) and **Taverna Anatoli** (☎ 51 330) are good. The **Mayflower** (☎ 51 302) also nearby is also worth a look in. All three are cheap to medium priced. The older locals nearly all hang out for coffee and ouzo at **To Akteo**, an old-world style kafeneio on the waterfront.

Getting There & Around The only effective way to see the north quickly is on a day trip from Pigadia. Two caïques, *Chrysovalandou III* (mobile ☎ 09-4498 4424) and *Karpathos II* (mobile ☎ 09-4429 2634)

leave Pigadia at around 8.30 am and head for Diafani where a bus whisks visitors up to Olymbos and back. Basic (ie, unguided) tours cost 4000 dr, while guided tours cost 7000 dr. Possi Tours (see Travel Agencies in the Pigadia section) also organises bus tours from Lefkos to Olymbos (7000 dr).

From Diafani, excursion boats go to nearby beaches and occasionally to the uninhabited islet of Saria where there are some Byzantine remains. These caïque tours cost between 1000 dr and 3000 dr. See Orfanos Travel Holidays in Diafani for details.

Kasos Κάσος

☎ 0246 • postcode 858 00 • pop 1088

Kasos, 11km south of Karpathos, is really the end of the line. It's the last Dodecanese island before Crete and looking south, it is the last Greek island before Egypt. It is neither particularly easy to get to, nor to get away from if the weather in these parts is inclement. Kasos is a rocky little island with prickly pears, sparse olive and fig trees, drystone walls, and sheep and goats.

There is a dreamy, isolated feel about the place, yet the local Kasiots go about their lives without seeming to care about their perceived isolation. In fairness, the island does receive a steady stream of Kasiots from Athens or the USA during the summer months, as well as a trickle of curious foreign island hoppers wanting to tick this island off their map. Kasos is the perfect place to see something of traditional Greek island life, to take relaxing walks or to simply chill out at an unassuming destination where time moves just that little bit slower than elsewhere.

History

Despite being diminutive and remote, Kasos has an eventful and tragic history. During Turkish rule it flourished, and by 1820 it had 11,000 inhabitants and a large mercantile fleet. Mohammad Ali, the Turkish governor of Egypt, regarded this fleet as an impediment to his plan to establish a base on Crete from which to attack the Peloponnese and quell the uprising there. So, on 7 June 1824,

SOUTHERN DODECANESE

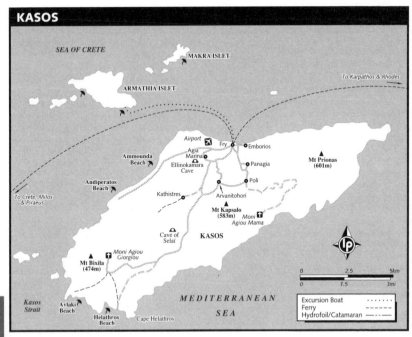

KASOS

Ali's men landed on Kasos and killed around 7000 inhabitants. This massacre is commemorated annually on the anniversary of the slaughter and Kasiots return from around the world to participate.

During the late 19th century, many Kasiots emigrated to Egypt and around 5000 of them helped build the Suez Canal. In the 20th century many emigrated to the USA. Today, many return in the summer months to make nostalgic visits to their diminutive homeland.

Getting There & Away

Air There are five flights weekly to Rhodes (13,400 dr), and five weekly to Karpathos (3500 dr). The Olympic Airways office (☎ 41 555) is on Fry's main street, Kritis.

Ferry The F/B *Vitsentzos Kornaros* and the F/B *Ierapetra* of LANE Lines of Crete stops at Kasos on its long, thrice-weekly 'milk run' from Rhodes to Piraeus.

The following table will give you an overview of services in high season.

destination	duration	price	frequency
Crete (Sitia)	2½ hours	2500 dr	3 weekly
Halki	6 hours	3300 dr	2 weekly
Karpathos (Pigadia)	3 hours	1800 dr	3 weekly
Milos	12 hours	5800 dr	3 weekly
Piraeus	17 hours	7800 dr	3 weekly
Rhodes	7 hours	5200 dr	3 weekly

Excursion Boat In summer there are excursion boats from Fry to the uninhabited Armathia Islet (1500 dr return), where there are sandy beaches.

Getting Around

There is no bus on Kasos. The airport is only a kilometre or so along the coast road from Fry. Ignore local road signs that suggest it is 4km. This may be just to drum up business for the local taxis.

There are two taxis on Kasos. One belongs to Giannis Nikolaou (☎ 41 158, mobile ☎ 09-7790 4632) and the other to Georgos Mondanos (☎ 41 278, mobile 09-4542 7308). Motorbikes can be rented from Frangiskos Motor Rentals (☎ 41 746).

While you can bring your car to Kasos – and visitors do – the paved road network is limited to the four main villages (see Around Kasos) all within 2km of Fry; the road to Andiperatos beach past the airport; and a paved road 11km to the south-west corner of the island from where there is foot access to Helathros beach.

FRY Φρυ

Fry (free), the island's capital and port, is a pleasant ramshackle kind of place with few concessions to tourism. There's not a lot to it and it can be thoroughly explored in under an hour. Its narrow whitewashed streets are usually busy with locals in animated discussion. Old men in American style baseball caps can often be heard switching from Greek to Brooklynese in mid-sentence, a reminder that many Kasiots left the island to find work in the USA, but still find time to visit or even retire in their old home.

The town's focal point is the picturesque old fishing harbour of Bouka where fishermen still gather to mend boats and nets and ply the sometimes choppy and open seas to make a living. Efforts to build a new and larger harbour east of Fry seem to have stalled, leaving a rather ugly and unfinished pile of cement blocks and earthworks in its place.

The suburb of Emborios is 1km to the east of Fry and makes a pleasant and easy evening stroll.

Orientation

Turn left when leaving the ferry quay to reach Bouka. Veer left, and then right, and continue along the waterfront to the central square of Plateia Iroön Kasou. Turn right here to reach Kritis, Fry's main street. To reach Emborios, continue along the waterfront passing the turn-off (signposted 'Agios Mamas') for Panagia, Poli and Agios Mamas.

The excellent 1:75,000 Freytag & Berndt map of *Karpathos & Kasos* is the best political map of Kasos while the locally produced *Kassos – The Tranquil Island* map is good on topographical relief but not as easy to follow. It also includes a town plan of Fry.

Information

Kasos does not have an EOT or tourist police, but Emmanouil Manousos at Kasos Maritime & Travel Agency (☎ 41 323, fax 41 036, ℮ emanousos@hellasnet.gr), Plateia Iroön Kasou, is helpful and speaks English. The agency sells ferry and air tickets, and will exchange money. Opening hours are 7.30 am to 3 pm and 5.30 to 11 pm.

Olympic Airways tickets can be obtained directly from the Olympic Airways office nearby (see the Getting There & Away chapter for more information).

The National Bank of Greece is represented by the supermarket on Kritis. There's a pharmacy across the road. There's also a stand-alone Commercial Bank ATM on the south side of Fry.

The post office is almost hidden away down a side street on the south side of town. The OTE is behind Plateia Dimokratias – you'll see the huge satellite dishes. There are a few card phones. Mobile phone users will be able to connect to all three of Greece's GSM mobile service providers.

The privately developed but helpful Web site at www.kassos-island.gr is worth checking for the latest information on the island.

The port police office (☎ 41 288) is behind the Church of Agios Spyridon. The police (☎ 41 222) are beyond the post office, on the opposite side.

Special Events

The Symi Festival hosts a few events in Kasos over three days, usually during the first week of August. See the Symi chapter for full details on this annual cultural festival.

Places to Stay

All of the island's limited accommodation is in Fry, except for the rooms at Moni Agiou Georgiou (see Monasteries in the Around

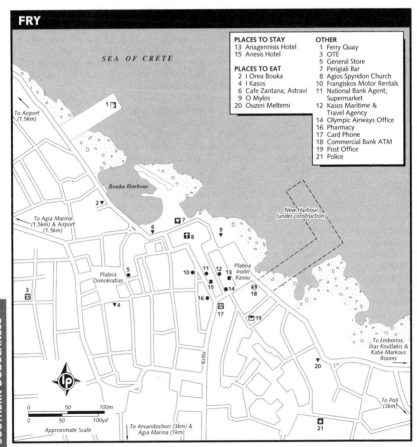

FRY

PLACES TO STAY
13 Anagennisis Hotel
15 Anesis Hotel

PLACES TO EAT
2 I Orea Bouka
4 I Kasos
6 Cafe Zantana; Astravi
9 O Mylos
20 Ouzeri Meltemi

OTHER
1 Ferry Quay
3 OTE
5 General Store
7 Perigiali Bar
8 Agios Spyridon Church
10 Frangiskos Motor Rentals
11 National Bank Agent;
   Supermarket
12 Kasos Maritime &
   Travel Agency
14 Olympic Airways Office
16 Pharmacy
17 Card Phone
18 Commercial Bank ATM
19 Post Office
21 Police

SEA OF CRETE

Bouka Harbour

New Harbour
(under construction)

To Airport
(1.5km)

To Agia Marina
(1.5km) & Airport
(1.5km)

Plateia
Iroön
Kasou

Plateia
Dimokratias

Kritis

To Emborios,
Ilias Koutlakis &
Katie Markous
Rooms

To Poli
(3km)

0   50   100m
0   50   100yd
Approximate Scale

To Arvanitochori (3km) &
Agia Marina (1km)

SOUTHERN DODECANESE

Kasos section). **Katie Markous** (☎ *41 613/498*) rents out doubles for 5000 dr, including kitchen. They're on the south side of the road to Emborios. Farther along this road, on the opposite side, **Ilias Koutlakis Rooms** (☎ *41 363*) costs 8000 dr a double with bathroom.

Anesis Hotel (☎ *41 234/201*), above the supermarket on Kritis, has singles/doubles for 6000/8000 dr with bathroom. **Anagennisis Hotel** (☎ *41 495, fax 41 036,* ℮ *emanousos@hellasnet.gr, Plateia Iroön Kasou*) has clean and comfortable double rooms with bathroom for 11,000 dr.

The owner of the Anagennisis Hotel, Emmanouil Manousos, also has well-equipped double/triple apartments called **Borianoula** for 15,000/18,000 dr in Emborios, just seven minutes' walk from Fry. They have two comfortable rooms each, a balcony with a sea view, and they're close to the nearby sandy beach.

Places to Eat

Fry has at least four restaurants and several snack bars. Perhaps the most enticing and interesting from a culinary aspect is **I Orea Bouka** (☎ *41 460*) overlooking

Bouka harbour, which offers up all the usual Greek fish and meat dishes, but on Wednesdays and Fridays dishes up some Egyptian specialities as well. Ask for *molohia* (a green soup) or *tamies* (similar to felafel). Also look out for Arab salads, rice and lentils, all concocted by chef and owner Foula Panayiotopoulou.

I Kasos (☎ 41 191, Plateia Dimokratias) is run by a women's cooperative. The food is well prepared and low-priced. The mezedes include *kritamos*, a plant that grows along the island's rocky shoreline.

O Mylos (☎ 41 825, Plateia Iroön Kasou) is also good, offering tasty casserole dishes and grilled meat and fish. It's more than likely to be open when others are closed.

Ouzeri Meltemi (☎ 41 888), on the road to Emborios, is also commendable, but only opens in high season.

There are several kafeneia in Fry, but young Kasiots congregate at the trendy *Cafe Zantana*, which overlooks Bouka harbour. Mihalis, the owner, makes excellent cappuccino and cocktails. It is open from 9 am until late. Upstairs from Cafe Zantana is the *Astravi* snack bar which dishes up pizzas and light snacks.

There's a *general store* for basic food items on Plateia Dimokratias.

Entertainment
Kasos' nightclub is *Perigiali Bar*, between Bouka and Plateia Iroön Kasou. The music played is predominantly Greek. *Alenti Bar*, on the road to Agia Marina, and *Marianthi Bar*, on the way to Emborios, are open only in high season.

AROUND KASOS
Beaches
Kasos' best beach is the isolated, pebbled cove of **Helathros**, near Moni Agiou Georgiou. There are no facilities at the beach. You can get there either along an 11km paved road and then a dirt track which bears left (downhill) from the road to the monastery, or along a slightly longer track from the monastery. **Avlaki** is another decent beach reached along a path from the monastery.

Nearest to Fry is the mediocre **Ammounda Beach**, beyond the airport, near the blue-domed church of Agios Konstantinos. There are slightly better beaches farther along this stretch of coast, notably the fine pebbled **Andiperatos Beach** at the end of the paved road system.

Agia Marina
Agia Marina, 1km south-west of Fry, is a pretty village with a gleaming white and blue church. On 17 July the Festival of Agia Marina is celebrated here. From Agia Marina the road continues to verdant **Arvanito-hori**, with fig and pomegranate trees.

Poli
Poli, 3km south-east of Fry, is the former capital, built on the ancient acropolis. **Panagia**, between Fry and Poli, has fewer than 50 inhabitants. Its once-grand sea captains' and ship owners' mansions are now derelict.

Caves
The curious may care to take a short walk past the village of Agia Marina to visit the rather undeveloped but still impressive **Ellinokamara Cave**, or to walk on a further hour and a half to the larger **Selaï Cave** with fairly impressive stalactites at its far end.

Monasteries
The island has two monasteries: **Moni Agiou Mama** and **Moni Agiou Georgiou**. The uninhabited Moni Agiou Mama on the south coast is a 1½ hour walk from Fry. Take the Poli road and just before the village turn left (signposted 'Agios Mamas'). The road winds uphill through a dramatic, eroded landscape of rock-strewn mountains, crumbling terraces and soaring cliffs. Eventually you will come to a sharp turn right (signposted again). Hold onto your hat here, as it's known locally as *aeras* (air) – it's the windiest spot on the island. From here the track descends to the blue and white monastery.

A new 11km asphalt road leads from Fry to Moni Agiou Georgiou. There are no monks, but there is a resident caretaker for most of the year, and basic (free) accommodation for visitors.

Kastellorizo

Καστελλόριζο

☎ 0246 • postcode 851 11 • pop 275

It takes a certain amount of decisiveness and a sense of adventure to come to tiny, rocky Kastellorizo (kah-stel-**o**-rih-zo). This mere speck on the map is 118km east of Rhodes, its nearest Greek neighbour, yet only 2.5km from the southern coast of Turkey and its nearest neighbouring town Kaş. Kastellorizo is so-named for the 'red castle' that once dominated the main port, but is also known as 'Megisti' (the largest), for it is the largest of a group of 14 islets that surround this isolated Hellenic outpost. The island's remoteness has so far ensured that its tourism is low-key yet there are more Australian-Greek Kastellorizians here in summer than locals. This is an indication of a widespread diaspora of Kastellorizians, most of whom set up home Down Under after WWI. There are no beaches, but there are rocky inlets from where you can swim and snorkel in a crystal-clear sea.

The island featured in the Oscar-winning Italian film *Mediterraneo* (1991), which was based on a book by an Italian army sergeant. The little book *Capture Kastellorizo* by Marina Pitsonis is available on the island. The author is a Greek/Australian whose father came from Kastellorizo. The book features eight island walks.

History

The town you see today is a virtual ghost town compared to its heyday past. This is made all the more poignant by an awareness of the island's past greatness. Due to its strategic position, Dorians, Romans, crusaders, Egyptians, Turks, Venetians and pirates have all landed on its shores. The 20th century was no less traumatic, with French, British and Italian occupiers.

In 1552, Kastellorizo surrendered peacefully to the Turks and so was granted special privileges. It was allowed to preserve its language, religion and traditions. Its cargo fleet became the largest in the Dodecanese and the islanders achieved a high degree of culture and education.

Kastellorizo lost all strategic and economic importance after the 1923 population exchange. In 1928 it was ceded to the Italians, who severely oppressed the islanders; in contrast, Turkish rule must have seemed like the good old days. Many islanders emigrated to Perth, Australia, where some 10,000 of them live today.

During WWII, Kastellorizo suffered severe bombardment, and English commanders ordered the few remaining inhabitants to abandon their island. They fled to Cyprus, Palestine and Egypt, with no belongings. In October 1945, 300 islanders boarded the Australian ship, *Empire Control*, to return to Kastellorizo. Tragically, the ship caught fire and 35 people lost their lives. Two months later the remaining refugees returned to their island to find that most of their houses had been destroyed by bombing and the remainder ransacked by the occupying troops. Not surprisingly, more islanders emigrated. Most of the houses that escaped the bombing in WWII stand empty.

Despite this gloomy picture, Kastellorizo's waterfront is surprisingly lively. Kastellorizo

KASTELLORIZO

To Ro & Rhodes

Moni Agiou Stefanou

0   500   1000m
0   500   1000yd

Kastellorizo Town

To Kaş & Turkey

Knights of St John Castle

To Strongyli

Moni Agias Triadas

Paleokastro   ▲ Vikla (273m)

Mandraki

Horafia

Airport

KASTELLORIZO   Moni Agiou Georgiou

Blue Cave

MEDITERRANEAN SEA

Excursion Boat ·······
Ferry ——————
Hydrofoil/Catamaran – – – – –

SOUTHERN DODECANESE

today survives on tourism, government subsidies and remittances from Kastellorizians who have made it big in the outside world.

Getting There & Away

Air In July and August there are daily flights to and from Rhodes (10,900 dr), dropping to three weekly at other times. You can buy tickets from Dizi Tours & Travel (☎/fax 49 240) in Kastellorizo Town. A ramshackle bus takes passengers to and from the airport and the port (500 dr).

Ferry Kastellorizo has the least ferry connections in the whole of the Dodecanese archipelago and what ferries do run are thanks to heavy government subsidies to keep this vital link open. At the time of research, only the F/B *Nisos Kalymnos* and the F/B *Milena* or F/B *Marina* (both belonging to G&A Ferries) were running to and from Kastellorizo, with additional links being provided up into the Dodecanese by the F/B *Nisos Kalymnos*.

Departure from Kastellorizo to Rhodes (5½ hours, 3400 dr) with the F/B *Nisos Kalymnos* is usually at 11.15 pm on Monday and Friday, while G&A's service departs once a week at the more convenient time of 4 pm and takes only four hours. These schedules are subject to yearly as well as seasonal change, so check locally with travel agents for the latest details.

Excursion Boat to Turkey Islanders go on frequent shopping trips to Kaş (Andifellos in Greek) in Turkey and day trips (5000 dr) are also offered to tourists. Look for the signs along the waterfront.

Note that for one-way travellers it is possible to enter and exit Greece legally via this route.

Getting Around

There is one bus on the island, which is used solely to transport people to and from the airport and the port (500 dr). There are no taxis.

Excursion boats go to the islets of **Ro**, **Agios Georgios** and **Strongyli**, and the spectacular **Blue Cave** (Parasta), which is named for its brilliant blue water due to refracted sunlight. All of these trips cost around 5000 dr.

KASTELLORIZO TOWN

Kastellorizo Town and the satellite neighbourhood of Mandraki, over the hill and to the west, is the only settlement on the island. Built around a U-shaped bay, its waterfront is skirted with imposing three-storey mansions with wooden balconies and red-tiled roofs. It is undoubtedly pretty nowadays, but black and white photos on display in harbourside shops and cafes depict a Kastellorizo that was once a booming, teeming metropolis and seaplane port. However, the alluring facade of today's waterfront contrasts starkly with backstreets of abandoned houses overgrown with ivy, crumbling stairways and stony pathways winding between them.

Since everyone on the island must pass through Kastellorizo Town at some point in

---

Mediterraneo – the Movie

If you have not seen the movie before you come to Kastellorizo, do so when you go home. You will enjoy it immensely. If you cannot recognise a lot of the places depicted in the film, don't be surprised. Many of the scenes depicting a 1940s Kastellorizo were shot away from today's busy waterfront and centred instead on Mandraki Bay and the square abutting the church of Agios Konstantinos & Eleni and the nearby school in the area known as Horafia. The famous soccer scene was shot at a then unpaved airport while other scenes were shot at locations along the coastline.

The legacy of the movie still lingers on and many Italians now come in search of the locations, or simply to satisfy their curiosity about an island that had so obviously enchanted the protagonists of this 1991 classic. The actor who portrayed one of the main characters of the movie, the unassuming Antonio (Claudio Bigagli) who married the prostitute Vasilissa (Vanna Barba), was spotted by this writer arriving, pack on back, at Kastellorizo airport in the summer of 2000. Some old habits die hard.

SOUTHERN DODECANESE

the day, within 24 hours you will inevitably be on nodding terms with all your fellow visitors and locals alike.

Orientation

The quay is at the eastern side of the bay. The central square, Plateia Ethelondon Kastellorizou, abuts the waterfront almost halfway round the bay, next to the yachting jetty. The suburbs of Horafia and Mandraki are reached by ascending the wide steps at the east side of the bay.

Information

There are no tourist offices on Kastellorizo, but in fairness you don't really need one, since choices are limited and generally covered in this chapter. The two travel agencies will fill you in on what you don't find here. Papoutsis Travel Agency (☎ 70 830, fax 49 286, e paptrv@rho.forthnet.gr), by the bus stop, sells tickets for both ferries while Dizi Tours & Travel (☎ 30 241, fax 49 240) on the waterfront is the Olympic Airways agent.

The National Bank of Greece (☎ 49 356) is in the middle of the waterfront, next to the ferry ticket agency and has an ATM.

The post office is on the western side of the bay. There is no OTE but there are plenty of card phones. Mobile phone users can pick up all three Greek GSM mobile service providers, as well as Turkcell GSM from Turkey.

The Kaz Bar (see Places to Eat) offers Internet access at around 1000 dr per hour.

The port police (☎ 49 333) are at the eastern tip of the bay while the police (☎ 49 333) are at the western side, near the post office.

Things to See

The **Knights of St John Castle** stands above the quay. A metal staircase leads to the top from where there are splendid views of Turkey and Kastellorizo Town. The **museum** within the castle houses a well displayed collection. Opening times are 7.30 am to 2.30 pm Tuesday to Sunday; entry is free. Beyond the museum, steps lead down to a coastal pathway, from where more steps go up the cliff to a **Lycian tomb** with a Doric facade. There are several along the Anatolian coast, but this is the only known one in Greece.

Special Events

The Symi Festival hosts a few events in Kastellorizo over one week towards the middle of August. See the Symi chapter for full details on this annual cultural festival.

Places to Stay – Budget

Accommodation is of a reasonably high standard though budget accommodation is not widely available and can be a bit pokey. Most *domatia* do not display signs, but it's not difficult to find the owners – that is, if they don't find *you* when you disembark.

Villa Kaserma (☎ 49 370, fax 49 365) is the red-and-white building standing above the western waterfront. The very pleasant double/triple rooms with bathrooms cost 9000/11,000 dr. Inquire about a room here at Lazarakis Restaurant (see Places to Eat).

Pension Palameria (☎ 49 282, fax 49 071) is a newly converted building on the small square at the north-western corner of the waterfront. Spotless doubles cost 10,000 dr with bathroom and kitchen/dining area. Inquire about these rooms at To Mikros Parisi restaurant.

I Anaviosi (☎ 49 302), above the Sydney Restaurant, has rates of 6000 dr for very average doubles with shared bathroom. The owner, Evangelos Polos, also has some better double rooms with bathroom for 10,000 dr.

Panorama Studios (☎ 49 098, mobile ☎ 09-7247 7186), over near Mandraki, were new in 2000 and offer roomy double/triple fridge-equipped studios for 12,000 dr. Some studios have balconies and views across to Kaş in Turkey.

Places to Stay – Mid-Range

Further around, the island's only hotel, the B-class *Hotel Megisti* (☎ 49 272, fax 49 221) has attractive singles/doubles for 14,500/19,000 dr. The friendly English-speaking manager, Nektarios Karavelatzis, owns *Karnagio Apartments* (☎/fax 49 266), housed in a beautifully restored red and ochre mansion near the top of the harbour's western side. These traditionally furnished double/triple apartments cost 15,000 dr and a five-person apartment is 20,000 dr.

Kastellorizo Hotel Apartments (☎ 49 044, fax 49 279, e kastel@otenet.gr) are beautiful, fully equipped rooms that go for around 15,000 dr, while farther along the western side of the bay, the rooms at *Pension Mediterraneo* (☎ 49 368) are equally well-appointed and go for 19,000 dr.

Places to Eat

There is no shortage of eating places in Kastellorizo and the good news is that each choice is within five minutes' walk of the next one. Standards are high and prices are reasonable. A filling meal with wine at most places will end up costing between 3000 dr and 4000 dr per person.

Some places cater more to yachties, have a prime location and offer up varied picture menus; others are home-style kitchens with no-nonsense fare and minimum frills. The busiest stretch is on the southern side of the harbour where restaurants interchange with

cafes and bars, while the northern side is more laid-back and less crowded.

To Mikro Parisi (☎ 49 282), on the north side on the waterfront, has been going strong for 30 years. It serves generous helpings of grilled fish and meat. *Sydney Restaurant* (☎ 49 302), a little farther along, is also highly commendable and serves similar fare. The chickpea patties *(revithokeftedhes)* are highly recommended. Closer to the square, *Lazarakis Restaurant* (☎ 49 370), on the waterfront opposite the jetty, excels in seafood and has tables invitingly set out on the jetty for romantic candle-lit dinners.

On the southern side, newcomer *Tis Ypomonis* (☎ 49 224) does a nightly roaring trade in souvlaki, sausage and steaks, while the ouzeri-cum-Internet bar, *Kaz Bar* (☎ 49 067), owned and run by Sydneysider Kostas (Colin Paull) Pavlidis, serves up slightly pricey, but well-made mezedes.

Orea Megisti (☎ 49 282, Plateia Ethelondon Kastellorizou) serves a range of well-prepared casserole dishes and spit-roast goat and lamb, both of which are superlative, especially when accompanied with rice cooked with herbs – a local speciality.

Restaurant Platania, on Plateia Mihail & Patricias Kaïli (known commonly as Plateia Horafion), is a laid-back unpretentious place which appeared in the film *Mediterraneo*, a fact it proudly proclaims in huge lettering on the outside wall. This is a good alternative spot for breakfast.

The *Megas Alexandros Grocery*, on the southern side of the harbour, is stocked with enough supplies to keep the hungriest traveller in food and drink.

Entertainment

There are several equally popular watering holes on the waterfront that are open all day, and at least one joint out by the old mosque that opens late and closes in the early hours.

The *Kaz Bar* is a good place to kick off since you can check your email first. The *Meltemi* next door has tempting waterside chairs and cold beers, while you can hardly miss the gaudily painted *Mythos Bar* whose

SOUTHERN DODECANESE

The Woman of Ro

The islet of Ro, one of Kastellorizo's 13 satellites, has been immortalised along with its last inhabitant, Despina Ahladioti, alias the Woman of Ro, who died in 1982. Despina and her shepherd husband were the only inhabitants of Ro. When her husband died, Despina remained alone on the island, staunchly hoisting the Greek flag every morning, and lowering it in the evening, in full view of the Turkish coast. The Woman of Ro has become a symbol of the Greek spirit of indomitability in the face of adversity. There are excursion boats to the islet; look for signs along the waterfront at Kastellorizo Town. There is also a bust of the Woman of Ro on Plateia Horafion.

'original' architecture probably had town planners gnashing their teeth when it was completed.

The *Aussie Bar*, out by the old mosque, opens at 10 pm and kicks on until everyone has had their fill and gone home.

AROUND KASTELLORIZO
Moni Agiou Georgiou
Moni Agiou Georgiou is the largest of the monasteries that dot the island. Within its church is the subterranean Chapel of Agios Haralambos reached by steep stone steps. Here, Greek children were given religious instruction during Turkish times. The church is kept locked; ask around the waterfront for the whereabouts of the caretaker. To reach the monastery climb the conspicuous zigzag white stone steps behind the town and at the top take the path straight ahead. The path looks steep and long, but can be undertaken by any reasonably fit walker in about 20 minutes. It's worth it just for the views from the top.

Moni Agiou Stefanou
Moni Agiou Stefanou, on the north coast, is the setting for one of the island's most important celebrations, Agios Stefanos Day on 1 August. The path to the little white monastery begins behind the post office. From the monastery a path leads to a bay where you can swim.

Paleokastro
Paleokastro was the island's ancient capital. Within its Hellenistic walls are an ancient tower, a water cistern and three churches. Concrete steps, just beyond a soldier's sentry box on the airport road, are the beginning of the steep path to Paleokastro.

Swimming
Kastellorizo is not endowed with beaches and if you attempt to swim off rocks randomly you will encounter sea urchins (see Cuts, Bites & Stings in the Facts for the Visitor chapter for more information). The best and most convenient spot is in front of the Hotel Megisti, where there is a large concrete sun bathing deck with umbrellas and loungers to hire (500 dr) and steps to enter the water.

Central Dodecanese

Symi Σύμη

☎ 0246 • postcode 856 00 • pop 2332

Symi is a rocky, dry island that lies within the geographical embrace of Turkey, only 10km from the Turkish peninsula of Datça. Some 24km north of Rhodes, the island has a scenic interior, dotted with pine and cypress woods. Its deeply indented coast with precipitous cliffs, and numerous small bays with pebbled beaches, make it enormously popular both with day-trippers from Rhodes and an active and buoyant British expat community who have made this beautiful island home.

Symi is an excellent base for a holiday, with good accommodation and food, excellent and easy transport links to the outside world, decent beaches and just the right balance of picturesqueness and modernity to make a week or more here an ideal break. On the downside, the island suffers from a severe water shortage and gets overrun with hoards of day-trippers from Rhodes. However, once they have left the island again, it reverts to its relatively tranquil existence.

The Dodecanese's most successful cultural event of the year is the summertime Symi Festival, which draws in the crowds of visitors seeking the best in music, drama and literature.

History

Symi has a long tradition of both sponge diving and shipbuilding. During Ottoman times it was granted the right to fish for sponges in Turkish waters. In return Symi supplied the sultan with first-class boat builders and top-quality sponges.

The sponge-diving business and a lucrative shipbuilding industry brought prosperity to the island. Gracious mansions were built and culture and education flourished. By the beginning of the 20th century the population was 22,500 and the island was

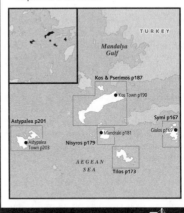

launching some 500 ships a year. But the Italian occupation, combined with the introduction of the steamship and Kalymnos' rise as the Aegean's principal sponge producer, put an end to Symi's prosperity.

The treaty surrendering the Dodecanese Islands to the Allies was signed on Symi on 8 May 1945.

Getting There & Away

Ferry Symi is not as well served by the main ferries heading north to the other Dodecanese islands and Piraeus. Both DANE (☎ 71 307) and G&A Ferries (☎ 71 320) send only one or two ferries each week via Symi to destinations north. The slower, Kalymnos-based F/B *Nisos Kalymnos* provides additional services plus links to Astypalea (via Kalymnos) and Kastellorizo (via Rhodes).

Services to Rhodes are much more frequent, with the local-based *Symi I* and faster *Symi II* boats running to and from Rhodes on a daily basis. ANES (☎ 71 100) runs these boats and has a ticket office on the north side of the harbour. See also Excursion Boats following.

The following table will give you an overview of the main destinations from Symi.

destination	duration	price	frequency
Astypalea	11 hours	3700 dr	2 weekly
Kalymnos	3¾ hours	2900 dr	4 weekly
Kastellorizo	7½ hours	3500 dr	2 weekly
Kos	1½ hours	2100 dr	4 weekly
Leros	5 hours	3700 dr	1 weekly
Patmos	7 hours	4200 dr	1 weekly
Piraeus	16¼ hours	7200 dr	4 weekly
Rhodes	1½ hours	1300 dr	7 weekly

Hydrofoil Symi is connected by hydrofoil to Kos (one hour, 4700 dr), Kalymnos (1½ hours, 6600 dr), Astypalea (four hours, 8250 dr) and Rhodes (50 minutes, 2950 dr). Departures in either direction (north or south) are usually on weekends (Saturday and Sunday).

The Symi-owned *Aigli* hydrofoil leaves Symi for Rhodes at 7.15 am and returns to Symi at 5 or 6 pm, depending on the day's schedule.

Catamaran The Rhodes-based *Dodekanisos Express* calls in at Symi on Saturday and Sunday in summer as the first stop on its daily run up the Dodecanese from Rhodes. Departures heading north from Symi are usually around 9.30 am, with arrival in Patmos at 2.10 pm. Departures heading south from Symi are usually around 6.45 pm, with arrival in Rhodes at 7.40 pm. Tickets can be bought at Symi Tours (☎ 71 307) in Gialos.

Using this catamaran is a good way to make a day trip to Symi from Rhodes and it gives you more time on the island than the slower tourist boats which arrive in Symi later and depart earlier.

Excursion Boat There are daily excursion boats running between Symi and Rhodes' Mandraki Harbour. The Symi-based *Symi I* and *Symi II* are the cheapest. They are owned cooperatively by the people of Symi, and operate as excursion boats as well as regular passenger boats. Tickets cost 3200 dr return and can be bought on board.

Symi Tours (☎ 71 307) has excursion trips to the town of Datça in Turkey on Saturday, which is market day. The cost is 10,000 dr return (including 4000 dr Turkish port tax). You must hand in your passport the day before.

Getting Around

Bus & Taxi A minibus makes frequent runs between Gialos and Pedi Beach (via Horio). Check the current schedule with Symi Tours. The fare is a flat 200 dr.

There are four taxi owners on Symi. They are Theodoris (mobile ☎ 09-4527 3842), Stamatis (mobile ☎ 09-4522 6348), Anastasia/Sotiris (mobile ☎ 09-4410 5596) and Kostas (mobile ☎ 09-4684 4417). Sample taxi tariffs are Horio (700 dr), Pedi (800 dr) and Nimborios (1300 dr). After midnight, fares attract a 400 dr surcharge.

The bus stop and taxi rank are on the east side of the harbour.

Car & Motorcycle There is not a large road network in Symi and while it is perfectly feasible to bring your car or motorbike to the island in order to get around, Symiots prefer that you do not. Instead, they like to promote an island atmosphere free of motorised transport wherever possible. That said, you can still hire a motorbike. Rent-a-Moto (☎ 71 926), on the north side of the harbour, will rent you motorbikes from about 6000 dr per day.

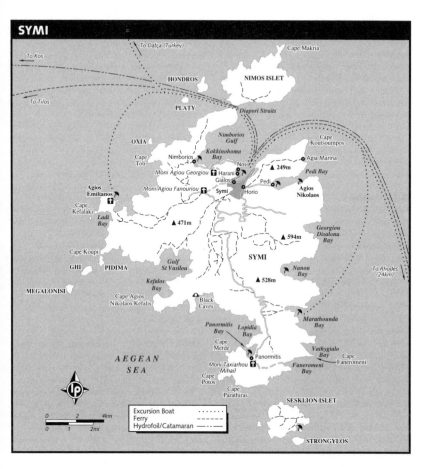

SYMI

To Kos
To Tilos
To Datça (Turkey)
Cape Makria
HONDROS
NIMOS ISLET
PLATY
Diapori Straits
Nimborios Gulf
OXIA
Cape Koutsoumpos
Cape Toli
Nimborios
Kokkinohoma Bay
Nos
Agia Marina
Moni Agiou Georgiou
Harani
Gialos
Pedi
Pedi Bay
249m
Moni Agiou Fanouriou
Symi
Horio
Agios Nikolaos
Agios Emilianos
Cape Kefalaki
Ladi Bay
471m
Georgiou Disalona Bay
Cape Koupi
594m
SYMI
To Rhodes (24km)
GHI
PIDIMA
Gulf St Vasilou
Nanou Bay
MEGALONISI
Kefalos Bay
528m
Cape Agios Nikolaos Kefalis
Black Caves
Marathounda Bay
Panormitis Bay
Lopidia Bay
Cape Merde
Panormitis
Vathygialo Bay
Cape Faneromeni
AEGEAN SEA
Moni Taxiarhou Mihail
Cape Potos
Faneromeni Bay
Cape Parathiras
SESKLION ISLET
Excursion Boat · · · · · ·
Ferry - - - - - -
Hydrofoil/Catamaran ———
0   2   4km
0   1   2mi
STRONGYLOS

Boats You can rent small motorised dinghies from Rent Boats Yiannis (☎ 71 931, mobile ☎ 09-4531 8916) for around 10,000 dr per day. Petrol costs are extra. Look for them on the Campanile jetty.

Excursion Boat Several excursion boats do trips to Moni Taxiarhou Mihail and Sesklia Islet where there's a shady beach. Check the boards for the best value tickets. Symi Tours also has trips to the monastery (10,000 dr).

Excursion boats also go to some of the island's more remote beaches.

Taxi Boats These small boats do trips to many of the island's beaches.

GIALOS

Gialos is undeniably pretty. As you enter the harbour you are surrounded on both sides by neoclassical mansions rising majestically and amphitheatrically around the steep hills that flank the narrow U-shaped harbour. Gialos was once a rich town, its wealth built up on the shipbuilding industry that supported a thriving population. When access to wood from the Turkish mainland became difficult following the secession from the Ottoman empire at the end of the 19th century and when steam ships began to be preferred over wooden sailboats, Gialos' fortunes took a nosedive. The once grand mansions were abandoned and began to crumble.

Today it is tourists and investors who have put money back into Gialos and the mansions are rising once again, painstakingly restored to their former glory. Behind the facade though, many buildings still lie in ruins. The town is divided into two parts: Gialos, the harbour, and Horio, above, crowned by the *kastro* (castle).

Orientation

Ferries, hydrofoils and the catamaran arrive and dock just south of the prominent Italian-era campanile (clock tower) at the north-eastern end of the harbour. Excursion boats dock a little farther along. Excursion boats to Symi's beaches leave from the top of the opposite side of the harbour. The centre of activity in Gialos is the promenade at the centre of the harbour. From the quay, walk left and round, crossing an ornamental stone bridge to reach the centre. The main square is a large open expanse just west of the stone bridge. The smaller Plateia tis Skalas is on the south side of the harbour. Kali Strata, a broad stairway, leads from here to Horio.

There is no decent map of Symi or Gialos Town available anywhere yet. The tourist map of Symi available in stores on the island is sufficient, but not brilliant. The *Symi Visitor* newspaper usually includes a hand-drawn map of Gialos, Horio and Pedi in its newspaper, showing advertiser locations.

Information

Tourist Office There is a Symi Visitor Office sharing space with the ANES ticket office on the northern side of the harbour.

Money The National Bank of Greece is near the centre of the harbourfront. The Ionian Bank on the waterfront, near the excursion boat quay, has an ATM. Opening hours are generally 8 am to 2 pm. Travel agencies will also exchange money.

Post & Communications The post office (☎ 71 315), at the north-eastern end of the harbour, is open from 7.30 am to 2 pm, Monday to Friday. The OTE (☎ 71 212) is signposted from the eastern side of the central square. Symi's Internet cafe is the Vapori Bar (☎ 72 082, e vapori@otenet.gr), near the beginning of Kali Strata. It is open from 4.30 pm onwards. Access charges are 1000 dr for 30 minutes or 1500 dr for one hour.

Internet Resources The best place to look for current information on the Web site at www.symi-island.gr. There is a wide range of information on the island as well as a rather stunning satellite photo of the Dodecanese.

Travel Agencies There is no EOT in Gialos, but the staff at Symi Tours (☎ 71 307, fax 72 292) or Kalodoukas Tours (☎ 71 077, fax 71 491, e information@kalodoukas.gr) are helpful. They are both near the beginning of Kali Strata.

Bookshops The foreign-language newspapers and tourist guides can be bought at the Foreign Press Agency on the south side of the harbour. The *Symi Visitor* (☎/fax 72 755, e symi-vis@otenet.gr) is an English-language newspaper published weekly and covering all aspects of life on the island from politics to real estate. The paper is free locally but is available overseas by subscription. The *Symi Visitor* office is just off the main square.

Kalodoukas Tours (see Travel Agencies) runs a small book exchange scheme.

Medical Services An on-call doctor can be summoned in Gialos (mobile ☎ 09-4634 8662), or in Horio (mobile ☎ 09-6558 8987). There is a pharmacy (☎ 71 888) near the taxi rank. It is open 9 am to 1 pm and 5 to 9.30 pm Monday to Saturday, and 9 am to 1 pm on Sunday.

Emergency The police (☎ 71 111) and port police (☎ 71 205) share the large white building beside the clock tower.

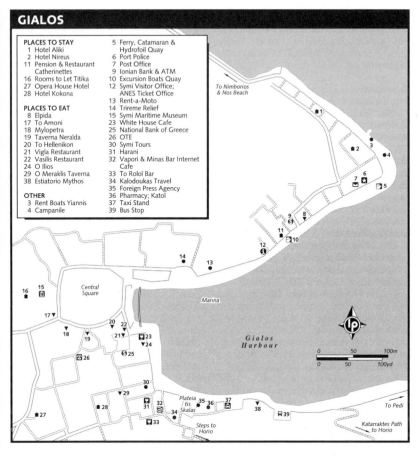

GIALOS

PLACES TO STAY		5	Ferry, Catamaran &
1	Hotel Aliki		Hydrofoil Quay
2	Hotel Nireus	6	Port Police
11	Pension & Restaurant	7	Post Office
	Catherinettes	9	Ionian Bank & ATM
16	Rooms to Let Titika	10	Excursion Boats Quay
27	Opera House Hotel	12	Symi Visitor Office;
28	Hotel Kokona		ANES Ticket Office
		13	Rent-a-Moto
PLACES TO EAT		14	Trireme Relief
8	Elpida	15	Symi Maritime Museum
17	To Amoni	23	White House Cafe
18	Mylopetra	25	National Bank of Greece
19	Taverna Neraïda	26	OTE
20	To Hellenikon	30	Symi Tours
21	Vigla Restaurant	31	Harani
22	Vasilis Restaurant	32	Vapori & Minas Bar Internet
24	O Ilios		Cafe
29	O Meraklis Taverna	33	To Roloï Bar
38	Estiatorio Mythos	34	Kalodoukas Travel
		35	Foreign Press Agency
OTHER		36	Pharmacy; Katoï
3	Rent Boats Yiannis	37	Taxi Stand
4	Campanile	39	Bus Stop

To Nimborios & Nos Beach

To Pedi

Central Square

Marina

Gialos Harbour

0   50   100m
0   50   100yd

Plateia tis Skalas

Steps to Horio

Katarraktes Path to Horio

Things to See & Do

Horio consists of narrow, labyrinthine streets crossed by crumbling archways. As you approach the kastro, the once-grand 19th-century neoclassical mansions give way to small, modest stone dwellings of the 18th century. The main way up is via the **Kali Strata**, a long but moderate climb up from behind the south side of Gialos. A more adventurous way up is to take the **Katarraktes Path**, which begins from the south-eastern side of the harbour. This steeper climb used to be the common route up to Horio before the Kali Strata was built in the 19th century.

The **Museum of Symi**, on the way to the castle, displays archaeological and folklore exhibits. Opening times are 10 am to 2 pm Tuesday to Sunday. Admission costs 500 dr. The castle incorporates blocks from the ancient acropolis of Gialos, and the **Church of Megali Panagia** is located within its walls.

The **Symi Maritime Museum**, behind the central square, is open 10 am to 2 pm Tuesday to Sunday. Admission is 500 dr. Look out for the **trireme relief** on the north harbour wall, which is a copy of the trireme relief in the Acropolis of Lindos.

CENTRAL DODECANESE

The multilingual guides from Symi Tours lead **walks** around the island. The publication *Walking on Symi* by Francis Noble (2000 dr) is on sale at Kalodoukas Travel at the beginning of Kali Strata.

Courses

There is a series of winter art courses run by the Symi Arts Workshop (☎ 72 755, e symi-vis@otenet.gr) including traditional stencilling and watercolour painting. Course fees include accommodation, breakfast, tuition, morning coffee and some mezes meals; it's part of a wider program designed to promote cultural tourism to Symi. Costs are variable and are available upon application.

Special Events

The Symi Festival is a colourful annual cultural event beginning in July and ending in September. This festival is held jointly by the municipalities of Symi, Kastellorizo, Halki, Kasos, Nisyros, Tilos and Astypalea and comprises musical, theatrical and literary performances from some of Greece's top artists. While most performances are held in Symi, there are between one and eight performances held on the other islands as well. Attendance at these concerts is free.

For current details check out the Web site www.symi-island.gr, or contact the organisers on ☎ 72 444, mobile ☎ 09-4538 7244, fax 71 344, or e festival@symi-island.gr.

Places to Stay – Budget

There is very little budget accommodation on Symi. The cheapest doubles cost around 9500 dr. Some accommodation owners meet the boats.

Rooms to Let Titika, located behind the Maritime Museum, has clean, nicely furnished air-conditioned double/triple rooms for 12,000/14,000 dr with bathrooms. You can make inquiries at Kostos Tourist Shop at the centre of the harbour. *Hotel Kokona* (☎ 71 549/451, fax 72620) has comfortable rooms with bathroom for 12,000/14,000 dr. The hotel is behind the southern side of the harbour, on the street to the left of the large church.

Pension Catherinettes (☎/fax 72 698, e marina-epe@rho.forthnet.gr) is on the north side, housed in the former town hall where the treaty granting the Dodecanese to the Allies was signed. Some of its rooms have magnificent painted ceilings. Doubles with a sea view are 15,000 dr, and those without are 9500 dr.

Hotel Fiona (☎/fax 72 755), in Horio, has lovely rooms with wood-panelled ceilings. Doubles/triples are 14,000/16,500 dr with bathroom. To reach the hotel, turn left off the Kali Strata at the top of the steps.

Nikolitsi Fotini Studios (☎ 71 780), near Nos Beach, are clean and comfortable with well-equipped kitchen areas. Doubles are 12,000 dr. If you call ahead the owner will pick you up from the harbour.

Places to Stay – Mid-Range

Opera House Hotel (☎ 72 034, fax 72 035), well signposted from the harbour, is an impressive cluster of buildings in a peaceful garden. Spacious double/triple studios are 22,000/27,000 dr. *Hotel Nireus* (☎ 72 400, fax 72 404), close to the ferry quay, has elegant, traditional double/triple rooms for 25,000/35,000 dr and double/triple suites for 35,000/37,000 dr, including breakfast. Farther along, the A-class *Hotel Aliki* (☎ 71 665, fax 71 655) is another traditional-style hotel. Singles/doubles are 26,000/32,000 dr.

Places to Eat – Budget

Many of Gialos' restaurants tend to be rather mediocre, catering for day-trippers. These tend to be clustered on the same side of the harbour as the ferry quay. However, here are some good exceptions.

Vigla Restaurant (☎ 72 056) and *Vasilis Restaurant* (☎ 72 753), both close to each other near the main square are good choices. *O Meraklis Taverna* (☎ 71 003), a block back from Symi Tours, is excellent and the low-priced *Taverna Neraïda*, also near the main square, is worth checking out.

Restaurant Les Catherinettes (☎ 72 698), below the pension, offers an extensive range of well-prepared dishes; the mixed mezedes plate plus retsina for two people costs 5000 dr.

English-run **O Ilios** (☎ 72 172), in the centre of the harbourfront, is a good vegetarian restaurant serving snacks during the day and three-course meals in the evening, but service can be very slow if it gets busy. **Elpida**, near the excursion boat quay, is a good spot for breakfast and tea, especially if you missed eating thanks to your early start from Rhodes.

Vapori & Minas Bar (☎ 72 082) serves good breakfasts and snacks and has free newspapers and magazines as well as Internet access (see Post & Communications earlier).

Places to Eat – Mid-Range

Near the main square, the classy **To Hellenikon** (☎ 72 455) has a cellar of 140 different Greek wines, and is known as the wine restaurant of Symi. The food offered is equally impressive. Unusual mezedes include sea urchin roe, snails with pesto and goat's cheese with mulberries. Desserts include a luscious concoction of ice cream, cream, dried fruits, red wine and rum. Expect to pay around 12,000 dr for a three-course meal with wine.

Quietly successful and operating without fuss is **Estiatorio Mythos** (☎ 71 488), on the south side of the harbour just before the bus stop. At lunchtime, Mythos serves mainly pasta dishes – see the daily blackboard specials. For evening harbourside dining, a variety of imaginative mezedes at around 1500 dr a serve, along with fine bottled wine, are recommended. Try calamari with fresh basil, mussels with garlic, white wine and saffron, or sea bream with fresh fennel.

To Amoni (☎ 72 540) is the only ouzeri in town and is another good dinner option, excelling in dolmades and other mezedes. It is next to the Maritime Museum. Finally, the fairly pricey **Mylopetra** (☎ 72 333) nearby is described as a 'Mediterranean restaurant' and offers top-class French-Greek fusion dishes at around 6000 dr per main course. It is open from 8 pm daily onwards.

Places to Eat – Horio

In Horio, there are only two restaurants worth a mention. They are both close to

each other on Kali Strata. **To Klima** (☎ 72 693) serves well-prepared traditional Greek dishes and an enticing vegetarian menu. **Restaurant Syllogos** (☎ 72 148), farther along, offers imaginative fare such as chicken with prunes and pork with leek. Prices at both restaurants are moderate.

Entertainment

There are several lively bars in the streets behind the south side of the harbour. The **White House Cafe** on the waterfront itself is the best spot for people watching, while the **Vapori & Minas Bar** (see Post & Communications) is also lively in the evenings, and sometimes features live music.

To Roloï Bar, near Kali Strata, is the place to go to play board games and have an English breakfast from 8.30 am to 5 pm (!). The **Harani** bar nearby pulls in the drinking crowd and runs its happy hour from 6.30 to 8.30 pm.

The expat-owned **Jean & Tonic** in Horio is a popular late night bar and is open from 8 pm to 6 am. Buy two cocktails for the price of one during 'cocktail hour' from 8 to 9 pm. At the top of the Kali Strata steps in Horio is the aptly named **Kali Strata**, ideally positioned for a cold Mythos beer after the long climb up from the harbour.

AROUND SYMI
Pedi

Pedi is a little fishing village and burgeoning holiday resort in a fertile valley 2km downhill from Horio. It has some sandy stretches on its narrow beach. There are domatia, hotels and tavernas. It's an easy walk downhill from Horio.

Pedi's best accommodation is the **Hotel Pedi Beach** (☎ 71 981, fax 71 982), with a pool, restaurant and car park. This two-storey resort hotel charges around 15,000 dr for a double room with all facilities.

There are also two or three tavernas lining the foreshore. One of the better ones is the **Ellinikon** (☎ 71 417) situated on a little jetty next to a small pebbly beach. There's a good range of dishes and some excellent value salads. Prices range from cheap to average.

CENTRAL DODECANESE

Beaches

Nos Beach is the closest beach to Gialos. It's about a five-minute walk north of the campanile. There is a taverna, and a bar and sun-beds to rent.

Nimborios is a long pebbled beach 3km west of Gialos. It has some natural shade as well as sun-beds and umbrellas. It's best reached by taxi or you can easily walk if you fancy the exercise.

Taxi boats go to **Agios Georgios Bay**; the more developed **Nanou Beach**, which has sun-beds, umbrellas and a taverna; and **Agia Marina**, which also has a taverna. These are all shingle beaches. Symi's only sandy beach is the tamarisk-shaded **Agios Nikolaos**.

The more remote **Marathounda** and **Agios Emilianos** beaches are best reached by excursion boat.

Moni Taxiarhou Mihail

Μονή Ταξιάρχου Μιχαήλ

Symi's principal sight is the large Moni Taxiarhou Mihail (Monastery of Michael of Panormitis) in Panormitis Bay, the stopping-off point for many of the day-trippers from Rhodes. A monastery was first built here in the 5th or 6th century, but the present building dates from the 18th century. The katholikon contains an intricately carved wooden iconostasis, frescoes, and an icon of St Michael, which supposedly appeared miraculously where the monastery now stands. St Michael is the patron saint of Symi, and protector of sailors.

The monastery complex comprises a museum, restaurant and basic guest rooms. Beds cost 3000 dr; reservations are necessary in July and August. Several excursion boats do trips here.

Tilos Τήλος

☎ 0246 • postcode 850 02 • pop 342

Tilos is one of the few islands left in the Dodecanese that still retains something of its traditional self and where tourism has not yet widely impacted on the slow and generally carefree lifestyle of the islanders. Tilos is 65km west of Rhodes but could well be 650km away for the difference that the two display. The island offers to the visitor good, uncrowded beaches, an abandoned ghost village, a well kept monastery at the end of a spectacularly scenic road, a castle and the remains of mini elephants that once roamed this demure, little-visited island. Tilos is also terrific for walkers, with vistas of high cliffs, rocky inlets, the sea, valleys of cypress, walnut and almond trees, and meadows with well-fed cattle.

However, Tilos' agricultural potential has not been utilised. Rather than work the land for a pittance, young Tiliots have long preferred to leave for the mainland or emigrate to Australia or the USA. Nowadays the accents of Brooklyn or Bondi can be heard during the summer months when Tiliot emigres and their children often return to the island for a summer of sun and fun in their ancestral home.

History

Traces of the first inhabitants of Tilos can still be found today. Thought to have first settled here during the Stone Age, their lives seem to have been inextricably intertwined with that of the elephants that roamed the island during this period. Over time, these animals evolved into a smaller species of midget elephants, adapting to the limited food supply available on the island. Fossils of these elephants can still be found today in the Harkadio Cave, between Livadia and Megalo Horio. According to archaeologists, these fossils are dated between 4,500 and 3,500 BC.

Erinna, one of the least-known of ancient Greece's female poets, lived on Tilos in the 4th century BC. Elephants and poetry apart, Tilos' history shares the same catalogue of invasions and occupations as the rest of the Dodecanese archipelago.

Getting There & Away

Ferry Tilos is served by G&A Ferries and DANE Sea Lines, as well as the slower, Kalymnos-based F/B *Nisos Kalymnos*. Tickets can be bought at Stefanakis Travel Agency (☎ 44 360) in Livadia. The following table will give you an overview of the main destinations from Tilos.

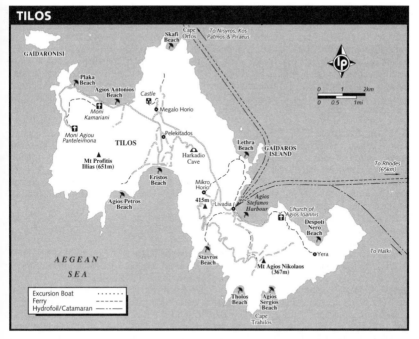

TILOS

GAÏDARONISI

Skafi Beach
Cape Orfos
To Nisyros, Kos Patmos & Piraeus

Plaka Beach
Agios Antonios Beach
Castle
Moni Kamariani
Megalo Horio
Moni Agiou Panteleimona
TILOS
Pelekitados
Lethra Beach
GAÏDAROS ISLAND
To Rhodes (65km)
Mt Profitis Illias (651m)
Harkadio Cave
Eristos Beach
Mikro Horio
415m
Livadia
Agios Stefanos Harbour
Church of Agios Ioannis
Despoti Nero Beach
To Halki
AEGEAN SEA
Agios Petros Beach
Stavros Beach
Mt Agios Nikolaos (367m)
Yera

0 1 2km
0 0.5 1mi

Excursion Boat · · · · · ·
Ferry – – – – –
Hydrofoil/Catamaran — · — · —

Tholos Beach
Agios Sergios Beach
Cape Trahilos

destination	duration	price	frequency
Astypalea	8½ hours	2280 dr	2 weekly
Kalymnos	3½ hours	2700 dr	3 weekly
Kastellorizo	10 hours	3260 dr	2 weekly
Kos	2 hours	1900 dr	4 weekly
Nisyros	1½ hours	1500 dr	2 weekly
Patmos	6½ hours	3800 dr	2 weekly
Piraeus	17 hours	7400 dr	2 weekly
Rhodes	4 hours	2800 dr	4 weekly

Hydrofoil On Wednesday a hydrofoil from Kalymnos via Kos and Nisyros arrives at Tilos at 9.50 am and then continues to Rhodes (1¼ hours, 5350 dr). It follows the same route back, arriving at Tilos at 7.30 pm and continuing to Nisyros (40 minutes, 2900 dr) and Kos (1½ hours, 3700 dr). On Sunday there is an afternoon hydrofoil to Rhodes and to Kos.

Catamaran The sleek and Tilos-owned *Sea Star* (☎ 77 048, 44 000) connects Tilos daily

with Nisyros and Rhodes. With its ingenious stabiliser curtains protecting the twin hulls of this modern craft, this is one of the most stable vessels ploughing the Aegean seas. *Sea Star* leaves Tilos for Nisyros daily at 10.30 am (35 minutes, 3200 dr) and for Rhodes at 5.30 pm (55 minutes, 5500 dr).

The Rhodes-based *Dodekanisos Express* calls in at Tilos two to three times a week in summer as an intermediate stop on its daily run up the Dodecanese from Rhodes. Departures heading north from Tilos are usually around 10.45 am, with arrival in Patmos at 1.30 pm. Departures heading south from Tilos are usually around 6.40 pm with arrival in Rhodes at 7 or 8.50 pm, depending on whether there is a stop in Halki. Tickets can be bought at Stefanakis Travel Agency (☎ 44 360) in Livadia.

Excursion Boat There are a number of excursions advertised around Livadia. Among them is a 'Beach BBQ' from 10 am to 5 pm

CENTRAL DODECANESE

on Tuesday and Thursday; the 6000 dr cost includes drink and food. The 'Tilos Odyssey' from 10 am to 5 pm costs 5000 dr, but does not include food and drink. A high-speed inflatable boat goes to numerous small beaches around the island, but it costs a pricey 7500 dr per person. Make inquiries at Taverna Blue Sky (see Places to Eat in the Livadia section).

Getting Around

Tilos' public transport consists of two buses: a minibus and a full-sized bus. There are seven services daily from Livadia to Megalo Horio, Agios Antonios and Eristos. Fares are either 300 dr or 400 dr, depending on the distance travelled. On Sunday there is a special excursion bus to Moni Agiou Panteleimona (1000 dr return), which leaves Livadia at 11 am and gives you one hour at the monastery.

Tilos has two taxis: Taxi Mike (☎ 44 169, mobile 09-4520 0436) and Nikos Logothetis (☎ 44 059, mobile 09-4498 1727). Both are available at any time. Sample fares from Livadia are Megalo Horio (1700 dr), Eristos beach (2300 dr) and Moni Agiou Panteleimona (10,000 dr return). This last fare also includes 30 minutes' waiting time. All taxi fares are displayed at the taxi stand in Livadia.

There are three motorcycle rental outlets in Livadia. An easy one to find is David Rentals in the centre of town. Bikes here rent out for 6000 dr a day. Bicycles can be rented at Taverna Michalis for 2000 dr per day.

LIVADIA Λειβάδια

Livadia is the main town and port, though not the island's capital: that honour belongs to Megalo Horio. It's a sleepy, pleasant enough place, though it tends to be a bit more hot and humid than other parts of the island. The town's beach is pebbly and rather mediocre, though things do get better towards the eastern side of the bay where most tourist tend to congregate. In Livadia you will find most services and shops and the greater bulk of the island's accommodation.

Orientation

Ferries, catamarans and hydrofoils all arrive at the small port at the northern end of Livadia. From the quay, turn left, ascend the steps beside Stefanakis Travel, and continue ahead to the central square. If you continue straight ahead, the road curves towards the beach and then turns right, passing the Church of Agios Nikolaos. Turn right at the main square to take the road to Megalo Horio.

There is no decent map of Livadia available anywhere on the island. The best map is the detailed topographic map of Tilos, produced by Barry 'Paris' Ward (the 5th edition was published in 2000). You can normally find this in the Kosmos shop for 500 dr. You can also view the 4th edition of the map on the Web site www.greekhotel .com/dodecane/tilos/info/map.htm.

Information

Money Take note. There is no bank and no ATM on Tilos. Getting money from an ATM entails a trip to Rhodes. Visa cash advances and currency exchange can be made at Stefanakis Travel (see Travel Agencies). The post office does not cash travellers cheques. Bring enough cash to cover at least your initial expenses.

Post & Communications The post office and OTE are on the central square. There are plenty of card phones and all three Greek mobile services can be picked up from Livadia. You can even pick up the Turkish Turkcell GSM mobile phone network from here.

You can check your email (no surfing or extended Web work) at Kosmos (☎ 44 074, e pnut@otenet.gr). Kosmos is open from 9 am to 1.30 pm and from 7.30 to 11.30 pm. Access costs 1500 dr for 15 minutes of computer use.

Internet Resources There is not a lot of Tilos information on the Web, but the site at www.greekhotel.com/dodecane/tilos/info/ home.htm lists a couple of hotels (also listed under Places to Stay) and shows a recent version of Ward's Tilos map, mentioned under Orientation. There is also some general background information on Tilos plus a few photos.

Travel Agencies Tilos has no EOT but the staff at both Stefanakis Travel (☎ 44 310, [e] stefanakis@rho.forthnet.gr) and Tilos Travel Agency (☎ 44 259), opposite the quay, are helpful.

Bookshops English-language newspapers and some magazines can be bought at the agency opposite David Rentals. English-language books can be swapped at Kosmos.

Emergency The port police (☎ 44 322) share the white Italianate building at the quay with the regular police (☎ 44 222).

Walks Around Livadia

There are a couple of popular walks that can easily be made from Livadia. One is an out and back hike to **Stavros Beach**, an hour's steady walk along a well-marked trail that starts from near the Tilos Mare Hotel in Livadia. This is the easiest and perhaps more accessible of the walks, with the lure of a dip at the fine pebble beach enough to attract a steady line of walkers. Note that there is no shade and no facilities.

A second walk is a longer out and back track to the small abandoned settlement of **Yera** and its accompanying beach access at **Despoti Nero**. From Livadia follow the road past Agios Stefanos on the east side of the bay and keep walking. Allow half a day for this hike. Both trails are marked on Ward's Tilos map (see Orientation).

Special Events

The Symi Festival hosts a few events in Tilos during the last days of August. See the Symi section earlier in this chapter for full details on this annual cultural festival.

Places to Stay

The information kiosk at the harbour is open whenever a ferry arrives and has photographs and prices of Livadia's accommodation in Tilos. They do not list every place though, and have a tendency to favour establishments in Livadia. Freelance *camping*

is permitted on the beaches – Plaka Beach is good if you have your own transport, but there are no facilities or drinking water. Eristos Beach is better and has a small facilities block, but charges 500 dr per tent.

In Livadia, *Paraskevi Rooms (☎ 44 280)* is the best of the three domatia on the beach, with clean, nicely furnished doubles with bathrooms and well-equipped kitchens for 10,000 dr. *Rena Rooms (☎ 44 274)*, two blocks back from the sea, offers one triple (10,700 dr) and two double rooms (9000 dr). The rooms are large and clean and have a fridge. This place is one of the few that is open all year

The A-class *Apollo Studios (☎ 44 379)*, on the road to Megalo Horio, has seven double rooms with kitchenette and fan. They are smallish but adequate enough and go for 12,000 dr. The expansive A-class *Olympos Studios (☎ 44 365)*, a little farther south, are a better option though a bit more expensive at 13,000 dr per fully equipped double room.

Casa Italiana Rooms (☎ 44 253/259), overlooking the quay, has well-kept doubles with bathrooms and refrigerators for 8000 dr, and a four-person apartment for 15,000 dr. *Stefanakis Studios (☎ 44 310/384)*, above Stefanakis Travel, is equally commendable with triple rooms for 11,000 dr.

Manos Hatzifoundas Studios (☎ 44 259), past Sofia's Taverna on the beach road, has pleasant doubles for 12,000 dr. Telephone in advance and Manos will meet the boat; alternatively, you'll find him in Taverna Blue Sky (see Places to Eat). *Hotel Eleni (☎ 44 062, fax 44 063)*, 400m along the beach road, has beautiful, tastefully furnished rooms with bathrooms, refrigerator and telephone. The rate for singles/doubles is 9000/ 12,000 dr, including breakfast.

Places to Eat

Livadia has a number of very reasonable eating options, and prices are low to mid-range. There are more places than the ones listed here, but try these for starters.

Joanna's Cafe (☎ 44 145) is very popular for breakfast and lunch. Joanna and husband Andrea serve excellent Italian coffee, best taken with home-made cakes such as chocolate fudge pudding or lunch drizzle cake. They also serve great Italian wines and alcoholic sundaes. 'Andrea's punch', heavily dosed with *pampero* rum is also recommended. *Kafeneion Omonias*, next to the post office, is a favourite place for breakfast, or an evening ouzo or two over mezedes. This is where the locals mostly hang out.

Sofia's Restaurant (☎ 44 340), 20m along the beach road, serves delicious, low-priced food; and *Taverna Michalis* (☎ 44 359), near the church, offers dining in a pleasant tree-shaded garden. This is where most of the Laskarina tour group crowd from the UK tend to congregate. *Taverna Blue Sky*, on the harbour near the quay, is good for grilled fish.

Restaurant Irina (☎ 44 206), with its relaxing waterside location overlooking Pebble Beach, has great home-made food including excellent mousakas and *papoutsakia* (aubergine slippers). *Zorba's Taverna* (☎ 44 015) is a bit out of the way, beyond the Irini Hotel on the beach road; it serves tasty grilled meat. The zany owner of Zorba's may break into a song and dance routine while taking your order.

Entertainment
La Luna, at the quay, and *Cafe Bar Bozi*, a little way past Zorba's Taverna on the waterfront, are the local hot spots. However, these change with the season's trends so ask around.

Shopping
You can pick up 'great Greek gear' at Kosmos (☎ 44 074), according to owners Paul and Helen from Manchester. Sandals, ceramics, designer stationery from Thessaloniki, sarongs, hats, bags and T-shirts – all Greek-made – are available at this friendly, handy shop which also offers Internet access (see Post & Communications earlier).

LIVADIA TO MEGALO HORIO
Livadia is linked to Megalo Horio with one of the Dodecanese's fastest and better constructed island highways – a real surprise, given the relative size of Tilos. The island's most accessible petrol station is halfway along this road (there is also a small one at Agios Antonios in the north).

Mikro Horio
Mikro Horio was once a thriving island population centre until the 1950s when mismanagement of water resources and a general drift to the harbour of Livadia was the death knell for this once attractive village. It is now a ghost village. Its stone houses, mostly roofless and crumbling, echo only to the bleating of goats and the crunch of the boots of curious visitors who come to gaze upon a modern day archaeological curiosity. There have been modest efforts to kickstart the village's revival with one or two houses being restored by former owners. The church is functional and fully restored, and is used on occasion, but the most unusual revival comes in the form of a summer night-time bar that brings in hoards of revellers seeking an unusual night out.

The *Mikro Horio Music Bar* kicks in late and belts out music till 4 am during the summer months. This place really is a buzz. It is the only inhabited building (other than the church and a house or two) in the otherwise abandoned village. You could easily imagine spirits of another sort in the spooky, dark alleyways of Mikro Horio, after a hard night on the vodka and shots.

Mikro Horio is signposted off the Livadia-Megalo Horio road (1km) and can also be spotted from the main road, even though its stone ruins now seem to blend imperceptibly into the surrounding dry rocks of the hills on which it is built. A minibus of sorts ferries people on demand to and from Livadia.

Harkadio Cave
It is in this remote cave in the centre of the island where the bones of the island's symbol – the dwarf elephant *(to elefantaki)* – were discovered by archaeologists in 1971. In the Pleiocene Age, dwarf elephants roamed Tilos until their unexplained extinction at some point in the distant past. The cave, though signposted off the main road, was closed in late 2000 pending its eventual re-opening after the completion of excavations. Meanwhile, you can view the bones of the

A lone fisherman plies the still waters off Nisyros.

A Tilos local honours the past.

Visitors eat, drink and are merry in Nikea village square, Nisyros.

The well-preserved frescoes in Tilos' Moni Agiou Panteleimona are a feast for the eyes.

Some like it hot: volcanic Nisyros

The Symi trailer carries bags and backpacks on the waterfront.

Gialos' grand seafront hides crumbling mansions in the backblocks.

A wall painting in Kos celebrates traditional cooking methods.

'elefantaki' in a partial reconstruction of the animal in the small Megalo Horio **museum** (see Megalo Horio later in this section).

Walks

Lethra Beach is a long, pebble beach an hour's walk along a path going north from Livadia. Alternatively, a track runs from **Mikro Horio** to Lethra, intersecting the main road (though not obviously) just south of the petrol station. From Mikro Horio it is about a 20 minute hike down to the main road and a further hour or so to the beach itself, following a usually dry stream bed that leads through the **Potami Canyon**.

Another walk, mostly bypassing the main road system, leads from Livadia to **Mikro Horio**. This will take about 45 minutes. The track is clearly marked on Ward's Tilos map (see Orientation).

There's a walking track to Stavros Beach from Livadia, and you can also get down to the isolated Agios Sergios beach farther to the east via a rough track.

MEGALO HORIO Μεγαλο Χωριο

Megalo Horio is a serene whitewashed village and is the island's capital. Its narrow alleyways are fun to explore and the village makes a great alternative base if you are looking for a taste of rural life in Tilos. There are domatia, a couple of restaurants and two lively, atmospheric bars to keep visitors bedded, fed and suitably watered.

The Knight's Castle & Ancient Settlement

Megalo Horio's main attraction is its hard-to-miss Knight's Castle, which is spectacularly illuminated at night. To reach it, follow the track behind the prominent Tilos FM sign at the north end of the village. The walk up should take no more than 45 minutes, but it gets fairly steep and rocky towards the end and you will need to wear stout shoes. Attempt it only if you are reasonably fit.

On the way up you will pass the remains of the ancient settlement of Megalo Horio – a scattering of ruined houses and buildings which, like the castle above, must have taken some considerable effort to construct given the elevation and the steep terrain. The castle itself is a jumbled ruin, yet contains a battered 16th-century chapel with some badly eroded frescoes. The spectacular views are best enjoyed in the early morning or early evening.

The Museum

The little museum on the main street houses finds from the Harkadio Cave including a partial reconstruction of the midget elephant. It's open from 8.30 am to 2.30 pm, Monday to Friday, and is free. The video about Tilos (in English or Greek), on sale in the museum, is well produced and a worthwhile souvenir to take home.

Places to Stay & Eat

Megalo Horio has three comfortable places to stay. *Pension Sevasti* (☎ 44 237), just beyond the Eristos Beach turn-off, has singles/doubles for 5000/5500 dr, and *Milou Rooms & Apartments* (☎ 44 204) has similar prices. *Elefantakia Studios* (☎ 44 242), next door on the main street, offers five double rooms with kitchenette and fridge for 8000 dr.

There are two places to eat in Megalo Horio. The better of the two is *To Kastro* (☎ 44 232), on the south side of the village overlooking the Eristos plain below. Great BBQ grilled meats and home cooking are the highlights here. After dark you may just get some spontaneous singing or musical instrument playing from the locals.

Entertainment

Megalo Horio has two atmospheric bars. *Ilakati*, on the steep road signposted to Kastro, plays rock and blues; and *Anemona*, at the top of the steps by the To Kastro restaurant, plays Greek music.

AROUND MEGALO HORIO

Just before Megalo Horio, a turn-off to the left leads in 2.5km to the pleasant, tamarisk-shaded **Eristos Beach** – a mixture of gritty sand and shingle. Camping here in summer is limited to 30 tents, with a cost of 500 dr per tent. There is a solitary cantina for food and drinks, toilets and beach umbrellas for hire. Nudism is tolerated at the eastern end of the beach.

CENTRAL DODECANESE

Agios Antonios, a kilometre or so farther north of Megalo Horio, is a rather desultory settlement with two seasonal tavernas, some domatia, but unfortunately not much of a beach. A restored **windmill**, which is now a private home, is about the most attractive thing about Agios Antonios, though the swimming in front of the windmill is not bad. There are some small **sea caves** here, with the **petrified remains** of a couple of hapless humans who were baked *in situ* after the explosion of the volcano in 1422 on neighbouring and clearly visible Nisyros.

Things get better 3km farther west where **Plaka Beach** is easily accessible by car or motorbike. It's made up of fine pebbles and sand, the water is shallow and clean, and there is some shade from trees. There are no facilities but campers make informal use of the raised flat land at the rear of the beach to stake out the odd tent or two.

The 18th-century **Moni Agiou Panteleimona** is 5km beyond here, along a scenic, sealed road. It is well maintained and has fine 18th-century frescoes. There is a small cafe here, also. The island's minibus driver takes groups of visitors here on Sunday (see Getting Around). A three-day festival takes place at the monastery, beginning on 25 July. A marked **walking track** starting from near the signposted **Moni Kamariani**, 1km from Agios Antonios, shortcuts the vehicle road and leads hikers to Moni Agiou Panteleimona in about two hours.

Places to Stay & Eat

Tropicana Taverna & Rooms (☎ 44 223), on the Eristos road, has doubles/triples for 6000/7500 dr as well as a reasonable eating place; the '60s timewarp *Nausika Taverna & Rooms*, to the left of Eristos Beach (signposted), has similar rates. The *Eristos Beach Hotel* (☎/fax 44 024), right on the beach, has excellent, airy studios for up to four people with fridge and kitchenette for 10,000 dr.

The ageing D class *Hotel Australia* (☎ 44 296) at Agios Antonios is, in essence, a small complex of ordinary domatia, though much-needed renovations were slated for 2001. Small doubles/triples with bathroom

are 7000/8000 dr. There is an attached seasonal taverna here, too.

The best accommodation here is the luxury apartments of *Filoxenia* (☎ 64 732, mobile 09-4679 8681), halfway between Megalo Horio and Eristos at Pelekitados. These four comfortable studios, which accommodate up to four people, are set in a relaxing citrus orchard and offer all expected facilities. There's a large verandah for breakfast, a separate lounge and bedroom, air-conditioning and TV. The lower studios go for 20,000 dr and the upper studios for 25,000 dr. They operate from 1 July to 31 September only.

Nisyros Νίσυρος

☎ 0242 • postcode 853 03 • pop 913

Nisyros (**nee-sih-ros**) is one of those quirky Greek Islands that you only really learn about when you get there. It's not on the usual island hopping circuit, has no stunning sandy beaches and supports a rather low-key tourist infrastructure that favours individuals, yachties, lost souls and those in search of something completely different.

Nisyros is an almost round, rocky island and has something that no other Greek island has – its own volcano. At the same time, the landscape is rocky, lush and green, yet it has no natural water. Its fecundity is due to the mineral-rich earth, which supports stands of olives, figs, citrus fruit and almonds.

The lunar landscape of the interior is offset by craggy peaks and rolling hillsides, which lead down to brown pebbly beaches that see relatively few visitors. The island's settlements are Mandraki, the capital; the fishing village of Pali; and the crater-top villages of Emborios and Nikea.

Many visitors come on day trips from Kos and increasingly from Rhodes and Tilos, and yachties regularly drop anchor off the north coast. However, few stay overnight. This is a pity because Nisyros offers an excellent antidote to the creeping commercialism found just across the water in Kos. Nisyros needs just that little bit of extra time to reveal its subtle attractions.

NISYROS

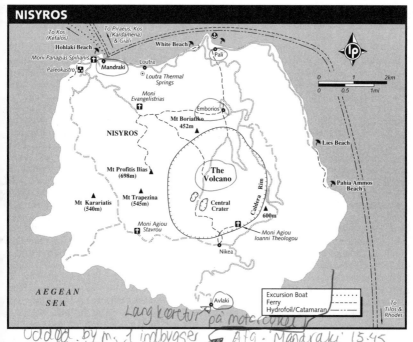

To Kos
(Kefalos)
To Piraeus, Kos
(Kardamena)
& Giali
Hohlaki Beach
White Beach
Moni Panagias Spilianis
Pali
Loutra
Mandraki
Paleokastro
Loutra Thermal
Springs
Moni
Evangelistrias
Emborios
Mt Boriatiko
452m
NISYROS
Mt Profitis Ilias
(698m)
The
Volcano
Lies Beach
Caldera Rim
Pahia Ammos
Beach
Mt Karariatis
(540m)
Mt Trapezina
(545m)
Central
Crater
600m
Moni Agiou
Stavrou
Moni Agiou
Ioanni Theologou
Nikea
AEGEAN
SEA
Avlaki
Excursion Boat
Ferry
Hydrofoil/Catamaran
To
Tilos &
Rhodes

0   1   2km
0   0.5   1mi

History

Nisyros' historical legacy has more to do with fiction than fact. This explains why – to popular belief at least – the island is sitting on an essentially dormant volcano.

According to mythology, during the Great War between the Gods and the Titans, the Titan Polyvotis annoyed Poseidon so much that Poseidon tore off a chunk of Kos and threw it at Polyvotis. This rock pinned Polyvotis underneath it and the rock became the island of Nisyros. From that day, the hapless Polyvotis has been groaning and sighing while trying to escape – hence the volcano.

Aside from such mythical beginnings Nisyros has had a quiet history, its main tangible legacy being the massive walls of Paleokastro, probably dating from settlement in the Mycenaean era. The threat of volcanic eruptions no doubt limited commercial development and kept the population in check. The most disastrous volcano on record was in 1422 when the current moonscape-like interior was created. Today, the volcanic pumice from the satellite island of Giali, along with a moderate tourist industry, provides income for the island's inhabitants.

Getting There & Away

Ferry Nisyros is served by G&A Ferries, DANE Sea Lines and the F/B *Nisos Kalymnos*. The following table gives an overview of the main destinations from Nisyros. Tickets can be bought at Diakomihalis Tours (see Travel Agencies) in Mandraki.

destination	duration	price	frequency
Astypalea	6½ hours	1820 dr	2 weekly
Kalymnos	3 hours	2230 dr	4 weekly
Kastellorizo	11½ hours	3300 dr	2 weekly
Kos	1¼ hours	1500 dr	7 weekly
Patmos	5½ hours	2410 dr	3 weekly
Piraeus	14 hours	7370 dr	3 weekly
Rhodes	6 hours	2320 dr	4 weekly
Tilos	1½ hours	2530 dr	3 weekly

CENTRAL DODECANESE

Services heading south tend to leave in the early morning and north in the late afternoon.

There is an additional service to Kardamena on Kos run by the local caïque *Chrysoula* on Monday, Wednesday, Thursday and Friday. Departure is around 7 am and the return trip from Kardamena is at 2.30 pm. A one-way ticket costs 1000 dr.

Hydrofoil There are two hydrofoils a week heading both north and south. On Saturday there are services to Kos (50 minutes, 3300 dr), Tilos (40 minutes, 2900 dr), and Rhodes (two hours, 5250 dr). On Sunday there is a further service to Tilos and Rhodes.

Catamaran The sleek *Sea Star* connects Nisyros with Tilos and Rhodes daily. *Sea Star* leaves Nisyros for Tilos daily at 1.45 pm (35 minutes, 3200 dr) and leaves Tilos for Rhodes at 5.30 pm (a further 55 minutes, 5500 dr). Tickets are sold at the quay prior to departure, or at Enetikon Travel (see Travel Agencies).

The Rhodes-based *Dodekanisos Express* calls in at Nisyros two to three times a week in summer. Tickets can be bought at Diakomihalis Tours (see Travel Agencies) in Mandraki.

Excursion Boat In summer there are daily excursion boats to Kardamena, Kefalos and Kos Town on Kos (3000 dr to 5500 dr).

Getting Around

Bus There are at least two excursion buses every day to the volcano (2000 dr return with 40 minutes waiting time) at 9.30 am and 5 pm. In addition, there are three daily buses to Nikea (via Pali, 500 dr) at 7 am, 1.45 and 8 pm, and an extra bus to Pali only (300 dr) at 11.45 am. The bus terminal is at the quay.

Motorcycle There are three motorcycle-rental outlets on Mandraki's main street.

Taxi There are two taxis on Nisyros: Babis Taxi (☎ 31 460) and Irene's Taxi (☎ 31 474). In practice Babis is the only one you will easily find and is the most reliable of the two drivers. A sample of tariffs are: the volcano

(6000 dr return with 40 minutes waiting time), Lies (2500 dr), Emborios (2500 dr), Nikea (3500 dr) and Pali (1500 dr).

Excursion Boat From June to September there are excursion boats (2500 dr return) to the pumice-stone islet of Giali where there is a good sandy beach.

MANDRAKI Μανδράκι

Mandraki is the attractive port and capital of Nisyros. Its two-storey houses have brightly painted wooden balconies. Some are whitewashed but many are painted in bright colours, predominantly ochre and turquoise. The web of streets huddled below the monastery and the central square are especially charming. It's a great place to hang around in for a few days and the still authentic atmosphere, apparent once the day-trippers have left, gets under your skin after a while.

Orientation

To reach Mandraki's centre, walk straight ahead from the quay. At the fork bear right; the left fork leads to Hotel Porfyris. Beyond here a large square adjoins the main street, which proceeds to Plateia Aristotelous Fotiadou, then continues diagonally opposite, passing the town hall. Turn left at the T-junction for the central square of Plateia Elikiomini.

There are one or two commercially available tourist maps of Nisyros, which you can find in most tourist shops. The Toubi's 1:25.000 map of the island also has a fair map of Mandraki. The best map of the island, however, is a computer-generated map drawn by German cartographer, Dr Jürgen Franke. It is available freely at tourist offices and some hotels on Nisyros.

Information

Tourist Offices Tourist information is willingly dispensed by Nisyrian Travel (☎ 31 204) at the quay, open 10 am to 1 pm and 6 to 8 pm daily. The staff here, and at Enetikon Travel (☎ 31 180, fax 31 168), on the main street, are helpful. The latter has a good library of used books.

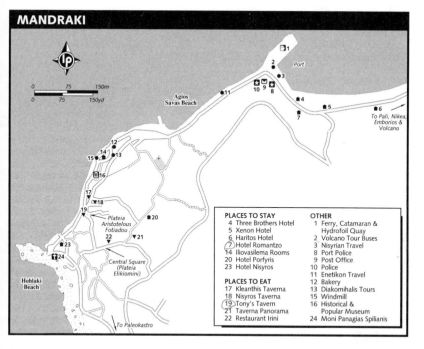

MANDRAKI

PLACES TO STAY	OTHER
4 Three Brothers Hotel	1 Ferry, Catamaran &
5 Xenon Hotel	Hydrofoil Quay
6 Haritos Hotel	2 Volcano Tour Buses
7 Hotel Romantzo	3 Nisyrian Travel
14 Iliovasilema Rooms	8 Port Police
20 Hotel Porfyris	9 Post Office
23 Hotel Nisyros	10 Police
	11 Enetikon Travel
PLACES TO EAT	12 Bakery
17 Kleanthis Taverna	13 Diakomihalis Tours
18 Nisyros Taverna	15 Windmill
19 Tony's Tavern	16 Historical &
21 Taverna Panorama	Popular Museum
22 Restaurant Irini	24 Moni Panagias Spilianis

Money There is no bank and no ATM on Nisyros. The National Bank of Greece is represented by Diakomihalis Tours (see Travel Agencies following) on the main street, and offers banking service from 9 am to 1 pm. Travel agencies will usually exchange money with no hassles.

Post & Communications The post office shares the same building as the port and regular police opposite the quay. There is no OTE, but there are plenty of card phones. Mobile phone users will pick up all three Greek mobile networks with no problem, and will probably also pick up the Turkish Turkcell GSM network as well.

Internet Resources The only Web site with any current information on Nisyros is at www.nisyros.com. This site is maintained and owned by a proud Nisyrian-American who has heavily laced the information with family stories.

Travel Agencies Volcano Tour operators meet all incoming caïques every morning and sell tours on the spot. Air and sea tickets can be bought at Diakomihalis Tours (☎ 31 459, fax 31 527), while sea tickets can be bought at Enetikon Travel (☎ 31 180, fax 31 168). G&A ferry tickets are sold only at Eleni Kendri Agency (☎ 31 230, fax 31 227).

Emergency The port police (☎ 31 222) and the regular police (☎ 31 201) share premises opposite the quay.

Things to See & Do
Mandraki's greatest tourist attraction is the cliff-top 14th-century **Moni Panagias Spilianis** (Virgin of the Cave), crammed with ecclesiastical paraphernalia. The monastery's opening times are 10.30 am to 3 pm daily, and admission is free. Turn right at the end of the main street to reach the steps up to the monastery.

CENTRAL DODECANESE

The **Historical & Popular Museum** is on the waterfront. Opening times are erratic, but there's no admission fee.

The impressive ancient acropolis of **Paleokastro** (Old Kastro), above Mandraki, has well-preserved Cyclopean walls built of massive blocks of volcanic rock. Follow the route signposted 'kastro', near the monastery steps. This eventually becomes a path. After about 15 minutes' walk, you will meet the main road from Mandraki. At this road turn right and the kastro is on the left.

Hohlaki is a beach of black stones. Its 'Heath Robinson' house was built by a local artist. To get there, walk to the end of the waterfront, go up the steps and turn right onto a path.

Special Events

The Symi Festival hosts a few events in Nisyros over three days during the middle of August. See the Symi section earlier in this chapter for full details on this annual cultural festival.

Places to Stay

Mandraki has a fair amount of accommodation but, unusually, owners do not meet the ferries. There is no camping ground. There is a cluster of hotels to the left as you leave the harbour, while the others are scattered throughout Mandraki.

Three Brothers Hotel (☎ 31 344, fax 31 009), left from the quay, has single/double rooms with bathrooms and fridge for 6000/10,000 dr. This hotel is open all year. Diagonally opposite is *Hotel Romantzo* (☎/fax 31 340), with clean, well-kept rooms for 10,000/12,000 dr with bathroom. The rooms are above a snack bar and there is a large communal terrace with a refrigerator, tables and chairs. Further along on the left is the *Xenon Hotel* (☎ 31 012, fax 31 204), with rooms for 6000/8500 dr.

In Mandraki itself is the fairly basic *Hotel Nisyros* (☎ 31 052), with unassuming rooms for 6500/7500 dr, while on the waterfront is *Iliovasilema Rooms* (☎ 31 159), with doubles for 7000 dr.

The C-class *Hotel Porfyris* (☎/fax 31 376), on the inland side of Mandraki, boasts a swimming pool and has pleasant rooms for 9000/14,000 dr.

Farther along on the right is the plush *Haritos Hotel* (☎ 31 322, 31 122), with well-appointed double/triple rooms for 15,000/ 18,000 dr, all with fridge, TV, telephone and air-conditioning (1000 dr extra). This place is open all year.

Places to Eat

Eating in Mandraki is pleasurable and there is a wide choice of places to eat. Be sure to try the nonalcoholic local beverage called *soumada*, made from almond extract. Another speciality of the island is *pittia* (chickpea and onion patties).

Nisyros Taverna (☎ 31 460), just off the main street, is a small, cheap and cheerful place that really fills up in the evening. Get in early if you want a table. *Tony's Tavern* (☎ 31 509), on the waterfront, has great breakfasts for 800 dr, and superb meat dishes. Former Melbournian Tony also has the island's best gyros (300 dr) and a good selection of vegetarian dishes.

Kleanthis Taverna (☎ 31 484), also on the waterfront, is popular with Greeks and has good mezedes. Up on the central square is *Restaurant Irini* (☎ 31 365), which serves economically-priced home-made dishes such as stuffed vegetables and grilled liver, and for vegetarians, okra, peas and mixed vegetables.

Taverna Panorama (☎ 31 185), a short walk from the central square, is also commendable and has tables overlooking a leafy garden. There's a *bakery* on Plateia Aristotelous Fotiadou.

AROUND NISYROS
Loutra Λουτρά

Loutra, east of Mandraki, has a thermal spa (☎ 31 284), with two spa buildings. One is derelict, but the other still functions. If you fancy a curative dip you'll need a quick health check at the medical clinic (☎ 31 217) near Hotel Porfyris first.

Pali & Lies Πάλι & Λιές

Pali (pah-lee) is a small harbour and village 4km east of Mandraki. It makes an

Koif g. Pali

ideal alternative base to Mandraki and puts at least one beach within walking distance of visitors. The village is strung out around a small attractive bay, and is host to a surprisingly large clutch of restaurants, a couple of sets of domatia masquerading as 'hotels' and not much else in the way of tourist facilities. That is perhaps Pali's attraction. It is a very relaxing place and attracts a constantly changing yachtie set who drop anchor here throughout the summer.

On a clear day you can see the mountains of Kalymnos looming over the narrow midriff of Kos to the south. The enormous stone building visible 1km east of Pali is destined to be a **therapeutic spa resort** once funding is found and restoration is completed. Meantime, it stands half-completed and depressingly empty. Four buses a day make the run from Mandraki to Pali (see Getting Around).

Pali's beach 200m to the east of the harbour is a narrow affair and is made up of fine pebbles and gravel. The water is clear and clean, if a little prone to strands of seaweed. Another 5.5km farther along, after driving a sealed, then unsealed road for 1.5km, you will reach **Lies** (lee-ez) beach, made up of brown sand and fine pebbles. There is no shade and no facilities other than a seasonal cantina. **Pahia Ammos** beach is 15 minutes' walk from here along a coastal track. This beach is much wider than Lies beach, but again there is no shade or facilities.

Places to Stay *Afroditi Rooms (☎ 31 242)*, over the restaurant of the same name, are reasonable and very handy. Expect to pay around 9000 dr for a double. Next door is the *Hotel Ellinis (☎ 31 453)*, essentially a collection of rooms without the usual facilities of a hotel; small and fairly basic doubles with bathroom cost 9000 dr.

About 1.5km before Pali and not quite as convenient as the two previous places is the *Lefki Ammos Hotel (☎ 31 497)* overlooking Yialiskari Beach and almost hidden from the main road. This is a conventional hotel, but usually caters to package groups. A double room here will cost around 15,000 dr in high season.

Places to Eat Visitors to Pali have a choice of five restaurants, and most have prices a shade on the high side. This is a reflection of the clientele – well-healed yachties who frequently drop by Pali for land-based R&R.

The most prominent eateries are the *Afroditi (☎ 31 242)* and *Taverna Ellinis (☎ 31 454)* restaurants, which both serve up a good selection of food. Afroditi probably has the edge in food quality and table service, while Ellinis has a better location.

The *Captain's House (☎ 31 016)* has tourist picture menus (!) but seems to act more as the locals' kafeneio and ouzeri and is the cheapest of the bunch. There are two quieter places at the eastern end of Pali: the *Astradeni (☎ 31 294)* and the *Angistri (☎ 31 114)*. Both offer much the same fare as the other Pali eateries – steaks and seafood.

The best bread on the island, including scrumptious brown bread, can be bought at Pali's *bakery*, 200m on the right along the Lies road. The *Oasis* is the seasonal permanent cantina at Lies beach.

Island Walks

Nisyros has some excellent walking and the distances are not huge nor the terrain too intimidating. Using the Jürgen Franke map (see Orientation earlier) as a basic guide you can spot the walks all marked in blue. A popular starting point is beside the pepper tree at **Moni Evangelistrias** 3km southeast from Mandraki. Three obvious trails start from here. While you can walk up to Moni Evangelistrias it is better to take a taxi or hitch a ride to the starting point.

The first is an occasionally rough 45-minute hike to Emborios direct and follows the north side of **Mt Boriatiko**. Look for the paint-marked stones on the east side of the pepper tree marking the start of the path and use a compass if you can. From Emborios you can hike down to Pali, or bus it back.

The second is an out and back hike to the summit of **Profitis Ilias** (689m). This will take about two hours there and back. The track is faint in parts, but generally easy to follow.

The third hike is probably the most popular and can be taken in either direction. This

CENTRAL DODECANESE

[handwritten annotation: virkel'? impønererne – sma/store bobler fra hullerne i jord. Varme op fra jord.]

is the **Evangelistrias-Volcano track** which cuts through a defile between Profitis Ilias and Boriatiko in a generally south-south-east direction. This will take you about 1½ hours to reach the sealed vehicle road, 1km from the volcano ticket office itself.

Alternatively, you can start your hikes in Nikea. One **day-long hike** would be to start in Nikea at around 8 am (take the 7 am bus from Mandraki) and hike into the caldera down a well-marked and downhill trail to the crater floor (45 minutes), visit the volcano and return to Mandraki via the Volcano-Evangelistrias track described previously.

The Volcano

Nisyros is on a volcanic line that passes through the islands of Aegina, Paros, Milos, Santorini, Nisyros, Giali and Kos. The island originally culminated in a mountain of 850m, but the centre collapsed 30,000–40,000 years ago after three violent eruptions. Their legacy is the white and orange pumice stones which can still be seen on the northern, eastern and southern flanks of the island, and the large lava flow which covers an area in the south-west of the island near Nikea Village. The first eruption partially blew off the top of the ancestral cone, but the sinking of the central part of the island came about mostly as a result of the removal of magma from within the reservoir underground.

Another violent eruption occurred in 1422 on the western side of the caldera depression (called Lakki), but this, like all others since, emitted steam, gases and mud, but no lava. The islanders call the volcano Polyvotis, because the Polyvotis crater on the western side of the caldera floor was the site of the eruptions in 1873, 1874 and 1888, and remains the most active of the craters.

There are five craters in the caldera. A path descends into the largest one, Stefanos, where you can examine the multicoloured fumaroles, listen to their hissing and smell their sulphurous vapours. The surface is soft and hot, making sturdy footwear essential.

If you arrive by bus you'll be with hordes of day-trippers, which detracts from the extraordinary sight. Also, the bus does not

allow you long enough to wander around and savour a glass of soumada from the cafe. It's a good idea to walk either to or from the crater from Nikea or via a longer route to/from Mandraki via Moni Evangelistrias (see Island Walks previously).

There is a charge of around 250 dr to view the volcano. Facilities include a cafe, toilets and car/bus parking. At the time of writing, a stone footpath was being built, which will lead to a new mini-amphitheatre where future Symi Festival events will be held.

Emborios & Nikea
[handwritten annotation: Ved by-start. Natur" Sauna]
Εμπορειός & Νίκαια *[handwritten: -varme/dag P, δra Vulkan]*
Emborios (Em-boh-**ryos**) and Nikea (**Ni**-ke-a) are perched on the volcano's rim. From each, there are stunning views down into the caldera. Only 20 inhabitants linger on in Emborios. You may encounter a few elderly women sitting on their doorsteps crocheting, and their husbands at the kafeneio. However, generally, the winding, stepped streets are empty, the silence broken only by the occasional braying of a donkey or the grunting of pigs.

In contrast to Emborios, picturesque Nikea, with 50 inhabitants, buzzes with life. It has dazzling white houses with vibrant gardens and a central square with a lovely pebble mosaic. The bus terminates on Plateia Nikolaou Hartofyli. Nikea's main street links its two squares.

The steep path down to the volcano begins from Plateia Nikolaou Hartofyli. It takes about 45 minutes one way. Near the beginning you can detour to **Moni Agiou Ioanni Theologou**, a monastery perched precariously on the crater rim offering shade and a different view of the everfascinating caldera.

Places to Stay & Eat Emborios has no accommodation for tourists, but the owner of its only taverna *To Balkoni* (☎ 31 607) with good views over the caldera can rustle up a tasty meal.

Nikea's only accommodation is a *Community Hostel* (☎ 31 285, Plateia Nikolaou Hartofyli), managed by Panayiotis Mastromihalis the owner of the *Plateia Taverna* just off the main square. Doubles cost 6500 dr. Another restaurant is the *Nikia* which is the first place you will come to on the left as you walk from the bus stop. The views over to Tilos from here are stunning.

Kos Κως

☎ 0242 • postcode 853 00 (Psalidi 852 00) • pop 26,379

Kos is the third-largest and one of the most fertile and well watered island of the Dodecanese. It lies only 5km from the Turkish peninsula of Bodrum. It is second only to Rhodes in both its wealth of archaeological remains and its tourist development, with most of its beautiful beaches wall-to-wall with sun beds and parasols. It's a long, narrow island with a mountainous spine. *se slde 206*

Pserimos is a small island between Kos and Kalymnos. It has a good sandy beach, but unfortunately can become a little overrun with day-trippers from both of its larger neighbours.

History
Kos' fertile land attracted settlers from the earliest times. So many people lived here in the Mycenaean era that it was able to send 30 ships to the Trojan War. During the 7th and 6th centuries BC, Kos flourished as an ally of the powerful Rhodian cities of Ialysos, Kamiros and Lindos. In 477 BC, after suffering an earthquake and subjugation to the Persians, it joined the Delian League and flourished once more.

Hippocrates (460–377 BC), the father of medicine, was born and lived on the island. After Hippocrates' death, the Sanctuary of Asklepios and a medical school were built, which perpetuated his teachings and made Kos famous throughout the Greek world.

Ptolemy II of Egypt was born on Kos, thus securing it the protection of Egypt, under which it became a prosperous trading centre. In 130 BC, Kos came under Roman domination, and in the 1st century AD it was put under the administration of Rhodes, with which it came to share the same vicissitudes, right up to the tourist deluge of the present day.

Hippocrates – the First GP

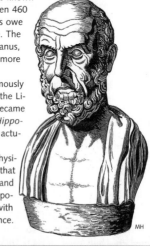

Hippocrates is often called the father of medicine yet little is known for certain about his life. He is believed to have lived between 460 and 380 BC, but 'facts' about his birth and medical practices owe more to mythology and legends than to hard-core evidence. The earliest known biography of him is *Life of Hippocrates*, by Soranus, a Roman physician. This work was published about AD 100, more than 400 years after Hippocrates' death.

Hippocrates' fame probably resulted from about 80 anonymously written medical works that became part of the collection of the Library of Alexandria after about 200 BC. Those writings became linked with Hippocrates and are known by scholars as the *Hippocratic corpus*. However, it cannot be proved that Hippocrates actually wrote any of these works.

Hippocrates' medicine challenged the methods of many physicians who used magic and witchcraft to treat disease. It taught that diseases had natural causes and could therefore be studied and possibly cured according to the workings of nature. Under Hippocratic medicine, a well-trained physician could cure illness with knowledge gained from medical writings or from experience. Modern medicine is still based on this assumption.

MH

CENTRAL DODECANESE

Getting There & Away

Air There are three flights daily to Athens (28,900 dr). The Olympic Airways office (☎ 28 330) is at Vasileos Pavlou 22, in Kos Town. The airport (☎ 51 229) is 27.5km from Kos Town near the village of Andimahia.

Charter flights from many European destinations fly into Kos from April through to the end of October, but there are no scheduled international flights. It may be possible to pick up one-way tickets on returning charter flights. Check with local travel agents.

Ferry – Domestic Kos is well connected with Piraeus and all the islands in the Dodecanese. In summer there is a weekly ferry service to Samos and Thessaloniki. The following table gives you an overview of services offered by the three major companies operating out of Kos, DANE Sealines (☎ 27 311), G&A Ferries (☎ 28 545) and the F/B *Nisos Kalymnos* (☎ 28 545).

destination	duration	price	frequency
Astypalea	4½ hours	2500 dr	2 weekly
Kalymnos	1¼ hours	1200 dr	7 weekly
Kastellorizo	11½ hours	3600 dr	1 weekly
Leros	3¼ hours	3500 dr	7 weekly
Nisyros	1¼ hours	1500 dr	7 weekly
Patmos	1¼ hours	4600 dr	7 weekly
Rhodes	3½ hours	2900 dr	7 weekly
Samos	4 hours	3400 dr	1 weekly
Thessaloniki	19 hours	10,100 dr	1 weekly
Tilos	2 hours	1600 dr	4 weekly

Services heading south tend to leave at the ungodly hour between 3 and 4 am, but heading north, services are much more amenable with departures in the late afternoon.

Kos is also linked via a thrice daily local ferry from Mastihari to Pothia in Kalymnos, and a caïque from Kardamena to Mandraki in Nisyros that makes the trip four times a week. See The North Coast and Southern Kos sections for details.

Ferry – International There are daily ferries in summer from Kos Town to Bodrum (ancient Halicarnassus) in Turkey (one hour, 13,000 dr return, including Turkish port tax). Boats leave at 8.30 am and return at 4 pm. Many travel agents around Kos Town sell tickets.

Hydrofoil Kos is served by Kyriacoulis Hydrofoils (☎ 25 920, fax 26 228). In high season there are daily shuttles, morning and evening, to and from Rhodes, (two hours, 6500 dr), with good connections to all the major islands in the Dodecanese. In addition, there are connections to Samos (3½ hours, 5600 dr), Ikaria (four hours, 7000 dr) and Fourni (3½ hours, 6800 dr) in the North-Eastern Aegean. From Samos you can easily connect with the Cyclades.

Information and tickets are readily available from the many travel agents.

Catamaran The Rhodes-based *Dodekanisos Express* calls in at Kos Town daily in summer on its daily run up the Dodecanese from Rhodes. Departures heading north from Kos Town are usually around 10.45 am with arrival in Patmos at 1.30 pm. Departures heading south from Kos are usually around 5 pm with arrival in Rhodes at 7 or 8.50 pm, depending on the number of intermediate stops. Tickets can be bought at Exas Travel (☎ 29 900) in Kos Town.

Excursion Boat From Kos Town there are many boat excursions, both around the island and to other islands. Some examples of return fares include: Kalymnos (3000 dr); Pserimos, Kalymnos and Platy (6000 dr); and Nisyros and Giali (5500 dr). There is also a daily excursion boat from Kardamena to Nisyros (3000 dr return) and from Mastihari to Pserimos and Kalymnos.

Getting Around

To/From the Airport An Olympic Airways bus (1000 dr) leaves the airline's office two hours before each flight and ferries arriving passengers back to Kos Town. The airport is 27.5km south-west of Kos Town, near the village of Andimahia, and is poorly served by public transport, though buses to and from Kardamena and Kefalos stop at the roundabout nearby. Many travellers choose to share a taxi into town (4000 dr).

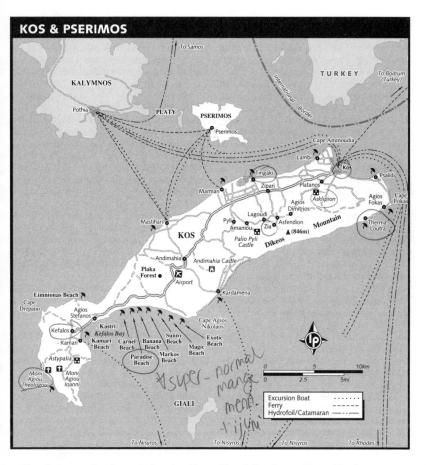

KOS & PSERIMOS

To Samos
TURKEY
To Bodrum (Turkey)
International Border
KALYMNOS
Pothia
PLATY
PSERIMOS
Pserimos
Cape Ammoudia
Lambi
Kos
Psalidi
Tingaki
Zipari
Platanos
Marmari
Asklipion
Agios Fokas
Cape Fokas
Agios Dimitrios
Mastihari
Pyli
Lagoudi
Amaniou
Zia
Asfendion
Therma Loutra
KOS
Palio Pyli Castle
Dikeos
Mountain
▲ (846m)
Andimahia
Andimahia Castle
Plaka Forest
Airport
Kardamena
Limnionas Beach
Cape Drepano
Agios Stefanos
Cape Agios Nikolaos
Kastri
Kefalos Bay
Sunny Beach
Exotic Beach
Kefalos
Kamari
Kamari Beach
Carnel Beach
Banana Beach
Magic Beach
Astypalia
Paradise Beach
Markos Beach
Moni Agiou Theologou
Moni Agiou Ioanni
super-normal mange mean tijiini

GIALI

| | 0 | 5 | 10km |
| 0 | 2.5 | 5mi | |

Excursion Boat ·······
Ferry – – – –
Hydrofoil/Catamaran — ·· — ·· —

To Nisyros   To Nisyros   To Nisyros   To Rhodes

The airport on Kos is modern and well-appointed. There is a 24-hour Telebank ATM in the arrival hall and an Acropole foreign exchange desk that opens for all arrivals. Four car hire companies maintain booths here and there are credit and card phones. Baggage trolleys are free.

Bus The bus station (☎ 22 292, fax 20 263) is at Kleopatras 7, just west of the Olympic Airways office. There are frequent local buses to the Asklipion, Lambi and Agios Fokas from the bus stop on Akti Koundourioti. Buy your tickets on board.

The following table will give you an overview of the local bus services operating on Kos:

destination	duration	price	Mon-Sat	Sun
Kardamena	45 minutes	600 dr	6 daily	3 daily
Kefalos	one hour	800 dr	6 daily	3 daily
Mastihari	45 minutes	550 dr	5 daily	3 daily
Paradise Beach	50 minutes	800 dr	6 daily	3 daily
Pyli	30 minutes	350 dr	5 daily	3 daily
Tingaki	20 minutes	350 dr	12 daily	7 daily
Zia	40 minutes	350 dr	3 daily	

euro currency converter 1000dr = €2.93

Car, Motorcycle & Bicycle There are numerous car, motorcycle and moped rental outlets. Prices are competitive and start at around 9000 dr a day for a small car or 5000 dr a day for a decent scooter.

You'll be tripping over bikes to rent. Mountain bikes can be hired at Power Moto Rentals (☎ 27 825, mobile ☎ 09-4453 2254), on the corner of Makrygianni & Harmilou, for 1000 dr per day, 6000 dr per week or 20,000 dr per month.

Excursion Boat These boats line the southern side of Akti Koundourioti in Kos Town and make trips around the island.

There's a caïque from Kos that drops you off at Mandraki harbour in Nisyros, where you are whisked by a waiting bus to the volcano for a 40-minute visit. The cost is around 4000 dr all-inclusive.

Taxi While taxis can be flagged down anywhere on the island, they can also be found awaiting customers at the taxi rank in Kos Town at the eastern end of Akti Koundourioti.

KOS TOWN

Kos Town, on the north-east coast, is the island's capital and main port. The old town of Kos was destroyed by an earthquake in 1933. The new town, although modern, is picturesque and lush, with palms, pines, oleander and hibiscus everywhere. The Castle of the Knights dominates the port, and Hellenistic and Roman ruins are strewn everywhere. It's a pleasant enough place and can easily be covered on foot in half a day.

Orientation

The ferry quay is north of the castle. Excursion boats dock on Akti Koundourioti to the south-west of the castle. The central square of Plateia Eleftherias is south of Akti Koundourioti along Vasileos Pavlou. Kos' so-called Old Town is on Ifestou, but its souvenir shops, jewellers and boutiques denude it of any old-world charm.

South-east of the castle, the waterfront is called Akti Miaouli. It continues as Vasileos Georgiou and then G Papandreou, which leads to the beaches of Psalidi, Agios Fokas and Therma Loutra.

Road Editions' 1:60,000 map *Kos* is the best map available of the whole island. It also includes a town map of Kos and a map of the Asklipion.

Information

Tourist Offices Kos Town's municipal tourist office (☎ 24 460, fax 21 111, e dotkos@hol.gr) is at Vasileos Georgiou 1. The staff are efficient and helpful. From May to October the office is open 8 am to 8 pm Monday to Friday and 8 am to 3 pm on weekends.

Money Both the National Bank of Greece, on Antinavarhou Ioannidi, and the Ionian Bank, on El Venizelou, have ATMs. The Alpha Credit Bank on Akti Koundourioti has a 24-hour automatic exchange machine.

Post & Communications The post office is on Vasileos Pavlou and the OTE is at Vyronos 6.

Kos Town has a few Internet cafes worth checking out. The best is Internet Cafe Del Mare (☎ 24 244, e sotiris@cybercafe.gr) at Megalou Alexandrou 4. It's open all year from 9 am until after midnight and rates are 1000 dr for 30 minutes or 1500 dr for one hour. There are 14 terminals. The second place is Multi Tech Internet Access (☎ 23 584, e info@multitech.gr) at El Venizelou 55. This place opens all year from 9 am to 9 pm and has the same rates as the Del Mare.

Internet Resources The Municipality of Kos Tourist Organization maintains a useful Web site at www.hippocrates.gr.

Travel Agencies Central Kos Town is wall to wall full of travel agencies, all offering much the same product. Exas Travel & Shipping (☎ 29 900, fax 24 864, e exas@ exas.com), at Ioannidi 4, was helpful during the research of this chapter.

Consulates The UK consulate (☎ 26 203, fax 21 540) is at Laoumtzi 8 and the Italian consulate (☎ 21 991) is on Ippokratous.

Laundry The Happy Wash laundrette is at Mitropolis 20 and the Laundromat Center is at Alikarnasou 124.

Medical Services & Emergency The hospital (☎ 22 300) is at Ippokratous 32. The port police (☎ 28 507) is at the corner of Akti Koundourioti and Megalou Alexandrou. The tourist police (☎ 22 444) and regular police (☎ 22 222) share the yellow building opposite the quay.

Things to See

The **archaeological museum** (☎ 28 326), on Plateia Eleftherias, has a fine 3rd-century mosaic in the vestibule and many statues from various periods. The most renowned is the statue of Hippocrates. The museum is open 8.30 am to 3 pm Tuesday to Sunday. Admission is 800 dr.

The **ancient agora** is an open site south of the castle. A massive 3rd-century BC stoa, with some reconstructed columns, stands on its western side. On the north side are the ruins of the **Shrine of Aphrodite**, the **Temple of Hercules** and a 5th century **Christian basilica**. There is no admission charge.

North of the agora is the lovely cobblestone Plateia Platanou where you can pay your respects to the **Hippocrates Plane Tree**. Under this tree, according to the EOT brochure, Hippocrates taught his pupils. Plane trees don't usually live for more than 200 years, though in all fairness it is certainly one of Europe's oldest. This once-magnificent tree is held up with scaffolding, and looks to be in its death throes. Beneath it is an old sarcophagus which the Turks converted into a fountain. Opposite the tree is the well-preserved 18th-century **Mosque of Gazi Hassan Pasha**, its ground floor loggia now converted into souvenir shops.

From Plateia Platanou a bridge leads across Finikon (called the Avenue of Palms) to the **Castle of the Knights**, known officially as the Neratzia Fortress. Along with the castles of Rhodes City and Bodrum, this impregnable fortress was the knights' most stalwart defence against the encroaching Ottomans. The castle, which had massive outer walls and an inner keep, was built in the 14th century. Damaged by an earthquake in 1495, it was restored by Grand Masters d'Aubuisson and d'Amboise (each a master of a 'tongue' of knights) in the 16th century. The keep was originally separated from the town by a moat (now Finikon). Opening times are 8.30 am to 3 pm Tuesday to Sunday. Admission is 800 dr.

The other ruins are mostly in the southern part of town. Walk along Vasileos Pavlou to Grigoriou and cross over to the restored **Casa Romana**, an opulent 3rd century Roman villa which was built on the site of a larger 1st-century Hellenistic house. It is open 8.30 am to 3 pm Tuesday to Sunday. Admission is 500 dr. Opposite are the scant ruins of the 3rd-century **Temple of Dionysos**.

Facing Grigoriou, turn right to reach the western excavation site. Two wooden shelters at the back of the site protect the 3rd-century **mosaics of the House of Europa**. The best preserved mosaic depicts Europa's abduction by Zeus in the guise of a bull. In front of here an exposed section of the Decumanus Maximus (the Roman city's main thoroughfare) runs parallel to the modern road, then turns right towards the **xysto**, a large Hellenistic **gymnasium**, with some restored columns, and the **nymphaeum**, which consisted of once-lavish public latrines. On the opposite side of Grigoriou is the restored 3rd-century **odeion**, which was used as a general entertainment complex.

Places to Stay – Budget

Kos' one camp site is **_Kos Camping_** (☎ 23 910), 3km along the eastern waterfront. It's a well-kept, shaded site with a taverna, snack bar, minimarket, kitchen and laundry. Rates are 1500 dr per person and 800 dr per tent.

The convivial **_Pension Alexis_** (☎ 28 798, fax 25 797, Irodotou 9) is highly recommended. Clean singles/doubles cost 5500/8000 dr. The friendly English-speaking Alexis promises never to turn anyone away, and he's a mine of information. A little farther east, **_Hotel Afendoulis_** (☎/fax 25 797, Evripilou 1) has tastefully furnished rooms with bathroom for 8000/11,000 dr. Laundry for guests costs 2000 dr a load.

CENTRAL DODECANESE

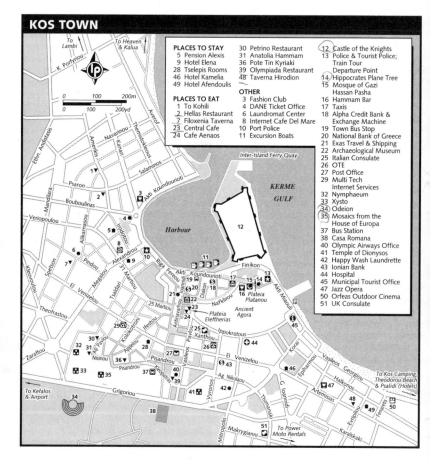

KOS TOWN

PLACES TO STAY
5 Pension Alexis
9 Hotel Elena
28 Tselepis Rooms
46 Hotel Kamelia
49 Hotel Afendoulis

PLACES TO EAT
1 To Kohili
2 Hellas Restaurant
7 Filoxenia Taverna
23 Central Cafe
24 Cafe Aenaos

30 Petrino Restaurant
31 Anatolia Hammam
36 Pote Tin Kyriaki
39 Olympiada Restaurant
48 Taverna Hirodion

OTHER
3 Fashion Club
4 DANE Ticket Office
6 Laundromat Center
8 Internet Cafe Del Mare
10 Port Police
11 Excursion Boats

12 Castle of the Knights
13 Police & Tourist Police;
   Train Tour
   Departure Point
14 Hippocrates Plane Tree
15 Mosque of Gazi
   Hassan Pasha
16 Hammam Bar
17 Taxis
18 Alpha Credit Bank &
   Exchange Machine
19 Town Bus Stop
20 National Bank of Greece
21 Exas Travel & Shipping
22 Archaeological Museum
25 Italian Consulate
26 OTE
27 Post Office
29 Multi Tech
   Internet Services
32 Nymphaeum
33 Xysto
34 Odeion
35 Mosaics from the
   House of Europa
37 Bus Station
38 Casa Romana
40 Olympic Airways Office
41 Temple of Dionysos
42 Happy Wash Laundrette
43 Ionian Bank
44 Hospital
45 Municipal Tourist Office
47 Jazz Opera
50 Orfeas Outdoor Cinema
51 UK Consulate

Other commendable budget options include the D-class *Hotel Elena* (☎ *22 740, Megalou Alexandrou 7*), with doubles/triples with bathroom for 8000/10,000 dr; and *Tselepis Rooms* (☎ *28 896, Metsovou 8*), where rooms cost 10,000/12,000 dr with bathroom.

The C-class *Hotel Kamelia* (☎ *28 983, fax 27 391, [e] kamelia_hotel@hotmail .com*) is open all year and is located on a quiet tree-lined street. Its very comfortable single/double rooms costs around 8000/14,000 dr, while the continental breakfast will knock you back an extra 1000 dr.

Places to Stay – Mid-Range & Top End

The B-class *Theodorou Beach* (☎ *23 363, G Papandreou*), east of the waterfront, has a cool, spacious interior and nicely furnished rooms. Singles/doubles cost 13,500/17,000 dr with bathroom.

Most of Kos' top-end hotels are on the beaches to either side of town. The luxurious *Kipriotis Village* (☎ *27 640, fax 23 590, [e] kipriotis@kos.forthnet.gr*), at Psalidi, 4km east of town, has rooms for 45,000/55,000 dr and apartments for up to three people for 60,000 dr. The A-class *Platanista*

CENTRAL DODECANESE

Hotel (☎ 22 400, fax 25 029), also at Psalidi, is an architecturally interesting, crenellated building. Rooms are 22,000/27,800 dr.

Places to Eat – Budget

There is no shortage of places to eat in Kos Town but the variety ranges from dreadful to excellent. Prices can be somewhat inflated, but need not be if you do some assiduous choosing. As a general rule, the restaurants lining the central waterfront are expensive and of poor value. Keep away.

In the back streets *Taverna Hirodion* (*Artemisias 27*) serves good, inexpensive food, though it's a little out of the way. The *Olympiada Restaurant* (☎ 23 031, Kleopatras 2) is an unpretentious place serving reasonably priced, tasty food.

Filoxenia Taverna (☎ 24 967, cnr Pindou & Alikarnasou) has a good reputation for traditional home-cooked food. *Hellas Restaurant* (☎ 22 609, Psaron 7) and the very untouristy ouzeri, *Pote tin Kyriaki* (☎ 27 872, Pisandrou 9), open in the evening, but 'never on a Sunday', are also highly commendable.

Cafe Aenaos (☎ 26 044, Plateia Eleftherias), housed in a former mosque opposite the market, and the *Central Cafe* (☎ 25 302, Vasileos Pavlou 6) nearby are popular meeting places for locals and tourists alike.

Places to Eat – Mid-Range

Budget for around 10,000 dr for a good meal for two with wine and dessert at the following three choices. The *Petrino Restaurant* (☎ 27 251, Plateia Ioannou Theologou) is a stylish place in a stone mansion, with outdoor eating in a romantic garden setting. It offers a wide range of well-prepared food.

To Kohili (☎ 25 000, Amerikis 64) is an old renovated house that has been converted into an intimate taverna featuring fish and other seafood dishes. It's open evenings only.

Anatolia Hammam (☎ 28 323, Plateia Diagora) is one of Kos' more atmospheric restaurants located in an old Turkish bathhouse. Cuisine is Greek-European and there is an extensive wine selection. It's open evenings only.

Entertainment

There are plenty of places to have fun in Kos Town, with around five major discos and some 15 or so bars and clubs. Two streets of bars, Diakon and Nafklirou – locally known as Bar Alley – positively pulsate in high season. Most belt out techno, but *Hammam Bar* (*Akti Koundourioti 1*) plays Greek music. *Jazz Opera* (☎ 21 448, Arseniou 5) is popular with locals and tourists.

Kos Town has five discos. Of these, *Heaven* (☎ 23 874, Akti Zouroudi 5) plays mostly house. At *Kalua* (☎ 24 938), next door, the music is more mixed and includes R&B. Both are outdoor and have swimming pools. The indoor *Fashion Club* (☎ 22 592, Kanari 2) has three air-conditioned bars.

The *Orfeas* outdoor cinema is on Vasileos Georgiou and operates in summer only. Tickets to films cost 1700 dr. Films generally have Greek subtitles with the original soundtrack.

Getting Around

Other than walking, which is the best way to see Kos Town, you can take the Train Tour (☎ 26 276) that leaves from the Municipality Building. The 20-minute tour around the city streets costs 500 dr (250 dr for children) and takes in all the main sights.

Parking can be a problem in Kos Town, but there is an easily accessible and very handy car park on the east side of the Old Town very close to the tourist office.

EASTERN KOS

The far eastern tip of Kos includes the strip of coastline hosting most of Kos' luxury hotels as well as its only camp site, a couple of lower-key resorts and rather rough-and-ready, but very popular, natural thermal baths. Kos' most famous archaeological site is located here, a short way inland from Kos Town. Nearby is the only village in Kos with a marked Turkish influence.

CENTRAL DODECANESE

Kos' most important
ancient site, the Asklipion,
as it might have looked
2000 years ago.

Asklipion Ασκληπιείον

The Asklipion (☎ 28 763), built on a pine-covered hill 4km south-west of Kos Town, is the island's most important ancient site. From the top there is a wonderful view of Kos Town and Turkey. The Asklipion consisted of a religious sanctuary to Asklepios, the god of healing, a healing centre, and a school of medicine, where trainees followed the teachings of Hippocrates.

Hippocrates was the first doctor to have a rational approach to diagnosing and treating illnesses. Until AD 554 people came from far and wide to be treated here, as well as for medical training.

The ruins occupy three levels. The **propylaea**, the Roman-era **public baths** and the remains of guestrooms are on the first level. On the next level is a 4th century BC **altar of Kyparissios Apollo**. West of this is the **first Temple of Asklepios**, built in the 4th century BC. To the east is the 1st century BC **Temple to Apollo**; seven of its graceful columns have been re-erected. On the third level are the remains of the once-magnificent 2nd century BC **Temple of Asklepios**. The site is open 8.30 am to 3 pm Tuesday to Sunday. Admission is 800 dr.

Frequent buses go to the site, but it is pleasant to cycle or walk there.

Lambi

Lambi (lam-**bi**) is a small resort at the far northern tip of Kos about 3km from Kos Town's port. Half the stretch from Kos Town to Lambi is built up with a succession of shops, restaurants and rental outlets. There are fairly good but always very crowded

public beaches. The actual tip of the island, **Cape Ammoudia** is a military base.

From **Lambi beach** you feel as though you could reach out and touch the Turkish coast opposite. Swimming here is not recommended as the water is very rough and there are strong currents. Still, there is beach life of sorts and if you like your sunbathing to be 'brisk', Lambi is your spot.

Therma Loutra

Therma Loutra (ther-**ma** lou-**tra**) is 11.5km south-east of Kos Town and is at the end of the paved road in this part of the island. A driveable track from the bus stop leads down to a couple of pebbly beaches, the last one of which is a natural thermal spa.

From a cleft in the rocks a stream of hot mineral water gurgles forth along an artificially cut channel into a rough rockpool on the beach. At any time of the day you will find enthusiastic bathers enjoying a warm and presumably very therapeutic bath for free. You'll find that Therma Loutra is a low-key and most enjoyable thermal spa. Buses ply to and from Kos Town every 25 minutes or so (200 dr). There is a cantina by the bus stop and a restaurant at the spa beach itself.

THE NORTH COAST
Tingaki & Marmari
Τιγκάκι & Μαρμάρι

The two villages of Tingaki (tin-**ga**-ki) and Marmari (mar-**ma**-ri) are popular with windsurfers and German tourists. The Germans also seem to dominate most of the accommodation which is geared towards package tourists, though there is a perceptible British

CENTRAL DODECANESE

C Yule

contingent here too. Windsurfers like it because of the stiff breezes, which can almost always be relied on.

The long sandy, dune-backed beaches are very pretty and the beach facilities at both centres are well organised, with boardwalks, beach showers, rental umbrellas and loungers, and the usual profusion of restaurants, cafes, hire outlets and shops. Tingaki Beach proudly sports an EU 'Blue Flag' award for the cleanliness of its beach, though on windy days there can be a fair bit of seaweed offshore. However this is one region where beach loungers and umbrellas tend to face inland away from the sea – so as to avoid the strong breezes preferred by the windsurfers. Not surprisingly, windsurfing hire outlets proliferate.

Tingaki and Marmari make ideal destinations for cyclists on relaxed day jaunts out of Kos Town. Both are easily accessible by regular local buses. While independent accommodation may be hard to pin down, there is no shortage of places to eat, or you could stock up on picnic items.

Cycling Kos is the sole island among the Dodecanese Islands to developed bicycle riding. This is due almost entirely to its ideal terrain, its excellent weather and easy access to beaches under your own pedal power. While cycling in Kos Town is possible, traffic is still busy; for a much more rewarding experience it's better to get out of town and hit the open roads. The main area of cycling activity is the north coast section between Kos Town and Tingaki, though many cyclists extend their forays as far as Marmari.

Getting out of Kos Town is a bit confusing and you are advised to get a copy of Road Edition's *Kos* map (see Orientation in Kos Town earlier) to get an overview. The preferred cycle route heads out along the back roads, through unmarked small settlements towards Tingaki (9km). The road – more like a country lane – is very pleasant cycling, there is little motorised traffic and bicycles far outnumber vehicles.

The extension of the route takes you to Marmari (14 km), bypassing the large saltworks that separate the two villages.

Places to Eat In Marmari leave the waterfront and walk about 1km inland to find both *Dimitris* (☎ *41 122*) and *Apostolis* (☎ *41 403*), next to each other near the road junction to Tingaki. Dimitris offers a wide range of *mayirefta* (ready-made) dishes, while Apostolis has a similar menu, which is pitched more at the German tourist market.

On the way to Dimitris and Apostolis you'll pass the big *Konstantinos Supermarket* on your right, where you can stock up on picnic goodies. It is open from 8 am to 10.30 pm daily.

In Tingaki seek out *Plori* (☎ *69 686*) at the far western end of the beachfront restaurant strip for a mainly fish-based menu. Dine in comfortable surroundings in stylish cane chairs under bamboo shading. Prices are moderate to more expensive.

Getting There & Away There are almost hourly buses to Kos Town from both Marmari (35 minutes, 350 dr) and Tingaki (20 minutes, 350 dr).

Mastihari Μαστιχάρι

Mastihari (mas-ti-**ha**-ri), north of Andimahia and 30km from Kos Town, is a fairly important village in its own right. It is a resort destination and also the arrival and departure point for local ferries to Pothia on Kalymnos. It is also better equipped to cater for independent travellers, with a good selection of domatia available. Moreover Mastihari is just that little bit more 'Greek' than its resort neighbours Marmari and Tingaki farther east.

Kos' international airport is just a short 10-minute bus ride away, making Mastihari a handy base for mobile travellers. There are the usual restaurants, cafes, a disco, car hire outlets, but no ATM. The nearest ATM is at the airport. Money can easily be exchanged at any of the travel agencies.

The beach on the west side is wide and sandy, while bathing on the east side is from rocks. Mastihari is also favoured by windsurfers. If all that wasn't enough, you can take day trips to both Kalymnos and Pserimos from here.

Places to Stay There's loads of accommodation in Mastihari and at decent prices. Walk inland along the main road to *Rooms to Rent Anna (☎ 59 041)*, on the left, where doubles are 8000 dr. Farther up on the right, *Pension Elena (☎ 59 010)* has doubles for 6500 dr. Next door, *Rooms to Let David (☎ 59 122)* has doubles for 8000 dr.

Closer to the west side beach are *Rooms Panorama (☎/fax 59 145)*. Owner Kalliopi has seven tidy double studios, with kitchenette for 10,000 dr; most overlook the beach.

Places to Eat In Mastihari the *Kali Kardia Restaurant (☎ 52 289)*, on the central square, has particularly good fish dishes, while *O Makis (☎ 51 592)*, one block back from the harbourfront, is also worth a look. Both places are moderately priced.

Entertainment It's a good sign when local Greeks head to Mastihari for a night out. Its one disco is the *Vyvlos Night Club*, a five-minute walk up the road towards the airport, near the petrol station. It opens after 11.30 pm and plays Greek and English music. Entry is free.

Kafe Plo, also in Mastihari, serves sangria (800 dr) and cocktails (1200 dr) onto tasteful marble topped tables. It's east off the main street down a little lane. Look for the rocks and pots at the front of the cafe.

The *Acid Jazz Cafe* is another good place to hang loose. Cocktails retail for 1200 dr and Mythos beer for 500 dr.

Getting There & Away The F/B *Olympios Apollon* leaves Mastihari daily at 9.30 am, 5.30 and 10.45 pm for its run across to Pothia in Kalymnos (one hour, 900 dr).

Buses from Mastihari to Kos Town run five times a day at 8, 9.40 and 10.40 am and 3.40 and 5.20 pm (45 minutes, 550 dr).

Taxis can more easily be found in Mastihari during arrival and departure times of the Kalymnos ferry.

CENTRAL KOS

Kos' mountain villages in inland Kos are a refreshing break from the sun and sea scene of the coast. There are several villages nestling along the northern slopes of **Mt Dikeos** (843m), an alpine-like mountain range that dominates the south-eastern quadrant of Kos. They are best taken as a leisurely day trip, though many visitors come at sunset for the view and others come for 'genuine' Greek evenings that involve much eating, drinking and occasional plate smashing. Oddly perhaps, given the villages' attraction, places to stay are pretty much non-existent. The villages are all within walking distance of one another and it is also possible to climb Mt Dikeos from here.

Zipari

Zipari (zi-**pa**-ri) lies 7.5km from the capital and is the best starting point for visitors from Kos Town. It's a busy agricultural town on the main highway which offers little to tempt visitors. A signposted road to the south-east leads to **Asfendion**. From Asfendion, a turn-off to the left leads to the pristine and little visited hamlet of **Agios Dimitrios**.

Zia

Zia (**zee**-ah) is the target of most visitors to the mountain villages and many of them come in large tourist buses that pile up at the entrance to the village. The place is very touristy. It is also undeniably attractive and if you look beyond the kitsch and commercial you will find some useful things to take home – like local honey, or bags of spices or mixed peppercorns that all grow or are produced locally.

Zia is also the starting point for hikers wishing to walk up to the summit of Mt Dikeos, a half-day undertaking for reasonably fit people.

Places to Eat Zia is well-endowed with restaurants, most touting sunset dinners. Choose prudently if you are not in a group, or you may be swamped by a coachload or two.

The *Oromedon (☎ 23 750)* gets this writer's vote for the best views and the most tasteful decor. *Taverna Olympia (☎ 69 121)* doesn't have a view, but cashes in on its solid, reliable local cuisine, moderate prices and repeat clientele. It is also open all year.

Herbs

Wherever the land in the Dodecanese is uncultivated and denuded of trees, vegetation has degenerated to a tangle of shrubs, bushes and a profusion of herbs. The most common herbs in the region are basil, rosemary, oregano, sage, bay, dill and garlic, but many others can be found. The evocative, all-pervading aroma of these herbs is something that lingers in the memory for a long time.

Herbs, more than any other ingredient, used wisely and in moderation, can transform a mundane dish into a gourmet feast.

Tourist-oriented shops selling traditional products, including dried herbs, are springing up all over the Dodecanese, particularly in the mountain villages of Kos and Karpathos, but you will find the same herbs at a lower price in street markets and supermarkets. Dried herbs are a poor substitute for freshly picked ones, but if you must use them they keep best in a cool, dark cupboard. They can be reconstituted in lemon juice, for use in salads.

Since ancient times herbs have been used in the Dodecanese for medicinal purposes. This custom continues today, particularly in rural areas. Oregano, a member of the marjoram family, but with a more pungent flavour, is the most widely used herb in Greek cooking. It is an important ingredient in tomato sauce and many oven-baked dishes. Finely chopped oregano is sprinkled on souvlaki, salads and feta cheese.

Basil is not used much in cooking in the Dodecanese, but is sprinkled on salads, especially tomatoes. Almost every house will have a pot of basil on the balcony, as it makes an excellent insect repellent. Rosemary is a sweet-scented, strong-tasting herb, which the Greeks sprinkle liberally on roast meat, particularly lamb.

Bay leaves are widely used to flavour stews and soups. Dill is a highly aromatic herb and both the leaves and seeds are used in cooking. Chopped fresh dill leaves are used in salads, and are an important ingredient in tzatziki. *Skordalia*, a strong garlic sauce, is served with fried cod. Garlic is also used in many baked dishes, as well as being an essential ingredient in tzatziki. It is said to aid digestion, build up immunity to colds and lower blood pressure.

If you've enjoyed your holiday in the Dodecanese, then hope that someone will give you some basil, because a parting gift of this herb, according to the Greeks, ensures that you will return.

For traditional sweets, tea, coffee and heavenly yogurt with honey, *Marianthi* (☎ *68 313)* in Zia's main street is the place to visit.

Lagoudi & Around

Lagoudi (la-**ghou**-dhi) is a small, unspoilt village west of Zia. From here you can continue to **Amaniou** (just before modern Pyli), where there is a left turn to **Palio Pyli**, a ruined Byzantine castle perched high on a lofty crag surveying the open plains of Kos to the north. This is definitely worth the side trip. Despite the apparent inaccessibility of the castle you *can* reach the top. Take the paved path from the car park and keep walking left (if you head right you'll come to other ruined buildings and a relatively open space below the castle, where access

is not so obvious). A side diversion from the access path up and into the castle walls will take you to the top, after a 15-minute scramble. From here, the views are magnificent, but watch out for dangerous holes that open into hidden chambers. Access is free.

Pyli

Pyli (pi-**lee**) is the next major village of the region and is strung out sinuously along its main street. People come here to wander around, have a bite to eat and visit the **Harmylio**, a grave monument from the early 3rd century AD that shares space with the small Byzantine **chapel of the Holy Cross**. Both are signposted from Pyli's main square and are an easy 700m walk south.

Taverna Pyli (☎ *41 377)*, on the main square, is a popular and reliable eatery, while

CENTRAL DODECANESE

Palia Pigi (☎ *41 510*), a small cafe 50m from the square, has the shadiest spot in the village under an enormous plane tree and next to the village's old water spring *(palia pigi)*. Both are cheap to moderate in price.

From Pyli you can return to the main trans-island highway (3km), take a circuitous back route to the highway farther south (7km), or even head for Kardamena (11.5km) on the south coast.

Buses to and from Pyli and Kos Town run four or five times a day (three times on Sunday) in either direction (350 dr, 30 minutes). From Kos Town, they leave at 7 and 10 am, 1, 3 and 7.30 pm, returning to Kos Town from Pyli 30 minutes later.

SOUTHERN KOS

Southern Kos is defined here as the area generally south of the airport village of Andimahia and is home to the island's best beaches, a strung-out low-key package resort and the remotest and least-developed section of the island. Independent travellers will probably find more attractions here than in the highly packaged North Coast and Kos Town tourist enclaves.

Iniand Kos is often crossed with undue haste by travellers heading for the southern beaches, but it's worth taking time out to stop and view the landscape. It's a land of rolling, dusty fields inhabited by large brown cows, gulches and canyons – some hiding military camps – a hidden forest and even a surprisingly impressive castle. The airport is almost within a lager can's throw of a tacky, but inexplicably popular down-market package resort.

Andimahia

Andimahia (andi-**ma**-hia) is a major cross-roads village with two large roundabouts. The village is rarely visited, though it is virtually on top of the airport. Its 'sight' as such is a fairly impressive windmill which the postcards usually depict with full sail. The mill was a fully operational corn grinding unit until fairly recently.

A worthwhile detour is to **Andimahia Castle** along a turn-off to the left, 1km before Andimahia. This is a deceptively large

and well-preserved Knight's structure that dates from the 14th century. The ruined settlement within its walls hosts a couple of chapels – those of Agios Nikolaos and Agia Paraskevi. From the southern ramparts you can look down onto the resort of Kardamena across the Kos badlands – rough, uninhabited and uncultivated terrain – and spot the islands of Nisyros and Tilos shimmering on the southern horizon.

The Plaka Forest

The Plaka Forest, signposted off the main road just south of the airport, is a beautiful, virtually 'hidden' surprise tucked away in the cool folds of the otherwise dry canyons and gullies of inland Kos. It is a small, cool and shady pine forest, ideal for a picnic away from the beach for a change. While there is ample space for picnickers to spread out, there are only two fixed picnic tables and benches and a desultory trickle of water from a ground spring. There are two BBQ pits, so you can roast a lamb or goat if you are sufficiently well prepared.

Kardamena

Kardamena (kar-**dha**-me-na), 27km from Kos Town, and 5km south-east of Andimahia, is essentially an over-developed, tacky resort over-favoured by northern Europeans on cheap two-week, sex, sun and booze package holidays. It could have been a pleasant place and in fairness it does have its scattered moments, but the lure of the fast buck has destroyed any kind of authenticity this once quiet fishing village enjoyed.

Kardamena is now claustrophobic and its narrow beaches packed and generally tatty. Even so, you can at least get decent fish and chips and Woodpecker cider, if you feel you've overdosed on retsina and souvlaki, and you'll never miss out on the live English soccer matches beamed into virtually every bar worth its pint glasses.

Things are marginally better along the long coastal strip east of Kardamena where the beach body count is perceptibly lower, the grass greener and the sand seemingly more mellow.

CENTRAL DODECANESE

Places to Eat If you find yourself stuck in Kardamena, do not despair. There is some salvation to be found at **_Kardamos Ouzeri_**, where the oldies sip on ouzo and snack on Greek mezedes. **_Loustros_** nearby advertises vegetarian dishes such as vegetable risotto and spinach rice, while **_Taverna Restaurant Andreas_** is about as Greek as it's going to get. The affable owner Andreas may even break out into song. All three places are close to each other on the main harbourfront.

Entertainment Kardamena would have the highest percentage of watering holes per square kilometre than any place south of Kos Town. Forget the British-style bars and make for 'cocktail alley', 100m east of the main harbour.

Adams, *Sky Line*, *Artemis* and the *Athinaio Bar* are four fairly plush joints with tables under cool, shaded awnings next to the water. They all serve up exotic pre-dinner cocktails with suggestive names costing anywhere between 1200 dr and 2000 dr.

Getting There & Away Kardamena is a convenient spot from which to take a day trip to Nisyros. Or exit Kos altogether on the Nisyros-based caïque *Chrysoula*, which makes the run across to Nisyros four times a week at 2.30 pm on Monday, Wednesday, Thursday and Friday (1000 dr one way).

There are also buses to/from Kardamena (45 minutes, 600 dr) six times a day (three times on Sunday) in either direction.

Beaches

Kos' biggest attraction in the south is its long sandy beaches. Swarms of scantily-clad youths on scooters can be seen heading out this way daily, and with around eight beaches to choose from you can have a new one each day of the week and still keep an extra one for Sunday. In practice nearly the whole coastline of the rounded underbelly of Kos is one long sandy beach, but beach centres have developed on separate sections of the coast and all are prominently signposted and approached from the main highway. Some are quiet and relatively untouched, others

Mass Tourism

Although the beaches of Kos' south-eastern coast are among the best in the Dodecanese, the beach and resort of Kardamena sets a new standard of kitsch and tackiness. The local population has been submersed in a tidal wave of sleazy commercialism. From frozen fish 'n' chips to draft Watneys Ale, imported 'Greek' ceramics and machine-made weavings in souvenir shops, there's nothing authentic or even particularly Greek about the place.

Unlike most of the rest of the island, the music in bars and tavernas is either western or the most westernised Greek music available. Don't understand the Greek signs? Don't worry. You won't see a single one in Kardamena. All signs are in Roman letters. Fish and chip stands, cafes with names like 'Cheers' and 'Union Jack', video bars playing British sitcoms or beaming in the latest British football matches, seem designed to shield visitors from the horrible realisation that they are actually in a foreign country.

Although Kos does have some genuinely pleasant places, for some inexplicable reason Kardamena has been ruined. The crowds here are predominantly young and you'll feel old if you are over 22. If you have come to Kardamena, it is assumed that you will consume copious quantities of alcohol and then try to engage in some free-for-all sex, or fall asleep on the pavement or, if your aim is better, on the beach. Don't be put off – Kos is a big island and the rest of it is just fine. Just choose your crowd carefully.

have a fine balance of development and quietness and at least one is a major beach destination in its own right. The water quality at all of them is good to excellent. In the following sections, 'facilities' refer to anything from simple beach showers to fully fledged restaurants.

Starting from the northern end you can visit the following beaches.

Exotic Beach Less prosaic than it sounds, the only exotic things about this beach are the straw beach umbrellas and the on-sand

CENTRAL DODECANESE

parking for car owners. The scrub-covered sand dunes offer some natural shade, but there are no facilities otherwise.

Magic Beach Magic Beach, 500m west of Exotic Beach, is reached by the same approach road as its neighbour and is very similar. Car owners can park on this wide open expanse of sand. There's no natural shade and no facilities. It is known locally as **Poleni beach**.

Sunny Beach This beach enjoys a good access road and ample car parking. There is a restaurant, umbrellas and loungers to rent, low-key water sports facilities, and beach showers. Cars can also park on the beach.

Markos Beach Yet further along is this wide sandy beach, with shade from rented umbrellas only, though a scraggly row of bamboo planted along the back of the beach will eventually provide some extra shade and protection. There are water sports on offer and a restaurant with bamboo shade mats protecting diners from the sun.

Banana Beach Known locally as **Langada Beach**, this is a narrow stretch of sand with very clean water. It's not too crowded and has a fresh water beach shower. A mobile cantina provides snacks and drinks. This is one of the better beaches on the island.

Paradise Beach Known also as **Tigani Beach**, this is the big daddy of all beaches down here. It's a strip of end-to-end umbrellas and *Baywatch* babe wannabes. It's sandy and clean, there's plenty of parking and it has at least one half-decent place to eat – the ***Paradise Beach Restaurant*** (☎ 71 263). It's all yours if you are prepared to share it with the hundreds of other sun-worshippers.

Camel Beach Further west round a small headland, this beach doesn't have any hump-backed dromedaries on offer, but it does have a couple of discrete strands sandwiched between two rocky headlands. In the middle is a half-demolished diving platform built over the rocks. There is no shade other than from rental umbrellas and there is no cantina or restaurant. Come prepared with food and drink.

Bay of Kefalos

The tourist centre that has developed around the attractive **Bay of Kefalos** is less frenetic than the beach areas nearer Kos Town, better protected from the winds than the North Coast resorts and better suited for vacationers wanting to relax, or young couples looking for a romantic and uncomplicated holiday. The beaches are at their best at the eastern end of the bay while at the southern end they tend to be pebbly but less crowded.

Agios Stefanos and **Kamari** are essentially two communities that merge imperceptibly into one long strip. Tourism is the key to livelihood here. In the winter, restaurateurs and shop owners retire to Kos Town or **Kefalos** high on the bluff above, and the area is virtually dead. In summer it is lively enough to provide for all your needs, while there are enough wining and dining options in both centres to give you room to breathe.

Agios Stefanos Agios Stefanos (**agh**-ios ste-fa-nos) takes its name from the little church on the island of **Kastri** that you can see floating off the sandy shore at the eastern end and the eponymous **5th-century basilica of Agios Stefanos** with its restored columns and still visible mosaic floors.

Agios Stefanos Beach is sandy and clean and is signposted off the main road. ***Restaurant Katerina*** at the back of the car park will provide sustenance. Club Med has a huge resort here, though most guests rarely venture out beyond the palm trees and grassy lawns of their closed compound. Note that the section of beach backed by Club Med is public and can also be accessed by a barely noticeable concrete road next to the Club Med entrance signposted simply 'Basilica'.

There is a handy Infocenter (☎ 71 755, e kastri@hol.gr), where you can access the

Internet for 1000 dr for 30 minutes. It is open from 9 am to 1 pm and 6.30 to 9.30 pm daily from May to October. The centre is on the right hand side of the main road as you come in from Kos Town.

Villa Soula (☎ 71 446, fax 71 788) offers three-person studios for 7000 dr.

Kamari Kamari (ka-**ma**-ri) is the strip of restaurants and studios that runs around from the middle of the bay and ends at the small **harbour** at the far southern end. It is quieter than Agios Stefanos and seems to be preferred by young couples who enjoy its subdued ambience. Its beach is narrower and on the whole pebbly.

Day **excursions to Nisyros** leave from a small jetty here (see also under Kardamena earlier). There is an abundance of generally mediocre restaurants with unchallenging picture menus, bars for people who like to relax with a beer in a comfy chair and a scattering of rental studios. Kamari is probably the best base in the southern half of the island for independent travellers.

There is no ATM in Kamari but Sebastian Tours (☎ 71 767) near the jetty exchanges money and sells most types of ferry tickets as well as day trips to Nisyros and 'Greek nights' in Zia. The minimket next door sells British newspapers.

Most of the accommodation in Kefalos Bay is monopolised by tour groups, but there is some hope for independents. *Hotel Sydney (☎ 71 286, 71 786)* in Kamari has 20 reasonable doubles for around 10,000 dr. If you prefer self-contained accommodation, there are a couple of good choices here also. *Anthoula Studios (☎ 71 904)* are a block of spotless ground-floor apartments with kitchen, fridge and balcony with loungers. These go for around 14,000 dr for two people. *Rooms to Let Katerina (☎ 71 397)* nearby are a little smaller, but also a good choice. Rates are 13,000 dr for a double studio. Both are on the seafront about 200m on the right from Sebastian Tours.

Kamari offers perhaps the best dining possibilities in the region. Most restaurants are on the land side of the beach road, but a couple have beachfront dining. *Captain*

John's (☎ 71 152), reliable though not exceptional, has a pleasant location next to the excursion boat jetty. A meal of *spetsofaï*, chips and beer cost this writer only 2000 dr.

About 50m from Captain John's and also enjoying a beachfront location is *Stamatia (☎ 71 245)*, which has been in business since 1935. Fresh fish and meat dishes are their stock in trade. Prices are also reasonable.

Supermarket Tiras, on the promenade, is the best stocked in the village. It is open until late.

The *Sydney Bar* serves up ice-cold Fosters lager while the *Mundial* is a cafe-cum-snack bar that is popular at night with the few locals who dare venture into otherwise solid tourist territory.

+ special – weekly

Kefalos Kefalos (ke-fa-los), 43km south of Kos Town, is the sprawling village perched high above Kamari Beach. It's a pleasant place with few concessions to tourism. The central square, where the bus terminates, is at the top of the 2km road from the coast.

The main reason to come to Kefalos is for the post office (open 10.15 am to 1.15 pm) and the National Bank ATM, both of which are close to each other near the bus stop.

Buses to and from Kefalos and Kos Town run five times a day (three times on Sunday) in either direction (800 dr, one hour), stopping at the major southern beaches along the route. Buses from Kos Town depart at 9.10 and 10 am, 1, 2.30, 4.30 and 9 pm. From Kefalos to Kos Town buses depart at 7.30, 10 and 11 am, 3.15 and 6 pm.

Fin standard + sten Hell fantastic

The Southern Peninsula

The Southern Peninsula has the island's most wild and rugged scenery. **Moni Agiou Theologou** is on the east coast, 4km from Kefalos, just beyond a sand and pebble beach. Sunsets here are spectacular and on a clear day you can see the island of **Astypalea** to the south-west, as well as the uninhabited islands of **Kandeliousa** and **Syrna** farther south. To the north-west you may also spot the islets of **Levitha** and **Kinaros**, both also uninhabited and better spotted before the road from Kefalos makes the descent to **Agios Theologos**.

CENTRAL DODECANESE

Moni Agiou Ioanni is at the end of the trans-island road and is 7km south of Kefalos. A narrow but sealed road from here leads curious riders and drivers on towards the prominent radio masts perched on the mountaintop at 427m. Unfortunately, the final leg is blocked by a military camp so you can't make it to the top, but the views on the way down are stunning.

Along the way back to Kefalos and just after the turn-off to Agios Theologos, look out for signs to the **palatia** (palaces), the site of the original **Astypalia** or 'ancient city'. This was the original capital of Kos, which was abandoned in 366 BC. Access and entry is unlimited and free.

Places to Eat *Restaurant Agios Theologos*, abutting Agios Theologos beach, serves excellent main dishes and delicious home-made traditional cakes. This is the spot for soothing sunset dinners. Canadian-Greek owner Haralambos is as gregarious as he is charming and will look after you. Prices are average. This is also the writer's favourite whistle-wetting spot, where a glass of ice cold Kourtaki retsina at sunset is as close to perfection as it gets after a hot day in the sun.

Astypalea
Αστυπάλαια

☎ 0243 • postcode 859 00 • pop 1100

Astypalea (ah-stih-**pah**-lia), the most westerly island of the archipelago, is geographically and architecturally more akin to the Cyclades, but administratively it's a Dodecanese island. Sited more or less equidistant between its nearest Cycladic neighbour, Amorgos to the west, and its fellow Dodecanese island, Kos to the east, Astypalea effectively has a foot in both camps. This in turn affects its mainstream popularity with the island-hopper set, with sea links either too short in supply or hopelessly inconvenient to travellers. Nonetheless, the island has a reasonably regular air link and Athenians come here in droves in high season –

perhaps because foreigners are so few in number. Thus, you'll find a disproportionately busy tourist scene for four or five weeks in July and August compared to the relatively quiet and serene times outside this domestic tourist onslaught.

Astypalea is intriguingly shaped like a butterfly, with its svelte waist being barely 100m wide at the narrowest point. With a wonderfully picturesque hilltop Hora, and bare, gently contoured hills, high mountains, green valleys and sheltered coves, Astypalea is a destination waiting to be discovered. The beaches aren't brilliant, the nightlife is very low-key, but there is good dining to be enjoyed and some truly excellent mid-range to more expensive accommodation for people looking for a do-it-yourself, get-away-from-the-rat-race vacation on an island that is still uniquely Greek.

History

Astypalea has a long history, though like many places in Greece its earliest history is more mythology than fact. What is known for certain is that the name of the island has been variously Pylea, Ichthyoessa and Stampalia. The name Astypalea means 'ancient city' and indeed the first colonisers of the island were the Karians who gradually came from the Anatolian mainland to the Aegean islands between 5500 and 1150 BC. They were succeeded in turn by the Cretans and finally Dorian settlers from the Argolis peninsula in the Peloponnese. This is borne out by linguistic elements of the Dorian dialect in the spoken vernacular on the island today.

Archaeological finds, including coins, ceramics and inscriptions, testify to a rich period of activity and a strong maritime infrastructure in the classical period when Astypalea was subject to Athens. During the Hellenistic period Astypalea belonged to the Ptolemies of Egypt, but during the Roman era the island remained essentially independent after concluding a pact with Rome that gave them a large degree of autonomy. The course of events during the era of Byzantium is largely uncharted, due partly to the depredations of piratism that were affecting

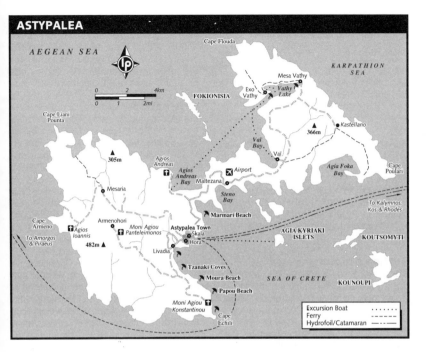

ASTYPALEA

AEGEAN SEA

KARPATHION SEA

Cape Flouda

Mesa Vathy

Exo Vathy · Vathy Lake

FOKIONISIA

0   2   4km
0 1 2mi

Cape Liani Pounta

366m

Kastellano

Vaï Bay

Vaï

305m

Agios Andreas

Agios Andreas Bay

Airport

Maltezana

Agia Foka Bay

Cape Poulari

Mesaria

Steno Bay

To Kalymnos, Kos & Rhodes

Marmari Beach

Cape Armeno

Armenohori

Moni Agiou Panteleimonos

Astypalea Town

Skala

AGIA KYRIAKI ISLETS

KOUTSOMYTI

Agios Ioannis

Hora

To Amorgos & Piraeus

482m

Livadia

Tzanaki Coves

Moura Beach

SEA OF CRETE

KOUNOUPI

Papou Beach

Moni Agiou Konstantinou

Cape Echili

Excursion Boat   ·······
Ferry   -------
Hydrofoil/Catamaran - - - -

the Aegean islands. Astypalea only really came to the forefront again in 1207 AD when it was taken over by the Quirini family from Venice. Their rule lasted until 1522. It was during this time that the Castle in Hora was built.

During the Ottoman rule from 1540 to 1912 Astypalea enjoyed a certain degree of free rule, but joined in the Greek War of Independence in 1821. It enjoyed independence until occupied by Italy in 1912, the first Dodecanese Island to succumb to Italian rule.

Getting There & Away

Links to the outside world are not too good, with relatively few ferries linked to sometimes inconvenient arrival or departure times.

Aircraft flying to Astypalea are of the larger ATR 42, 50-seater type, as opposed to the more common Dornier 18-seaters that flit around the smaller islands of the Aegean. Thus, the chances of securing a

seat at busy times are higher. However, the only services are to and from Athens.

The once-weekly hydrofoil is particularly prone to the vagaries of the weather that affect the open sea between Astypalea and Kos, and may be cancelled. Always allow for possible 'maroon time' on Astypalea.

Air There are four flights weekly from Astypalea to Athens (20,100 dr). Astypalea Tours in Astypalea Town, is the agent for Olympic Airways.

Ferry Lying between the Cyclades and the Dodecanese, Astypalea is the most easterly destination of some Cyclades services, and the most westerly of the Dodecanese services. Departure times are more favourable when heading west and north.

The F/B *Nisos Kalymnos* does a round-trip to Astypalea from Kalymnos on Tuesday and Saturday. Other services are provided by DANE Sealines and G&A Ferries.

CENTRAL DODECANESE

The general sailing patterns can best be summarised by the following table.

destination	duration	price	frequency
Amorgos	2¼ hours	2700 dr	4 weekly
Donousa	4 hours	2800 dr	2 weekly
Kalymnos	2 hours	2600 dr	5 weekly
Kos	3½ hours	3000 dr	2 weekly
Naxos	5¼ hours	4000 dr	4 weekly
Paros	5¾ hours	4700 dr	4 weekly
Piraeus	12 hours	6700 dr	5 weekly
Rhodes	7½ hours	5000 dr	2 weekly
Symi	4½ hours	4300 dr	2 weekly

Hydrofoil Between June and September one weekly hydrofoil plies its way on a round-trip from Rhodes (5½ hours, 9400 dr) to Astypalea via Symi, Kos and Kalymnos.

Getting Around
Bus From Skala a bus travels fairly frequently to Hora and Livadia (200 dr), and from Hora and Skala to Maltezana (300 dr) via Marmari.

Car & Motorcycle Lakis & Manolis Moto Center (☎ 61 263, fax 61 540), close to the OTE in Skala, rents out bikes and cars. Prices tend to be somewhat higher than on other islands and may still be expensive out of season. Count on a minimum of 10,000 dr per day for a car (Seat Marbella) and about half that for a scooter.

Excursion Boat In summer there are daily excursion boats to the island's less accessible beaches and to Agia Kyriaki Islet (2000 dr). Tickets can be bought from the stalls next to the excursion boats.

ASTYPALEA TOWN
Astypalea Town, the capital, consists of the port of Skala and the hilltop district of Hora, crowned by a fortress. Skala can be a noisy busy place, despite its small size, and few linger here to relax. Most visitors head uphill to Hora to so-called Windmill Square to sit around nursing cold beers, or refreshing frappé coffees at comfortable cafes. The windmills lining the square are perhaps

Hora's most enduring feature. Hora also has narrow streets of dazzling-white cubic houses with brightly painted wooden balconies, doors and banisters. The castle peering above this jumble of houses and balconies completes the picture.

Orientation
From Skala's quay, turn right to reach the waterfront. The steep road to Hora begins beyond the white Italianate building. In Skala the waterfront road skirts the beach and then veers right to continue along the coast to Marmari and beyond.

No reasonably accurate map of the island exists. The Toubis 1:45,000 tourist map *Astypalea* is about the best you'll find, but that shows no contours and does not accurately depict the state of the road system.

Information
A municipal tourist office adjoins the quayside cafe. The owner of Astypalea Tours (☎ 61 571, fax 61 328) is helpful and is the agent for Olympic Airways and ferry lines; you'll find it under Vivamare Apartments. Paradisos Ferries Agency (☎ 61 224, fax 61 450) on the seafront also sells tickets.

The Commercial Bank, with an ATM, is on the waterfront. One traveller has reported the ATM as being temperamental and having a tendency to retain cards. Don't entrust your card to it, if you are likely to need it again soon.

The post office is at the top of the Skala-Hora road. The OTE is close to the Hotel Paradisos on the waterfront. There was no Internet cafe on Astypalea at the time of research, though this will no doubt have changed by now.

Mobile phone users can easily pick up all three Greek GSM mobile service providers.

The Web site at www.astypalaia.com is fairly well put together, with hotel, restaurant and shop listings. However, it is selective and does not show all possibilities. You can view and book rooms and studios online. There are also several useful location maps.

There is a pharmacy 200m along the Hora road on the right. Both the police

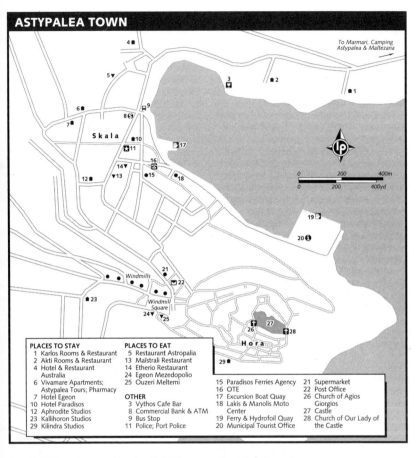

ASTYPALEA TOWN

To Marmari, Camping
Astypalea & Maltezana

Skala

Windmills

Windmill
Square

Hora

PLACES TO STAY	PLACES TO EAT
1 Karlos Rooms & Restaurant	5 Restaurant Astropalia
2 Akti Rooms & Restaurant	13 Maïstrali Restaurant
4 Hotel & Restaurant	14 Etherio Restaurant
Australia	24 Egeon Mezedopolio
6 Vivamare Apartments;	25 Ouzeri Meltemi
Astypalea Tours; Pharmacy	
7 Hotel Egeon	
10 Hotel Paradisos	OTHER
12 Aphrodite Studios	3 Vythos Cafe Bar
23 Kallihoron Studios	8 Commercial Bank & ATM
29 Kilindra Studios	9 Bus Stop
	11 Police; Port Police

15 Paradisos Ferries Agency	21 Supermarket
16 OTE	22 Post Office
17 Excursion Boat Quay	26 Church of Agios
18 Lakis & Manolis Moto	Giorgios
Center	27 Castle
19 Ferry & Hydrofoil Quay	28 Church of Our Lady of
20 Municipal Tourist Office	the Castle

(☎ 61 207) and port police (☎ 61 208) are in the Italianate building.

Venetian Castle

During the time of the Knights of St John, Astypalea was occupied by the Venetian Quirini family, who built the imposing castle. In the Middle Ages the population lived within its walls, but gradually the settlement outgrew them. The last inhabitants left in 1948 and the stone houses are now in ruins. Above the entrance is the Church of Our Lady of the Castle and within the walls is the Church of Agios Giorgios.

Special Events

The Symi Festival hosts a few events in Astypalea during the last days of August. See the Symi section earlier in this chapter for full details on this annual cultural festival.

Places to Stay

Skala *Camping Astypalea* (☎ 61 338) is 3km east of Skala and is next to a pebble beach. This well-shaded camping ground costs 1200 dr to pitch a tent and an extra 600 dr per person.

Hotel and domatia owners meet incoming boats. *Hotel Australia* (☎ 61 067, 61 275), on the waterfront, has well-kept doubles/triples for 11,000/12,000 dr, and friendly Greek-Australian owners, Manolis & Maria Stavla. A set of luxury studios are also available for rental for 15,000 dr each.

At the eastern end of the harbour, *Karlos Rooms (☎ 61 330)* has rates of 11,000/12,000 dr. *Akti Rooms (☎ 61 281/168, e astrooms@ otenet.gr)*, near Karlos Rooms, has attractive rooms for 10,000/13,000 dr and good sea views from the communal terrace.

Hotel Egeon (☎ 61 236), on the Skala-Hora road, has singles/doubles for 7000/10,000 dr. The ageing but well-maintained *Hotel Paradisos (☎ 61 224/256)* has comfortable doubles/triples with bathroom for 12,000/13,000 dr.

Vivamare Apartments (☎ 61 571/572), a little way up the Skala-Hora road, has rather run-down double/triple studios for 10,000/12,000 dr.

Aphrodite Studios (☎ 61 478/086, fax 61 087), between Skala and Hora, has beautiful, well-equipped double/triple studios for 12,000/14,000 dr. Take the Hora road, turn left after the shoe shop and it's on the left.

Hora *Kilindra Studios (☎ 61 966, fax 61 181, e lemis@mland.gr)*, beautifully appointed and fully equipped, are on the west side of the castle in Hora. There's even a swimming pool. Rates are between 24,000 dr and 28,000 dr for a two- to three-person studio.

· *Kallihoron Studios (☎ 61 937, mobile ☎ 09-7788 0857, e kolidaki@klm.forthnet .gr)* are also a good choice and are very close to the Windmill square. Rates are around 20,000 dr for a very comfortable studio for two.

Places to Eat

Skala Eating in Astypalea is generally quite good and moderately expensive. Fish tends to predominate and most restaurants worth their salt will do a variation on the island's speciality: lobster with pasta. Try it at least once when you are here.

Restaurant Australia (☎ 61 067), below Hotel Australia, serves delicious fish; the speciality is lobster and macaroni. *Restaurant*

Astropalia is also commendable and has wonderful views down to Skala from its terrace. *Etherio Restaurant* is a trendy place serving a range of imaginative mezedes and main courses.

Maïstrali Restaurant (☎ 61 691), run by Froso and Dimitris Kondaratos, specialises in seafood but also has a wide range of mayirefta dishes and is more than likely to be open out of season as well. This is a good place for breakfast.

The *Karlos Restaurant* and *Akti Restaurant* are both eating establishments joined to their accommodation options (see Places to Stay).

Hora *Ouzeri Meltemi*, opposite the windmills, is a popular hang-out with Astypalea's young crowd. The *Egeon Mezedopolio (☎ 61 730)* next door serves up excellent snacks and mezedes and is just the place to hang out with a frappé on a hot day.

There is a *supermarket* near the post office in Hora.

Entertainment

The liveliest entertainment you will find is at the rather hip and trendy *Vythos Cafe Bar* in Skala. Its underwater-themed decor will appeal to lovers of seahorses and mermaids, which liberally decorate the interior of this place. It is open from 7 pm until late and hosts a DJ in summer.

LIVADIA Λειβάδια

The little resort of Livadia lies in a fertile valley 2km from Hora. Its beach is the best on the island, but also the most crowded. Still, it's an easy walk (signposted from near the windmills in Hora) and it is a good alternative base for your stay on the island.

Places to Stay

There's plenty of accommodation in Livadia. Pleasant budget options are *Gerani Rooms (☎ 61 484/337)*, where doubles/triples go for 10,000/11,000 dr with bathrooms and refrigerators; and *Kaloudis Domatia (☎ 61 318/336)*, with doubles for 10,000 dr and a communal kitchen overlooking a large courtyard garden. Both are on the dirt road (a dried-up riverbed) that runs inland from the waterfront.

A sign at the end of the beach road points to **Jim Venetos Studios & Apartments** (☎ 61 490/150), where attractive double studios cost 13,000 dr and four-person apartments are 18,000 dr.

Rooms Drosia (☎ 61 497) has doubles/triples for 10,000/11,000 dr with small balconies at the front for breakfast, and a small vegetable garden with home-grown tomatoes. The rooms aren't signposted; ask for directions from anyone in Livadia.

Places to Eat

H Kalamia (☎ 61 468), the first taverna on the waterfront, serves good food under the cool shade of tamarisk trees. Its speciality is rice-stuffed goat. **Kafestiatorio Eleftherios Angelis** (☎ 61 497) dishes up fresh fish and BBQ grilled meat dishes cooked on an outside spit. **To Gerani** (☎ 61 484), combined with a domatia of the same name, cooks up a variety of home-style dishes and is probably the best choice here. All three are medium priced.

OTHER BEACHES

Astypalea's remaining beaches are nothing to rave about. They are somewhat scraggly and often covered with flotsam and jetsam. Some are reachable by road or path, others can only be reached conveniently by caïque. Caïque owners run trips to various beaches, and the destinations often vary annually.

Marmari, 2km north-east of Skala, has three bays with pebble and sand beaches. The island's only camp site is located in the first bay. **Maltezana**, known officially as Analipsi, is 7km beyond Marmari in a fertile valley on the isthmus. It's a scattered, pleasantly laid-back settlement, but its two beaches are grubby. There are some remains of Roman baths with mosaics on the settlement's outskirts. It was once the refuge of Medieval Maltese pirates – hence the unofficial name.

The road from Maltezana is reasonable as far as **Vaï**, but gets rougher beyond here. However, it is driveable or rideable with due care. Local maps may show a supposed settlement called Kastellano. Forget it; there's basically nothing here. **Mesa Vathy** is a fishing hamlet with a beach at the end of a long narrow inlet and is used occasionally as an alternative ferry port. It takes about 1½ hours to walk here from Vaï. From Mesa Vathy a footpath leads to **Exo Vathy**, another hamlet with a beach.

Tzanaki Coves is about 15 minutes' walk south of Livadia. These three small, pebbly coves are sheltered by the coastal cliffs and are frequented by nudists. There are three more beaches south of Tzanaki. The first two, **Moura** and **Papou**, are rocky,

---

Tops or Bottoms

Greeks have a long tradition of welcoming foreigners, which has made them tolerant of different customs. Although Greek women are less likely to go topless, in most places topless sunbathing is allowed, albeit tacitly. The best bet is to assess what is happening on a beach-by-beach basis and disrobe or top-up accordingly. Even once frumpy Patmos basically shrugs its shoulder and turns a blind eye to discrete topless bathing.

Although naturism is not widely practised and not officially allowed, you will find a sprinkling of naturists on at least one beach on each of the Dodecanese islands, usually the most remote and least accessible beach. Nude beaches change from year to year. Sometimes a small taverna or cantina turns up on one beach, only to have the naturists move on and turn up somewhere else. Beaches that are currently popular with naturists are the North Beach on Telendos, Monodendri Beach on Lipsi, Tzanaki Beach on Astypalea, Eristos Beach on Tilos and generally any remote beach where you are the only person enjoying it.

CENTRAL DODECANESE

prone to large amounts of seaweed and are best avoided. The third beach, **Agios Konstantinos** (named after the nearby church), is somewhat better with a 200m sandy gravel beach offering some shade and one seasonal taverna. The rough access track ends here.

The south coast beach of **Kaminakia** is considered the island's best and is a 150m stretch of sheltered sand and pebble with a seasonal cantina. There are some explorable sea caves on the east side of the bay. **Vatses Beach** is farther to the east but there are no facilities here, the water can get rough and is also prone to seaweed infestation. Both beaches are best reached by caique from Skala though there are rideable (just) access roads into both of them.

On the far west side is **Agios Ioannis Beach**, a small pebbly affair best taken as part of a visit to the eponymous **church** and its surrounding orchards and nearby ruined **Byzantine Castle**. The climb down to the beach is a little tiring but probably worth it

if you have made the two-hour walk (or 35 minute motorbike ride) this far out from Skala.

Places to Stay & Eat

There are plenty of accommodation options in Maltezana, but many only operate during summer. *Maltezana Rooms* (☎ 61 446), to the left of the quay, has doubles for 8000 dr. *Ovelix Studios* (☎ 61 260), belonging to the restaurant of the same name, consists of 10 three-person studios with kitchenette and fridge for around 12,000 dr.

Hotel Castillo (☎/fax 61 552/553), a complex of self-contained units on both sides of the main road, has beautifully furnished, immaculate studios with a well-equipped kitchen area, TV and telephone. Doubles cost 10,000 dr and four-person apartments are 13,000 dr.

Ovelix Taverna (☎ 61 260), in a cool shaded courtyard, and *Armera Restaurant* are recommended; their fish dishes are especially good.

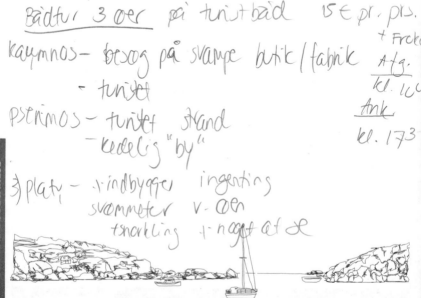

Kalymnos Κάλυμνος

☎ 0243 • postcode 852 00 • pop 18,200

Kalymnos (**kah**-lim-nos), only 2.5km south of Leros, is a mountainous, arid island, speckled with fertile valleys. Kalymnos is renowned as the 'sponge-fishing island', but with the demise of this industry it is now exploiting its tourist potential. It faces a tough job. While there is plenty on offer to entice travellers – good food, accommodation and rugged scenery – neighbouring Kos has the pull on the package tourism industry and the majority of people flying into the region stay there. The modest numbers that do make it across to Kalymnos via the thrice daily connecting ferry find an island that is still in touch with its traditions and where the drachma goes just that little bit further.

History

Kalymnos is believed to have been first settled by a Dorian colony from Epidaurus in the Peloponnese. The island minted its own money and took part in the first and second Athenian leagues in the 5th and 4th centuries BC. It was conquered in 332 BC by Alexander the Great and was later annexed by Rome. Until 1310 it was occupied by the Venetians who were in turn succeeded by the Knights of Rhodes. The Turks captured Kalymnos in 1523 (along with the rest of the Dodecanese) and it remained in their hands until overtaken by the Italians in 1912. The Kalymnians resisted the Italian occupation and during WWII many fled to Turkey.

As in classical times, sponge fishing is still a key industry, with the sponge fleet away to the North African coast for up to six months each year after Easter. Towards the centre of the island, the volcanic valley of Vathys – irrigated from springs – supports citrus, olives, figs, and vines. The island is the seat of a metropolitan bishop of the Greek Orthodox Church.

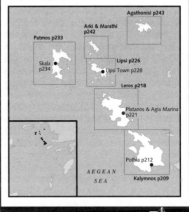

Getting There & Away

Kalymnos is well connected by sea to the rest of the Dodecanese islands. Pothia is the main port, where there are ferry, hydrofoil and catamaran services, but there is also a caïque service from Myrties to Xirokambos on Leros. There is no functioning airport.

Air Kalymnos' airport was completed as far back as 1993 but has yet to see a commercial aircraft land on it. Byzantine local politics, lack of further funding, or perhaps even lobbying from its rival Kos have to date kept it inoperative. Most people wishing to fly to Kalymnos fly to Kos and transfer to the Mastihari–Pothia local ferry.

Olympic Airways is represented by Kapellas Travel (☎ 29 265) in Pothia.

Ferry Kalymnos is on the main north–south route for ferries to and from Rhodes and Piraeus and is reasonably well serviced with at least one and sometimes more daily departures from Pothia. Services are provided by DANE Lines, G&A Ferries and the F/B *Nisos Kalymnos*.

Ferries heading south tend to depart at unsocial hours – between midnight and 6 am. Departures north are usually in the late evening. The slower, Kalymnos-based F/B *Nisos Kalymnos'* departure times are a little more manageable, with both north and south departures during daylight or evening hours.

The following table will give you an overview of the main departures.

destination	duration	price	frequency
Agathonisi	6 hours	2600 dr	2 weekly
Astypalea	3 hours	2500 dr	3 weekly
Kastellorizo	15 hours	4100 dr	2 weekly
Leros	1½ hours	1900 dr	7 weekly
Lipsi	2 hours	1800 dr	3 weekly
Patmos	2½ hours	2500 dr	8 weekly
Rhodes	5 hours	4300 dr	8 weekly
Samos	7½ hours	3100 dr	1 weekly

The 'landing craft' type car and passenger ferry, F/B *Olympios Apollon* leaves three times daily from Pothia to Mastihari on Kos (50 minutes, 900 dr) at 7 am, 4 and 8.30 pm. A car costs 3800 dr and a motorbike 750 dr. This is the cheapest way to get to Kos and the best way to get to Kos airport.

Hydrofoil Kalymnos is currently only served by Kyriacoulis Hydrofoils. In high season there is a morning service daily to Kos (35 minutes, 2620 dr), with a connection to Rhodes (three hours, 8055 dr), returning

every evening. There are good connections to all the major islands in the group, as well as Samos, Ikaria and Fourni in the North-Eastern Aegean. From Samos you can easily connect with the Cyclades. Buy tickets from Magos Travel (see Travel Agencies).

Catamaran The Rhodes-based *Dodekanisos Express* calls in at Kalymnos daily in summer as an intermediate stop on its run up the Dodecanese from Rhodes. Departures heading north from Kalymnos are usually around 11.30 am with arrival in Patmos at 1.30 pm. Departures heading south from Kalymnos are usually around 4.10 pm with arrival in Rhodes at 7 or 8.50 pm depending on the number of intermediate stops. Tickets can be bought at the Dodekanisos Shipping Agency in Pothia (☎ 28 651). See 'The Cost of the Catamaran' boxed text in the Getting Around chapter.

Excursion Boat In summer there are three excursion boats daily from Pothia to Mastihari on Kos.

There are also weekly excursions to Turkey for 11,000 dr (including Turkish port tax). There are daily excursions from Myrties to Xirokambos on Leros (3000 dr return).

All excursion boats run from the harbourfront in Pothia. Tickets are sold at the boats.

Getting Around

Bus In summer there is a bus on the hour to Massouri (250 dr) via Myrties; to Emborios (300 dr) at 8 am and 4 pm daily; and to Vathys (300 dr) at 6.30 and 10 am, 2 and 6 pm Monday to Saturday, and 7 am, 1.30 and 6 pm Sunday. There are buses to Vlyhadia (200 dr) at 8 and 11 am and 2, 4, 5.30, 6.30 and 7.30 pm, and Platys Gialos (250 dr) at 9.15 am, 12.15, 3 and 4.45 pm. Buy tickets from Themis Minimarket, as they're not available on the bus.

Motorcycle There are several motorcycle rental outlets along Pothia's waterfront. Look out for Rent A Moto Kostas (☎ 50 105) and Scootermania (☎ 50 193, mobile ☎ 09-3240 6964) who have a reasonable selection of bikes and scooters at reasonable prices.

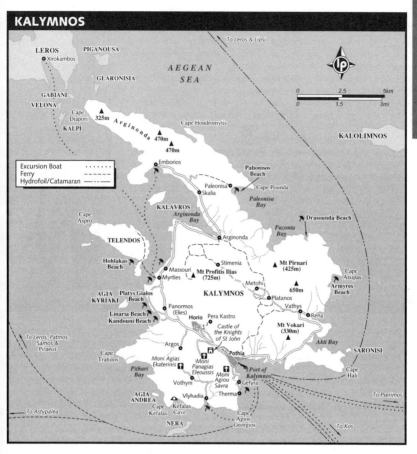

KALYMNOS

Taxi Shared taxis are an unusual feature of Kalymnos and cost just a little more than buses. They travel from Pothia to Massouri, leaving from the taxi rank on Plateia Kyprou (☎ 50 300). These taxis can be hard to bag in summer when they are busy with conventional passengers. It is better to wait at the bus stop near the taxi station and flag one down – or do so en route. Make it very clear that you want a taxi bus. The fare from Pothia to Massouri is around 300 dr per person.

Regular (non-shared) taxis to Myrties cost 1500 dr, to Emborios 4000 dr and to Vathys 3000 dr. Taxis from the ferry quay will be up to 500 dr more expensive and all journeys will be twice the price between midnight and 6 am.

Excursion Boat From Myrties there are daily excursion boats to Emborios (5000 dr). The caïque *Irini* also runs excursions to Nera, Vlyhadia, Platys Island, Akti, Vathys and Kefala Cave. It departs from the quay at Myrties; tickets are sold on board. For further information call ☎ 33 442, or mobile ☎ 09-4471 4663. Day trips to Kefala Cave (6000 dr) run from both Pothia and Myrties.

Sponge Fishing

Kalymnians have long dominated the ancient trade of sponge diving. In the 19th century a fleet of 300 boats worked the Aegean and Mediterranean right down to North Africa.

Traditionally, divers worked naked, holding a stone attached by a rope to the boat and staying underwater for as long as their breath held out. From 1869 the *skafandro* – a diving suit with a heavy bronze helmet – allowed them to stay down longer and gather more sponges but thousands paid the terrible price of death or disability from decompression sickness, the 'bends'.

Now modern equipment is used and training is obligatory at Greece's only commercial diving school located on the quay in Pothia. But the trade itself has been decimated by the introduction of synthetic sponges and by a mystery virus that struck the natural sponge population in 1986.

The sponges have since recovered and Kalymnos retains its proud tradition with about 15 boats. Obviously, the island is still the best place to buy sponges and in Pothia's workshops you can see how they are taken black from the sea and processed. Once used as a contraceptive device and for padding suits of armour, it's most practical these days for showering, make-up or the weekly car wash!

Faith Warn

MH

Daily excursion boats leave Pothia at 10 am for the beach island of Pserimos (2000 dr return), returning at 4 pm.

POTHIA Πόθια

Pothia (**poth**-ya), the port and capital of Kalymnos, is fairly large by Dodecanese standards. The town is built amphitheatrically around the slopes of the surrounding hills and valley, and its visually arresting melange of colourful mansions and houses draped over the hills make it a photogenic sight for visitors.

While Pothia can be brash and busy and its narrow vehicle- and motorbike-plagued streets can be a challenge to pedestrians, the island capital is not without its charm. There are pleasant restaurants and backstreet ouzeria and the shops are designed more for local consumer needs than for the whims of tourists. All the island's major services are based here and unless you enter and exit Kalymnos via Myrties to Leros, you will pass through Pothia at some stage in your visit to the island.

Orientation

Pothia's ferry quay is at the southern side of the port. To reach the town centre, turn right at the end of the quay. Follow the waterfront for 200m and you will reach the main promenade at the north-eastern end, where you will find the prominent Cathedral of Agios Hristos and the sandstone coloured Italianate municipal buildings. The main thoroughfare, Venizelou, runs north from here to Plateia Kyprou and on to destinations in the north and west of the island. Another busy street, Patriarhou Maximimou, also runs from the waterfront to this square.

The tourist maps of the island sold in some waterfront shops will suffice for most needs.

Information

Tourist Office In the middle of the central promenade is a temporary tourist information kiosk (☎ 50 879), which is open from 7.30 am to 10 pm in summer. Whether it is to remain here or not was unknown at the time of research. The material supplied is mainly transport timetables and the colourful but not very practical *Kalymnos – Island of Sponge Divers* booklet.

Money The National Bank of Greece, at the bottom of Patriarhou Maximimou, and the Ionian Bank, 100m farther north along on the waterfront, both have ATMs. There is a third ATM at the commercial bank on Patriarhou Maximimou.

Post & Communications North of Plateia Kyprou are the OTE, on Venizelou, and the post office on Patriarhou Maximimou. Mobile phone users will pick up all three mobile service providers in Kalymnos.

There are two Internet cafes in Pothia, both owned by the same people. The newer Neon Internet Cafe 3 (☎ 28 343) is easy to find and more conveniently located on the main promenade. It has four terminals with fast ISDN connections. Neon Internet Cafe 2 (☎ 48 318), to the north of town, is older and had only one terminal at the time of research, though more were planned. Access charges are 500 dr for 30 minutes; it is open all year from 8.30 am to midnight.

Internet Resources Kalymnos' Web site at www.kalymnos-isl.gr is rather underdeveloped at the moment, but does have some good photo images of the island.

Travel Agencies The office for the F/B *Nisos Kalymnos* (☎ 29 612, fax 24 144) is on 25 Martiou. DANE Lines is represented by Kalymnia Travel (☎ 23 083, fax 29 125) nearby and G&A Ferries by Magos Travel (☎ 28 777, fax 22 608), near the ferry quay on 25 Martiou.

Emergency The police (☎ 29 301) are on Patriarhou Maximimou before the post office while the port police (☎ 29 304) are at the start of the quay.

Things to See & Do

The **Archaeological Museum** (☎ 23 113), housed in a neoclassical mansion which once belonged to a wealthy sponge merchant, Mr Vouvalis, is north-east of Plateia Kyprou. In one room there are some Neolithic and Bronze Age objects. Other rooms are reconstructed as they were when the Vouvalis family lived here. The museum is open 10 am to 2 pm Tuesday to Sunday. Admission is currently free.

The **Nautical & Folklore Museum** is in the centre of the waterfront. It is open 8 am to 2 pm daily. Admission is 500 dr.

You can hire **yachts** from Kalymna Yachting (☎ 24 083, fax 29 125), 50m north-east of the quay.

Places to Stay

Domatia owners usually meet the ferries but there are enough options around town to make finding a place to stay an easy task. In truth most visitors usually head for one of the beach resorts, but Pothia is pleasant and lively enough to make a stay here for a few days quite worthwhile.

A pleasant budget option open all year is *Pension Greek House* (☎ 29 559, 23 752), inland from the port near the Astor Sponge Factory. It has cosy wood-panelled singles/doubles with bathroom and kitchen facilities for 5500/7000 dr. Norma Delapoutou rents out well-kept *domatia* (☎ 24 054, 48 145) behind the Astor Sponge Factory. Double rooms with kitchen and verandah are 6500 dr.

Hotel Panorama (☎ 22 138), high up and enjoying one of the better views in Pothia is clean and breezy and has a pleasant breakfast area. Each of its 13 rooms go for 10,000 dr including breakfast.

Archontiko Hotel (☎/fax 24 149), at the north-eastern end of the quay, is a cool and pleasant hotel in a renovated century-old mansion. Immaculate single/double rooms with fridges, TV and phone go for a reasonable 9000/12,000 dr, breakfast included. The hotel is open all year.

Olympic Hotel (☎ 51 710, fax 51 71) on the harbourfront is open all year and has decent rooms with phone, TV, fan and fridge for 9000/14,000 dr.

Villa Themelina (☎ 22 682, fax 23 920), next door to the well signposted archaeological museum, is a 19th-century pink-coloured mansion with swimming pool and garden. Spacious, traditionally furnished

NORTHERN DODECANESE

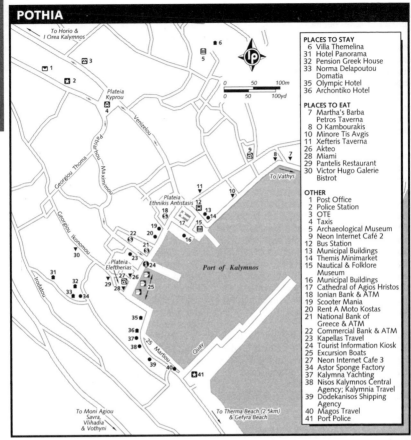

POTHIA

To Horio &
I Orea Kalymnos

Plateia
Kyprou

Venizelou

Georgiou Thoma

Patrarkhou Maximinou

Georgiou Konomou

Iroidou

Plateia
Ethnikis Antistasis

Plateia
Eleftherias

To Vathys

Port of Kalymnos

Quay

Marliou

To Moni Agiou
Savra,
Vlihadia
& Vothyni

To Therma Beach (2.5km)
& Gefyra Beach

0   50   100m
0   50   100yd

PLACES TO STAY
6   Villa Themelina
31 Hotel Panorama
32 Pension Greek House
33 Norma Delapoutou
    Domatia
35 Olympic Hotel
36 Archontiko Hotel

PLACES TO EAT
7   Martha's Barba
    Petros Taverna
8   O Kambourakis
10 Minore Tis Avgis
11 Xefteris Taverna
26 Akteo
28 Miami
29 Pantelis Restaurant
30 Victor Hugo Galerie
    Bistrot

OTHER
1   Post Office
2   Police Station
3   OTE
4   Taxis
5   Archaeological Museum
9   Neon Internet Café 2
12 Bus Station
13 Municipal Buildings
14 Themis Minimarket
15 Nautical & Folklore
    Museum
16 Municipal Buildings
17 Cathedral of Agios Hristos
18 Ionian Bank & ATM
19 Scooter Mania
20 Rent A Moto Kostas
21 National Bank of
    Greece & ATM
22 Commercial Bank & ATM
23 Kapellas Travel
24 Tourist Information Kiosk
25 Excursion Boats
27 Neon Internet Cafe 3
34 Astor Sponge Factory
37 Kalymna Yachting
38 Nisos Kalymnos Central
    Agency; Kalymnia Travel
39 Dodekanisos Shipping
    Agency
40 Magos Travel
41 Port Police

doubles/triples cost 16,000/19,500 dr with bathroom. In summer the mansion is often booked by tour operators.

Places to Eat

The stretch of promenade north-east of the main port is home to a line of fish restaurants and tavernas that pull in mostly local crowds at night. One of the longer standing and popular places at the far northern end is the curiously named *Martha's Barba Petros Taverna* (☎ 29 678); the crab salad is a delicious starter. *O Kambourakis* (☎ 29 879) is primarily an ouzeri and has probably the

best location, being one of the few places with harbourside tables. Fish and mezedes will cost a bit more than usual: bank on a minimum of 4000 dr for a fish-based meal or mezedes selection here. Not far away and on an equal footing from the point of view of quality and price is *Minore tis Avgis* (☎ 29 869), with its main emphasis on fish.

A block back from the waterside is the century-old *Xefteris Taverna* (☎ 28 642), just off Venizelou, which serves delicious, inexpensive food; you'll be taken into the kitchen to choose from the pots. Highly recommended by a local hotel owner is the busy *Pantelis Restaurant (☎ 51 508)* on Plateia Eleftherias. This reasonably priced, homely eatery is open all year and all day and its specialities are goat in red wine sauce and home-made dolmadhes. A decent feed at either of these two places should not set you back more than 2500 dr.

The owner of *Victor Hugo Galerie Bistrot (☎ 50 013, Georgiou Ikonomou)* is Sakellarios Koulouriotis, a professional photographer. He has travelled widely but returned to his island to 'do something for its young people'. Here, young locals are given the opportunity to exhibit their art work and stage live music performances. Coffee, soft and alcoholic drinks and snacks are served and visitors are warmly welcomed. It is open from 10.30 am to 2 pm and from 6 pm until late.

The waterfront opposite the excursion boats quay is packed with cafeterias and equally packed with young Greeks eyeing each other up over a forest of frappé straws. *Akteo* and *Miami* seem to pull in the most crowds, but the establishments are all ultimately busy.

AROUND POTHIA

The ruined **Castle of the Knights of St John** (or Kastro Hrysoherias) looms to the left of the Pothia-Horio road. There is a small **church** inside the battlements.

Pera Kastro was a pirate-proof village inhabited until the 18th century. Within the crumbling walls are the ruins of stone houses and six tiny, well-kept churches. Steps lead up to Pera Kastro from Horio. It's a strenuous climb but the splendid views make it worthwhile.

A tree-lined road continues from Horio to **Panormos** (panorama), a pretty village 5km from Pothia. Its pre-war name of Elies (olives) derived from its abundant olive groves, which were destroyed in WWII. An enterprising post-war mayor planted abundant trees and flowers to create beautiful panoramas wherever you look – hence its present name.

The monastery **Moni Agiou Savra** is reached along a turn-off left from the Vothyni and Vlihadia road. You can enter the monastery but a strict dress code is enforced, so wear long sleeves and a long skirt or trousers.

Beaches

There are about four beaches within striking distance of Pothia and all offer something different. First up and within walking distance (2.5km) of Pothia is **Therma Beach**, a small pebbly beach with some shade and sun beds to rent at 500 dr. You will also pass the minuscule **Gefyra Beach** along the way.

Vlyhadia is a small settlement on the south coast, easily reached by a sealed road, or by caïque from Pothia. It sports two beaches – one sandy and one pebbly – and both are enclosed in a pretty protected cove. The whimsical Museum of Sea World (☎ 50 662) is here and houses a mixed collection of sea-related items as well as model caïques. **Kafala Cave**, nearby, has impressive stalactites and stalagmites.

Round Cape Trahilos you come to **Kandouni Beach**, which is a shade too scruffy with hard-packed, seaweed-strewn sand. Kandouni looks a bit rundown thanks to a few abandoned shops and houses and attracts mainly locals. **Linaria** and **Platys Gialos** Beaches, a kilometre or so along, are better choices. Both are sandy with shade from tamarisk trees and again have a mainly Greek clientele.

Places to Eat Each beach has somewhere to eat though quality varies. *Akrogiali (☎ 28 670)* at Therma Beach is big and rather impersonal, but there is no other choice. At Vlyhadia, *Paradisos Restaurant* is the longest established and most reliable. Stuffed tomatoes or stifado are good bets. Prices are average.

At Kandouni the *Trata (☎ 48 340)*, about 300m inland, is probably the best bet. At Linaria Beach the *Aegean Cafe (☎ 48 666)* is good for breakfast and *To Steki tis Fanis (☎ 47 317)*, up the hill and left for 15m up some stairs, offers local dishes not found easily elsewhere. Try the pot-baked lamb *(mouri)*, or unusual salad called *mermizelli* made of greens, feta cheese and rusks. Prices are 5% or so higher than elsewhere.

Getting There & Away Regular buses from Pothia serve both Vlyhadia (seven per day, 200 dr) as well as Platys Gialos (four per day, 250 dr). Caïques from Pothia also visit Vlyhadia, but charge considerably more since they are considered excursions.

MYRTIES & MASSOURI
Μυρτιές & Μασσούρι

The busy twin centres of **Myrties** (myr-**tyez**) and **Massouri** (mah-**soo**-ri) host the lion's share of Kalymnos' package holiday industry. The two resorts are essentially one long street packed head to tail with restaurants, bars, souvenir shops and minimarkets. On the land side, apartments and studios – most block-booked by tour companies – fill the hillside, while on the sea side a dark, volcanic sand beach stretches around the headland punctuated only by the small caldera of an extinct mini-volcano.

If you like to be sociable on your holiday then come here; if not, then you should probably stay away. You can easily spend a week or two here and not need to move except perhaps to find an ATM in Pothia to withdraw more funds to spend on eating and drinking. There are exchange bureaus, car and motorbike rental outlets and even an Internet cafe.

Places to Stay

Despite most places being pre-booked you can usually find a spare studio or room with kitchenette and fridge by simply asking around. In Massouri, *Ambience Studios* (☎ 47 882) is a largish complex of studios built right down to the water's edge. These luxury apartments cost around 17,000 dr and are fully equipped.

Pension Graziella (☎ 47 314), signposted from the main road in Panormos, has comfortable doubles for around 7000 dr, double studios for 9000 dr and five-person apartments for 15,000 dr. The owner, the dynamic English-speaking Menelaos, enjoys informing guests of the delights of Kalymnos. Just outside Panormos on the road to Myrties, *Hotel Kamari* (☎ 47 278) has great views and well-kept singles/doubles for 6500/8000 dr.

Kalymnian Cuisine

Look out for a couple of local specialities in Kalymnos, or follow the recipes to create them yourself.

Mermizelli is a Kalymnian salad made using *kouloura* – hard, dried brown rolls. Soak these in water until they are just damp. Break them into small pieces, and mix in some freshly chopped tomatoes, sliced cucumber, coarsely chopped onions and chunks of feta cheese. Dress it all with olive oil, wine vinegar, oregano, salt and pepper.

Mouri is the Kalymnian Easter lamb dish, though it is sometimes cooked as a special dish in better restaurants. Take a whole lamb or goat (minus head and entrails used for soup) and stuff it with a mixture of rice, tomatoes, chopped liver, butter and herbs. Placed the stuffed lamb or goat in a large tin or clay pot and slow roast it overnight in a wood-fired brick oven.

Places to Eat

There is no shortage of eateries and the competition to lure you in is fierce. One place worth being lured into is *To Iliovasilema* (☎ 47 683) in Massouri. The service is truly excellent and the food equally so. The *kontosouvli* (Cypriot-style, spit-roasted meat) is top class since the cook, Panagiotis Koullias, is also the local butcher. A filling meal for two will just top 6000 dr.

In Myrties, head down the road that leads to the harbour and seek out *Taverna i Galazia Limni* (☎ 47 016) with its mainly Greek patrons. Octopus balls, squid and *saganaki* mussels are all recommended dishes. Prices are moderate, with main meat dishes costing around 1500 dr each. Diagonally opposite is *I Drosia* (☎ 48 745) with better harbour views. It's an ouzeri-style eatery with sea-based mezedes featuring prominently on the menu. Prices are similar to the Galazia Limni.

Entertainment

There are probably more bars than restaurants here so you are spoiled for choice and style; most are in Massouri. The *Scorpion Cafe Bar* specialises in '60s and '70s music and generally appeals to the over-25s. You can also play cards and Connect 4 if you get bored.

The **Ambience Cafe Bar**, with its starry ceiling, icy Bacardi Breezers and trendy aluminium chairs, is a Greek music club that plays favourites by singers Glykeria and Notis Sfakianakis, among others. Imbibers enjoy good views over to Telendos. Grab a Red Bull and vodka at the **Palms**, a bar that appeals mainly to Scandinavians and is open from 6 pm until late. You can play billiards as well as surf at the **Neon Cafe Internet** (☎ 48 318) in Massouri. It is open from 10 am until late. Access to one of its three terminals costs 1000 dr an hour.

Getting There & Around
Buses run hourly through the day to Pothia (250 dr). Taxis can always be found cruising the main street.

Lakis Motor Bike Rentals (☎ 29 704, mobile 09-4417 6364), just down from the main road in Myrties, is as good a rental outfit as any. Bikes and scooters range in price from 4900 dr to 5500 dr per day.

Drivers should note that the main through road is one way from south to north. To reach Massouri you have to take the upper road, which bypasses the centre.

TELENDOS ISLET
Νήσος Τέλενδος
The tranquil and traffic-free islet of Telendos (teh-len-dhos), with a little quayside hamlet, was part of Kalymnos until separated by an earthquake in AD 554. If you look carefully at the southern rocky profile of the island, you will make out the shape (eyes, nose and chin) of the **Princess of Telendos**, best viewed in the early morning. Telendos is a great place to chill out for a few days (if Kalymnos wasn't already enough), with good eating, sleeping and swimming to hand. The caïques to the island pull in at the mid-point of the long harbourfront.

You can walk either left or right from the Telendos quay. If you turn right you will pass the ruins of a **Byzantine basilica**. Farther on, beyond On the Rocks Cafe, there are several pebble and sand beaches, the

last of which is used by nudists. To reach the far superior 100m long and fine pebbly **Hohlakas Beach**, turn left from the quay and then right at the sign to the beach. Follow the paved path up and over the hill for 10 minutes. Beach loungers and umbrellas are for hire at 1500 dr for two people. Snorkelling is good here. Note the remains of the 6th century AD **Church of the Holy Trinity** overlooking the beach.

Places to Stay
Telendos has several domatia. All have pleasant, clean rooms with bathroom. Opposite the quay, **Pension & Restaurant Uncle George** (☎/fax 47 502, e uncle georgeingreece@hotmail.com) has studios for 8000 dr. Next door at **Pension Rita** (☎ 47 914, fax 47 927) the rates are the same, and there are also double studios for 8000 dr. To the right of the quay, **Nicky Rooms** (☎ 47 584) has doubles for 6000 dr while **Galanomatis Fotini Rooms** (☎ 47 401) charges 7000 dr.

Hotel Porto Potha (☎ 47 321, fax 48 108, e portopotha@klm.forthnet.gr), beyond On the Rocks Cafe, has very comfortable doubles/triples for 9000/12,000 dr and a large, tempting swimming pool. The **On The Rocks Cafe Rooms** (☎ 48 260, fax 48 261, e otr@telendos.com) offers spacious doubles/triples with fridge for 10,000/16,000 dr including breakfast.

Places to Eat
'Enter once, friends forever' says the welcoming sign at **On the Rocks Cafe** (☎ 48 260), where Greek-Australian owner George serves well-prepared meat and fish dishes as well as vegetarian mousakas and souvlaki. In the evening it becomes a lively music bar and on Friday and Monday evenings it's 'Greek Night'. Don't miss spouse Popi executing a mean zeïmbekiko dance, while George makes some imaginative cocktails.

Barba Stathis (☎ 47 953) is open for breakfast, lunch and dinner and does a great version of octopus in red sauce (ohtapodi stifado) and octopus rissoles (ohtapodokeft-edhes). The tables are set out invitingly in a little lane behind the waterfront and prices are mid-range. *Pension & Restaurant Uncle George* (see Places to Stay earlier) doubles also as a fine taverna serving up fish and meat dishes at reasonable prices.

Getting There & Away

Telendos is reached by a regular caïque service from Myrties (400 dr each way), running every half hour from 8 am to midnight. If you are stuck after midnight, restaurant owners are usually willing to give you a lift back to Myrties.

EMBORIOS Εμπορειοσ

North of Massouri settlements rapidly thin out and a long, sealed road leads northwards to the last settlement on the island, the relaxed village of Emborios (em-bor-**yos**). Along the way the road curves around the fjord-like **Arginonda Bay** which is home to a thriving fish farming industry. The fish pens can be seen along the southern edge of the bay. The village of Arginonda itself is rather spread out but attracts a few bathers to its pebbly beach. Most visitors plough on to the end of the line past a rugged landscape that seems to support more goats than humans.

Emborios attracts a loyal band of followers who come here to get away from it all. There are enough eating and sleeping options to make the trip out here worthwhile – either for a day trip, or for a few days relaxation. The pebble beach is presentable and tree-shaded and there is none of the commercial hype that you will find back in Massouri or Myrties.

Places to Stay & Eat

One of the most pleasant places to stay is *Harry's Apartments* (☎ 40 062) where modern double/triple kitchen-equipped apartments cost 9000/10,800 dr. They are set around a cool and peaceful garden. Harry's also doubles as an excellent restaurant which does a good line in vegetarian dishes such as chickpea croquettes *(revithokeftedhes)* and pies *(pittes)* with fillings such as aubergine, onion and various other vegetables.

There are two restaurants by the beach: *To Kastri* (☎ 40 110) and *Kapetan Kostas Psarotaverna* (☎ 47 277). Both offer prime positions but offer little in the way of a cosy ambience. The latter is watched over by a full-sized dummy sponge diver. Ask for their version of the Kalymnian speciality, mermizelli. *Mbarba Nikolas* (☎ 40 064), 250m north of the jetty (follow the signs), has the best view of Asprokyklia Beach.

In Arginonda, you might well make a lunch or dinner stop at *Katerina Restaurant* on the Emborios side of the bay. Look for the place with tables on both sides of the road.

Getting There & Away

The caïque *Aï Nikolas* makes a daily trip from Myrties to Emborios (2000 dr return), leaving at 10 am and returning from Emborios at 4 pm. Two buses daily make the run from Pothia (300 dr) at 8 am and 4 pm and return from Emborios at 9 am and 5 pm respectively. Hitching a ride should not present too much difficulty if you really get stuck.

VATHYS & RENA Βαθύς & Ρένα

A winding but now fully sealed road leads from Pothia's tatty shipyard district past an unpromising landscape that, apart from being barren and dry, is also home to the island's rubbish dump and power station. The first indication that things may be improving is a sign pointing down to **Akti Beach** about 7km out of Pothia. There is a taverna here as well as reasonable swimming.

Over the last rise the impressive fjord of **Vathys** (vah-**this**) comes into view and with it an excellent photo opportunity. The road winds down to a valley of citrus orchards and *koumoula* (high, white protective walls that used to protect the individual landholdings from trespassers). Vathys, 11km from Pothia, is the scattered settlement 1km inland from the harbour of **Rena** (re-na) and the usual destination of visitors here. You can swim at the far end of the south side of the bay in a designated swimming area, but the water is sometimes a little oily from the many water taxis that flit in and out and the tourist caïques that come from Pothia and even Kos.

Water taxis (☎ 31 316) from Rena take visitors to cleaner but generally unshaded beaches such as **Armyres**, **Drasounda** and **Palionisos**. Come well prepared for trips to these beaches. Bring food and drink and your own shade.

Places to Stay & Eat
In Rena, the C-class *Hotel Galini (☎ 31 241)* has well-kept doubles for 8000 dr with bathroom and balcony, breakfast included. *Pension Manolis (☎ 31 300)*, above the south side of the harbour, has beautiful singles/doubles for 6000/7000 dr with bathroom. There is a communal kitchen and terraces surrounded by an attractive garden. The English-speaking Manolis is a tour guide and is knowledgeable about the area.

Poppy's Taverna (☎ 31 260) serves reasonably priced, well prepared food and, according to one customer, the best dolmahdes he's ever tasted. *Harbour Taverna (☎ 22 485)* is housed in a pretty stone building, and in defiance of the 'plastic fantastic' culture of many restaurants, still seats its diners on wood and cane chairs. The food is good and moderately priced. *Faros Restaurant (☎ 31 347)*, by the end of the south side of the harbour, has the best position and usually pulls in the yachties and day-trippers. The food is also good, but a bit more expensive.

Getting There & Around
There are four buses daily (300 dr) from Pothia to Vathys at 6.30 and 10 am, and 2 and 6 pm, leaving Vathys 30 minutes later. Taxis back to Pothia can be difficult to find, but you can usually hitch a ride back with no difficulty.

INLAND
The more adventurous might like to head inland through the villages of **Platanos**, so-named because of the huge plane tree straddling the road; **Metohi**, where the asphalt turns to gravel; and as far as **Stimenia**, a scattered, isolated community that sees few visitors. The only real reason for coming out here is so that walkers can tackle the two-hour **hike** from Stimenia across the shoulder of Kalymnos and down to Arginonda, where

you can catch a bus (at about 5.25 pm) back to Pothia. Walkers can also tackle a two-hour hike from Platanos across the bare mountain ridges back to Pothia, where you will emerge behind the archaeological museum. This track used to be used in the days before the 11km coastal road was built.

Leros Λέρος

☎ 0247 • postcode 854 00 • pop 8059
Travellers looking for an island that is still relatively untouched by mass commercial tourism will find it on Leros, a surprisingly little-known destination for the international community, though well-known for years by the discerning Greek public. Leros is a medium-sized island in the Northern Dodecanese offering an attractive mix of sun, sea, rest and recreation, a stunning medieval castle and some fine dining that will not overtax your budget.

The island offers gentle, hilly countryside dotted with small holdings and huge, impressive, almost landlocked bays, which look more like lakes than open sea. Leros was also the principal naval base of the Italians in the eastern Mediterranean in the immense natural harbour at Lakki, which is now a curious living architectural museum of Italian Fascist art-deco buildings.

History
It is believed that the islands of Leros and Kalymnos, just to the south-east, comprise the Kalydnian Isles referred to in Homer's *Iliad (2.677)*; it was famous in ancient times for its honey and for a temple of Artemis. Leros was first inhabited by Carians, then successively by Cretans, Ionians, Byzantines and Rhodians; the last two quarrelled over it until Rhodes took possession of Leros in 1319. Leros' fate was much the same as that of its neighbour Kalymnos, passing from Rhodian into Turkish and finally Italian hands. The island was fought over in November 1943 when the Italian and British garrison then occupying the island were dislodged by superior German forces. It was during that battle that the Greek

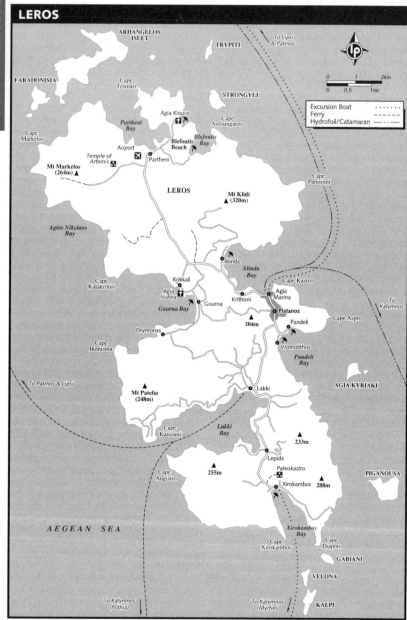

LEROS

NORTHERN DODECANESE

ARHANGELOS ISLET

TRYPITI

To Lipsi & Patmos

FARADONISIA

Cape Tesmari

STRONGYLI

Agia Kioura

Par
theni
Bay

Cape Asfoungaros

Cape Markelos

Blefoutis Beach

Blefoutis Bay

Temple of Artemis

Airport

Partheni

Cape Panosimi

Mt Markelos (264m) ▲

LEROS

Mt Klidi ▲ (320m)

Agios Nikolaos Bay

Alinda

Alinda Bay

Cape Kastro

To Kalymnos

Cape Katakrotiri

Kokkali

Agia Isidora

Krithoni

Agia Marina

Gourna Bay

Gourna

Platanos

Cape Aspro

204m ▲

Pandeli

Drymonas

Vromolithos

Cape Ikonisma

Pandeli Bay

AGIA KYRIAKI

To Patmos & Lipsi

Mt Patelia (248m) ▲

Lakki

Lakki Bay

Cape Katsouni

233m ▲

255m ▲

Lepida

Cape Angistro

Paleokastro

Xirokambos

288m ▲

PIGANOUSA

AEGEAN SEA

Xirokambos Bay

Cape Xirokambos

Cape Diapori

GABIANI

VELONA

To Kalymnos (Pothia)

To Kalymnos (Myrties)

KALPI

Excursion Boat · · · · · ·
Ferry − − − − −
Hydrofoil/Catamaran − · − · −

0   1   2km
0   0.5   1mi

euro currency converter €1 = 340.75dr

battleship *Queen Olga* was destroyed and sunk in Lakki harbour. Like the rest of the Dodecanese islands, Leros joined the Greek State in 1947 following the end of the war.

The island was used as a place of internal exile for political detainees by the infamous Colonels' Junta from 1967 to 1974, and is the current location for Greece's largest psychiatric institution, one of Leros' largest employers.

Getting There & Away

Leros is well-connected by sea to the rest of the Dodecanese islands and has daily flights to and from Athens in summer. Lakki is the main port of Leros, but the hydrofoils and daily catamaran use the Agia Marina port, and the caïque from Myrties on Kalymnos docks at Xirokambos.

Air There is one flight daily to Athens (21,400 dr) serviced by an 18-seater Dornier. The Olympic Airways office (☎ 22 844) is in Platanos, just before the turn-off for Pandeli. The airport (☎ 22 777) is in the north of the island at Partheni. There is no airport bus.

Ferry Leros is on the main north-south route for ferries to and from Rhodes and Piraeus and is reasonably well serviced with at least one and sometimes more daily departures from Lakki. Services are provided by DANE Lines (☎ 22 500), G&A Ferries (☎ 22 154) and the F/B *Nisos Kalymnos* (☎ 22 154).

Ferries heading south tend to depart at unsocial hours – between midnight and 6 am. The slower F/B *Nisos Kalymnos*' departure times are a little more manageable, with both north and south departures coming during daylight or evening hours.

The following table will give you an overview of the main departures.

destination	duration	price	frequency
Agathonisi	4 hours	2200 dr	2 weekly
Kalymnos	1½ hours	1800 dr	8 weekly
Lipsi	1 hour	1300 dr	4 weekly
Patmos	2 hours	1550 dr	9 weekly
Piraeus	11 hours	6300 dr	9 weekly
Rhodes	7¼ hours	4650 dr	8 weekly

Hydrofoil In summer there are hydrofoils every day to Patmos (45 minutes, 3000 dr), Lipsi (20 minutes, 2650 dr), Samos (two hours, 5000 dr), Kos (one hour, 4100 dr) and Rhodes (3¼ hours, 9300 dr); and almost every day to Agathonisi (1½ hours, 4460 dr) via Patmos and Fourni (1¾ hours, 4600 dr). Hydrofoils leave from Agia Marina.

Catamaran The Rhodes-based *Dodekanisos Express* calls in at Leros daily in summer as an intermediate stop on its run up the Dodecanese from Rhodes. Departures heading north from Leros are usually around 12.30 pm with arrival in Patmos at 1.30 pm. Departures heading south from Leros are usually around 3.20 pm, with arrival in Rhodes at 7 or 8.50 pm depending on the number of intermediate stops. Tickets can be bought at the Dodekanisos Shipping Agency in Lakki (☎ 22 145). See 'The Cost of the Catamaran' boxed text in the Getting Around chapter for more details.

Excursion Boat The caïque leaves Xirokambos at 7.30 am daily for Myrties on Kalymnos (1500 dr one way). In summer the Lipsi-based *Anna Express* makes daily trips between Agia Marina and Lipsi, and the *Captain Makis* runs on Tuesday and Thursday. Both cost 5000 dr return.

Getting Around

The hub for Leros' buses is Platanos. There are four buses daily to Partheni via Alinda and six buses to Xirokambos via Lakki. There is a flat rate of 200 dr per trip.

There are three main taxi stands on Leros. They are Lakki (☎ 22 550), Platanos (☎ 23 070) and Agia Marina (☎ 23 340).

There's no shortage of car, motorcycle and bicycle rentals around the island, though they tend to be centred on the resort areas of Alinda/Krithoni and Pandeli/Vromolithos.

SOUTHERN LEROS Νοτια Λέρος
Lakki Λακκί

Arriving at Lakki (lah-**kee**) by boat is like stepping into an abandoned Fellini film set. The grandiose buildings and wide tree-lined boulevards dotted around the Dodecanese are best (or worst) represented here, for Lakki was built as a Fascist showpiece during the Italian occupation. Lakki is one of the most un-Greek looking ports and you may justifiably wonder where you are. Many of the buildings look rather rundown, but to the credit of the Lakkiotes, slow restoration work is now in progress and once completed, will give Lakki a much-needed facelift.

Few people linger in Lakki, though it has decent accommodation and restaurants and there are some secluded swimming opportunities nearby. Locals are miffed that the hydrofoil and catamaran have chosen Agia Marina as their port. The only activity the port sees these days is in the late evening and after midnight when the big ferries call in on their way to Piraeus or Rhodes.

Orientation & Information Ferries dock at the far western end of the harbour from where it is a 15-minute walk round the bay to the centre. The once-functioning tourist office at the quay now seems to be permanently closed, but taxis meet all incoming ferries so, unless you plan to stay in Lakki, you can move on to your destination fairly painlessly.

There is a National Bank of Greece and ATM about 300m along the harbour road leading to the centre and a Commercial Bank and ATM on the left of the signposted road leading from Lakki to Platanos. The post office is prominently located on the corner of Vasileos Pavlou and 7 Martiou two blocks inland from the harbourfront. G&A and DANE ferry ticket offices are located here on the harbourfront near the taxi stands.

Places to Stay Perhaps the most pleasant place to stay in Lakki is the E-class *Hotel Katerina* (☎ 22 460) on 7 Martiou. Despite its low rating, the hotel has been extensively renovated and is modern, clean and airy. Rooms have TV and telephone plus heating and air-conditioning. They are good value at 8000/10,000 dr for singles/doubles and the hotel is open all year. It is one block back from the waterfront.

One of the longer-standing hotels in Lakki, also open all year, is the D-class *Hotel Mira Mare* (☎ 22 053, fax 22 469) on 7 Martiou. Rooms are 9000/11,000 dr and have TV, telephone and refrigerator. Neither hotel includes breakfast in the room price. The small C-class *Artemis Hotel*, four blocks back from the harbour, charges a rather hefty 15,000 dr for one of its eight double rooms.

Places to Eat The most obvious traditional eating place is *Petrino* on Vasileos Pavlou, on the same block as the post office. Standard fare food is served under a shaded streetside patio. Prices are cheap to medium.

For a fast snack or breakfast try *Restaurant Woody* (☎ 22 778) on a broad, palm tree ringed square on the Platanos road. English breakfasts are 1600 dr, while a cheap 'X-Burger' is 600 dr.

Past the harbour towards signposted Merikia are three places that the locals recommend and seek out. *Merikia Fish Restaurant* (mobile ☎ 09-3707 1778) is in a pleasant shaded location about 2km from Lakki next to a shingly beach. Opposite each other not too far away are *Apanemo* (☎ 25 295) and *Koulouki Restaurant*, where there is live bouzouki music on Friday and Saturday night.

The island's best supermarket, the well-stocked *Spanos*, is about 200m north on the right hand side of Platanos road in Lakki.

Xirokambos Χηρόκαμπος

Xirokambos (xi-**roh**-kam-bos) Bay, in the south of the island, is a low-key resort with some good spots for snorkelling. The main reason to come here is for the diving (see Activities later) or to catch the caïque to Myrties in Kalymnos. There is a pebbly, clean and sheltered beach, though harbour works on the west side to create a naval anchorage may change Xirokambos' relatively undisturbed status. There are a sprinkling of rooms to let and at least one very attractive waterside restaurant to tempt you for lunch.

The only attraction as such is the ruined fortress of **Paleokastro** signposted on a road just before the camping ground. The views are more impressive than the actual remains – you can see both Lakki and Xirokambos.

Activities The Panos Diving Club (☎ 23 372, mobile ☎ 09-4763 3146) is based in Xirokambos at the camping ground. Owner Panos Sideris offers an introductory dive for 20,000 dr and regular dives for 17,000 dr. There are bottle refill facilities and full technical support. A 10-dive package to ancient wrecks, WWII wrecks and marine caves, over six days, costs 120,000 dr all-inclusive. Diving is best in September.

Places to Stay & Eat The island's only camping ground, *Camping Leros (☎ 23 372)*, is signposted on the right coming from Lakki. It's pleasant and shaded (there are 218 olive trees) though the ground is a little hard. Camping costs 1500 dr per person plus 700 dr per tent. Electricity, hot water and cooking facilities are available for campers and there is a small restaurant and bar.

There are some easy to spot *domatia (☎ 23 148)* for around 7000 dr a double on the main road from Lakki. *Villa Alexandros (☎ 22 202)*, about 100m from the beach, offers better options for around 12,000 dr a double.

The most pleasant (and newest) place to eat is the tastefully furnished *To Kyma (☎ 25 248)* straddling the road at the eastern side of the bay. Its waterside tables and blue cane chairs are set out under the shade of tamarisk trees. Try delicious fried calamari or a dish from their daily *mayirefta* selection. It's open all day; prices are average.

CENTRAL LEROS Κεντρική Λέρος
Platanos & Agia Marina
Πλάτανος & Αγία Μαρίνα
Platanos (**plah**-ta-nos), the capital of Leros, is 3km north of Lakki. It's a picturesque little place spilling over a narrow hill pouring down to the port of Agia Marina (ay-**i**-a ma-**ri**-na) to the north, and Pandeli to the south, both within walking distance. Platanos is the main shopping area for the island and while it doesn't offer much in the way of eating or accommodation options, it's a

very pleasant place to spend a leisurely hour or so browsing. It is also the starting point for the path up to the Castle of Pandeli.

Orientation The focal point of Platanos is the lively central square, Plateia Nikolaou Roussou. Harami links this square with Agia Marina. Its southern extension eventually leads down to Lakki. A higher bypass road leads through-traffic around Platanos. Use this if you are just passing through as the streets are quite narrow and congested. Agia Marina is spread out around the bay. To the right as you come down from Platanos is the quay and to the left the road leads to Alinda.

Information There is a tourist information kiosk at the Agia Marina quay though its offerings are mainly limited to hydrofoil and catamaran schedules, accommodation listings and the odd colourful but not so useful tourist brochure.

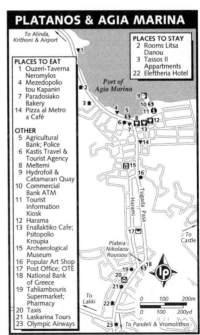

PLATANOS & AGIA MARINA

PLACES TO STAY
2 Rooms Litsa Danou
3 Tassos II Appartments
22 Eleftheria Hotel

PLACES TO EAT
1 Ouzeri-Taverna Neromylos
4 Mezedopolio tou Kapaniri
7 Paradosiako Bakery
14 Pizza al Metro a Café

OTHER
5 Agricultural Bank; Police
6 Kastis Travel & Tourist Agency
8 Meltemi
9 Hydrofoil & Catamaran Quay
10 Commercial Bank ATM
11 Tourist Information Kiosk
12 Harama
13 Enallaktiko Cafe; Psitopolio Kroupia
15 Archaeological Museum
16 Popular Art Shop
17 Post Office; OTE
18 National Bank of Greece
19 Tahliambouris Supermarket; Pharmacy
20 Taxis
21 Laskarina Tours
23 Olympic Airways

To Alinda, Krithoni & Airport
Port of Agia Marina
Tsigada Pasa
Harami
Plateia Nikolaou Roussou
To Lakki
To Castle
To Pandeli & Vromolithos

0   100   200m
0   100   200yd

Laskarina Tours (☎ 24 550, fax 24 551), at the Eleftheria Hotel in Platanos, and Kastis Travel & Tourist Agency (☎ 22 140), near the quay in Agia Marina, are very helpful. Laskarina Tours organises trips around the island for 5000 dr, or picnic cruises including a BBQ lunch for 7000 dr.

The National Bank of Greece is on the central square in Platanos. There is a free-standing Commercial Bank ATM on the quay in Agia Marina and an Agricultural Bank nearby.

The post office and OTE share premises on the right side of Harami. You can access the Internet at Enallaktiko Cafe (☎ 25 746) in Agia Marina. There are only two terminals and access charges are 500 dr for 15 minutes or 1500 dr for an hour. It is open from 8 am to after midnight daily.

There are a couple of convenient pharmacies in Platanos that are open after hours on a rotating basis.

The police station (☎ 22 222) is in Agia Marina on the Alinda road.

Things to See & Do On the east side of Platanos, houses are stacked up a hillside topped by the massive **Castle of Pandeli**. To reach the castle you can either climb up 370 steps, or walk or drive 2km along an asphalt road. The views from the top are very impressive. You can see the broad expanses of the bays of Gourna, Alinda and Lakki simultaneously. Photography is best here in the early morning or at sunset. It is open from 8 am to 1 pm and from 4 to 7.30 pm. Entry is 500 dr.

The small collection at the **Archaeological Museum** can easily be visited in between strolls to and from Platanos. It is open from 8 am to 2.30 pm Tuesday to Sunday. Entry is free.

Places to Stay Pickings in Platanos are limited to the C-class *Eleftheria Hotel* (☎ 23 551), near the taxi rank, which has pleasant, well-kept double rooms for around 10,000 dr with bathroom.

Options in Agia Marina are similarly limited, but are decidedly more atmospheric. *Rooms Litsa Danou* (☎ 23 739), on the waterfront as you walk towards the prominent water mill housing Ouzeri-Taverna Neromylos (see also Places to Eat). The three rooms available are large, airy, overlook the beach and go for 15,000 dr in high season.

Tassos II Appartments (☎/fax 22 769) offers fully equipped studios with kitchen, ironing facilities, satellite TV, coffee maker, air-conditioning, money safe and hair drier. They are excellent value at 13,000/16,000 dr for doubles/triples. They are on the left along the main road leading to Alinda.

Places to Eat The windmill in the water is featured in many travel brochures to Leros and is unique to the Mediterranean. Today it is home to the *Ouzeri-Taverna Neromylos* (☎ 24 894), run by a proud Takis Koutsounaris, who cooks some fine dishes such as 'special prawns', stuffed calamari and his own mousakas. Although open all day, night-time dining is best when lights illuminate the watermill to its best effect. Prices are mid-range.

The *Mezedopolio tou Kapaniri* (☎ 22 750) on the main road to Alinda and right on the waterfront is open all day and offers breakfast. The owners suggest diners try their *haloumi* (a soft rubbery cheese) for 1000 dr and *mydia saganaki* (mussels in melted cheese) for 1700 dr.

For the best pizza and pasta as well as filling focaccia sandwiches, Italian-owned *Pizza al Metro a Café* (☎ 24 888), on Harami, is your best bet. You'll get some cheap and filling sausages, souvlaki and hot dogs at *Psitopolio Kroupia* on the little waterfront square heading towards Agia Marina's quay. Bread and sweet lovers should duck into the *Paradosiako Bakery*, on the corner of Harami and the harbourfront street, for the best the island has to offer. Ask for *soumada* syrup (made of sweet and bitter almonds) to take home. Add water to a small spoonful and slurp it.

Entertainment Frappé drinkers or chronic chair warmers might want to hang around *Harama*, a little bar/cafe that sees quite a bit of activity during the evening. Other options include *Meltemi* and *Enallaktiko Cafe*, which doubles as an Internet cafe (see Information earlier).

Shopping The exquisite collection of high class popular art, paintings, antiques, silverware and even Indonesian batik and carvings from the Popular Art Shop (☎ 24 331) on Tsigada Pasa is definitely worth a look. It is owned and run by locals Kostas and Paraskevi Dekoulis, themselves frequent travellers, who will make you very welcome.

Getting Around The bus station and the Platanos taxi rank (☎ 23 070) are both on the Lakki-Platanos road, just before the central square.

Krithoni & Alinda
Κριθώνι & Αλιντα
West of Agia Marina and running north around Alinda Bay are the low-key resorts of Krithoni (kri-**tho**-ni) and Alinda (a-**lin**-da). Krithoni is less obviously a resort as it stretches out a little more tenuously along the bay road and does not have a centre as such. It merges imperceptibly into Alinda, which begins to feel more like a resort just after the turn-off for the road to the airport.

Swimming is best along the narrow shoreline of Alinda where the water is generally sheltered and the beach is a mixture of gravel and sand. Here you will find most restaurants and accommodation as well as motorbike rental outlets. The stretch of road running alongside the beach at Alinda is a bit of a 'kamikaze strip' in high summer, with young Greeks tearing up and down on motorbikes and scooters. Pedestrians should exercise caution.

Orientation & Information There is no bank or ATM and no post office, but you can change money at the Kastis Travel Agency (☎ 22 305) on the waterfront in Alinda.

Motoland (☎ 23 145), on the Alinda waterfront, rents out reasonable-looking though not so late model motorcycles and scooters. Right next door, Alinda Seasport (☎ 24 584) rents out all kinds of water sports equipment.

Things To See & Do The well presented **Historical & Folkloric Museum** (Bellenis Museum; ☎ 25 040), right in the middle of the waterfront promenade in a towered and turreted former Italian mansion, houses a mixed bag of folkloric exhibits. These range from ink paintings on stones made by political prisoner Kyriakos Tsakiris between 1967 and 1972, to musical instruments and *objets* from the public pharmacy of 1899. There is an exhibition on the battle of Leros fought by the British and Italians against the Germans in 1943, as well as objects from the *Vasilissa Olga*, which was sunk during the course of this battle. It is open from 10 am to 1 pm and 6 to 9 pm daily. Entry costs 1000 dr.

On Krithoni's waterfront there is a poignant, well-kept **war cemetery**. After the Italian surrender in WWII, Leros saw fierce fighting between German and British forces. The cemetery contains the graves of 179 British, two Canadian and two South African soldiers.

Places to Stay The *Hotel Kostantinos* (☎ 22 904), on the right coming from Agia Marina, has comfortable singles/doubles with bathrooms for 6000/8000 dr. Just beyond the war cemetery on Krithoni's waterfront, a road veers left to *Hotel Gianna* (☎/fax 24 135), which has nicely furnished singles/doubles for 9000/13,000 dr. The sparkling, pine-furnished *Studios & Apartments Diamantis* (☎ 22 378), located behind the cemetery, charges rates of around 12,000/14,000 dr.

Boulafendis Bungalows (☎ 23 515, fax 24 533) has some beautiful self-contained studios and bungalows for 16,000 dr for two people and 24,000 dr for a fully equipped bungalow for four or five people. It's on the left just before Odos Aschaim, the turn-off for the airport.

A bit farther along from the Hotel Kostantinos, the B-class *Crithoni Paradise Hotel* (☎ 25 120, fax 24 680, e lerosparadise@hotmail.com), complete with bars, restaurant and swimming pool, has singles/doubles for 23,500/30,800 dr and suites for 45,000 dr.

Places to Eat Alinda's waterfront *Finikas Taverna (☎ 22 695)* offers up 15 types of salad and 16 different mezedes and has an equally extensive menu of well-prepared Greek specialities; mezedes are 800 dr to 1400 dr and souvlaki is 1800 dr. *Taverna Kostantinos (☎ 24 630)*, adjacent to Finikas, offers much the same in menu choices. *To Fanari*, halfway along the beach strip, is newish and reasonably reliable for good food.

Restaurant Alinda is a larger, posher place with terrace and garden dining and is a bit more expensive. It is popular with the small tour groups that are based here. *Argo Pizzeria & Bar*, at the northern end of the beach strip, is good for pizza and drinks and has tables actually on the beach.

Sweet-toothed travellers should head for the *Zaharoplastio to Elliniko*, halfway along the beach strip and housed in an impressive stand-alone building. Customers can eat in or take away. The cafe crowd clusters mainly around *Palatino Cocktail Bar* at the south end – the forest of motorbikes and scooters parked outside betray its location. The *Alaloum* and *Kosmopolitan* nearby also pull in their own fair share of cafe trade.

At the other end of the strip the *Zubuli Bar*, by the boat anchorages, is better for a quieter drink, especially since fewer motorbikes make it this far up.

Two *minimarkets* on the waterfront provide basic supplies including 1.5L bottles of cold Cambas retsina which go down well mixed with *Souroti* soda and taken on your balcony as the sun goes down.

Pandeli & Vromolithos
Παντέλι & Βρωμόλιθος

The two smaller resorts of Pandeli (pan-**deh**-li) and Vromolithos (vro-**mo**-lith-os) huddle round Pandeli Bay on the south side of the peninsula straddled by Platanos. Many visitors prefer this cosy bay as their base since there is more of a village feel to it and the water is a bit more sheltered when the wind is up. The two centres are separated by a small headland, but they are connected to one another by a track. Drivers and bike riders must backtrack up the hill to get from one side to the other.

The only blight is an unsightly stack of concrete blocks – supposedly to be used one day to extend the harbour – at the northern end of the harbour in Pandeli. It's been there so long that they call it the Pandeli Playpark.

Orientation & Information Pandeli has most of the accommodation and restaurants and the beach is more easily accessible. Vromolithos is more scattered and the access road runs behind the waterfront restaurants and accommodation. There is the usual sprinkling of minimarkets and small gift shops plus the odd motorbike rental outfit.

Places to Stay In Pandeli, the waterfront *Pension Roza (☎ 22 798)* has doubles/triples for 6000/8000 dr. A bit farther along, *Rooms to Rent Kavos (☎ 23 247)* has double room rates of 10,000 dr. *Pension Happiness (☎ 23 498)*, on the left of the road down from Platanos, has modern, sunny rooms with bathroom for 9000/10,000 dr.

An excellent and popular choice open all year is the *Pension Rodon (☎ 22 075)*, located up near the main road halfway between Pandeli and Vromolithos. Doubles range in price from 8000 dr to 10,000 dr and more expensive five-person apartments are available.

Set back high above Pandeli are two fairly obvious restored windmills. You can stay in one of these for 20,000 dr. The delightful and unusual *I Anemomyli (☎ 25 549)* tends to be block-booked much of the summer, but is open all year; you may be lucky to secure your own mill with a view with a bit of foresight.

Places to Eat The *Dimitris Taverna (☎ 25 626)* is probably Leros' best taverna with great views from its dining balcony. Its delicious mezedes (up to 30) include cheese courgettes, stuffed calamari, and onion and cheese pies. Main courses include chicken in retsina and pork in red sauce for around 1800 dr. Take the road to Vromolithos from Platanos, turn left at a shop a little way down, and the taverna is on the right.

In Pandeli, *Zorbas* and *Psarapoula* are popular tavernas, but the unpretentious little *Taverna Drosia* is good value and offers

A quiet moment to reflect, before continuing on to Kefalos Bay, Kos Island

Going to chapel in Mandraki

Where better to sit back, relax and watch the Zia village locals go by

Dominating Kos Town is the ruins of the 15th-century Castle of the Knights of St John.

The bustling port town of Pothia, Kalymnos

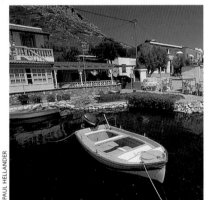

The peaceful traffic-free islet of Telendos

Take a seat: Hohlakas Beach, Telendos

A solo swimmer enjoys a refreshing dip in Rena Harbour on Kalymnos.

string beans for 800 dr and lamb with rice for 1500 dr, among other dishes. Similarly unpretentious is **Stou Tzouma**, a little waterfront ouzeri offering grilled octopus. Wash it down with Samiotiko ouzo, or Liokri retsina.

Entertainment In Pandeli, *Savana Bar* is open from mid-afternoon until late and has a great music policy: you can choose what you want. Sample the Blue Savana cocktail (vodka, tequila, apple schnapps, Grand Marnier and grapefruit juice) and figure out how they got the motorbike on the wall.

Gourna Γούρνα
The wide bay of Gourna (**ghour**-na), on the west coast, has a similar beach to Alinda but is less developed and is somewhat more exposed to the winds. You will need a motorbike to get here as it is not served by public transport. At the northern side, the chapel of **Agia Isidora** is on a tranquil islet reached by a causeway. There is a pleasant, little used route to Lakki via Drymonas.

NORTHERN LEROS
Northern Leros sees fewer tourists due, in part, to its general lack of infrastructure. This may have resulted from the area's former role as the principal place used to incarcerate political prisoners (see History earlier), its current role as a military base and its general lack of stunning beaches.

Parentheni is a scattered settlement north of the airport. Despite having a large army camp, it's an attractive area of hills, olive groves, fields of beehives and two large bays.

Artemis, the goddess of the hunt, was worshipped on Leros in ancient times. Just before the airport there's a signposted left turn to the **Temple of Artemis**. A dirt track turns right 300m along it. Where the track peters out, clamber up to the left and you will see the derelict **Chapel of Agia Irini**. There's little in the way of ancient ruins but it's a strangely evocative place.

Farther along the main road there is a turn-off to the right to **Blefoutis Bay**, which has a shaded sand and pebble beach and a reasonable taverna, *Thea Artemis* (*☎ 24 253*). Beyond this turn-off, the main road

skirts Partheni Bay and its poor beach. But if you continue straight ahead, turn right at the T-junction, go through a gate to pass the Chapel of Agia Kioura, then through another gate and bear right, you'll come to a secluded pebbled cove. There are no facilities, only one tree for shade and it is just accessible by car along a dusty, bumpy road.

Lipsi Λειψοί

☎ 0247 • postcode 850 01 • pop 700

Lipsi (lip-**see**), 12km east of Patmos and 11km north of Leros, is the kind of place that few people know about, but once they have discovered it they feel disinclined to share their discovery with others. It's a friendly, cheery place with the right balance of remoteness and 'civilisation'. It has comfortable accommodation, a pleasing choice of quality restaurants and a good selection of underpopulated beaches. Apart from the two or three days a year when pilgrims and revellers descend upon Lipsi for its major festival, you can have most of it for yourself.

In recent years Lipsi has become increasingly popular with Italian visitors and the French seem to have found Lipsi as well. The only tour operator currently making inroads is Laskarina, but it's still definitely low-key. Lipsi is an ideal place to unwind, engage in some contemplative navel gazing and pull out that long-unread novel. Get in now while the going's still good.

History
Lipsi of antiquity was also known as Lipso and Lipsiai, but its history is shrouded in mystery, due primarily to the lack of historical records of any stature. What is known is that its ancient history followed much the same pattern of colonisation and settlement as the neighbouring islands of Patmos, Leros and Kalymnos. First came Karians in about 1370 BC, followed by Dorians in 1200 BC who were succeeded by Ionians from Miletus in Asia Minor. Archaeological finds from the Mycenaean period (1600–1100 BC) and the Geometric period (1110–800 BC) testify to the island's settlement during this time.

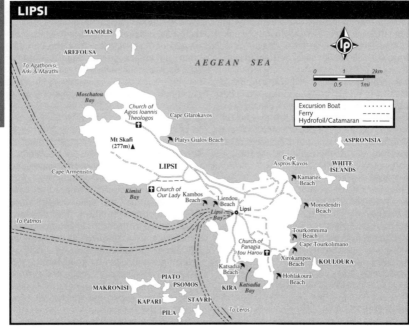

It is recorded that during the Peloponnesian War opposing forces occasionally anchored their ships in the sheltered harbour of Lipsi. In the 11th century BC, Lipsi – along with Patmos – was granted to the Blessed Christodoulos by the emperor Alexis Komninos I, and became a monastic community. Lipsi subsequently suffered depredations at the hands of pirates, Ottoman colonisation and a gradual population loss as people emigrated or abandoned the island. Today, Lipsi supports no more than 700 permanent inhabitants.

Getting There & Away

Ferry Although Lipsi is theoretically well positioned to receive ferries on the main Piraeus-Rhodes run, not all ferries stop here so services are rather limited. The Kalymnos-based and slower F/B *Nisos Kalymnos* makes up for the deficit somewhat with at least two extra links per week in either direction.

The following table will give you an overview of the main departures.

destination	duration	price	frequency
Agathonisi	1¾ hours	1550 dr	4 weekly
Astypalea	6 hours	4000 dr	2 weekly
Kalymnos	3 hours	1800 dr	3 weekly
Kos	4 hours	3000 dr	1 weekly
Leros	1 hour	1300 dr	4 weekly
Patmos	1 hour	1200 dr	5 weekly
Piraeus	10 hours	8900 dr	1 weekly
Rhodes	7½ hours	5000 dr	1 weekly
Samos	4½ hours	1800 dr	3 weekly

The Patmos-based *Patmos Express* leaves for Patmos at 4 pm daily (one hour, 2000 dr) but doesn't return until 10 am the following day. This is more suited for day-trippers from Patmos to Lipsi, rather than the other way round.

Hydrofoil In summer, hydrofoils call at Lipsi at least twice daily on their routes north and south between Samos, in the North-Eastern Aegean, and Rhodes. Sample destinations and fares are as follows: Samos-Pythagorio (1½ hours, 3600 dr), Patmos (20 minutes, 2400 dr), Leros (20 minutes, 2600 dr), Kalymnos (1½ hours, 3700 dr), Kos (two hours, 3300 dr) and Rhodes (4½ hours, 10,100 dr).

Catamaran The Rhodes-based *Dodekanisos Express* calls in at Lipsi three times a week in summer as an intermediate stop on its daily run up the Dodecanese from Rhodes. Departures from Lipsi to Patmos and Rhodes are usually between 1 and 3 pm. Patmos is only 30 minutes from Lipsi and Rhodes is 4½ hours. Tickets can be bought at the Dodekanisos Shipping Agency in the port (☎ 41 209). See 'The Cost of the Catamaran' boxed text in the Getting Around chapter for more details.

Excursion Boat The *Captain Makis* and *Anna Express* do daily trips in summer to Agia Marina on Leros and to Skala on Patmos (both 5000 dr return). *Black Beauty* and *Margarita* do 'Five Island' trips around Lipsi for around the same price. All four excursion boats can be found at the small quay and all depart at around 10 am each day.

Getting Around
Lipsi has three modern minibuses which go to Platys Gialos (300 dr), Katsadia and Hohlakoura (both 250 dr). They leave on the hour from 10 am to 5 pm (July and August) from an unmarked stop near the police station. Out of these months the times are reduced.

A couple of taxis should also be in operation in 2001.

There are two motorcycle rental outlets in Lipsi. Markos & Maria (☎ 41 358, 41 130), on the far side of the harbour, has a modern range of motorbikes for rent from 3000 dr to 4000 dr per day. It also rents out bicycles for 1000 dr per day. George Bikes (☎ 41 340) rents out bikes at a similar price from an office just behind the Flisvos Pension.

LIPSI TOWN
Orientation
All boats dock at one of the two quays in Lipsi Town. The ferries, hydrofoils and catamaran all dock at the larger outer jetty, while excursion boats dock at a smaller jetty near the centre of Lipsi Town.

From the large quay, facing inland, turn right. Continue along the waterfront to the large Plateia Nikiforias, which is just beyond Hotel Calypso. Ascend the wide steps at the far side of Plateia Nikiforias and bear right to reach the central square. The left fork leads to a second, smaller square.

Laskarina Holidays has produced a rough map of Lipsi Town for its own clients. The Lipsi tourist map, on sale at some tourist shops, shows all the major points of reference and beaches.

Information
The municipal tourist office (☎ 41 288) is on the central square and has a limited amount of tourist material but enthusiastic staff. You may find Laid Back Holidays (☎ 41 141, fax 41 343) or Paradisis Travel (☎ 41 120, fax 41 110) more helpful.

There is a freestanding Commercial Bank ATM near the wide steps. At busy times this sometimes runs out of money, so come prepared with extra cash. You can also change money and cash Eurocheques at travel agencies or the post office.

The post office and OTE are on the central square. A number of cardphones are scattered around Lipsi Town. Mobile phone users will find that only Cosmote provides coverage on Lipsi, unless you stand on the large quay where the other providers can sometimes be picked up. There is a rather good Web site maintained by Laid Back Holidays at www.otenet.gr/lbh.

The police (☎ 41 222) are in the large white building on the waterfront. The port police (☎ 41 133) are in the long white building to the right of the wide steps.

Things to See & Do
Lipsi is the kind of place where most visitors are content to do very little. There are no stunning sites or momentous cultural

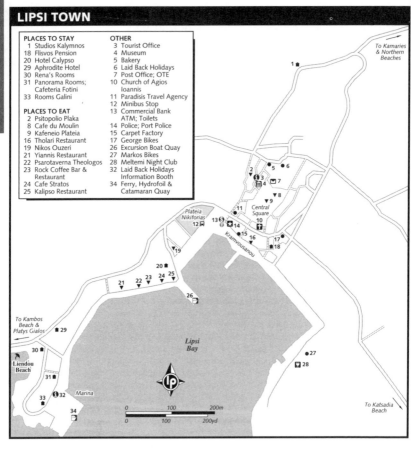

LIPSI TOWN

PLACES TO STAY	OTHER
1 Studios Kalymnos	3 Tourist Office
18 Flisvos Pension	4 Museum
20 Hotel Calypso	5 Bakery
29 Aphrodite Hotel	6 Laid Back Holidays
30 Rena's Rooms	7 Post Office; OTE
31 Panorama Rooms;	10 Church of Agios
Cafeteria Fotini	Ioannis
33 Rooms Galini	11 Paradisis Travel Agency
	12 Minibus Stop
PLACES TO EAT	13 Commercial Bank
2 Psitopolio Plaka	ATM; Toilets
8 Cafe du Moulin	14 Police; Port Police
9 Kafeneio Plateia	15 Carpet Factory
16 Tholari Restaurant	17 George Bikes
19 Nikos Ouzeri	26 Excursion Boat Quay
21 Yiannis Restaurant	27 Markos Bikes
22 Psarotaverna Theologos	28 Meltemi Night Club
23 Rock Coffee Bar &	32 Laid Back Holidays
Restaurant	Information Booth
24 Cafe Stratos	34 Ferry, Hydrofoil &
25 Kalipso Restaurant	Catamaran Quay

activities taking place. The island's biggest event is the yearly feast of Panagia tou Harou which takes place on or around August 22 each year, when the island is literally swamped with pilgrims and the curious. The ensuing feast in the harbourside park is a riot of dancing, eating and drinking and usually only splutters to an end at around 6 am the next day.

Lipsi's **museum** is on the central square. Its somewhat underwhelming exhibits include pebbles and plastic bottles of holy water from around the world. Admission is free, and opening times are 11 am to 1 pm

daily. There is a **carpet factory** in the same building as the port police. The hand-woven carpets are not for sale here but you can see them being made. It's open 8.30 am to 3.30 pm Monday to Friday.

Places to Stay – Budget

There is not a huge choice of accommodation on Lipsi and it is centred upon Lipsi Town. Visitors will not usually have trouble finding a place to stay except during the feast of Panagia tou Harou. Accommodation or even getting off the island can then be problematic. Book well in advance.

One of the more appealing and certainly the most friendly place to stay in Lipsi is **Studios Kalymnos** (☎ *41 141, fax 41 343,* [e] *lbh@otenet.gr)*, a 10-minute walk from the harbour. These neat and airy studios are set in a cool garden with a BBQ for guests. Double studios are available for 10,000 dr. Owner Nick Hristodoulou or his Canadian wife Anna can usually be found at the Laid Back Holidays office or the harbour information kiosk.

The D-class **Hotel Calypso** (☎ *41 420, fax 41 242)* has comfy doubles/triples for 8000/9000 dr with bathroom. **Rena's Rooms** (☎ *41 363)*, owned by Greek-Americans John and Rena Paradisis (of Paradisis Travel), are spotless, beautifully furnished and spacious. Rooms are 9000/10,000 dr with bathroom. There is a communal refrigerator and electric hot plates, and a terrace overlooking Liendou Beach.

Rooms Galini (☎ *41 212)*, opposite the large quay, has lovely light rooms with bathroom, fridge, electric ring and balcony for 12,000/13,000 dr. Owner Nikos takes guests on fishing trips upon request. Nearby, above Cafeteria Fotini, **Panorama Rooms** (☎ *41 235, 42 254)* are equally agreeable, with room rates of 11,000/12,000 dr.

Flisvos Pension (☎ *41 261)*, just beyond the carpet factory, has doubles/triples for 10,000/12,000 dr.

Places to Stay – Mid-Range
The A-class **Aphrodite Hotel** (☎ *41 394, fax 41 000)*, overlooking Liendou Beach, has luxurious double studios for 20,000 dr and four-person apartments for 28,000 dr.

Places to Eat
There is a clutch of eateries along the stretch of harbourside leading from the port to the main square. You will first meet **Cafeteria Fotini** (☎ *41 235)*, with pizza, snacks and cakes on offer. It's very handy if you are staying at the Panorama Studios upstairs. **Yiannis Restaurant** (☎ *45 395)* is probably the most popular of the harbourside eateries. The food is wholesome and not too expensive. **Psarotaverna Theologos** (☎ *41 248)*, a blue and white painted

The Miracle of Lipsi
Every year a small miracle happens on the small island of Lipsi. An icon of the Virgin Mary, in the blue-domed church of Agios Ioannis in Lipsi Town, is encased within the glass with a small sprig of dried lilies. Every year on August 24 the dried lily sprig comes to life and a cluster of white buds appears and blossoms. Amid much pomp and ceremony, the icon is taken in procession from the church of Agios Ioannis to the small chapel of the Panagia tou Harou – the curiously-named Virgin of Charon, so-called because this is the only icon in the Orthodox world that shows the Virgin holding Jesus dead. Here a ceremony, attended by nearly all the islanders and hundreds of visiting pilgrims, takes place. The religious ceremony is followed by a night-long feast *(paniyiri)*.

The story goes that a young woman once prayed for assistance for her son from the Virgin. Her prayer was duly answered and, in gratitude, she left a small bouquet of lilies near the icon of the Virgin. The lilies withered in due course, but on August 24, the same day of the Virgin's Assumption into Heaven, the lilies sprang to life once more and have done so ever since. This once sceptical writer took part in the procession and did indeed spy the revitalised lily buds popping up under the protective glass. Sleight-of-hand, or a true miracle? Decide for yourselves next August 24.

fish tavern with a fishing caïque usually tied up outside, only opens when the owner has fish to cook and that is not every day. Keep your eyes open for signs of activity: the fish is guaranteed to be fresh.

The **Rock Coffee Bar & Restaurant** (☎ *41 180)* is next along, offering coffee and ouzo with unusual mezedes such as sea urchins. Check their specials board to see what else is on offer. **Cafe Stratos**, next along, is the place to come for ice creams, pastries and excellent coffee as well as breakfast. **Kalipso Restaurant** (☎ *41 060)*, also on the seafront, is a smidgin touristy, but otherwise popular, reliable enough and not too expensive.

Not obviously marked but easy enough to spot is *Nikos Ouzeri* next to the little park. This is the place to come for a pre-dinner ouzo and grilled octopus, or if you really get mellow on the ouzo, just order more mezedes and have dinner here. It's not overly cheap, so keep an eye on the mezes tab.

New in 2000 and still finding its feet is the *Tholari Restaurant (☎ 41 230)*, on Kramvousanou, on the waterfront in front of the church. It seems to have garnered a loyal local following with its range of fish and grill-based dishes. It's moderately expensive.

Cafe du Moulin (☎ 41 416) in the main square is the best of the two eateries here. The staff are French- and Greek-speaking. It's good for light lunches – omelettes, mousakas and the like.

Tucked away down a side street off the main square, *Psitopolio Plaka (☎ 41 065)* is a popular and cheap *rôterie* and souvlaki shop which pulls in a regular evening crowd of fast diners.

There are a couple of bakeries selling bread, pitties and other baked delicacies close to the main square, and a couple of small, but well-stocked supermarkets.

Entertainment
Night owls head for the *Meltemi Night Club* for music and drinks. Greek music usually kicks in later on and it stays open until late – or early, depending on how you view your day.

AROUND LIPSI
There are a number of beaches on Lipsi. Getting to them makes for pleasant walks, passing through countryside dotted with smallholdings, olive groves and cypresses but buses also go to most of them.

Liendou Beach is the most accessible and naturally most popular beach. The water is very shallow and calm and is the best beach for children. It's very handy for the hotels at this south-west side of Lipsi Town.

Next along is sandy **Kambos Beach**, a 1km, 15-minute walk along the same road that leads to Platys Gialos. There is some shade available.

Beyond Kambos Beach the road takes you another 40 minutes along to **Platys Gialos**, a lovely, but narrow sandy beach. The water is shallow and ideal for children. Some people free camp under the olive trees backing the beach. While this is unofficial, it is quietly tolerated by the owners of the land. The minibus runs here if you don't fancy the walk. *Kostas Restaurant*, above the beach, is an excellent place and owner Kostas Makris dishes up some excellent fish and grill dishes. It is open from 8 am to 6 pm every day in July and August.

The sand and pebble **Katsadia Beach**, 2km south of Lipsi Town, is perhaps the next best beach on the island after Platys Gialos. It is shaded with tamarisk trees and is easily reached on foot (40 minutes), or by the hourly minibus from Lipsi Town. The water is clean and protected by the confines of the bay.

The small, rustic *Gambieris Taverna (☎ 41 087)* at Katsadia Beach is owned by an elderly couple who serve simple, low-priced meat and fish dishes. Nearer the beach, the modern *Dilaila Cafe Restaurant (☎ 41 041)* is owned by their son, Hristodoulos, who has travelled widely and speaks English. Good, reasonably priced food is served, and music from Hristodoulos' eclectic collection is played.

Tourkomnima Beach is a sandy beach 3km and 50 minutes' walk away from Lipsi. It is best reached by taking a side road from near Hohlakoura Beach.

The pebble **Hohlakoura Beach**, to the east of Katsadia, is near the **Church of Panagia Harou** (The Virgin of Charon). It offers neither shade nor facilities. Farther north, **Monodendri** (One Tree) is the island's unofficial nudist beach. It stands on a rocky peninsula, the neck of which is pebbled. There are no facilities. It is a 3km, 50-minute walk to get there, though it is reachable by motorbike. You'll know you've reached it when you see the solitary tree, which offers limited shade.

KIMISI Κοίμηση
Kimisi (ki-mi-si) is a little bay on the south-west coast. A hermit monk lives here beside the little **Church of Our Lady**. If you visit,

behave appropriately with respect for his peace and holiness. In Ottoman times monks hid in a cave here, choosing death from starvation rather than capture by the Turks. A casket in the church contains their bones.

To walk there, take the Platys Gialos road, and veer left onto the uphill track by a stone wall, opposite the asphalt road to the right. Go through a gap in the stone wall, continue ahead and you will eventually come to the Church of the Virgin of the Cross, from where an asphalt road leads down to Kimisi. There is also a pebble beach here if you feel like a swim.

Patmos Πάτμος

☎ 0247 • postcode 855 00 • pop 2663

Patmos could well be the ideal Greek island destination. It has a beguiling mix of qualities that make it an inexplicably pleasant vacation destination. It appeals in equal doses to the culturally inclined, the religiously motivated, gastronomes and sun-worshippers, shoppers, yachties, bookaholics and travellers simply seeking to unwind. It is not too far from Athens (eight hours by boat), yet suitably cut off from the mainstream world (there is no airport). Patmos boasts some fine but never crowded beaches, excellent food, and for the serious shopper some of the classiest artwork and jewellery in the Aegean. It also has an intangible spirit of place evolving in part from its white Cycladic architectural feel, juxtaposed by the ever-visible blue Aegean and the subtle, but never dominating religious atmosphere that draws Christian pilgrims from all over the world. It was here, after all, that God delivered to St John the text of the Apocalypse, that damningly ominous explanation of the end of the world. Patmos is instantly palatable and entices the visitor to linger and to almost certainly return another time.

History

In AD 95, St John the Divine was banished to Patmos from Ephesus by the pagan Roman Emperor Domitian. While residing in a cave on the island, St John wrote the *Book of Revelations*. In 1088 the Blessed Christodoulos, an abbot who came from Asia Minor to Patmos, obtained permission from the Byzantine Emperor Alexis I Komninos to build a monastery to commemorate St John. Pirate raids necessitated powerful fortifications, so the monastery looks like a mighty castle.

Under the Duke of Naxos, Patmos became a semi-autonomous monastic state, and achieved such wealth and influence that it was able to resist Turkish oppression. In the early 18th century, a school of theology and philosophy was founded by Makarios Kalogeras and it flourished until the 19th century.

Gradually the island's wealth polarised into secular and monastic entities. The secular wealth was acquired through shipbuilding, an industry which diminished with the arrival of the steam ship.

MH
A church belltower on Patmos reflects the island's strong spiritual atmosphere.

Getting There & Away

Ferry Patmos is on the main north-south route for ferries to and from Rhodes and Piraeus and is reasonably well serviced with at least one and sometimes more daily departures from Skala. Services are provided by DANE Lines and G&A Ferries while the F/B *Nisos Kalymnos* provides additional links to Agathonisi and Samos.

Ferries heading south tend to depart between midnight and 1 am. Departures north are usually in the late evening. The slower F/B *Nisos Kalymnos'* departures times are a little more manageable, with both north and south departures coming during daylight or evening hours.

The following table will give you an overview of the main departures.

destination	duration	price	frequency
Agathonisi	1¾ hours	1600 dr	4 weekly
Astypalea	7 hours	4300 dr	2 weekly
Kalymnos	3 hours	2450 dr	8 weekly
Kos	4 hours	2700 dr	8 weekly
Leros	2 hours	1550 dr	9 weekly
Lipsi	45 minutes	1200 dr	5 weekly
Piraeus	9 hours	6700 dr	8 weekly
Rhodes	8½ hours	5400 dr	8 weekly
Samos	3 hours	1750 dr	4 weekly

Hydrofoil There are daily hydrofoils to Rhodes (five hours, 10,300 dr), via Kalymnos (1½ hours, 4700 dr) and Kos (2¼ hours, 5300 dr), and to Fourni (40 minutes, 3200 dr), Ikaria (1¼ hours, 3400 dr) and Samos (one hour, 3400 dr) in the North-Eastern Aegean. Twice a week, a hydrofoil runs to and from Agathonisi (40 minutes, 3200 dr).

Catamaran The Rhodes-based *Dodekanisos Express* calls in at Patmos six times a week in summer as the last stop on its daily run up the Dodecanese from Rhodes. The first port of call on the return leg is Leros with intermediate stops at Lipsi twice a week. Departures from Patmos are usually around 2 pm with arrival in Rhodes at 7 pm and intermediate stops in between those times. Tickets can be bought at the Dodekanisos Shipping Agency (☎ 29 303) in Skala. For details on fares see the boxed text 'The Cost of the Catamaran' in the Getting Around chapter.

Excursion Boat The local *Patmos Express* leaves daily for Lipsi at 10 am (2000 dr return) and returns from Lipsi at 4 pm.

The Patmos-based *Delfini* (☎ 31 995/371) goes to Marathi every day in high season – Monday and Thursday at other times. Twice a week it also calls in at Arki. From Marathi a local caïque will take you across to Arki.

Getting Around

Bus From Skala there are eleven buses daily in July and August to Hora (210 dr), eight to Grikos (230 dr) and four to Kambos (230 dr). The frequency drops off during the rest of the year. There is no bus service to Lambi.

Car & Motorcycle Rental There are lots of motorcycle and car rental outlets in Skala. Competition is fierce, so shop around. Agencies you might want to try are Moto Rent Express (☎ 32 088) or Theo & Giorgio (☎ 32 066). Prices start at around 5000 dr per day. Theo & Giorgio also rents out bicycles.

Taxi From Skala's taxi rank, examples of tariffs are: Meloï Beach (800 dr), Lambi (1500 dr), Grikos (1200 dr) and Hora (1000 dr).

Excursion Boat Boats go to all the island's beaches from Skala, leaving about 11 am and returning about 4 pm.

SKALA Σκάλα

Patmos' port is Skala (**ska**-la), a bright and glitzy town draped around a large curving bay and only visible from arriving ships once the protective headland has been rounded. It's a fairly busy port; large cruise ships are often anchored offshore and the smaller ones are at Skala's harbour. Once the cruise ships have departed and the daily ferries have come and gone, Skala reverts to being a fairly normal, livable port town. It has a wide range of accommodation and restaurants and all the island's major facilities are here. If you are not bent on staying next to a beach, Skala is as good a base as any for your visit to Patmos.

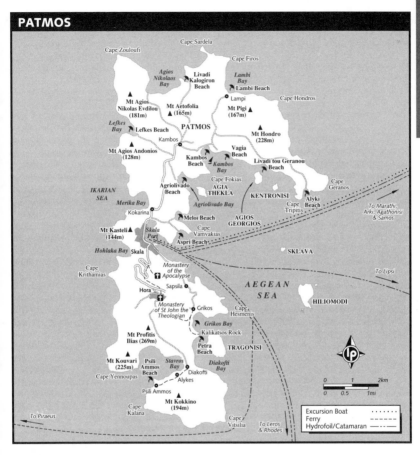

PATMOS

Orientation

All boats, hydrofoils and the catamaran conveniently dock more or less in the middle of the Skala waterfront. Taxis and local buses all depart from just beyond the arrivals area. Upon disembarking turn left (south) for the hotels in the Konsolato quarter and turn right (north) for hotels and studios in the Netia quarter. If you want to reach Hora, turn left and right again at the small roundabout by Taverna Grigoris. Most of the accommodation listed for Skala is within five to 10 minutes' walking distance from the ferry quay.

Excursion boats depart from a separate area 200m north of the ferry quay. The large Italianate building facing you as you disembark houses the police and post office, while the port police are on the main ferry quay.

The simplistic tourist maps handed out by motor rental agencies in Skala will suffice for most purposes.

Information

Tourist Offices The unhelpful and poorly stocked municipal tourist office (☎ 31 666, e dpatmos@rho.forthnet.gr) shares the Italianate building with the post office and police station. It's open from 9 am to midnight in summer only, but don't bother with it if you are looking for solid information.

Money The National Bank of Greece on the central square has an ATM. There is another ATM and Commercial Bank at the northern end of the waterfront next to Hotel Chris. Travel agencies will exchange money as well. Look for signs advertising their services.

Post & Communications The post office is housed in the Italianate building on the main square and maintains regular opening hours. The OTE – for what it is worth nowadays – is located some way away from the centre, but there are cardphones aplenty all over Skala. Mobile phone users on global roaming can easily pick up any of the three domestic mobile networks.

There are two Internet centres in Skala. One is in the Hotel Blue Bay (see Places to Stay for details), open from 8 am to 8 pm. It offers two terminals with the option of connecting your own laptop; access charges are 600 dr per 20 minutes.

The Millennium Internet Cafe (☎ 29 300, ⓔ millenniumcafepatmos@hotmail.com) is

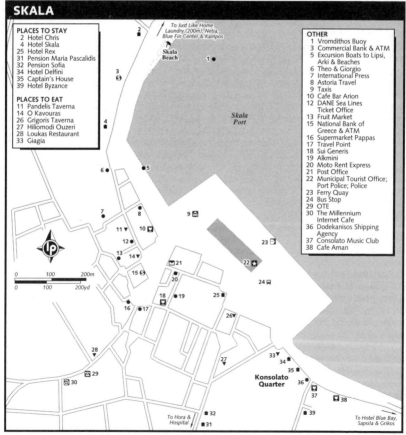

SKALA

PLACES TO STAY
2 Hotel Chris
4 Hotel Skala
25 Hotel Rex
31 Pension Maria Pascalidis
32 Pension Sofia
34 Hotel Delfini
35 Captain's House
39 Hotel Byzance

PLACES TO EAT
11 Pandelis Taverna
14 O Kavouras
26 Grigoris Taverna
27 Hiliomodi Ouzeri
28 Loukas Restaurant
33 Giagia

OTHER
1 Vromdithos Buoy
3 Commercial Bank & ATM
5 Excursion Boats to Lipsi, Arki & Beaches
6 Theo & Giorgio
7 International Press
8 Astoria Travel
9 Taxis
10 Cafe Bar Arion
12 DANE Sea Lines Ticket Office
13 Fruit Market
15 National Bank of Greece & ATM
16 Supermarket Pappas
17 Travel Point
18 Sui Generis
19 Alkmini
20 Moto Rent Express
21 Post Office
22 Municipal Tourist Office; Port Police; Police
23 Ferry Quay
24 Bus Stop
29 OTE
30 The Millennium Internet Cafe
36 Dodekanisos Shipping Agency
37 Consolato Music Club
38 Cafe Aman

To Just Like Home Laundry (200m), Netia, Blue Fin Center & Kampos

Skala Beach

Skala Port

0   100   200m
0   100   200yd

Konsolato Quarter

To Hora & Hospital

To Hotel Blue Bay, Sapsila & Grikos

the second, and is 50m past the OTE. Access charges here are a steeper 1500 dr for 30 minutes, or 2000 dr for one hour. It is open from 8.30 am to 10.30 pm daily and the access price includes a coffee or soft drink.

Travel Agencies Astoria Travel (☎ 31 205, fax 31 975), on the waterfront near the quay, and Travel Point (☎ 32 801, fax 32 802, e info@travelpoint.gr), just inland from the central square, are helpful. The latter has a room-finding service. The Dodekanisos Shipping Agency (☎ 31 314), at the southern end of the waterfront, sells tickets for the *Dodekanisos Express* catamaran. Tickets for DANE Lines and the *Nisos Kalymnos* are sold by agencies near the main square. Hydrofoil tickets are sold by a number of agencies, while G&A Ferries are handled by Astoria Travel.

Laundry Just Like Home Laundry (☎ 33 170) is at the northern end of the waterfront. Turn left up a small side street immediately after Skala's beach.

Medical Services The hospital (☎ 31 211) is 2km along the road to Hora.

Things to See & Do
If you look carefully at the northern end of the port you will see a solitary red buoy some 100m off the small town beach. This marks the location of the **vromolithos** (smelly rock), the underwater rock hazard said to be the petrified remains of the wicked Patmian wizard Yennoupas. See the boxed text 'The Evil Wizard of Patmos'.

Behind the town rises the **acropolis**, a rocky outcrop that once supported the island's original settlement (signposted from north of the harbour). Other than a more recent church and some ancient stone walls there is not much to see up here but the walk up and the views from the top are worth the effort.

Places to Stay – Budget
Patmos offers a wide range of accommodation catering to all tastes and pocket depths. However, owing to its popularity, Patmos can

The Evil Wizard of Patmos

At the northern end of Skala harbour on Patmos floats a red buoy, a few swimming strokes offshore, widely believed to mark the petrified remains of Patmos' own sorcerer, the evil wizard Yennoupas. Lying just beneath the surface of the water, this stack of rock is a potential shipping hazard, which not even drilling or dynamiting has been able to remove. Legend has it that while St John was on Patmos writing up his Gospel, a local wizard-cum-sorcerer by the name of Kynops ('dog-faced' in Greek) used to retrieve effigies of the dead from the seabed as a form of gruesome local entertainment. Kynops (known today by the derivative name Yennoupas) challenged John to a duel of miracles. John's response was to petrify Kynops while he was still searching for effigies underwater. The rock has since refused to be dislodged and it is believed that fish caught near here taste foul. A volcanic cave on the now inaccessible Cape Yennoupas is believed to have been Kynops/Yennoupas' lair when he was still fit to practise his own macabre form of Patmian sorcery.

be a hard place to find accommodation in July and August and advance bookings are highly recommended. Domatia owners usually gather en masse to meet the boats, hydrofoil and catamaran outside of high season.

Central If you are not scooped up by one of these domatia owners, there are several budget places along the Hora road. *Pension Sofia* (☎ 31 876), 250m up the Hora road on the left, has double/triple rooms with bathroom and balcony for 7500/8500 dr. The domatia sign is not obvious. Look high up and you will see it. A bit farther up the road, the *Pension Maria Pascalidis* (☎ 32 152) has comfortable single/double rooms available for 6500/8500 dr.

The long-standing budget option in the port is the D-class *Hotel Rex* (☎ 31 242) which offers basic, but reasonable single/double rooms for 7000/8500 dr with bathroom. It's on a narrow street opposite the cafeteria/passenger-transit building.

Netia If you turn right as you disembark into the port and walk about 800m past the yacht marina and power station you will come to the quieter Netia district which is home to a clutch of pleasant domatia or studios and at least one hotel. This is probably the best bet for visitors looking for reasonably priced accommodation and a modicum of peace and quiet.

Pension Sydney (☎ 31 689, fax 32 118), signposted from the main road, has single/double rooms for 10,000/12,000 dr with bathroom. The nearby *Pension Avgerinos* (☎/fax 32 118, mobile ☎ 09-4593 3632), run by the same family, has doubles with superb views and bathroom for the same price.

Villa Knossos (☎ 32 189, fax 32 284), in a lovely garden, has immaculate rooms with bathroom, fridge and balcony. Doubles/triples are 14,000/15,000 dr. This place is also prominently signposted off the waterfront road. *Australis Appartments* (☎ 32 562, fax 32 284), in the same cluster of small hotels and run by the same owners, are well-appointed and easy to find. Apartments with a TV and fully equipped kitchenette are 15,000 dr for two people.

Australis Hotel (☎ 32 189), set amidst a leafy garden, offers standard hotel-sized singles/doubles for 12,500/15,000 dr, including breakfast. They also have larger rooms for up to six people.

Places to Stay – Mid-Range
One of the more pleasant and welcoming places to stay is *Hotel Blue Bay* (☎ 31 165, fax 32 303, e bluebayhotel@yahoo.com). This modern, breezy low-rise complex has clean, tastefully furnished air-conditioned single/double rooms for 14,500/18,000 dr. Manager Anna Karas lived in Australia for many years and now offers Aussie guests Vegemite at breakfast. An Internet service is available here (see Information earlier). Turn left at the quay and the hotel is 150m along on the right around the last bend in the road.

The C-class *Hotel Delfini* (☎ 32 060, fax 32 061) is one of a clutch of small hotels in the Konsolato quarter about 300m south of the ferry quay. This pleasant hotel has well-kept double rooms ranging in price from 12,000 dr to 18,500 dr. The front rooms have individual balconies with blue and white tables and cane chairs overlooking the street action. Immediately next door is the *Captain's House* (☎ 31 793, fax 34 077) with rates of 12,000/18,500 dr for singles/doubles. Almost hidden in a side street around the corner, *Hotel Byzance* (☎ 31 052, fax 31 663, e byzance@hol.gr) charges around 18,000/19,000 dr for its single/double rooms.

Moving northwards towards the Netia quarter, but more conveniently sited for access to the central action, is *Hotel Chris* (☎ 31 403, fax 31 877). Its rooms go for 11,000/17,000 dr. The small Skala Beach is almost right in front of the hotel, making it ideal for water lovers who don't want to go far to swim.

Skala's best hotel is the B-class *Hotel Skala* (☎ 31 343, fax 31 747), discretely set back from the waterfront. Rates are 20,000/27,000 dr, including breakfast, and there's a swimming pool.

Places to Eat
There is a wide range of eating choices in Skala. Reckon on about 2000 dr to 3000 dr per person for a meat-based meal with salad and wine.

For excellent seafood, sea urchins and a variety of imaginative mezedes try *Hiliomodi Ouzeri* (☎ 34 080), 50m up the Hora road. Dining is in a leafy, narrow street at the back of the restaurant. The tasty 'variety of mezedes plate' is excellent value at 2200 dr.

Grigoris Taverna (☎ 31 515), on the corner of the Hora road by the ferry quay, gets a universal thumbs-up from Greeks and foreign visitors alike. Its wide variety of *mayirefta* and grilled dishes and its food quality and prices – not to mention its busy streetside location close to the harbour – make it an excellent choice for either lunch or dinner. Main dishes go for around 1300 dr.

O Kavouras (☎ 31 422) is unassuming and unpretentious, though its central location on the main square does attract more than its share of the tourist trade. *Pandelis Taverna* (☎ 31 230), one block inland from the waterfront, caters admirably well to cruise groups and tourists with efficient service and busy street dining. In the back streets away from the bustle is the less frenetic and more relaxed *Loukas Restaurant* (☎ 31 832) where grilled dishes are served in a leafy, shaded garden. Prices at all three are mid-range.

For an upmarket change try the following three places. *Giagia* (☎ 33 226) is a classy Indonesian restaurant in the Konsolato quarter. Run by Dutch couple Fred and Sophie Brinkman, you can sample excellent *nasi goreng* for 2800 dr or a beef *rendang* for 2500 dr. About 2km south of Skala, at Sapsila, *Benetos* (☎ 33 089) is considered by many to be Patmos' premier restaurant. This waterside eatery is on the expensive side, but offers a wide range of imaginative Mediterranean-influenced dishes.

The best fish on the island is to be had at *To Kyma* (☎ 31 192) on the minuscule Aspri Beach, about 30 to 40 minutes' walk from Skala. This rather out-of-the-way and little-known fish taverna has perhaps the most evocative dining ambience on the island. Tables sit next to the water on a rock-enclosed dining area. It's open in the evening only.

Self-catering
There are two excellent *bakeries* on the square and the *Supermarket Pappas*, 50m west of the main square, is remarkably well-stocked with items not normally found on Greek islands. You can even find coconut milk and spices if you fancy rustling up a South-east Asian dish of your own. Nearby is a busy fruit market.

Entertainment
The waterfront *Cafe Bar Arion* is great for people-watching, and is a popular evening haunt for young people, Greek and foreign alike. It also serves decent snacks. Skala's music nightlife revolves around *Sui Generis,* a prominently signposted music bar in central Skala. With its interior wooden balconies, stone arches and funky blue, high wooden chairs, Sui Generis is a hip joint to meet and be met.

Cafe Aman, in Konsolato, is more a place to sit outside on the tree-shaded patio and relax to music while nursing a cold Heineken or cocktail. It also serves food, but delivery can be very slow on busy nights. It's open all day. Almost next door is the *Consolato Music Club*. Like Sui Generis, this place caters more to the party crowd and opens late to even later.

Shopping
Shoppers will love Patmos. There is an eclectic choice of shops and boutiques purveying items such as Lalaounis jewellery and worry beads. Your choice is only limited or enhanced by your budget. Fine ceramics and pottery, paintings and etchings, rugs and wall hangings are for sale. Byzantine art and silverware can be found at the classy Alkmini (☎ 33 109) very close to the main square. Australian-Greek owner Mina Karavis might give you her own tips on where to eat and what to see.

Skin divers and snorkellers might want to check out the good stock of equipment at the Blue Fin Center (☎/fax 31 251), halfway between central Skala and Netia.

MONASTERIES & HORA
The immense **Monastery of St John the Theologian**, with buttressed grey walls, crowns the island of Patmos. In 1999 this splendid edifice and the hilltop village of Hora were accorded Unesco World Heritage listing. A 4km asphalt road leads in from Skala, but many people prefer to walk up the Byzantine path. To do this, walk up the Skala-Hora road and take the steps to the right, 100m beyond the far side of the football field. The path begins opposite the top of these steps.

A little way along, a dirt path to the left leads through pine trees to the **Monastery of the Apocalypse**, built around the cave where St John received his divine revelation. It is in all honesty a fairly spiritual place, despite the constant procession of visitors, and you may be fortunate to chance upon a religious service taking place. The detailed and fascinating description of the cave delivered in hushed and measured tones by the lay custodian in both English and Greek is worth listening to. Opening times are 8 am to 1 pm Monday to Saturday,

8 am to noon Sunday and 4 to 6 pm on Tuesday, Thursday and Sunday. Photography is not allowed inside the cave.

To rejoin the Byzantine path, walk across the monastery's carpark and bear left onto the (uphill) asphalt road. After 60m, turn sharp left onto an asphalt road, and almost immediately the path veers off to the right. Soon you will reach the main road again. Cross straight over and continue ahead to reach Hora and the Monastery of St John the Theologian.

The finest frescoes of this monastery are those in the outer narthex. The priceless contents in the monastery's treasury include icons, ecclesiastical ornaments, embroideries and pendants made of precious stones. Opening times are the same as for the Monastery of the Apocalypse. Admission to the treasury is 1000 dr.

Huddled around the monastery are the immaculate whitewashed houses of **Hora**. The houses are a legacy of the island's great wealth of the 17th and 18th centuries. Some of them have been bought and renovated by wealthy Greeks and foreigners. Strolling these narrow streets at any time of the day and especially at night is a marvellous activity, for no brash tourist displays pervade here. During the day you could almost be forgiven for thinking that you are the only person in Hora, such is the all-pervading quiet and stillness.

Places to Stay

There are no signs for hotels or independent domatia in Hora. There is accommodation but it is expensive and the best places are pre-booked months in advance. If you wish to stay in Hora, contact Travel Point in Skala (see Information in the Skala section for details). They have at least 10 traditional houses in Hora that can be booked online. They accommodate four to eight people and range in price from 46,000 dr to 125,000 dr per day in high season. You can view and book them yourself at www.travelpoint.gr.

Places to Eat – Budget

The Aphrodite Pastry Shop on the ramp leading up to the monastery is cheap and quick, with filling spinach turnovers and cheese pies. Follow that with coffee and ice cream. Nearby and enjoying good views down to Skala is *Pantheon Cafe Restaurant* where the owner grills octopus on a mini barbecue and also serves up excellent kalamari and meatballs. Prices are very reasonable. On the road leading from here to the signposted main square (Centric Sqare) is *Estiatorio Ipiros*, a small place that doesn't get too busy. The grilled octopus on a barbecue is best washed down with a small carafe (or two) of ouzo.

The best dining views from Hora are afforded by *To Balkoni* (☎ 32 115), meaning 'balcony'. The views at night down to Skala are stunning. The food is not too expensive – main dishes run from 1600 dr to 2000 dr – and beef liver with onions (1600 dr) is one of their specials.

Places to Eat – Mid-Range

Vangelis Taverna (☎ 31 967), on the central square, with a roof garden at the back, is deservedly popular. Reaching this restaurant at night is like stepping into an illuminated film set with tables and chairs spread out around the square. Good menu choices are *bekri mezes* (pork cubes in a spicy sauce with vegetables) and *spetsofaï* (similar, but with rustic sausage instead of pork). The best bet is *gourounopoulo se ladoharto* (suckling pig roasted in greaseproof paper, a slow-cooked, succulent dish). Expect to pay around 10,000 dr for a good meal for two with a bottle of wine.

The elegant *Patmian House* (☎ 31 180) on Plateia Xanthou is in a restored mansion and is another excellent restaurant, albeit in a quieter and slightly less colourful quarter of Hora. The cuisine is a French-Greek melange with delicacies such as pan-seared jumbo prawns flamed in ouzo (3900 dr), fillet of beef flambé (4200 dr), or a simple mousakas (1900 dr). It's open evenings only from 7.30 pm onwards. Reservations are recommended.

Entertainment

Hora has at least a couple of decent bars that make the trip up here at night worthwhile.

The *Stoa*, sharing space on the central square with Vangelis Taverna, is an arty, neat night spot with arched stone interior walls or tables out on the square. Before you reach Stoa, *Atsivi* is upstairs in an old traditional Hora house and is favoured mainly by locals.

Shopping

Like Skala, Hora has its fair share of arty boutiques. Sokaki (☎ 34 119), near the Pantheon Cafe Restaurant, is one of the better ones with an eclectic collection of Byzantine icons and candle holders as well as other high-class Byzantine artefacts.

NORTH OF SKALA

The area north of Skala attracts the greater proportion of visitors by far. Most of Patmos' beaches are here along with the village of Kambos, its third major settlement, and a series of small farming communities and sometimes exposed bays that see little tourism. All are easily accessible by motorbike or scooter. Car drivers may have some difficulty in parking or turning in the often narrow confines near the sheltered beaches of the south side of the northern peninsula of Patmos.

Meloï Beach

The pleasant, tree-shaded Meloï Beach is just 2km to the north-east of Skala, along a turn-off from the main road. It's easily reached on foot (30 minutes) and is home to Patmos' only camping ground, *Stefanos Camping* (☎ 31 821). It has bamboo-shaded sites, a minimarket, cafe/bar and motorcycle rental facilities. Camping rates are 1300 dr for an adult and 600 dr for a tent. The rainbow-coloured minibus meets most boats. Next to the well signposted Taverna Meloï there are basic *domatia* (☎ 31 213, 31 247), with doubles for 7000 dr. There are some newer rooms nearby, where doubles with bathroom are 9000 dr. The luxury B-class *Porto Scoutari* (☎ 33 124, fax 33 175, e elias@12net.gr) at Meloï has double/ triple studios for around 26,000/30,000 dr. The excellent *Taverna Meloï* (☎ 31 888) on Meloï Beach serves up tasty traditional Greek dishes.

Backtrack to the main road and travel another 2km and you will reach the popular **Agriolivado Beach**, via a signposted turn-off to the right. There are beach umbrellas and loungers for hire and ample parking. The beach is a pebble and sand mix and the water is clean and sheltered from prevailing winds. *Glaros Taverna* (☎ 32 348) on Agriolivado Beach is worth a visit.

Kambos Beach

The next beach along is Kambos Beach, the sea annexe of the eponymous village you pass through before descending to the sea. This is Patmos' most lively beach and attracts a domestic, mainly young, Greek clientele as well as a scattering of foreign visitors. The beach is gravelly sand, but affords ample natural shade and is well served by bars and restaurants as well as public transport. Water sports can be enjoyed here too, with windsurfing and tube rides being prominently on offer.

The owners of *George's Place* snack bar (☎ 31 881) offer an unofficial room-letting service. The luxurious B-class *Patmos Paradise* (☎ 32 624, fax 32 740) has singles/ doubles for 22,000/27,000 dr.

There are a couple of places on the main square for lunch or an evening meal. Of the two, *Panagos Restaurant* (☎ 31 076) is the better, or at least keeps more predictable hours. The *Kafe* next door serves breakfast and doubles as a bar in the evening. On Kambos Beach there is a wider choice. Of the eateries *Ta Kavourakia* (☎ 31 745) at the northern end seems to pull the most customers. *George's Place* (☎ 31 881), hidden away slightly on the northern end of the beach, serves light snacks and drinks and attracts a mainly Greek clientele who gather to play backgammon to a background of hip, laid-back music.

Other Beaches

Vagia Beach, next along, is reached by a steepish cement-paved road. There is limited vehicle parking, but good natural shade from a stand of trees backing the pebbly beach. *Cafe Vagia* (☎ 31 658), overlooking Vagia Beach, has great food and views.

Livadi tou Geranou Beach is not obviously signposted but can be seen down to the right as you skirt the bay. More obvious but again with tricky parking and turning is the eastern extension of Livadi tou Geranou Beach where there is a restaurant as well as umbrellas and loungers for hire. The small islet of **Agios Georgios**, with its tiny chapel opposite the beach, is a good swimming spot. This is probably the best beach for snorkelling.

The north coast beaches are less appealing, mainly because they are not as well developed and are more exposed to the prevailing north wind. **Lambi Beach** attracts the bulk of visitors and can be very calm on the rare occasions when the wind comes from the south. It is covered in many small multi-hued pebbles, has some basic accommodation and a couple of seasonal tavernas. *Psistaria Leonidas (☎ 31 490)* rustles up a wide range of home-made mayirefta dishes, various fish of the day plates and highly recommended saganaki.

Livadi Kalogiron Beach is an exposed, seaweed-strewn stretch of sand and pebbles with one caravan-style cantina serving the few visitors that make it this far out of the way. **Lefkes Beach**, reached by a signposted road before Kambos is an undeveloped gravelly beach with no facilities whatsoever, though there is a small boat anchorage and tree shade for its few visitors.

SOUTH OF SKALA
The area to the south of Skala offers more opportunities for exploration, a small self-contained resort village for those who like it quiet, some excellent if slightly remote accommodation options suited to visitors with independent transport, and the chance to take a brisk stroll to one of Patmos' better if less accessible beaches.

Sapsila
Sapsila is the first community you come to about 3km south of Skala. It's a rather scattered village with no real centre, but boasts a small, scraggly beach, some excellent studios/domatia and at least one upmarket accommodation option.

The beautiful rooms at *Mathios Studios (☎ 32 119, 32 583)* are *the* place to stay. There are seven self-contained studios set in a quiet, leafy garden set back 200m from Sapsila Beach. Double/triple studios go for 10,000/13,000 dr. Follow the sign near Mathios Studios to reach *Ennea Mouses (☎ 34 079, fax 33 151)*, a complex of tastefully and individually designed bungalows, each bearing names such as *Efterpi, Kalliopi* or *Erato*. The complex has a pool and bar/snack bar. Breakfast is delivered to your apartment. Rooms are a pricey 44,000 dr per double and pre-booking is recommended.

Grikos
Over the hill from Sapsila you come to Grikos, a small fishing village now serving as a rather low-key package resort with many of its studios and apartments being pre-booked by low-key tour groups. Grikos is primarily a family village and its beach offers shallow, warm water ideal for toddlers and timid bathers.

The cheapest accommodation in Grikos are the *domatia (☎ 31 302)* of Restaurant o Stamatis, with double rooms for a still expensive 12,000 dr. Right on the beach, *Hotel Silver Beach (☎ 32 652, fax 32 826)* has 16 rooms – eight with sea views and eight with breezier garden views. The rooms are smallish but otherwise comfortable and clean. Doubles/triples are 15,000/19,000 dr.

Rooms Flisvos & Apolafsi (☎ 31 380, fax 32 094) are in fact two separate complexes comprising comfortable and airy rooms for two people with shared bathroom (8000 dr) and fully equipped three-person studio apartments with great views for 15,000 dr. These are run by the owners of the Flisvos restaurant, Floros and Pavlos Vamvakos.

The *Restaurant o Stamatis (☎ 31 302)* is the most obvious eating choice in Grikos. The food is good and medium-priced, but the dark brown decor is a little grim. For a lighter touch, look to the *Oasis (☎ 31 847)*, 50m to the right on the beach. Its blue and white decor complements its breezy beachside appeal while fish features prominently on the menu. Worth the extra effort to find is the *Flisvos Restaurant (☎ 31 764)* on the

The views overlooking Platanos on Leros are well worth the walk.

Windmill, Agia Marina

With annual miracles and flocks of pilgrims, religion still plays an important role on Lipsi.

Fishing for dinner in Leros

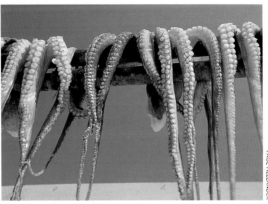

Throw it on the grill until crispy and serve with a glass of ouzo.

Idyllic Tiganakia Bay, Arki

The distinctive multi-coloured pebbles on Patmos' Lambi Beach

On the town, Patmos

And the band played on, Lipsi

A mini fleet of caiques await passengers at Marathi Island harbour.

bend at the high point overlooking Grikos Bay. It's a well-shaded, modern eatery where you can still eat cheaply. Stuffed aubergine slippers, chips and a half-litre carafe of fruity, slightly spritzig draft wine will cost no more than 2300 dr.

Other Beaches
Farther south past the Flisvos Restaurant in Grikos, the beach widens out and is shaded by a long stand of tamarisk trees. **Petra Beach**, 1km along, is pebbly and has no shade other than that provided by rented umbrellas. The strange **Kalikatsos Rock**, a large volcanic outcrop to the east side of the beach, provides some distraction for active limbs to climb on. There are small caves in the rock tunnelled out by Paleo-Christian hermits.

The trans-island road eventually winds down to the small shipyard settlement of **Diakofti** past a promising-looking beach settlement at **Alykes** (salt pans), which has neither restaurant nor accommodation. Diakofti has a small restaurant on the south side of **Stavros Bay** just before the small parking lot that marks the start of a walking trail to **Psili Ammos Beach**. The trail is rocky but generally easy – solid shoes are recommended – and it takes about 40 minutes to reach Psili Ammos. The fine sand beach (as per its Greek name) sports a well-patronised seasonal taverna for hungry bathers.

The tourist maps optimistically show a road leading to **Yennoupas Cave**, the supposed lair of the evil wizard (see boxed text 'The Evil Wizard of Patmos' earlier). In practice the whole peninsula on which the cave is located is now a large quarry and is closed off to visitors, so a drive out here will lead to nought.

Arki & Marathi
Αρκοί & Μαράθι

ARKI Αρκοί
☎ 0247 • 850 01 • pop 50

Tiny and almost forgotten, Arki (ar-**kee**) is home to a small number of souls who eke out a living from fishing and tourism. The short tourist season attracts a surprising number of people for solitude, walking, eating, sleeping and drinking. Yachties have discovered Arki and it is not uncommon to come across luxurious yachts bobbing at anchor in Arki's small harbour. Accommodation is limited but quite adequate and there is a steady stream of intrepid travellers – mainly Italians – who come for the simple offerings of a remote, rocky island in the sun. Away from its little settlement, the island seems almost mystical in its peace and stillness.

Orientation & Information
Arki, 5km north of Lipsi, is hilly with low shrubs but few trees. Its only settlement, the little port on the west coast, is also called Arki. One cement road links the port of Arki

Harley Heavies

On a hot summer's day in August in the mid-1990s, a small caïque hove to in the little harbour of Arki and with great difficulty off-loaded a large Harley Davidson motorcycle with Italian registration plates. The leather-clad owner, an Italian designer from Milan, was spending his summer island-hopping on his 'Hog' and was determined not to let a single island escape his rumbling attentions. To the great amusement of the gathered islanders he set about preparing for his great ride on Arki – an island he had heard was very popular among his fellow countrymen.

When he gestured to the now totally absorbed fishermen which was the highway out of town they pointed vaguely in the direction of Tiganakia Bay towards the south – essentially the only road out of the village. With a roar the Harley Hog took off and disappeared into a cloud of dust. Within 10 minutes the puzzled rider was back looking quite lost. 'Where is the highway?' demanded the driver. 'There is no highway!' replied the islanders, with a shrug of their communal shoulders.

Unabashed, the leather-clad biker took off his gloves and helmet, parked his now useless Hog on the quayside, pulled out a book and ordered a beer. He stayed two weeks and never rode his bike on Arki again.

with a small settlement to the south. There is one car on the island, a battered red Honda that the owner uses to transport goods to and from the port and his house. There's also an abandoned and rusting Land Rover.

There is no post office, OTE or police on the island, but there is a cardphone, which is quite often out of order. Mobile phone users can only pick up Cosmote from the harbour, but you should be able to pick up Telestet or Panafon if you walk up higher to the Church of Metamorfosis. Forget the Internet for a while if you come to Arki.

Things to See & Do

The **Church of Metamorfosis** stands on a hill behind the settlement. From its terrace there are superb views of Arki and its surrounding islets. The cement road between Taverna Trypas and Taverna Nikolaos leads to the path up to the church. The church is kept locked but ask a local if it's possible to look inside.

Several secluded sandy coves can be reached along a path skirting the north (right) side of the bay. To reach the path, walk around the last house at the far right of the bay, go through a little wooden gate in the stone wall near the sea and continue ahead.

Tiganakia Bay on the south-east coast has a good sandy beach. To walk there from Arki Village, take the cement road which skirts the left side of the bay. Continue along the dirt track passing the blue-domed church. At the end of the track, take the path ahead and go through a gate at the seaward end of a stone wall. Tiganakia Bay, reached by a network of goat tracks, lies at the far side of the headland. You will recognise it by the incredibly bright turquoise water and the offshore islets.

Places to Stay & Eat

Arki has three tavernas, two of which have double rooms with bathroom for 8000 dr per night for two nights or 10,000 dr for one night. *O Trypas Taverna & Rooms* (☎ 32 230) is to the right of the quay, as you face inland. The owner, Manolis, speaks English and treats diners to a soothing array of eclectic music that seems to emanate from the trees. He starts with New Age in the morning and reaches jazz level by early evening. Good menu suggestions are *fasolia mavromatika* (black-eyed beans) and *pastos tou Trypa* (a kind of salted fish dish).

Taverna Nikolaos Rooms (☎ 32 477) is adjacent to it. Try his potatoes *au gratin*. This place is open all year and has rooms to rent for a similar rate as O Trypas. The third taverna, *Taverna Manolas*, opposite the quay, is also highly commendable. Nektaria, the delightful owner, doesn't speak English, but enjoys giving customers impromptu Greek lessons.

Getting There & Away

It is not easy to get to Arki. The best way is by the twice-weekly summer caïque *Delfini* (☎ 31 995/371) from Patmos. The trip takes about 1½ hours, costs 4000 dr return and can get very choppy in the open waters between Patmos and the small islet of Marathi that you reach before Arki itself. On the other days you disembark at the island of Marathi and transfer to a local caïque, run by the Zorba lookalike, Captain Vasilis. His caïque meets the *Delfini* and leaves Marathi at 11.30 am. It returns to Marathi from Arki at 2.45 pm. The short trip takes only 15 minutes.

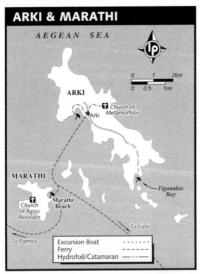

ARKI & MARATHI

AEGEAN SEA

0   1   2km
0   0.5   1mi

ARKI

Church of Metamorfosis

Arki

MARATHI

Church of Agios Nikolaos

Marathi Beach

Tiganakia Bay

To Lipsi

To Patmos

Excursion Boat ......
Ferry ——
Hydrofoil/Catamaran — — —

In theory the F/B *Nisos Kalymnos* calls on Wednesday but this depends entirely on the weather. The small harbour is too small for large boats so you are supposed to transfer to a local caïque to get to Arki. This means pre-warning the captain of the *Nisos Kalymnos* who has to radio ahead for a rendezvous and he is not always keen to do this if the weather is rough.

Sturdy and often luxurious yachts make their way to Arki and you may be able to hitch a ride in or out on one of these if you are persistent, or just plain lucky.

A new harbour is slowly being built to accommodate larger boats and hydrofoils, but don't hold your breath. It is likely to be a while before it is completed.

MARATHI Μαράθι
☎ 0247 • 850 01 • pop 4

Marathi (mah-**ra**-thi) is the largest of Arki's satellite islets. Before WWII it had a dozen or so inhabitants, but now has only one family. The old settlement, with the immaculate little chapel of Agios Nikolaos, stands on a hill above the harbour reached by the grandly-named Leoforos Agiou Nikolaou (St Nikolaos' Avenue), a duck-, hen- and goat-riddled alleyway which you follow for 10 minutes to reach the summit of the island. Marathi has a long, narrow sandy beach and clean languid water, but there is little to do on the island except unwind, eat, drink, sleep and swim. Bring plenty of books if you want to keep your mind occupied.

Marathi has two tavernas, both of which rent out rooms. *Taverna Mihalis (☎ 31 580)*, owned by the island's only permanent inhabitants, is the most obvious place immediately in front of the landing jetty. Hirsute owner Mihalis is a bit of a bohemian character (you would have to be to live on Marathi permanently), but makes you feel very welcome. His rooms are 8000 dr for a double. The other taverna and domatia owner prefers not to be listed in this guidebook.

Getting There & Away
Marathi shares the same transport links as Arki, but has no plans to receive larger boats or hydrofoils in the foreseeable future.

Agathonisi
Αγαθονήσι

☎ 0247 • postcode 850 01 • pop 112

If you are really looking for a getaway place with enough creature comforts to satisfy your basic needs – eating and sleeping – and minimum distractions to remind you that there is a busy frenetic world beyond the horizon then come to Agathonisi (agha-tho-**ni**-si). This sun-bleached, often ignored speck of rock just over an hour's sail south of Samos attracts yachties, serious island hoppers, the plain curious and latter-day Robinson Crusoes all seeking what Agathonisi has to offer – simple peace and quiet. Bring a stack of novels to this island and relax.

Agathonisi, meaning 'Virtuous Island', is the most northerly isle in the Dodecanese archipelago. The island was known historically as 'Yetoussa' and alternatively as 'Gaïdouronisi' (*gaïdaros* means donkey in Greek), ostensibly for its tenuous similarity with the outline of a donkey. There are only three settlements of any stature on the island: the little port of Agios Georgios, the

AGATHONISI

Excursion Boat ·······
Ferry
Hydrofoil/Catamaran — — —

AEGEAN
SEA

0   1   2km
0 0.5 1mi

PSATHONISI

Katholiko

AGATHONISI

Agios Georgios
Hohlia   Mikro
Bay   Horio
Megalo Horio   Church of
Agios Nikolaos
Spilia Beach

To Samos
Tholos Beach

To Lipsi & Patmos

KOUNELONISI

uphill and inland village of Megalo Horio and the smaller settlement of Mikro Horio – all of which are less than 1km apart.

Getting There & Away

Ferry Despite being off the main routes Agathonisi gets just enough transport links to keep the island in touch with the outside world, though only two small ferry companies keep this link open. They are Kalymnos Shipping, who run the F/B *Nisos Kalymnos*, and Miniotis Lines (☎ 0271-24 670, fax 25 371, e miniotis@compulink.gr), who usually send along the smaller F/B *Hioni*.

The following table will give you an overview of the main departures.

destination	duration	price	frequency
Astypalea	9 hours	4500 dr	2 weekly
Chios	8 hours	4000 dr	2 weekly
Kalymnos	5¾ hours	2600 dr	2 weekly
Leros	4¼ hours	2200 dr	2 weekly
Patmos	1¾ hours	1600 dr	4 weekly
Samos	1¼ hours	1450 dr	4 weekly

The twice-weekly supply boat from Samos also takes passengers, but its schedule is subject to change – check with the police officer or locals.

Hydrofoil A hydrofoil running to and from Samos-Pythagorio (30 minutes, 2800 dr), Patmos (one hour, 3200 dr), Lipsi (1½ hours, 3000 dr), Leros (1¾ hours, 4300 dr), Kalymnos (2½ hours, 5000 dr) and Kos (3¼ hours, 5200 dr) calls in every day in summer except Sunday.

Adventurous day-trippers from Patmos can visit Agathonisi using either the hydrofoil or the F/B *Nisos Kalymnos*. This will give you between three and four hours respectively to visit the island before returning to Patmos. This is enough time for an exploratory walk, a swim and a relaxed lunch.

Getting Around

There is no public transport. It takes 25 minutes of solid uphill walking to reach Megalo Horio – no mean feat on a hot day. There are cars on the island though most islanders use more practical flatbed utility trucks for shift-

ing goods – and islanders – up and down the steep road linking Agios Georgios with Megalo Horio. An asphalt road links Megalo Horio with the desultory harbour of Katholiko on the northern side of the island.

AGIOS GEORGIOS
Άγιος Γεώργιος

The village of Agios Georgios (**agh**-ios ye-or-yi-os) is where most of your activity (or inactivity) will take place. It hosts the only accommodation on the island and most of the restaurants. The village is draped attractively around the end of a short fjord-like bay on the south side of the island. The arrival of the ferry or hydrofoil is the most exciting event of the day. When that has departed the village reverts to its almost dreamlike torpor and visitors settle down once more to a book and a beer, or an indolent swim at the pebbly beach. The more active visitors may walk round to **Spilia Beach**, reached along the track around the west side of the bay.

Orientation & Information

Boats dock at Agios Georgios from where cement roads ascend steeply right (facing inland) to Megalo Horio and left to Mikro Horio. There is no tourist information office, post office, bank or OTE, but there are cardphones.

Ferry and hydrofoil tickets are sold by the roaming agent Savvas Kamitsis (mobile ☎ 09-3257 5121) who can normally be found selling tickets at either Pension Maria Kamitsi or at the Glaros Restaurant.

The one police officer, who is also the port police officer and customs officer, has an office in the white building at the beginning of the Megalo Horio road.

Places to Stay

All the accommodation in Agathonisi is based at the port of Agios Georgios. While it is basic, it's all clean and comfortable. The tourist season is nominally only during July and August, but most if not all of these places will be open from as early as April until at least October.

Agios Georgios has four pensions. *Pension Maria Kamitsi (☎/fax 29 003)* is run by former mayor of Agathonisi and ferry ticket agent Savvas Kamitsis and his wife Maria. The establishment is easy to find and is pleasant and friendly. Double rooms are 7000 dr. *Theologias Rooms* (☎ 29 005) is next door on the harbourfront and is another good option. Double rooms are 7000 dr.

Domatia Giannis (☎ 29 062) has the newest rooms on the scene and charge a little extra (8000 dr) for one of seven comfortable rooms, each of which takes between three and four people. They are above the restaurant of the same name. *George's Pension* (☎ 29 007) is set back a little from the harbourfront and tends to operate only when there is an overspill of guests from the other establishments. George charges 7000 dr for a double room.

Places to Eat

There are four restaurants, all close to each other and all clustered around the east side of the little port. *Glaros Restaurant* (☎ 29 062) probably has the best location and most appealing ambience. The barbecue-grilled fish is excellent and the owners suggest diners ask for *markakia* when available. These are feta cheese fingers rolled in vine leaves with a special sauce (1400 dr). The owners, Voula and Giannis, speak English.

George's Taverna (☎ 29 007) is nearest the ferry quay and is also a very good restaurant by all accounts. George and his German wife speak English. *Restaurant Limanaki* (☎ 29 066), between the two, is the locals' favourite, serving well prepared grilled fish. *Restaurant I Irini* (☎ 29 054) is open all year round.

AROUND AGATHONISI

Megalo Horio is Agathonisi's biggest village. It's a no-nonsense workaday village, not used to many outsiders but always happy and curious to see them. The main reason for coming here is to see what the village looks like and perhaps to change venue once in a while for lunch or dinner.

Restaurant I Irini (☎ 29 054), named after the owner's daughter Irini, is an obvious choice and is open all year. Close by on the small central square is another small eatery, *Kafeneio/Pantopoleio Ta 13 Adelfia*, run by a proud elderly couple who have produced 13 children – they will pronounce with a big smile that all are alive and well.

Tholos Beach and **Katholiko** are reached by taking the cement road from Megalo Horio. At the T-junction turn left to reach Tholos Beach, near the fish farm that supplies Italy with produce. You can also visit the little **Church of Agios Nikolaos**; ask a local if it's possible to look inside.

Katholiko, an abandoned fishing hamlet, is reached by turning left at the T-junction. There's not much to see but the walk is worth it for the views.

Language

The Greek language is probably the oldest European language, with an oral tradition of 4000 years and a written tradition of approximately 3000 years. Its evolution over the four millennia was characterised by its strength during the golden age of Athens and the Democracy (mid-5th century BC); its use as a lingua franca throughout the Middle Eastern world, spread by Alexander the Great and his successors as far as India during the Hellenistic period (330 BC to AD100); its adaptation as the language of the new religion, Christianity; its use as the official language of the Eastern Roman Empire; and its eventual proclamation as the language of the Byzantine Empire (380–1453).

Greek maintained its status and prestige during the rise of the European Renaissance and was employed as the linguistic perspective for all contemporary sciences and terminologies during the period of Enlightenment. Today, Greek constitutes a large part of the vocabulary of any Indo-European language, and much of the lexicon of any scientific repertoire.

The modern Greek language is a southern Greek dialect which is now used by most Greek speakers both in Greece and abroad. It is the result of an intralinguistic influence and synthesis of the ancient vocabulary combined with words from Greek regional dialects, namely Cretan, Cypriot and Macedonian.

Those wishing to delve a little deeper into the language should get a copy of Lonely Planet's *Greek phrasebook*.

Pronunciation

All Greek words of two or more syllables have an acute accent which indicates where the stress falls. For instance, άγαλμα (statue) is pronounced **agh**alma, and αγάπη (love) is pronounced *agh**api***. In the following transliterations, bold lettering indicates word stress. Note also that **dh** is pronounced as 'th' in 'then', and **gh** is a softer, slightly guttural version of 'g'.

Greetings & Civilities

Hello.
| **ya**sas | Γειά σας. |
| **ya**su | Γειά σου. (informal) |

Goodbye.
| *andio* | Αντίο. |

Good morning.
| *kali**mera*** | Καλημέρα. |

Good afternoon.
| **he**rete | Χαίρετε. |

Good evening.
| *kalis**pera*** | Καλησπέρα. |

Good night.
| *kali**nihta*** | Καληνύχτα. |

Please.
| *paraka**lo*** | Παρακαλώ. |

Thank you.
| *efhari**sto*** | Ευχαριστώ. |

Yes.
| *ne* | Ναι. |

No.
| **ohi** | Οχι. |

Sorry. (excuse me, forgive me)
| *sigh**nomi*** | Συγγνώμη. |

How are you?
| *ti **kanete**?* | Τι κάνετε; |
| *ti **kanis**?* | Τι κάνεις; (informal) |

I'm well, thanks.
| *kala efhari**sto*** | Καλά ευχαριστώ. |

Essentials

Do you speak English?
| *mi**late** angli**ka**?* | Μιλάτε Αγγλικά; |

I understand.
| *katala**veno*** | Καταλαβαίνω. |

I don't understand.
| *dhen katala**veno*** | Δεν καταλαβαίνω. |

Where is ...?
| *pou ine ...?* | Πού είναι ...; |

How much?
| **poso** kani? | Πόσο κάνει; |

When?
| **pote**? | Πότε; |

The Greek Alphabet & Pronunciation

Greek	Pronunciation Guide		Example		
A α	a	as in 'father'	αγάπη	*agha*pi	love
B β	v	as in 'vine'	βήμα	*vi*ma	step
Γ γ	gh	like a rough 'g'	γάτα	*gha*ta	cat
	y	as in 'yes'	για	*ya*	for
Δ δ	dh	as in 'there'	δέμα	*dhe*ma	parcel
E ε	e	as in 'egg'	ένας	*enas*	one (m)
Z ζ	z	as in 'zoo'	ζώο	*zoo*	animal
H η	i	as in 'feet'	ήταν	*itan*	was
Θ θ	th	as in 'throw'	θέμα	*the*ma	theme
I ι	i	as in 'feet'	ίδιος	*idhyos*	same
K κ	k	as in 'kite'	καλά	*kala*	well
Λ λ	l	as in 'leg'	λάθος	*la*thos	mistake
M μ	m	as in 'man'	μαμά	*mama*	mother
N ν	n	as in 'net'	νερό	*nero*	water
Ξ ξ	x	as in 'ox'	ξύδι	*ksi*dhi	vinegar
O o	o	as in 'hot'	όλα	*ola*	all
Π π	p	as in 'pup'	πάω	*pao*	I go
P ρ	r	as in 'road'	ρέμα	*re*ma	stream
		a slightly trilled 'r'	ρόδα	*ro*dha	tyre
Σ σ, ς	s	as in 'sand'	σημάδι	*sima*dhi	mark
T τ	t	as in 'tap'	τόπι	*to*pi	ball
Υ υ	i	as in 'feet'	ύστερα	*istera*	after
Φ φ	f	as in 'find'	φύλλο	*filo*	leaf
X χ	h	as the 'ch' in Scottish *loch*, or like a rough 'h'	χάνω	*ha*no	I lose
			χέρι	*he*ri	hand
Ψ ψ	ps	as in 'lapse'	ψωμί	*psomi*	bread
Ω ω	o	as in 'hot'	ώρα	*ora*	time

Combinations of Letters

The combinations of letters shown here are pronounced as follows:

Greek	Pronunciation Guide		Example		
ει	i	as in 'feet'	είδα	*idha*	I saw
οι	i	as in 'feet'	οικόπεδο	*iko*pedho	land
αι	e	as in 'bet'	αίμα	*ema*	blood
ου	u	as in 'mood'	πού	*pou*	who/what
μπ	b	as in 'beer'	μπάλα	*bala*	ball
	mb	as in 'amber'	κάμπος	*kam*bos	forest
ντ	d	as in 'dot'	ντουλάπα	*doula*pa	wardrobe
	nd	as in 'bend'	πέντε	*pen*de	five
γκ	g	as in 'God'	γκάζι	*ga*zi	gas
γγ	ng	as in 'angle'	αγγελία	*angeli*a	classified
γξ	ks	as in 'minks'	σφιγξ	*sfinks*	sphynx
τζ	dz	as in 'hands'	τζάκι	*dza*ki	fireplace

The pairs of vowels shown above are pronounced separately if the first has an acute accent, or the second a dieresis, as in the examples below:

γαϊδουράκι	*gaidhoura*ki	little donkey
Κάιρο	*kai*ro	Cairo

Some Greek consonant sounds have no English equivalent. The υ of the groups αυ, ευ and ηυ is generally pronounced 'v'. The Greek question mark is represented with the English equivalent of a semicolon ';'.

Small Talk

What's your name?
pos sas lene?   Πώς σας λένε;
My name is ...
me lene ...   Με λένε ...
Where are you from?
apo pou iste?   Από πού είστε;

I'm from ...
ime apo ...   Είμαι από ...
America
tin ameriki   την Αμερική
Australia
tin afstralia   την Αυστραλία
England
tin anglia   την Αγγλία
Ireland
tin irlandhia   την Ιρλανδία
New Zealand
ti nea zilandhia   τη Νέα Ζηλανδία
Scotland
ti skotia   τη Σκωτία

How old are you?
poson hronon iste?   Πόσων χρονών είστε;
I'm ... years old.
ime ... hronon   Είμαι ... χρονών.

Getting Around

What time does the ... leave/arrive?
ti ora fevyi/ ftani to ...?   Τι ώρα φεύγει/ φτάνει το ...;

boat	*karavi*	καράβι
bus	*astiko*	αστικό
plane	*aeroplano*	αεροπλάνο

I'd like ...
tha ithela ...   Θα ήθελα ...
a return ticket
isitirio me epistrofi   εισιτήριο με επιστροφή
two tickets
dhio isitiria   δυο εισιτήρια
a student's fare
fititiko isitirio   φοιτητικό εισιτήριο
first class
proti thesi   πρώτη θέση

Signs

ΕΙΣΟΔΟΣ	Entry
ΕΞΟΔΟΣ	Exit
ΩΘΗΣΑΤΕ	Push
ΣΥΡΑΤΕ	Pull
ΓΥΝΑΙΚΩΝ	Women (toilets)
ΑΝΔΡΩΝ	Men (toilets)
ΝΟΣΟΚΟΜΕΙΟ	Hospital
ΑΣΤΥΝΟΜΙΑ	Police
ΑΠΑΓΟΡΕΥΕΤΑΙ	Prohibited
ΕΙΣΙΤΗΡΙΑ	Tickets

economy
touristiki thesi   τουριστική θέση

timetable
dhromologio   δρομολόγιο
taxi
taxi   ταξί

Where can I hire a car?
pou boro na nikyaso ena aftokinito?
Πού μπορώ να νοικιάσω ένα αυτοκίνητο;

Directions

How do I get to ...?
pos tha pao sto/ sti ...?   Πώς θα πάω στο/ στη ...;
Where is ...?
pou ine ...?   Πού είναι...;
Is it near?
ine konda?   Είναι κοντά;
Is it far?
ine makria?   Είναι μακριά;

straight ahead	*efthia*	ευθεία
left	*aristera*	αριστερά
right	*dexia*	δεξιά
behind	*piso*	πίσω
far	*makria*	μακριά
near	*konda*	κοντά
opposite	*apenandi*	απέναντι

Can you show me on the map?
borite na mou to dhixete sto harti?
Μπορείτε να μου το δείξετε στο χάρτη;

Around Town

I'm looking for (the) ...
  psahno ya ...
  Ψάχνω για ...

bank	*trapeza*	τράπεζα
beach	*paralia*	παραλία
castle	*kastro*	κάστρο
church	*ekklisia*	εκκλησία
... embassy	*tin ... presvia*	την ... πρεσβεία
market	*aghora*	αγορά
museum	*musio*	μουσείο
police	*astynomia*	αστυνομία
post office	*tahydhromio*	ταχυδρομείο
ruins	*arhea*	αρχαία

I want to exchange some money.
  thelo na exaryiroso lefta
  Θέλω να εξαργυρώσω λεφτά.

Accommodation

Where is ...?
  pou ine ...? Πού είναι ...;
I'd like ...
  thelo ena ... Θέλω ένα ...

a cheap hotel
  ftino xenodohio φτηνό ξενοδοχείο
a clean room
  katharo dhomatio καθαρό δωμάτιο
a good hotel
  kalo xenodohio καλό ξενοδοχείο
a camp site
  kamping κάμπιγκ

single	*mono*	μονό
double	*dhiplo*	διπλό
room	*dhomatio*	δωμάτιο
with bathroom	*me banio*	με μπάνιο
key	*klidhi*	κλειδί

How much is it ...?
  poso kani ...? Πόσο κάνει ...;
per night
  ti vradhya τη βραδυά
for ... nights
  ya ... vradhyez για ... βραδυές

Help!
  voithya! Βοήθεια!
Police!
  astynomia! Αστυνομία!
There's been an accident!
  eyine atihima Εγινε ατύχημα!
Call a doctor!
  fonaxte ena yatro! Φωνάξτε ένα ιατρό!
Call an ambulance!
  tilefoniste ya asthenoforo! Τηλεφωνήστε για ασθενοφόρο!
I'm ill.
  ime arostos (m) Είμαι άρρωστος
  ime arosti (f) Είμαι άρρωστη
I'm lost.
  eho hathi Εχω χαθεί
Thief!
  klefti! Κλέφτη!
Go away!
  fiye! Φύγε!
I've been raped!
  me viase kapyos Με βίασε κάποιος!
I've been robbed!
  meklepse kapyos Μ'έκλεψε κάποιος!
Where are the toilets?
  pou ine i toualetez? Πού είναι οι τουαλέτες;

Is breakfast included?
  symberilamvani ke pro-ino? Συμπεριλαμβάνει και πρωϊνό;
May I see it?
  boro na to dho? Μπορώ να το δω;
Where is the bathroom?
  pou ine tobanio? Πού είναι το μπάνιο;
It's expensive.
  ine akrivo Είναι ακριβό.
I'm leaving today.
  fevgho simera Φεύγω σήμερα.

Food & Drinks

breakfast	*pro-ino*	πρωϊνό
lunch	*mesimvrino*	μεσημβρινό
dinner	*vradhyno*	βραδυνό
beef	*vodhino*	βοδινό
bread	*psomi*	ψωμί
beer	*byra*	μπύρα
cheese	*tyri*	τυρί
chicken	*kotopoulo*	κοτόπουλο
Greek coffee	*ellinikos kafes*	ελληνικός καφές
iced coffee	*frappe*	φραππέ
lamb	*arni*	αρνί
milk	*ghala*	γάλα
(mineral)	*(metalliko)*	(μεταλλικό)
water	*nero*	νερό
tea	*tsai*	τσάι
wine	*krasi*	κρασί

I'm a vegetarian.
ime hortofaghos Είμαι χορτοφάγος.

Shopping

How much is it?
poso kani?
Πόσο κάνει;
I'm just looking.
aplos kitazo
Απλώς κοιτάζω.
I'd like to buy ...
thelo n'aghoraso ...
Θέλω ν'αγοράσω ...
Do you accept credit cards?
pernete pistotikez kartez?
Παίρνετε πιστωτικές κάρτες;
Could you lower the price?
borite na mou kanete mya kaliteri timi?
Μπορείτε να μου κάνετε μια καλύτερη τιμή;

Time & Dates

What time is it?
ti ora ine? Τι ώρα είναι;

It's ...	*ine ...*	είναι ...
1 o'clock	*mia i ora*	μία η ώρα
2 o'clock	*dhio i ora*	δύο η ώρα
7.30	*efta ke misi*	εφτά και μισή
am	*to pro-i*	το πρωί
pm	*to apoyevma*	το απόγευμα
today	*simera*	σήμερα

tonight	*apopse*	απόψε
now	*tora*	τώρα
yesterday	*hthes*	χθες
tomorrow	*avrio*	αύριο
Sunday	*kyriaki*	Κυριακή
Monday	*dheftera*	Δευτέρα
Tuesday	*triti*	Τρίτη
Wednesday	*tetarti*	Τετάρτη
Thursday	*pempti*	Πέμπτη
Friday	*paraskevi*	Παρασκευή
Saturday	*savato*	Σάββατο
January	*ianouarios*	Ιανουάριος
February	*fevrouarios*	Φεβρουάριος
March	*martios*	Μάρτιος
April	*aprilios*	Απρίλιος
May	*maios*	Μάιος
June	*iounios*	Ιούνιος
July	*ioulios*	Ιούλιος
August	*avghoustos*	Αύγουστος
September	*septemvrios*	Σεπτέμβριος
October	*oktovrios*	Οκτώβριος
November	*noemvrios*	Νοέμβριος
December	*dhekemvrios*	Δεκέμβριος

Health

I need a doctor.
hriazome yatro Χρειάζομαι ιατρό.
Can you take me to hospital?
borite na me pate Μπορείτε να με πάτε
sto nosokomio? στο νοσοκομείο;
I want something for ...
thelo kati ya ... Θέλω κάτι για ...
diarrhoea
dhiaria διάρροια
insect bites
tsimbimata apo τσιμπήματα από
endoma έντομα
travel sickness
naftia taxidhiou ναυτία ταξιδιού

aspirin
aspirini ασπιρίνη
condoms
profylaktika προφυλακτικά
(kapotez) (καπότες)
contact lenses
faki epafis φακοί επαφής
medical insurance
yatriki asfalya ιατρική ασφάλεια

Numbers

0	*midhen*	μηδέν
1	*enas*	ένας (m)
	mia	μία (f)
	ena	ένα (n)
2	*dhio*	δύο
3	*tris*	τρεις (m & f)
	tria	τρία (n)
4	*teseris*	τέσσερεις (m & f)
	tesera	τέσσερα (n)
5	*pende*	πέντε
6	*exi*	έξη
7	*epta*	επτά
8	*ohto*	οχτώ
9	*enea*	εννέα
10	*dheka*	δέκα

20	*ikosi*	είκοσι
30	*trianda*	τριάντα
40	*saranda*	σαράντα
50	*peninda*	πενήντα
60	*exinda*	εξήντα
70	*evdhominda*	εβδομήντα
80	*oghdhonda*	ογδόντα
90	*eneninda*	ενενήντα
100	*ekato*	εκατό
1000	*hilii*	χίλιοι (m)
	hiliez	χίλιες (f)
	hilia	χίλια (n)

one million
ena ekatomyrio ένα εκατομμύριο

Glossary

Achaean civilisation – see *Mycenaean civilisation*

acropolis – highest point of an ancient city

agia (f), agios (m), agii (pl) – saint

agora – commercial area of an ancient city; shopping precinct in modern Greece

amphora – large two-handled vase in which wine or oil was kept

Archaic period (800–480 BC) – also known as the Middle Age; period in which the city-states emerged from the 'dark age' and traded their way to wealth and power; the city-states were unified by a Greek alphabet and common cultural pursuits, engendering a sense of national identity

architrave – part of the *entablature* which rests on the columns of a temple

arhondika – 17th and 18th century AD mansions which belonged to arhons, the leading citizens of a town

Asia Minor – the Aegean littoral of Turkey centred around Izmir but also including İstanbul; formerly populated by Greeks

baglamas – miniature *bouzouki* with a tinny sound

ballos – dance popular in the Dodecanese

basilica – early Christian church

bouleuterion – council house

bouzouki – stringed lute-like instrument associated with rembetika music

bouzoukia – 'bouzoukis'; used to mean any nightclub where the bouzouki is played and low-grade blues songs are sung; see *skyladika*

buttress – support built against the outside of a wall

Byzantine Empire – characterised by the merging of Hellenistic culture and Christianity and named after Byzantium, the city on the Bosphorus which became the capital of the Roman Empire in AD 324; when the Roman Empire was formally divided in AD 395, Rome went into decline and the eastern capital, renamed Constantinople after Emperor Constantine I, flourished; the Byzantine Empire dissolved after the fall of Constantinople to the Turks in 1453

caïque – small, sturdy fishing boat often used to carry passengers

capital – top of a column

cella – room in a temple where the cult statue stood

city-states – states comprising a sovereign city and its dependencies; the city-states of Athens and Sparta were famous rivals

classical Greece – period in which the city-states reached the height of their power after the defeat of the Persians in the 5th century BC; ended with the decline of the city-states after the Peloponnesian Wars, and the expansionist aspirations of Philip II, King of Macedon (ruled 359–336 BC), and his son, Alexander the Great (ruled 336–323 BC)

Corinthian – order of Greek architecture recognisable by columns with bell-shaped *capitals* with sculpted elaborate ornaments based on acanthus leaves

cornice – the upper part of the *entablature*, extending beyond the frieze

crypt – lowest part of a church, often a burial chamber

Cycladic civilisation (3000–1100 BC) – civilisation that emerged following the settlement of Phoenician colonists on the Cycladic islands

Cyclopes – mythical one-eyed giants

DANE – *Dodekanisiaki Anonymi Naftiliaki Eteria* (Dodecanese Anonymous Shipping Company); main shipping line to the Dodecanese

Dark Age (1200–800 BC) – period in which Greece was under *Dorian* rule

delfini – dolphin; commonly used as a name for hydrofoils

diglossy – the existence of two forms of one language within a country; has existed in Greece for most of its modern history

dimarhio – town hall

Dimotiki – Demotic Greek language; the official spoken language of Greece

domatio (s), domatia (pl) – room; a cheap accommodation option available in most tourist areas

Dodecanese – an administrative group of islands; originally meaning 'twelve islands' there are in fact some 18 inhabited islands in the archipelago

Dorians – Hellenic warriors who invaded Greece around 1200 BC, demolishing the city-states and destroying the Mycenaean civilisation; heralded Greece's 'dark age', when the artistic and cultural advancements of the Mycenaeans and Minoans were abandoned; the Dorians later developed into land-holding aristocrats which encouraged the resurgence of independent city-states led by wealthy aristocrats

Doric – order of Greek architecture characterised by a column which has no base, a *fluted* shaft and a relatively plain capital, when compared with the flourishes evident on *Ionic* and *Corinthian* capitals

ELPA – *Elliniki Leshi Periigiseon & Aftokinitou*; Greek motoring and touring club

ELTA – *Ellinika Tahydromia*; Greek post office

entablature – part of a temple between the tops of the columns and the roof

EOT – *Ellinikos Organismos Tourismou*; national tourism organisation which has offices in most major towns

epitafios – picture on cloth of Christ on his bier

estiatorio – restaurant serving ready-made food as well as a la carte dishes

ET – *Elliniki Tileorasi*; state television company

evzones – famous border guards from the northern Greek village of Evzoni; they also guard the parliament building in Athens

Filiki Eteria – friendly society; a group of Greeks in exile; formed during Ottoman rule to organise an uprising against the Turks

fluted – (of a column) having vertical indentations on the shaft

FPA – *foros prostithemenis axias*; Value Added Tax, or VAT

frappé – iced coffee

frieze – part of the *entablature* which is above the *architrave*

galaktopoleio (s), galaktopoleia (pl) – a shop which sells dairy products

Genoese – people from Genoa, commercial adventurers who settled in the Dodecanese in the Middle Ages

Geometric period (1200–800 BC) – period characterised by pottery decorated with geometric designs; sometimes referred to as Greece's 'dark age'

GNTO – Greek national Tourist Office; English acronym of EOT

giouvetsi – casserole of meat and pasta

haloumi – soft, rubbery cheese

helidonismata – 'swallow songs', demotic songs peculiar to Halki and Nisyros

Hellas, Ellas or Elladha – the Greek name for Greece

Hellenistic period – prosperous, influential period of Greek civilisation ushered in by Alexander the Great's empire-building and lasting until the Roman sacking of Corinth in 146 BC

Helots – original inhabitants of Lakonia whom the Spartans used as slaves

hohlaki – a striking pebbled floor mosaic found in churches and houses all over the Dodecanese

hora – main town (usually on an island)

iconostasis – altar screen embellished with icons

Ionic – order of Greek architecture characterised by a column with truncated flutes and *capitals* with ornaments resembling scrolls

kafeneio (s), kafeneia (pl) – traditionally a male-only coffee house where cards and backgammon are played

kafeteria – upmarket *kafeneio*, mainly for younger people

kalderimi – cobbled footpath

kantina – mobile drink and snack dispenser, often a caravan, set up on remote beaches

Karians – ancient people from the Anatolian mainland; original settlers of the Dodecanese Islands

kaseri – mild, slightly rubbery sheep's-milk cheese

kastro – walled-in town

Katharevousa – purist Greek language; very rarely used these days

katholikon – principal church of a monastic complex

kefi – an undefinable feeling of good spirit, without which no Greek can have a good time

KKE – *Kommounistiko Komma Elladhas*; Greek communist party

Knights, the – the Knights Hospitaller of St John; chivalric order that held sway over the Dodecanese from AD 1309 to AD 1523

Koine – Greek language used in pre-Byzantine times; the language of the church liturgy

kore – female statue of the Archaic period; see *kouros*

kouloura – hard bread rolls that are soaked in water in order to be eaten

kouros – male statue of the Archaic period, characterised by a stiff body posture and enigmatic smile

KTEL – *Kino Tamio Ispraxeon Leoforion*; national bus cooperative; runs all long-distance bus services

Kypriako – the 'Cyprus issue'; politically sensitive and never forgotten by Greeks and Greek Cypriots

LANE – *Lassithiotiki Anonymi Naftiliaki Eteria* (Lassithi Anonymous Shipping Company); shipping company that runs ferries between Crete and Rhodes

laouto – lute, stringed instrument with a long neck

libation – in ancient Greece, wine or food that was offered to the gods

li-lo – inflatable mattress for use in the water (UK)

limenarhio – port police

lyra – small violin-like instrument, played on the knee; common in Karpathian music

makarounes – handmade macaroni cooked with onions and cheese; culinary speciality of Karpathos

malakas – literally 'wanker'; used as a familiar term of address, or as an insult, depending on context

mangas – 'wide boy' or 'dude'; originally a person of the underworld, now any streetwise person

mandinadhes – songs made up of short rhyming couplets, often heard on Karpathos

mayirefta – 'cooked dishes', ready-made food found in many popular restaurants

mayiria – cook houses

megaron – central room of a Mycenaean palace

meltemi – north-easterly wind which blows throughout much of Greece during the summer

mermizelli – Kalymnian salad made of soaked rusks, tomatoes, cucumbers, onions and feta cheese

metope – the sculpted section of a *Doric frieze*

mezes (s), mezedes (pl) – appetiser

Middle Age – see *Archaic period*

mihanikos – poignant sponge divers' dance from Kalymnos

Minoan civilisation (3000–1100 BC) – Bronze Age culture of Crete named after the mythical king Minos and characterised by pottery and metalwork of great beauty and artisanship

moni – monastery or convent

mouri – whole lamb cooked overnight in a wood brick oven (Kalymnos)

mousakas – most well-known Greek dish; made from layers of minced meat, aubergines and potatoes, topped by béchamel sauce and baked in the oven

Mycenaean civilisation (1900–1100 BC) – first great civilisation of the Greek mainland, characterised by powerful independent city-states ruled by kings; also known as the *Achaean civilisation*

mydia saganaki – mussels fried with cheese in a small pan

myzithra – soft sheep's-milk cheese

narthex – porch of a church

nave – aisle of a church

Nea Dimokratia – New Democracy; conservative political party

necropolis – literally 'city of the dead'; ancient cemetery

nefos – cloud; usually used to refer to pollution in Athens

nisiotika – island songs, endemic to the Dodecanese and Cyclades islands

nomarhia – prefecture building

nomos (s), nomi (pl) – prefectures into which the regions and island groups of Greece are divided

nymfaion – in ancient Greece, building containing a fountain and often dedicated to nymphs

OA – *Olympiaki Aeroporia* or Olympic Airways; Greece's national airline and major domestic air carrier

odeion – ancient Greek indoor theatre

odos – street

ohi – 'no'; what the Greeks said to Mussolini's ultimatum when he said 'surrender or be invaded'; the Italians were subsequently repelled and the event is celebrated on 28 October

ohtapodokeftedhes – rissoles made from octopus meat

OSE – *Organismos Sidirodromon Ellados*; Greek railways organisation

OTE – *Organismos Tilepikinonion Ellados*; Greece's major telecommunications carrier

Ottoman Empire – Turkish-dominated empire that included all of present-day mainland Greece from 1453 to 1912

oud – a bulbous, stringed instrument with a sharply raked-back head

ouzeri (s), ouzeria (pl) – place which serves *ouzo* or *tsipouro* and light snacks *(mezedes)*

ouzo – a distilled spirit made from grapes and flavoured with aniseed

Panagia – Mother of God; name frequently used for churches

paniyiri – festival or feast with music, drinking and eating, usually associated with a religious feast

Pantokrator – painting or mosaic of Christ in the centre of the dome of a Byzantine church

pantopoleio – general store

paralia – waterfront

PASOK – *Panellinio Sosialistiko Komma*; Greek socialist party

pediment – triangular section (often filled with sculpture) above the columns, found at the front and back of a classical Greek temple

periptero (s), periptera (pl) – street kiosk

peristyle – columns surrounding a building (usually a temple) or courtyard

pithos (s), pithoi (pl) – large Minoan storage jar

pitties – chick pea patties

plateia – square

Politiki Anixi – Political Spring; centrist political party

Pontians – Greeks whose ancestral home was on the Black Sea coast of Turkey

propylon (s), propylaia (pl) – elaborately built main entrance to an ancient city or sanctuary; a propylon had one gateway and a propylaia more than one

psarotaverna – taverna specialising in seafood

psistaria – restaurant serving grilled food

rembetika – blues songs commonly associated with the underworld of the 1920s

retsina – resinated white or rosé wine

revithokeftedhes – chickpea patties

rhyton – another name for a libation vessel

Rodesli – Jewish Rhodians, a once thriving community now reduced to a few hundred

sacristy – room attached to a church where sacred vessels etc are kept

sandouri – hammered dulcimer from Asia Minor

skafandro – heavy diving suit used by sponge divers in Kalymnos

skala – literally 'stairway', but now meaning the port of an island *hora*

skyladika – literally 'dog songs'; popular, but not lyrically-challenging blues songs often sung in *bouzoukia* nightclubs

soumada – syrup made of bitter and sweet almonds

souvlaki (s), souvlakia (pl) – literally 'little skewer'; usually means skewered cubes of meat, grill roasted

spilia – cave

stazione marittima – ferry quay (It)

stele (s), stelae (pl) – slab or pillar standing upright, especially as gravestone

stoa – long colonnaded building, usually in an *agora*; used as a meeting place and shelter in ancient Greece

syrtos – a popular island dance, where participants move to the rhythm in a circle

taverna – traditional restaurant which serves food and wine

temblon – votive screen

tholos – Mycenaean tomb shaped like a beehive

toumberleki – small lap drum played with the fingers

trata – small fishing boat

triglyph – sections of a Doric frieze between the *metopes*

trireme – ancient Greek galley with three rows of oars on each side

tsambouna – kind of bagpipe used in the Dodecanese

tsikoudia – Cretan version of *tsipouro*

tsipouro – distilled spirit made from grapes

vaulted – having an arched roof, normally of brick or stone

Venetians – people from Venice, commercial adventurists who settled in the Dodecanese in the Middle Ages

volta – promenade; evening stroll

volute – spiral decoration on *Ionic* capitals

yiros – layers of meat compressed onto a large skewer and slowly grilled; the outside layers are cut off and served in pitta bread with tomatoes, cucumber and sauces

zaharoplastio (s), zaharoplastia (pl) – patisserie; a shop that sells cakes, chocolates, sweets and, sometimes, alcoholic drinks as well

zeïmbekiko – slow, improvised and solo blues dance

LONELY PLANET

You already know that Lonely Planet produces more than this one guidebook, but you might not be aware of the other products we have on this region. Here is a selection of titles that you may want to check out as well:

Europe on a shoestring
ISBN 1 86450 150 2
US$24.99 • UK£14.99

Mediterranean Europe
ISBN 1 86450 154 5
US$27.99 • UK£15.99

Read this First: Europe
ISBN 1 86450 136 7
US$14.99 • UK£8.99

Western Europe
ISBN 1 86450 163 4
US$27.99 • UK£15.99

Greece
ISBN 0 86442 682 8
US$19.95 • UK£12.99

Greek Islands
ISBN 1 86450 109 X
US$17.95 • UK£11.99

Greek phrasebook
ISBN 0 86442 683 6
US$7.99 • UK£4.50

Available wherever books are sold

LONELY PLANET

ON THE ROAD

Travel Guides explore cities, regions and countries, and supply information on transport, restaurants and accommodation, covering all budgets. They come with reliable, easy-to-use maps, practical advice, cultural and historical facts and a rundown on attractions both on and off the beaten track. There are over 200 titles in this classic series, covering nearly every country in the world.

 Lonely Planet Upgrades extend the shelf life of existing travel guides by detailing any changes that may affect travel in a region since a book has been published. Upgrades can be downloaded for free from **www.lonelyplanet.com/upgrades**

For travellers with more time than money, **Shoestring** guides offer dependable, first-hand information with hundreds of detailed maps, plus insider tips for stretching money as far as possible. Covering entire continents in most cases, the six-volume shoestring guides are known around the world as 'backpackers bibles'.

For the discerning short-term visitor, **Condensed** guides highlight the best a destination has to offer in a full-colour, pocket-sized format designed for quick access. They include everything from top sights and walking tours to opinionated reviews of where to eat, stay, shop and have fun.

CitySync lets travellers use their Palm™ or Visor™ hand-held computers to guide them through a city with handy tips on transport, history, cultural life, major sights, and shopping and entertainment options. It can also quickly search and sort hundreds of reviews of hotels, restaurants and attractions, and pinpoint their location on scrollable street maps. CitySync can be downloaded from **www.citysync.com**

MAPS & ATLASES

Lonely Planet's **City Maps** feature downtown and metropolitan maps, as well as transit routes and walking tours. The maps come complete with an index of streets, a listing of sights and a plastic coat for extra durability.

Road Atlases are an essential navigation tool for serious travellers. Cross-referenced with the guidebooks, they also feature distance and climate charts and a complete site index.

LONELY PLANET

ESSENTIALS

Read This First books help new travellers to hit the road with confidence. These invaluable predeparture guides give step-by-step advice on preparing for a trip, budgeting, arranging a visa, planning an itinerary and staying safe while still getting off the beaten track.

Healthy Travel pocket guides offer a regional rundown on disease hot spots and practical advice on predeparture health measures, staying well on the road and what to do in emergencies. The guides come with a user-friendly design and helpful diagrams and tables.

Lonely Planet's **Phrasebooks** cover the essential words and phrases travellers need when they're strangers in a strange land. They come in a pocket-sized format with colour tabs for quick reference, extensive vocabulary lists, easy-to-follow pronunciation keys and two-way dictionaries.

Miffed by blurry photos of the Taj Mahal? Tired of the classic 'top of the head cut off' shot? **Travel Photography: A Guide to Taking Better Pictures** will help you turn ordinary holiday snaps into striking images and give you the know-how to capture every scene, from frenetic festivals to peaceful beach sunrises.

Lonely Planet's **Travel Journal** is a lightweight but sturdy travel diary for jotting down all those on-the-road observations and significant travel moments. It comes with a handy time-zone wheel, a world map and useful travel information.

Lonely Planet's eKno is an all-in-one communication service developed especially for travellers. It offers low-cost international calls and free email and voicemail so that you can keep in touch while on the road. Check it out on **www.ekno.lonelyplanet.com**

FOOD & RESTAURANT GUIDES

Lonely Planet's **Out to Eat** guides recommend the brightest and best places to eat and drink in top international cities. These gourmet companions are arranged by neighbourhood, packed with dependable maps, garnished with scene-setting photos and served with quirky features.

For people who live to eat, drink and travel, **World Food** guides explore the culinary culture of each country. Entertaining and adventurous, each guide is packed with detail on staples and specialities, regional cuisine and local markets, as well as sumptuous recipes, comprehensive culinary dictionaries and lavish photos good enough to eat.

OUTDOOR GUIDES

For those who believe the best way to see the world is on foot, Lonely Planet's **Walking Guides** detail everything from family strolls to difficult treks, with 'when to go and how to do it' advice supplemented by reliable maps and essential travel information.

Cycling Guides map a destination's best bike tours, long and short, in day-by-day detail. They contain all the information a cyclist needs, including advice on bike maintenance, places to eat and stay, innovative maps with detailed cues to the rides, and elevation charts.

The **Watching Wildlife** series is perfect for travellers who want authoritative information but don't want to tote a heavy field guide. Packed with advice on where, when and how to view a region's wildlife, each title features photos of over 300 species and contains engaging comments on the local flora and fauna.

With underwater colour photos throughout, **Pisces Books** explore the world's best diving and snorkelling areas. Each book contains listings of diving services and dive resorts, detailed information on depth, visibility and difficulty of dives, and a roundup of the marine life you're likely to see through your mask.

OFF THE ROAD

Journeys, the travel literature series written by renowned travel authors, capture the spirit of a place or illuminate a culture with a journalist's attention to detail and a novelist's flair for words. These are tales to soak up while you're actually on the road or dip into as an at-home armchair indulgence.

The range of lavishly illustrated **Pictorial** books is just the ticket for both travellers and dreamers. Off-beat tales and vivid photographs bring the adventure of travel to your doorstep long before the journey begins and long after it is over.

Lonely Planet **Videos** encourage the same independent, tough-minded approach as the guidebooks. Currently airing throughout the world, this award-winning series features innovative footage and an original soundtrack.

Yes, we know, work is tough, so do a little bit of deskside dreaming with the spiral-bound Lonely Planet **Diary** or a Lonely Planet **Wall Calendar**, filled with great photos from around the world.

TRAVELLERS NETWORK

Lonely Planet Online. Lonely Planet's award-winning Web site has insider information on hundreds of destinations, from Amsterdam to Zimbabwe, complete with interactive maps and relevant links. The site also offers the latest travel news, recent reports from travellers on the road, guidebook upgrades, a travel links site, an online book-buying option and a lively traveller's bulletin board. It can be viewed at **www.lonelyplanet.com** or AOL keyword: lp.

Planet Talk is a quarterly print newsletter, full of gossip, advice, anecdotes and author articles. It provides an antidote to the being-at-home blues and lets you plan and dream for the next trip. Contact the nearest Lonely Planet office for your free copy.

Comet, the free Lonely Planet newsletter, comes via email once a month. It's loaded with travel news, advice, dispatches from authors, travel competitions and letters from readers. To subscribe, click on the Comet subscription link on the front page of the Web site.

LONELY PLANET

Guides by Region

Lonely Planet is known worldwide for publishing practical, reliable and no-nonsense travel information in our guides and on our Web site. The Lonely Planet list covers just about every accessible part of the world. Currently there are 16 series: Travel guides, Shoestring guides, Condensed guides, Phrasebooks, Read This First, Healthy Travel, Walking guides, Cycling guides, Watching Wildlife guides, Pisces Diving & Snorkeling guides, City Maps, Road Atlases, Out to Eat, World Food, Journeys travel literature and Pictorials.

AFRICA Africa on a shoestring • Cairo • Cairo City Map • Cape Town • Cape Town City Map • East Africa • Egypt • Egyptian Arabic phrasebook • Ethiopia, Eritrea & Djibouti • Ethiopian Amharic phrasebook • The Gambia & Senegal • Healthy Travel Africa • Kenya • Malawi • Morocco • Moroccan Arabic phrasebook • Mozambique • Read This First: Africa • South Africa, Lesotho & Swaziland • Southern Africa • Southern Africa Road Atlas • Swahili phrasebook • Tanzania, Zanzibar & Pemba • Trekking in East Africa • Tunisia • Watching Wildlife East Africa • Watching Wildlife Southern Africa • West Africa • World Food Morocco • Zimbabwe, Botswana & Namibia
Travel Literature: Mali Blues: Traveling to an African Beat • The Rainbird: A Central African Journey • Songs to an African Sunset: A Zimbabwean Story

AUSTRALIA & THE PACIFIC Auckland • Australia • Australian phrasebook • Australia Road Atlas • Cycling Australia • Cycling New Zealand • Fiji • Fijian phrasebook • Healthy Travel Australia, NZ & the Pacific • Islands of Australia's Great Barrier Reef • Melbourne • Melbourne City Map • Micronesia • New Caledonia • New South Wales • New Zealand • Northern Territory • Outback Australia • Out to Eat – Melbourne • Out to Eat – Sydney • Papua New Guinea • Pidgin phrasebook • Queensland • Rarotonga & the Cook Islands • Samoa • Solomon Islands • South Australia • South Pacific • South Pacific phrasebook • Sydney • Sydney City Map • Sydney Condensed • Tahiti & French Polynesia • Tasmania • Tonga • Tramping in New Zealand • Vanuatu • Victoria • Walking in Australia • Watching Wildlife Australia • Western Australia
Travel Literature: Islands in the Clouds: Travels in the Highlands of New Guinea • Kiwi Tracks: A New Zealand Journey • Sean & David's Long Drive

CENTRAL AMERICA & THE CARIBBEAN Bahamas, Turks & Caicos • Baja California • Belize, Guatemala & Yucatán • Bermuda • Central America on a shoestring • Costa Rica • Costa Rica Spanish phrasebook • Cuba • Dominican Republic & Haiti • Eastern Caribbean • Guatemala • Havana • Healthy Travel Central & South America • Jamaica • Mexico • Mexico City • Panama • Puerto Rico • Read This First: Central & South America • World Food Mexico • Yucatán
Travel Literature: Green Dreams: Travels in Central America

EUROPE Amsterdam • Amsterdam City Map • Amsterdam Condensed • Andalucía • Austria • Baltic States phrasebook • Barcelona • Barcelona City Map • Belgium & Luxembourg • Berlin • Berlin City Map • Britain • British phrasebook • Brussels, Bruges & Antwerp • Brussels City Map • Budapest • Budapest City Map • Canary Islands • Central Europe • Central Europe phrasebook • Copenhagen • Corfu & the Ionians • Corsica • Crete • Crete Condensed • Croatia • Cycling Britain • Cycling France • Cyprus • Czech & Slovak Republics • Denmark • Dublin • Dublin City Map • Eastern Europe • Eastern Europe phrasebook • Edinburgh • England • Estonia, Latvia & Lithuania • Europe on a shoestring • Europe phrasebook • Finland • Florence • France • Frankfurt Condensed • French phrasebook • Georgia, Armenia & Azerbaijan • Germany • German phrasebook • Greece • Greek Islands • Greek phrasebook • Hungary • Iceland, Greenland & the Faroe Islands • Ireland • Italian phrasebook • Italy • Krakow • Lisbon • The Loire • London • London City Map • London Condensed • Madrid • Malta • Mediterranean Europe • Mediterranean Europe phrasebook • Moscow • Munich • Netherlands • Normandy • Norway • Out to Eat – London • Out to Eat – Paris • Paris • Paris City Map • Paris Condensed • Poland • Polish phrasebook • Portugal • Portuguese phrasebook • Prague • Prague City Map • Provence & the Côte d'Azur • Read This First: Europe • Rhodes & the Dodecanese • Romania & Moldova • Rome • Rome City Map • Russia, Ukraine & Belarus • Russian phrasebook • Scandinavian & Baltic Europe • Scandinavian phrasebook • Scotland • Sicily • Slovenia • South-West France • Spain • Spanish phrasebook • St Petersburg • St Petersburg City Map • Sweden • Switzerland • Tuscany • Ukrainian phrasebook • Venice • Vienna • Walking in Britain • Walking in France • Walking in Ireland • Walking in Italy • Walking in Spain • Walking in Switzerland • Western Europe • World Food France • World Food Ireland • World Food Italy • World Food Spain
Travel Literature: After Yugoslavia • Love and War in the Apennines • The Olive Grove: Travels in Greece • On the Shores of the Mediterranean • Round Ireland in Low Gear • A Small Place in Italy

LONELY PLANET

Mail Order

Lonely Planet products are distributed worldwide.They are also available by mail order from Lonely Planet, so if you have difficulty finding a title please write to us. North and South American residents should write to 150 Linden St, Oakland, CA 94607, USA; European and African residents should write to 10a Spring Place, London NW5 3BH, UK; and residents of other countries to Locked Bag 1, Footscray, Victoria 3011, Australia.

INDIAN SUBCONTINENT & THE INDIAN OCEAN Bangladesh • Bengali phrasebook • Bhutan • Delhi • Goa • Healthy Travel Asia & India • Hindi & Urdu phrasebook • India • Indian Himalaya • Karakoram Highway • Kerala • Madagascar • Maldives • Mauritius, Réunion & Seychelles • Mumbai (Bombay) • Nepal • Nepali phrasebook • Pakistan • Rajasthan • Read This First: Asia & India • South India • Sri Lanka • Sri Lanka phrasebook • Tibet • Tibetan phrasebook • Trekking in the Indian Himalaya • Trekking in the Karakoram & Hindukush • Trekking in the Nepal Himalaya
Travel Literature: The Age of Kali: Indian Travels and Encounters • Hello Goodnight: A Life of Goa • In Rajasthan • Maverick in Madagascar • A Season in Heaven: True Tales from the Road to Kathmandu • Shopping for Buddhas • A Short Walk in the Hindu Kush • Slowly Down the Ganges

MIDDLE EAST & CENTRAL ASIA Bahrain, Kuwait & Qatar • Central Asia • Central Asia phrasebook • Dubai • Farsi (Persian) phrasebook • Hebrew phrasebook • Iran • Israel & the Palestinian Territories • Istanbul • Istanbul City Map • Istanbul to Cairo • Istanbul to Kathmandu • Jerusalem • Jerusalem City Map • Jordan • Lebanon • Middle East • Oman & the United Arab Emirates • Syria • Turkey • Turkish phrasebook • World Food Turkey • Yemen
Travel Literature: Black on Black: Iran Revisited • The Gates of Damascus • Kingdom of the Film Stars: Journey into Jordan

NORTH AMERICA Alaska • Boston • Boston City Map • Boston Condensed • British Columbia • California & Nevada • California Condensed • Canada • Chicago • Chicago City Map • Florida • Great Lakes • Hawaii • Hiking in Alaska • Hiking in the USA • Las Vegas • Los Angeles • Los Angeles City Map • Louisiana & the Deep South • Miami • Miami City Map • Montreal • New England • New Orleans • New York City • New York City City Map • New York City Condensed • New York, New Jersey & Pennsylvania • Oahu • Out to Eat – San Francisco • Pacific Northwest • Rocky Mountains • San Francisco • San Francisco City Map • Seattle • Southwest • Texas • Toronto • USA • USA phrasebook • Vancouver • Virginia & the Capital Region • Washington, DC • Washington, DC City Map • World Food New Orleans
Travel Literature: Caught Inside: A Surfer's Year on the California Coast • Drive Thru America

NORTH-EAST ASIA Beijing • Beijing City Map • Cantonese phrasebook • China • Hiking in Japan • Hong Kong • Hong Kong City Map • Hong Kong Condensed • Hong Kong, Macau & Guangzhou • Japan • Japanese phrasebook • Korea • Korean phrasebook • Kyoto • Mandarin phrasebook • Mongolia • Mongolian phrasebook • Seoul • Shanghai • South-West China • Taiwan • Tokyo • World Food Hong Kong
Travel Literature: In Xanadu: A Quest • Lost Japan

SOUTH AMERICA Argentina, Uruguay & Paraguay • Bolivia • Brazil • Brazilian phrasebook • Buenos Aires • Chile & Easter Island • Colombia • Ecuador & the Galapagos Islands • Healthy Travel Central & South America • Latin American Spanish phrasebook • Peru • Quechua phrasebook • Read This First: Central & South America • Rio de Janeiro • Rio de Janeiro City Map • Santiago de Chile • South America on a shoestring • Trekking in the Patagonian Andes • Venezuela
Travel Literature: Full Circle: A South American Journey

SOUTH-EAST ASIA Bali & Lombok • Bangkok • Bangkok City Map • Burmese phrasebook • Cambodia • Hanoi • Healthy Travel Asia & India • Hill Tribes phrasebook • Ho Chi Minh City • Indonesia • Indonesian phrasebook • Indonesia's Eastern Islands • Java • Lao phrasebook • Laos • Malay phrasebook • Malaysia, Singapore & Brunei • Myanmar (Burma) • Philippines • Pilipino (Tagalog) phrasebook • Read This First: Asia & India • Singapore • Singapore City Map • South-East Asia on a shoestring • South-East Asia phrasebook • Thailand • Thailand's Islands & Beaches • Thailand, Vietnam, Laos & Cambodia Road Atlas • Thai phrasebook • Vietnam • Vietnamese phrasebook • World Food Thailand • World Food Vietnam

ALSO AVAILABLE: Antarctica • The Arctic • The Blue Man: Tales of Travel, Love and Coffee • Brief Encounters: Stories of Love, Sex & Travel • Chasing Rickshaws • The Last Grain Race • Lonely Planet ... On the Edge: Adventurous Escapades from Around the World • Lonely Planet Unpacked • Not the Only Planet: Science Fiction Travel Stories • Sacred India • Travel Photography: A Guide to Taking Better Pictures • Travel with Children per

Kalymnos   flere interessante steder
                  1 1/4 t. på Kos
Telendos   - e rever siglos fra kalym
            noss ifm jordskælv

○ Asklepion — beh. sted for
            hipacvratn

            — 4km fra kos

○ Therma Loutra — kilder - gratis

○ marmari / tingaki
            god strand
            sejle til ø psenmos

Ank. fredag nat

Lordag : kos by + swimmingpool

søndag : Motorcykel til Asklipion, Tingaki
+ Zia

Mandag : sejltur 30er - Bytur nat

Tirsdag : øst kos
metorcykel til kefalos + Mani
agia Theologou + paradis beach

onsdag : Nisyros - motorcykel - vulkan +

Torsdag : Pali, embonios, nikia, avlaki

Fredag

Hjem nat / aften

Index

Abbreviations

Text

Boxed Text

MAP LEGEND

CITY ROUTES

Freeway .... Freeway	= = = = ... Unsealed Road
Highway ...... Primary Road	⇒⇒⇒ .... One Way Street
Road ...... Secondary Road	.... Pedestrian Street
Street .... Street	⊔⊔⊔⊔⊔ .... Stepped Street
Lane .... Lane	========= .... Footbridge

BOUNDARIES

▬ ∙ ▬ ∙ ▬ ∙∙∙ .... International
▬ ▬ ∙ ▬ ∙∙∙∙∙ .... Regional Border
⊥⊥⊥⊥⊥⊥ .... Cliff
◼▬▬▬ .... Fortified Wall

HYDROGRAPHY

.... River, Creek
.... Lake, Salt Lake
⊚ ⟿ .... Spring; Rapids
⑤ ⊣⊢ ◀ .... Waterfalls

REGIONAL ROUTES

▬▬▬ .....Tollway, Freeway	▬▬▬▬ .... Secondary Road
▬▬▬ .... Primary Road	= = = = ... Unsealed Road

TRANSPORT ROUTES & PATHS

∙ ∙ ∙ ∙ ∙ ∙ ▫ .... Excursion Boats	▬ ▬ ▬ ▬ .... Walking Trail
▬ ▬ ▬ ▫ .... Ferry	∙ ∙ ∙ ∙ ∙ ∙ ∙ .... Walking Tour
▬ ▬ ▫ .... Hydrofoil/ Catamaran	.... Path

AREA FEATURES

.... Building	.... Market	🖈 .... Beach
⊛ ...... Park, Gardens	⬭ ...... Sports Ground	+ + + ... Cemetery
		.... Plaza
		.... Swamp

POPULATION SYMBOLS

❂ **CAPITAL** .... National Capital	● **City** .... City	● Village .... Village
◉ **CAPITAL** .... Provincial Capital	○ **Town** .... Town	.... Urban Area

MAP SYMBOLS

◼ ....Place to Stay	▼ ....Place to Eat	● .... Point of Interest

☒ .... Airport	◣ .... Dive Site	▲ .... Mountain	⊠ ...... Shopping Centre
⊕ .... Anchorage	🖸 ..... Embassy, Consulate	🏛 .... Museum	⋩ ...... Surf Beach
⑤ .... Bank	⚓ .... Fountain	🄿 .... Parking	⊟ .... Taxi
🏛 ... Building of Interest	◉ .... Golf Course	)(............... Pass	⊡ .... Telephone
▣ .... Bus Terminal	✚ .... Hospital	✪ .... Police Station	⊙ .... Toilet
🄰 .... Castle	⊠ .... Internet Cafe	◪ .... Post Office	❶ .... Tourist Information
◰ 🕇 .... Church	✲ .... Lookout	⊡ .... Pub or Bar	▭ .... Transport
⊞ .... Cinema	⚲ .... Monument	◪ .... Ruins	◢ .... Windsurfing

Note: not all symbols displayed above appear in this book

LONELY PLANET OFFICES

Australia
Locked Bag 1, Footscray, Victoria 3011
☎ 03 8379 8000 fax 03 8379 8111
email: talk2us@lonelyplanet.com.au

USA
150 Linden St, Oakland, CA 94607
☎ 510 893 8555 TOLL FREE: 800 275 8555
fax 510 893 8572
email: info@lonelyplanet.com

UK
10a Spring Place, London NW5 3BH
☎ 020 7428 4800 fax 020 7428 4828
email: go@lonelyplanet.co.uk

France
1 rue du Dahomey, 75011 Paris
☎ 01 55 25 33 00 fax 01 55 25 33 01
email: bip@lonelyplanet.fr
www.lonelyplanet.fr

World Wide Web: www.lonelyplanet.com *or* AOL keyword: lp
Lonely Planet Images: lpi@lonelyplanet.com.au